Business Strategies and Ethical Challenges in the Digital Ecosystem

Business Strategies and Ethical Challenges in the Digital Ecosystem

EDITED BY

S. ASIEH H. TABAGHDEHI

Brunel University London, UK

AND

PANTEA FOROUDI

Brunel University London, UK

United Kingdom – North America – Japan – India – Malaysia – China

Emerald Publishing Limited
Emerald Publishing, Floor 5, Northspring, 21-23 Wellington Street, Leeds LS1 4DL

First edition 2025

Reprints and permissions service
Contact: www.copyright.com

British Library Cataloguing in Publication Data
A catalogue record for this book is available from the British Library

ISBN: 978-1-80455-070-0 (Print)
ISBN: 978-1-80455-069-4 (Online)
ISBN: 978-1-80455-071-7 (Epub)

Printed and bound by CPI Group (UK) Ltd, Croydon, CR0 4YY

INVESTOR IN PEOPLE

Contents

List of Figures and Tables

Figures

Tables

About the Editors

S. Asieh H. Tabaghdehi is an Associate Professor and an Academic Researcher in the field of strategy and digital economy, with a strong interest in ethical digital ecosystems. Dr Tabaghdehi's expertise lies in understanding the critical role of data and digital technologies in shaping the future of society and the economy. She is dedicated to developing evidence-led initiatives and strategies that emphasise the importance of ethics in fostering inclusive digital innovation and sustainability. She is an enthusiastic Economist and Social Value Practitioner who employs innovative methodologies in her research and consultancy work to promote the ethical use of digital data for business growth and sustainability initiatives. Her research and consultancy work in these areas help businesses, individuals and society at large navigate the complex challenges and opportunities of our digital age. Dr Tabaghdehi actively collaborates with government agencies to shape policies that are grounded in organisational theory and drive responsible digital innovation and transformation on a national and international scale. Her commitment to driving positive change and innovation in the digital world makes her a vital thought leader in this field.

Pantea Foroudi (PhD, SFHEA, MSc (Honours), MA, BA (Honours)) is the Business Manager and Solution Architect at Foroudi Consultancy and is a member of the Marketing and Branding Department, Brunel Business School, London. Pantea has been working in the field of design, branding and marketing since 1996, and she has experience as a creative innovator and practical problem-solver in visual identity, graphic design, and branding in different sectors. Her primary research interest has focused on consumer behaviour from a multidisciplinary approach based on two research streams: (i) corporate brand design and identity and (ii) sustainable development goals (SDGs). Pantea has been published widely in international academic journals, such as the *British Journal of Management, Journal of Business Research, European Journal of Marketing, International Journal of Hospitality Management* and others. She is the Associate/Senior Editor of the *International Journal of Hospitality Management, Journal of Business Research, International Journal of Hospitality Management, International Journal of Management Reviews, International Journal of Contemporary Hospitality Management* and *European Journal of International Management* (EJIM), among others.

About the Contributors

Alireza Aghakabiriha received his Master degree in Technological Entrepreneurship in 2023 from University of Tehran, Faculty of Entrepreneurship. His research interests include strategic management, new product development, innovation and organisational capabilities.

Morteza Akbari is an Associate Professor at the Faculty of Entrepreneurship, University of Tehran. He has published several papers on different aspects of entrepreneurship and technological entrepreneurship and innovation. His research interests are sharing behaviour, consumer psychology, food marketing, open innovation and technological entrepreneurship. His work has been published in various journals including *Journal of Cleaner Production, Journal of Nursing Scholarship, Current Issues in Tourism, European Journal of International Management, European Journal of Innovation Management, Journal of Engineering and Technology Management, British Food Journal, Innovation, Research in Transportation Business & Management, Transportation Research Record, Journal of Agricultural Science and Technology, Int. J. Business Innovation and Research, Social Responsibility Journal* and *Iranian Journal of Management Studies.*

Ozlem Ayaz received her PhD in Management and Organisations in 2016. She joined Brunel Business School in February 2020. Dr Ayaz has several years of management experience in strategic management, working at big companies in Turkey. Her research is embedded in the strategic management field specifically interested in the integration of management systems with different operational aims. Her interest also resides in the role of leadership, social and business value creation ethical organisations during the digital era started with Industry 4.0. Dr Ayaz has published widely in internationally well-regarded academic journals such as *Journal of Business Research, Decision Support Systems, Business Strategy* and the *Environment.* She has presented her research output at international conferences such as the Academy of Management Conference in 2016, 2018 and 2020.

Ramin Behbehani is a Lecturer in Operations Management at Brunel Business School. His research primarily explores the social dimensions of operations management, emphasising contemporary areas such as sustainability and green supply chain and their implications on organisational performance. Actively investigating the underlying social dynamics within operations, his work aims to drive sustainable practices and strengthen organisational efficiency in today's business landscape.

Guido Berens is an Assistant Professor at Rotterdam School of Management, Erasmus University. His research and teaching interests include corporate communication, consumer reactions to CSR and quantitative research methods. His research has been published in the *Journal of Marketing* and the *Journal of Management Studies*, among others.

Edem Kofi Boni is a third-year PhD student at Brunel University London Business School. His research explores how artificial intelligence is *reinventing the retail landscape,* the extent to which an AI application is customer-facing, the amount of value creation, whether the AI application is online and the extent of ethical concerns.

Ashley Braganza is the Dean of Brunel Business School and holds the Chair in Business Transformation. Prior to being appointed Dean, Professor Braganza was the Deputy Dean of the College of Business, Arts and Social Sciences. He is the Founder and co-Director of Brunel's interdisciplinary Research Centre for Artificial Intelligence, launched in 2018, which incorporates a dedicated AI Lab. The Centre and Lab are central to Brunel's wider AI Ecosystem, led by Professor Braganza. Most recently, Professor Braganza is part of a consortium that has won a €5.8 million bid for the ELOQUENCE EU project (2024–2027). Professor Braganza's scholarly contribution is to the field of change implementation and, specifically, leadership of strategic organisational transformation. His interest in the implementation of cross-functional change was sparked during his doctoral journey and continues to inform his research projects, teaching and consultancy assignments. AI technologies are, in his view, going to create the biggest changes in industry. His research is practice-based, underpinned by over 35 publications in high-ranking, peer-reviewed journals. Professor Braganza has led over 25 large consultancy transformation projects in global and national public and FT100 private sector organisations.

Ana Isabel Canhoto is a Professor of Digital Business at the University of Sussex, UK. Her research focuses on service automation and the role of digital technology (including AI) in customer interactions. She examines drivers of adoption, user experiences and consequences of adoption. Recent research has focused on health decision-making, smart technology in the home, AI-powered personalisation, chatbots and the digitalisation of SMEs. Ana is also committed to the pedagogical use of digital technology, including using machine learning to support pupil performance, creating quasi-simulations for experiential learning and training early career researchers to use social media to develop and disseminate their work.

Fahimeh Dousthosseini is a PhD researcher at Marketing Management, Alzahra University, Tehran, Iran. She is a member of the National Elite Foundation of Iran. She studied and works in business management since 2015. Her research interest is in green marketing, artificial intelligence, and consumer behavior. She has published many articles in academic journals and conferences.

Manijeh Haghighinasab is a Full Professor in Marketing Management at Alzahra state University. During the years, she had different positions in the private and governmental sectors. She was primarily involved in international activities. She had training courses in Italy's plastics industry, entrepreneurs' skills for SMEs in Greece, presenting papers in different Conferences in Malaysia, Russia, Turkey, Spain and India from trade to education and research. She was a Lecturer in Marketing at the Tourism School of the Universitat Autonoma de Barcelona in Spain as well as at Chandigarh University in India. Her expertise is in international marketing, digital marketing, electronic commerce, business to business marketing, services marketing and entrepreneurship. She has published several books, book chapters and many papers on these subjects.

Ming-yao Jen is a Lecturer in International Business at Brunel Business School, Brunel University. Her research interests include market research, third sectors, ESG, online consumer behaviour and governance mechanisms. Her works are published in *International Marketing Review*, etc.

Hossein Kalatian is a Lecturer in Marketing and Business Studies at University Northampton International College. He is a Consultant, Lecturer and Researcher in Strategy, Organisational Change and Development and Digital Marketing. In the last 6 years, Hossein has taught courses in Management, Marketing, Organisational Behaviour, Organisational Change and Development in the United Kingdom. He has also been involved in several research projects investigating the impact of digital platforms and social media on SMEs performance and growth.

Nikos Ioannis Kois is a Senior QC Analyst with extensive experience within the AML sector investigating and analysing company data on existing clients to identify potential risks and conduct the appropriate level of due diligence to ensure minimal risks to the bank. Apart from that, Nikolaos has an interest in management and potential ways to improve the efficiency of entities, which was the reason why he studied Economics and Management with Patway in Brand Management.

Ameneh Khadivar is an Associate Professor at the Faculty of Social Sciences and Economics, University of Al-Zahra University, Tehran, Iran. She has a BA in Industrial Management from Iran University of Science and Technology in Iran. She obtained her MA in Information Technology Management from Tarbiat Modares University in Iran. She also received her PhD in Systems Management from Tarbiat Modares University. Her research interests include expert system, business intelligence, knowledge management and system dynamics.

Maryam Khodayari is a PhD student in Entrepreneurship, University of Tehran. Her research interests are technological entrepreneurship and innovation, technology intelligence, sustainability and energy storage technologies. Her work has been published in several journals including *Sustainable Energy Technologies and*

Assessments, Journal of Business Research, European Journal of Innovation Management, Cogent Business and Management and *Journal of Technology Development Management.*

Lefteris Kretsos is a Senior Lecturer at Brunel Business School, Brunel University London. He has published articles and coedited books and book chapters in world-leading academic journals and academic presses. His teaching portfolio includes several business and management courses mainly in the area of employee relations and HRM, organizational behavior, and management of change. During 2015–2019, Lefteris served as a Cabinet Minister in Greece and as a Permanent Secretary responsible for Digital and Media Policy.

Kevin Lu is a Senior Lecturer, Business School, Brunel University. His research interests include marketing analytics, online customer behaviour and electronic business. His research has been supported by EPRSC, EU and KTP.

Shazia Luidens is a sustainability professional from Aruba. She holds a degree in Global Business and Sustainability from Rotterdam School of Management, Erasmus University, and has experience in the fashion and hospitality industry.

Danae Manika (PhD, University of Texas at Austin) is a Professor of Marketing at Brunel Business School and Deputy Dean of the College of Business, Arts and Social Sciences at Brunel University. She also leads the Behavioural Science Insights for Sustainability Lab within the Centre for Entrepreneurship and Sustainability at Brunel University. Danae's research profile includes sustained publications across several years on effective message construction for behaviour change within health, environmental and well-being contexts, while her research has been supported by £364,000+ of funding (e.g., CRUK, EPSRC/Innovate UK, NERC/NCAS, RED and Arrow/ERDF). Danae has also been involved in various consultancies (e.g., Harrow Council, Royal Borough of Kensington and Chelsea Council, RECOUP, Global Action Plan), with the aim of linking theory to practise (impact). She is a Section Editor for the *Journal of Business Ethics* (section: Marketing Ethics) which is a Financial Times 50 journal, and Associate Editor (AE) for *Business and Society*, and sits on the Editorial Review Boards of top journals. Adding to her external recognition, she has experience as a Funding Reviewer for Cancer Research UK (2015–2019) and track chair for top marketing conferences worldwide (Academy of Marketing Science World Marketing Congress Conference in 2023, the Transformative Consumer Research Conference in 2021 and the European Social Marketing Association Conference in 2016).

Mohammad Reza Meigounpoory received his PhD in Mechanical Engineering from Iran University of Science And Technology. At present, he is a faculty member of technological entrepreneurship at University of Tehran, Faculty of Entrepreneurship. He works on techno entrepreneurship and new product development.

Ayatolah Momayez is an Assistant Professor, Faculty of Entrepreneurship, University of Tehran, Tehran, Iran.

Waheed Mughal earned his PhD in Social and Policy Studies from Loughborough University. Dr Mughal has published research papers on the issue of out of school children and their engagement in entrepreneurship. His research interests also include social innovation, entrepreneurship for a family run business at a small scale. Dr Mughal has recently worked at Brunel University London as a Research Fellow with the principal investigators on the project titled SMEs digital footprints and their ethical implications during the COVID-19 outbreak and beyond.

Mostafa Oboudi is a PhD Student, Faculty of Entrepreneurship, University of Tehran, Tehran, Iran.

Hamid Padash is an Associate Professor at the Faculty of Entrepreneurship, University of Tehran. He has published several papers on economics and entrepreneurship. His research work has been published in various journals including *European Journal of Innovation Management, Research in Transportation Business & Management, Transportation Research Record, Journal of Agricultural Science and Technology, Social Responsibility Journal* and *Foods*.

Maria Palazzo (PhD, AFHEA, FHEA, MSc (Honours), MA, BA (Honours)) is an Associate Professor, Universitas Mercatorum (Italy) and a member of the 'Sustainability Communication Centre' (SCC) (http://dsc.unisa.it/scc/). She was a former Lecturer at the University of Bedfordshire, School of Business (London, Luton, UK), a Visiting Scholar at the University of Granada (Granada, Spain) and a Visiting Lecturer at the Universidad del Norte, Escuela de Negocios (Barranquilla, Colombia). Her articles have been published in *Journal of Cleaner Production, Current Issues in Tourism, Corporate Social Responsibility & Environmental Management, Qualitative Market Research: An International Journal, Journal of Business-to-Business Marketing, Journal of Brand Management* and in other academic outlets.

Mehdi Rahmani is a current Doctoral Researcher at Brunel Business School. He holds an MSc in Business Intelligence and Digital Marketing from Brunel University and a BS in Industrial Engineering. With over two decades of professional experience, Mehdi has served as the CEO of both an advertising and marketing agency and a consulting company, as well as worked as an Economic Journalist. His diverse professional background deeply informs his academic pursuits and research. Currently, his doctoral research explores the intersection of advanced technology, customer purchase behavior, customer engagement, and digital marketing.

Atta ur Rehman (MSc, BSc) is a Master's in Marketing graduate with merit from Brunel University. Atta has a profound passion for quantitative research with expertise in data analytics, brand management, and the intersection of technology in marketing. Their dissertation, 'Perceived Product Innovation and Brand Loyalty', extends the Technology Acceptance Model to highlight the relationship between technological innovation and adoption with brand loyalty. Committed to enhancing marketing strategies, Atta is dedicated to leveraging data-driven insights for impactful contributions to the field.

Ronny Reshef is a PhD Researcher and a Lecturer at Rotterdam School of Management, Erasmus University. Her research and teaching interests include early modern times government–nonprofit relations, religion and philanthropy and the longitudinal legitimacy of the third sector.

Ainurul Rosli is a Professor of Enterprise and Entrepreneurship and leads Business Engagement at Brunel Business School. She works on evidence-led social impact and co-creation initiatives to support SMEs various strategic agendas, including collaboration for digital adoption. Prof Rosli's work has been instrumental in supporting the UK Government Funded Small Business Support programmes (Small Business Leadership, Help To Grow Management). She chairs the Practice and Impact Special Interest Group at Institute of Small Business Enterprise (ISBE).

Nader Seyyedamiri is an Associate Professor, Faculty of Entrepreneurship, University of Tehran, Tehran, Iran.

Javad Shekarkhah is an Associate Professor in Accounting at Allameh Tabataba'i University. Javad holds a PhD from the Allameh Tabataba'i University. His research interests lie in the area of accounting, auditing and finance, focusing on managerial accounting, behavioural finance, enterprise wide risk management (EWRM), corporate governance, Islamic banking, financial statements fraud, audit quality and stock markets. His research work covers different areas such as stock market issues, future of corporate reporting, Islamic banking and corporate governance. He has published his work in Iranian leading and internationally academic journals. He serves on the editorial advisory board and is a Reviewer for the Iranian journals.

Leila Hosseini Tabaghdehi is a distinguished Lecturer specialising in Educational Management at Islamic Azad University. With a profound expertise in the field, she holds a PhD in Educational Management, reflecting her commitment to advancing knowledge and contributing to the academic community. Throughout her career, Dr Tabaghdehi has been dedicated to the principles of education and leadership, aiming to instill a passion for learning and effective management practices among her students. Her research and academic pursuits focus on the dynamic intersection of educational theory and practical management applications. Dr Tabaghdehi's academic journey has been marked by a deep-seated commitment to excellence in teaching, research and administration. Her extensive knowledge in educational management and quantitative data analysis not only enriches her classroom interactions but also informs her contributions to the broader educational landscape.

Prena Tambay is a Practitioner and engaged Scholar. She specialises in the role of HRM in the digital age, future of work and people analytics. She works for Kingston Business School London. She has published her work in the space of using AI and blockchain in reducing modern slavery. She has presented her work in academic conferences and at various forums like Chartered Institute of Personnel Development and British Computer Society. She has several years of industry experience. She is engaged in knowledge transfer and consulting.

Dorothy Yen is a Professor in Marketing at Brunel Business School, Brunel University London. Dorothy takes on a consumer-centric approach to understand and discuss marketing, branding and tourism matters. She is particularly interested in exploring how culture affects human behaviour, in both B2B and B2C domains. She studies cross-cultural business relationships, consumer acculturation, sojourners and migrants' food consumption and contributes to the debate of Anglo-Chinese business relationships. Her works are published in journals such as *Industrial Marketing Management*, *Journal of Business Research*, *International Marketing Review*, *European Journal of Marketing*, etc.

Zeinab Zamani is a Lecturer at the Faculty of Economics, Management and Social Sciences, University of Shiraz, Shiraz, Iran. She has a PhD in Marketing Management from Al-Zahra University in Iran. She also has an MA and a BA in Business Management from Persian Gulf University in Iran. Her research interests include marketing, tourism marketing, entrepreneurship, advertising campaign and message content strategy.

Chapter 1

Introduction: Business Strategies and Ethical Challenges in the Digital Ecosystem

S. Asieh H. Tabaghdehi and Pantea Foroudi

Brunel University London, UK

Business Strategies and Ethical Challenges in the Digital Ecosystem developed progressively and became vital in academic research and management practice in a new normal. The playing field for managers and entrepreneurs has changed and become progressively complex due to the technological advancements and social issues they have to deal with in the current international market. Artificial intelligence has been used to create pathways into the private spaces of consumers allowing the application of Big Data Analytics as a tool to monitor and interact with consumers, businesses, competitors and every other stakeholder to improve business performance. Being computer-savvy has become a must at all levels of the workforce. But technological advancements are not the only ones challenging traditional management and organisational theories. Concepts like open innovation, the share economy and sustainability are also pushing practitioners to think innovatively.

The development of platforms and infrastructures such as social media, crowdfunding/crowdsourcing, Internet of Things (IoT) and virtual workspaces has improved, worldwide, innovation, entrepreneurship and sustainability in substantial ways with broad managerial, organisational and policy implications. The emergence of new digital technologies, awareness of corporate social responsibility and the greater need for innovation and problem-solving skills are becoming a de-facto part of the everyday management agenda. Increasing globalisation has made the world smaller and more competitive. Sociocultural and sociopolitical issues affect businesses at an unprecedented speed, yet academic research is not evolving fast enough to develop concepts and techniques needed by practitioners, especially where it is needed in domains such as management.

Before COVID-19 swept over the globe, the term "technological adoption" was highly used in businesses which implied that a business was forward-thinking enough to embrace technology and evolve their operations, products and services to better appeal to modern needs. There was no particular urgency or real meaning attached to the term even a few months ago. But now, needless to say,

Business Strategies and Ethical Challenges in the Digital Ecosystem, 1–4
Copyright © 2025 S. Asieh H. Tabaghdehi and Pantea Foroudi
Published under exclusive licence by Emerald Publishing Limited
doi:10.1108/978-1-80455-069-420241001

the situation has changed. Technological adoption has suddenly become crucial for businesses across all industries. Those undergoing a tech-centric reimagining hope to achieve a new business model, tap new revenue streams or find new digital means to improve their products, extend their business reach and outfox their competitors. Digitally mature organisations enjoy increased efficiency, better consumer satisfaction, improved employee engagement and better product and service quality. Thus, there is the need to understand how "technological adoption" impacts on business strategy, organisational performance and consumers behaviour.

Digitally mature organisations enjoy increased efficiency, better consumer satisfaction, improved employee engagement, better product and service quality and revenue growth. This is where digital ethics and online reputation management comes into play. In a post-COVID world, remaining on that ever-important cutting-edge means being remote-friendly, keyed into a tech-reliant world and being capable of facilitating satisfying interactions between digitally connected employers and consumers. Online reputation management is the practice of ensuring that your online presence accurately conveys your business's image and any important digital evolutions it might have undergone.

Hence, in the contemporary landscape of business, the intersection of technological adoption and digital strategy has become a critical focal point, particularly in current rapidly growing digital society. As industries grapple with unprecedented challenges, the integration of smart technology and responsible digital innovation has emerged as a transformative force, reshaping the way organisations operate, strategise and connect ethically and responsibly with their stakeholders.

This book, *Business Strategies and Ethical Challenges in the Digital Business Ecosystem*, delves into a comprehensive exploration of this dynamic landscape, navigating through four distinct but interconnected parts that collectively illuminate the multifaceted dimensions of this digital paradigm shift. Part I focuses on 'The landscape of Technological Innovation', Part II emphasises 'Market Trends and Consumer Adoption', Part III focuses on 'Business Strategies for Technological Adoption' and Part IV emphasises 'Ethical and Strategic Challenges in the Digital Age'.

Our leading chapter was contributed by S. Asieh Hosseini Tabaghdehi, Ana Canhoto and Ashley Braganza, as provided (Chapter 2) and focused on the duality of smart technology in the current digital era. The chapter was driven from their policy recommendation that was presented to the UK policymakers; they specified that to pave the way for socially responsible smart technologies, companies must explore and address risks stemming from the connectivity and cognitive capabilities of smart systems throughout their lifecycle stages, encompassing data input, processing and output. Chapter 3 is contributed by Alireza Aghakabiriha, Mohammad Reza Meigounpoory and Pantea Foroudi. They focus on the innovation ambidexterity bibliometric analysis and explore further whether the technovation ambidexterity is a new agenda in future study. Atta ur Rehman, Danae Manika, Pantea Foroudi and Maria Palazzo in chapter 4 develop an understanding of how the perceived product innovation impacts on brand loyalty among UK Apple product users, with a focus on extending the technology acceptance model.

In part II, chapter 5 is provided by S. Asieh Hosseini Tabaghdehi, Nikolas Kois, Leila Hosseini Tabaghdehi and Hossein Kalatian. This chapter highlights the importance of the relationship between organisations and customers in the current digital age and how SMEs use social media as an opportunity to develop their enterprises. In their study, they conducted qualitative methods to explore the insights from a wider stakeholder perspective. Chapter 6 is provided by Fahimeh Dousthosseini, Manijeh Haghighinasab and Pantea. They delineate why and under what conditions consumers intend to buy green and what the consequences are. Relying on theories of reasoned action and theory of planned behaviour, the authors offer that the green purchase intention is impressed by environmental and personality components. Provide statements about the determinants and key implications of such market identification. Chapter 7 was developed by Mostafa Oboudi, Ayatolah Momayez, Nader Seyyed Amiri and Morteza Akbari. They review the IoT as a concept with bibliometric analysis using data selected from the Scopus database. The cited references included two clusters. Also, co-occurrence keyword analysis found four groups. The first cluster shows IoT adoption in agriculture, manufacturing, logistics and supply chain management. The second cluster includes behavioural models of IoT technology acceptance. The third cluster refers to the adoption of IoT and automation technology in intelligent buildings, smart homes, smart cities and healthcare. Finally, the fourth cluster contains information management.

In chapter 8, Mehdi Rahmani, Pantea Foroudi , S Asieh H Tabaghdehi and Ramin Behbehani investigated the specific features of advanced technology that shape customer purchase intention in greater depth. By investigating when and under what conditions customers choose advanced technology-based purchases, this chapter sheds light on the evolving landscape of consumer decision-making, and it seeks to quantify the transformative power of advanced technology in driving customer purchase intentions. Shazia Luidens, Guido Berens and Ronny Reshef in chapter 9 highlight the importance of the relationship between sustainable human resource practices and employee intentions to engage in sustainable behaviour within an eco-friendly hotel. Specifically, they examine the influence of internal sustainability orientation, supervisory support, training and rewards, as well as the mediating role of employees' knowledge of the resort's sustainability practices.

In Part III, Edem Boni and S Asieh Hosseini Tabaghdehi contributed to chapter 10 and explored further the impact of digitalisation on retail business models and understanding consumer purchasing habits during emergencies. They discussed in detail the influence of scarcity and competitive arousal on consumer choices, the effects of stock-outs on brand and store preferences, price sensitivity, waiting times and the shift towards online shopping. They addressed concerns about social exclusion in digital channels and the potential for bridging the gap between offline and online shopping experiences.

In Chapter 11, Zeinab Zamani, Ameneh Khadivar, Hamid Padash, Javad Shekarkhah and Morteza Akbari recognise and rank the factors that impact the adoption of mobile commerce (MC) by users. Their results showed that compatibility, perceived usefulness (PU), perceived risk (PR), mobility and perceived cost (PC) have a significant effect on the adoption of MC by users. The results of multilayer perceptron (MLP) showed that mobility, among other model variables, had the greatest impact on the adoption of MC, and perceived cost had the lowest effect on the adoption of MC. The comparison of the MLP model with linear regression illustrates that the predictive power of MLP outperforms the linear regression model in predicting MC adoption.

Next, Maryam Khodayari, Morteza Akbari and Pantea Foroudi in chapter 12 highlight the importance of the factors involved in and obstacles to sharing economy adoption have been studied with several methods, and several models have occurred to clarify the underlying procedure of SE adoption, which provide contradictory and scattered findings. This chapter seeks to offer a scientific outline of the academic structure of the SE adoption domain.

Chapter 13 is provided by Asieh Tabaghdehi, Ozlem Ayaz, Ainurul Rosli, Prena Tambay and Waheel Mughal. This chapter highlights the importance of digital adoption in SMEs and investigated further the ethical implications of digital footprints in SMEs performance and value creation. Chapter 14, provided by Lefteris Kretsos, S. Asieh H. Tabaghdehi and Ashley Braganza, discussed the Political Challenge of AI in Modern Society by focusing on various challenges from National AI Strategy to the Algorithmic Elections. Chapter 15, provided by Ming-yao Jen, Dorothy Yen and Kevin Lu, highlighted social trust and self-efficacy drive collaborative consumption. Chapter 16, provided by Hossein Kalatian and S. Asieh H. Tabaghdehi discussed the role of digital Customer Knowledge Management and Ethical Innovation Strategy in social value creation. Finally Chapter 17, provided by S. Asieh H. Tabaghdehi explored further the ethical governance of digital footprint data and how it is a critical domain, influencing privacy, trust, transparency, accountability and overall digital well-being. This chapter provides an overview of key considerations and challenges in this realm, emphasising the need for a robust ethical framework to guide the responsible use of digital footprint data. It explores the interconnected dimensions of trust, transparency, accountability and digital well-being in the context of digital footprint data. In essence, "Business Strategies and Ethical Challenges in the Digital Business Ecosystem" offers a comprehensive journey through the intricate web of technological evolution, digital innovation strategy, and ethical considerations as the key implication in this domain. By examining these interconnected parts, readers will gain valuable insights into the strategies and considerations essential for navigating the challenges and opportunities presented by the digital age.

Part I

The Landscape of Smart Technology and Digital Innovation

This part aims to set the stage by focusing on technological innovations and their immediate impact on consumer perceptions and behaviour.

Chapter 2

The Duality of Smart Technology

S. Asieh H. Tabaghdehi[a], Ana Isabel Canhoto[b] and Ashley Braganza[a]

[a]Brunel University London, UK
[b]University of Sussex, UK

Abstract

The advent of the smart technology era has brought forth unprecedented opportunities and challenging risks, extending beyond individual, organisational and societal boundaries. These vulnerabilities are deeply interconnected with contextual factors such as technology accessibility, user competence and the wide-ranging consequences of technology utilisation that necessitates context-aware solutions. In this policy recommendation that was presented to the UK policymakers, we specified that to pave the way for socially responsible smart technologies, companies must explore and address risks stemming from the connectivity and cognitive capabilities of smart systems throughout their lifecycle stages, encompassing data input, processing and output. We emphasised that effective risk management demands a multifaceted orchestration of proactive (push) and reactive (pull) measures to mitigate harm. Furthermore, we indicate that smart technology's transformative potential has the capacity to revolutionise competition across industries, redefining innovation. However, this transformation introduces substantial risks that extend beyond corporate boundaries, affecting individual well-being and safety. Consequently, responsible innovation and mitigation strategies are imperative. Finally, we highlighted that global consumer decisions about smart technology adoption tend to be influenced less by geopolitical factors and more by complex motivations that weigh technological promises against perceived risks. The pursuit of socially responsible smart technology represents a multilayered effort tackling challenges that transcend conventional boundaries while empowering technology developers to embrace innovation.

Business Strategies and Ethical Challenges in the Digital Ecosystem, 7–18
doi:10.1108/978-1-80455-069-420241002

Keywords: Smart technology; connected technology; datafication; digital vulnerability; digital exclusion; push and pull mechanism

Introduction: Unravelling the Impact of Smart and Connected Technology – Evaluating the Shift in Society

In today's rapidly evolving world, the pervasive influence of "Smart and connected technology" has emerged as a defining symbol of modern society. Smart and connected technology refers to a category of technological solutions and devices that are designed to be intelligent, interconnected and capable of collecting and sharing data for various purposes. These technologies often leverage the Internet of Things (IoT) and other advanced digital systems to provide innovative features and capabilities. These digital innovations and digital connectivity have revolutionised nearly every aspect of our lives, from our homes and workplaces to the ways we communicate, learn and interact with the world. The unique characteristics of current digital transformation are the unprecedented synergy between devices and the seamless exchange of data across a vast network of interconnected systems.

This chapter provides a reflective analysis of our recommendations to policymakers in the United Kingdom in 2022, focusing on the exposition of five critical issues:

(1) What have been or will be the most important impacts of increasingly prevalent smart and connected technology in our lives, including in the home, in the workplace and in our towns and cities, and are they necessarily better than current systems?

(2) Are there any groups in society who may particularly benefit from or be vulnerable to the increasing prevalence of smart technology, such as young or elderly people, people with disabilities and people likely to be digitally excluded?

(3) How can we incentivise or encourage design that is safe, secure, environmentally and user-friendly and human rights compliant?

(4) What are the key short- and long-term risks and threats, and how can we ensure the devices, systems and networks of individuals, businesses and organisations are digitally literate and cyber secure?

(5) How will current geopolitical concerns influence domestic consumers, e.g. regarding standards of imported goods or in how we can deal with cyber threats?

Here, we highlighted the impact of smart and connected technology on modern society discussing how technology has changed our daily routines and reshaped our expectations.

The arrival of smart technology ranging from smartphones to autonomous vehicles has expanded their conventional functions. The connected technology altered the way that we interact with devices, equipped with the ability to collect and transmit data through internet connectivity, and thus the world. Smart technology can collect and transmit data about how they are used, and/or about their context of use, with little or no interference from users. Some devices can also interact with each other, with no human interference, and learn from each other (e.g. self-driving cars), setting the stage for an autonomous future.

The most remarkable and revolutionary influence of smart technology is its capacity to transform everyday life into data, enabling its application across various aspects of our daily routines. This datafication process enhances our comprehension, monitoring and optimisation of different life facets. Consequently, it places data at the core of our daily experiences and decision-making processes. Thus, the most significant and transformative impact of smart technology lies in its role in the datafication of daily life. This phenomenon encompasses the systematic collection and processing of data concerning a wide array of human and non-human activities. What's particularly noteworthy is that these data collection often occurs without direct human intervention or, in some cases, without the conscious awareness of the individuals from whom the data is being gathered.

Smart technology has become an invisible yet persistent observer of our lives, recording all our behaviour, preferences and interactions. Whether it's tracking our steps, monitoring our energy consumption, or even predicting when our appliances require maintenance, datafication has developed a web of interconnected data points in relation to our daily routines and habits. This unprecedented level of data collection is redefining the boundaries of privacy, as individuals often find themselves in situations where they are oblivious to the data being harvested about them. This raises various questions about the ethical use of these data, the boundaries of surveillance, and the transparency that should be maintained in the era of datafication. This implies that datafication occurs at the individual, workplace and societal levels, considering both its potentials and privacy-related risks (Brodie et al., 2005), underscoring the need for a balance between personal optimisation and safeguarding sensitive information. For instance, health and fitness monitoring has been revolutionised by wearable devices.

In the workplace, datafication empowers evidence-informed decision-making, from predictive maintenance to designing optimal work shifts; and creates opportunities for innovation (Tabaghdehi, 2022). Such innovation drives productivity and efficiency but simultaneously reshapes the employment landscape, leading to professional alienation (Braganza et al., 2021) as certain job roles evolve or disappear. Yet, the promise of progress also raises concerns about uncontested surveillance (Mascheroni, 2020), compelling society to grapple with the balance between innovation and privacy. In this multifaceted era of datafication, society faces the complex task of integration innovation with privacy. This journey challenges us to explore responsible and ethical approaches in the age of smart technology. Therefore, in 'Inclusivity and Vulnerability: the Impact of Smart Technology on Diverse Groups in Society', we consider the risk and impact of smart technology in society. In the section 'Extended Strategies for Encouraging Safe, Secure and Human Rights-Compliant Design', we discuss a set of strategies that are essential for promoting safe, secure and human rights-compliant design. In 'Addressing Short- and Long-Term Risks in the Digital Landscape', we discussed the risks present in the digital landscape, both in the short and long term. In 'Influence of Geopolitical Concerns on Domestic Consumers', we explored the correlation between contemporary geopolitical factors and consumer behaviours in the digital age at the geopolitical level. The final Section concludes this chapter.

Inclusivity and Vulnerability: the Impact of Smart Technology on Diverse Groups in Society

In the rapidly evolving landscape of smart technology, one of the fundamental principles guiding our exploration is the belief that every citizen, in principle, should have the opportunity to gain the benefits of these innovative advancements. The potential advantages offered by smart technology are to enhance the personal convenience for improving overall quality of life. However, as smart technology is adopted, there is a significant concern or risk associated with its vulnerability, that could be exploited or pose a threat. Vulnerability, in this context, does not imply inability or exclusion but rather highlights the various factors that could impact an individual's ability to harness the full benefits of smart technology.

There are various attributes and conditions that might contribute to vulnerability in the context of smart technology. These attributes can be wide-ranging including factors such as digital literacy and socio-economic status. By recognising and understanding these potential vulnerabilities, we can begin to develop strategies and solutions that ensure equitable access and use of smart technology for all members of society. Beyond identification, it is crucial to consider the means by which we can address these vulnerabilities effectively such as developing inclusive design principles to policy recommendations, aimed at mitigating the impact of these vulnerabilities.

While some groups are at an increased risk of finding themselves in a vulnerable position (as per the list of protected characteristics already embedded in legislation), it is the context rather than personal characteristics that determines vulnerability (Canhoto & Dibb, 2016). For instance, a pensioner's vulnerability to online scams arises from their unfamiliarity with new technology, not their age. Expanding on this, it's essential to recognise that vulnerability in the context of smart technology is not solely determined by personal characteristics such as age, gender or disability, which are traditionally protected by existing legislation. This understanding emphasises the importance of assessing vulnerability on a case-by-case basis, considering the specific context and the individual's relationship with smart technology. It also highlights the need for targeted education and support to empower individuals to use technology safely, regardless of their personal characteristics.

Next, we will elaborate on the concept of vulnerability in the context of smart technology. Vulnerability may arise from the unavailability of technology, challenges in utilising the technology and potential consequences associated with its use.

Unavailability of Technology

The challenges related to unavailability of technology, include issues related to hardware, software and internet connection. I) The hardware related challenges, e.g. assistive technology relates to the physical devices required for utilising smart technology. Vulnerability can arise when individuals, especially those with disabilities, lack access to necessary hardware like screen readers, braille displays or specialised input devices. II) The software-related challenges such as lack of features and lack of compatibility are very important aspects when it comes to smart technology. Mainly because the software plays a crucial role in enabling smart technology to perform specific functions. III) Vulnerability may emerge when software lacks essential features or compatibility with certain devices or systems, preventing users from benefiting fully. Internet access is fundamental for using most smart technologies. Vulnerability can stem from the unavailability of a reliable internet connection, particularly in rural or remote areas where connectivity may be limited.

Inability to Use the Technology

Inability to use the technology could be due to various factors including: I) insufficient purchasing power, incompatibility with legacy technologies and lack of digital skills. Insufficient purchasing power, e.g. limited disposable income can rise individual's vulnerability if they cannot afford the necessary technology. Whereas, limited financial resources can result in an inability to purchase smartphones, tablets or other smart devices. II) Moreover, incompatibility with legacy technologies, e.g. old operating systems in mobile phones may arise when individuals own older technology that does not support newer smart devices. This incompatibility can lead to vulnerability due to the inability to access the latest features. III) Furthermore, lack of digital skills can cause vulnerability which includes not being aware of the existence of certain technologies or having an inadequate understanding of how to use them effectively (Stuart et al., 2022). IV) Additionally, lack of representation in dataset, e.g. particular accents can raise the issue of digital vulnerability particularly in a multicultural society. The data used to train smart technology systems may not adequately represent the diversity of users. Vulnerability can result when individuals with particular accents or unique linguistic characteristics face difficulties in using voice-activated smart systems that do not recognise their speech patterns.

Consequences of Using the Technology

Consequences of using the technology, including digital footprints and scams and frauds among many others. I) The issues related to digital footprints such as not understanding the risks of mismanagement of digital footprint such as cyber-bullying, cyber-dating violence and hacking are vital consequences of using technology. Vulnerability can emerge from a lack of awareness about the potential risks associated with digital footprints such as issues around privacy, trust, fairness and accountability. This includes not understanding the implications of one's online activities, such as sharing personal information on social media. II) Scams and frauds such as online hacking arising with the use of smart technology can lead to vulnerability through scams and fraudulent activities. For instance, individuals may become vulnerable to hacking or identity theft when they are not adequately informed or protected against such risks. Hence, vulnerability in the context of smart technology can result from many of the above factors. Understanding these facets is crucial for addressing and mitigating vulnerabilities in the digital age. Those citizens that find themselves at the intersection of two or more of the factors mentioned above are at an increased risk of vulnerability.

Extended Strategies for Encouraging Safe, Secure and Human Rights-Compliant Design

The pursuit of technology that is not only innovative but also safe, secure and compliant with human rights is a paramount concern in the digital age. It necessitates a comprehensive strategy that goes beyond traditional standards and rulings, focusing on proactive measures to prevent potential issues before they arise. Hence, it is crucial to put forward some principles and strategies for incentivising responsible design in the smart technology era.

Beyond Conventional Standards

While standards and rulings play a pivotal role in ensuring compliance, they are typically reactive, addressing issues after they have already surfaced. For example, regulations like the European Commission's mandate for USB-C charging ports in mobile devices aim to mitigate electronic waste and protect consumers (Stuart et al., 2022). However, such standards focus on the end product and are applied after the fact, often in response to real-world events, such as fatalities involving self-driving cars. To foster a more proactive approach, it is essential to shift the focus from end products to the entire system that underpins smart technology.

Proactive Risk Assessment

A more effective strategy involves early identification of the potential for value destruction within a technology system before it is deployed. This proactive assessment consists of two critical steps. Firstly, it requires a comprehensive mapping of all components within the system, encompassing inputs and the production process leading to the end product. Secondly, a careful analysis is conducted to understand how the system's connectivity, cognitive capabilities and imperceptibility can give rise to specific risks. For instance, connectivity may introduce the possibility of corrupted, incomplete or misleading data inputs. Moreover, processing algorithms may be chosen based on compatibility rather than performance, resulting in suboptimal outcomes. Poor-quality outputs can propagate rapidly, increasing the likelihood of errors and their potential risks and impact (Canhoto & Clear, 2020). This approach seeks to identify vulnerabilities before they can lead to detrimental consequences.

Implementing Push and Pull Mechanisms

To ensure that firms adopt a comprehensive assessment of the value destruction potential of their technologies, a combination of push and pull mechanisms is recommended. Push mechanisms entail the development of relevant guidelines and the establishment of audit and enforcement mechanisms. These mechanisms create a framework for firms to adhere to rigorous evaluation processes and uphold responsible design. On the other hand, pull mechanisms involve investments in resources aimed at identifying and managing risks. This includes educational initiatives and fostering a diverse workforce that can offer multifaceted perspectives on potential issues. Furthermore, behavioural changes can be instilled through certification programs that encourage firms to meet and exceed safety, security and compliance standards.

The extended strategies presented here highlight the importance of shifting from reactive measures to proactive, comprehensive approaches that aim to prevent issues before they emerge. By understanding the potential risks associated with smart technology and fostering a culture of responsible design, the digital landscape can evolve towards being safer, more secure and aligned with human rights and environmental considerations. These strategies empower technology developers to embrace innovation while minimising the negative consequences of rapid technological advancements.

Addressing Short- and Long-Term Risks in the Digital Landscape

In an ever-evolving digital landscape, understanding and mitigating short-term and long-term risks and threats is paramount. This section elaborates on different types of problems and discusses the key considerations for ensuring the digital literacy and cyber security of individuals, businesses and organisations.

Short-Term and Long-Term Cyber Risks

The rapid advancement of technology has given rise to a multitude of information security concerns and short-term cyber risks. These encompass issues such as cyber-bullying, cyber-dating violence and hacking. These immediate threats not only compromise the security of digital systems but also have extensive consequences. In the long term, they can lead to significant mental health risks, including depression, anxiety and psychological distress (Paat & Markham, 2021). These mental health implications highlight the pressing need for addressing these short-term concerns as a key social concern in the digital society. Strategies for cyber security must encompass not only the protection of systems and data but also the well-being of individuals who interact with these technologies.

Data Ownership and De Facto Monopolies

Data derived from smart devices represent a valuable asset in the digital ecosystem. However, data ownership introduces a complex dynamic known as data network effects (DNE), benefiting platform owners. Essentially, the more user data accumulated by a platform owner, the more valuable the platform becomes for each user (Gregory et al., 2021), creating a feedback loop. In the long term, this may result in de facto monopolies for smart device manufacturers. As a consequence, it is crucial to address the risks associated with DNE to maintain a competitive and diverse digital landscape that benefits both individuals and society.

Developing Digital Literacy and Safer Technology Use

One effective approach to foster digital literacy and encourage safer technology use is the utilisation of quasi-simulations. In these simulations, participants are tasked with assessing an uncertain environment, planning and executing actions and receiving feedback through the use of metrics. By engaging individuals in quasi-simulations (Canhoto & Murphy, 2016), participants are required to assess an uncertain environment; plan and execute their actions; and obtain feedback through the use of metrics (McIlwraith, 2021). This assists the users to gain practical experience in navigating digital challenges, improving their decision-making skills and enhancing their ability to interact with technology safely. These simulations offer a proactive and hands-on method for enhancing digital literacy and cyber security.

Hence, addressing short- and long-term risks and threats in the digital domain necessitates a multifaceted approach that encompasses not only the protection of digital systems but also the well-being of individuals, the regulation of data ownership dynamics and practical education to enhance digital literacy. By adopting such strategies, we can create a more secure, informed and resilient digital society.

Influence of Geopolitical Concerns on Domestic Consumers

Geopolitical concerns hold a significant influence over domestic consumers, impacting their choices related to imported goods and the approach to handling cyber threats. This section explores further the relationship between current geopolitical factors and consumer behaviours.

Consumer Brand Preferences and Sociopolitical Stance

Consumer brand preferences are not integrally persuaded by a brand's sociopolitical stance. For instance, consumers' opinions on contentious topics like Brexit do not significantly influence their intent to purchase brands that have relocated their production to the United Kingdom. However, their perceptions of such brands improved when the onshoring decision was deemed to improve the local economy or reduce carbon footprint (Dey et al., 2023). This reveals that the preference for domestic firms can be influenced when these companies emphasise their corporate social responsibility initiatives. Highlighting a commitment to ethical and sustainable practices can make a brand more appealing to consumers who value such considerations.

Influencing Preferences Through Economic and Performance Factors

Consumer preferences can be influenced by mechanisms that increase the cost of non-domestic options or raise performance-related risks. These mechanisms include taxation policies and sanctions. For example, the actions of political leaders can have a direct impact on consumer behaviour. A notable case is the blacklisting of Huawei by President Trump in 2019. This move led to a significant 47% decline in revenues in the consumer electronics segment of the business, although the company experienced growth in other areas (Kynge, 2021). Such actions demonstrate the power of geopolitical concerns in affecting consumer choices. The potential economic and security consequences related to geopolitical decisions can shape consumer preferences in favour of domestic options and away from brands or products associated with political controversies or national security concerns. Therefore, the influence of geopolitical concerns on domestic consumers is multidimensional. While sociopolitical stances of brands may not be the primary driver of consumer preferences, factors like corporate social responsibility initiatives and government actions can significantly impact consumer choices. Understanding these dynamics is vital for businesses and policymakers as they address the complex interplay between geopolitics and consumer behaviours.

Conclusion

In conclusion, here we shed light on crucial aspects of smart technology and its impact on society. The discussions on inclusivity and vulnerability highlight the need to consider diverse groups in the design and deployment of smart technology to ensure equitable benefits. The exploration of extended strategies for encouraging safe, secure and human rights-compliant design emphasises the importance of proactive measures in technology development. Additionally, the assessment of short- and long-term risks in the digital landscape highlights the necessity for comprehensive risk management strategies to safeguard individuals and organisations at the same time.

The influence of geopolitical concerns on domestic consumers reveals the complex interplay between international political dynamics and technology adoption, necessitating a nuanced understanding of global influences on local contexts. Hence, the exploration of artificial intelligence (AI) safety and the proposition for a global regulatory body emphasises the imperative of prioritising the protection of vulnerable individuals. The commendable initiative requiring AI companies to undergo pre-release product reviews is a positive step forward. However, the voluntary nature of this submission reveals an obvious absence of geopolitical commitment. It is noteworthy that, as of now, the United Kingdom lacks imminent legislative measures mandating companies to prioritise the safeguarding of vulnerable populations. Examining the geopolitical landscape expounded here reveals a stark contrast between governmental announcements about prioritising the safety of vulnerable citizens and the practical actions undertaken by major countries/continents such as the European Union, United States, China and India. These entities are charting distinctive paths, each establishing its own frameworks and regulations. This divergence introduces intricacies for AI companies and offers significant flexibility for them to adapt their strategies or, in some instances, withdraw services from specific markets. The prevailing geopolitical dynamics present formidable obstacles to the formulation of a unified, globally accepted approach to AI safety. As we move forward, embracing a holistic and adaptive approach to smart technology will be imperative in building a more resilient and equitable technological future.

Case Study

Navigating the Digital Divide: Unravelling the Complexities of Smart Technology Adoption

As the world rapidly embraces smart technology, the implications of this digital shift are felt across diverse societal segments. This case study discusses further the multifaceted landscape of smart technology adoption, exploring its interconnected aspects, such as connected technology, datafication, digital vulnerability, digital exclusion and the intricate mechanisms that propel or hinder its integration. In the fictional town of Techville, where a city-wide initiative has been launched to implement smart technology solutions for enhanced urban living, the initiative covers various aspects, from smart traffic management to connected healthcare services.

The city deploys an extensive network of connected devices and sensors to gather real-time data for optimising public services. Smart traffic lights, waste management systems and healthcare monitoring devices become integral components of this interconnected infrastructure. As the town immerses itself in the data-driven ecosystem, challenges arise concerning the ethical and responsible use of data. Citizens express concerns about data privacy, leading to a growing debate on the need for robust data governance and security measures.

Despite the promising advancements, the interconnected nature of smart technology exposes the town to digital vulnerabilities. A cyberattack disrupts critical systems, revealing the fragility of the digital infrastructure and prompting a re-evaluation of cybersecurity protocols. While the smart city initiative gains momentum, segments of the population, particularly elderly and economically disadvantaged residents, face challenges in adapting to the digital transformation. The case explores how digital exclusion exacerbates social inequalities and raises questions about inclusive smart technology implementation.

Case Study Questions

(1) How can Techville address citizens' concerns about data privacy and ensure the ethical and responsible use of data in its smart technology initiative?
(2) What measures should be taken to establish robust data governance?
(3) Following the cyberattack, what strategies should Techville employ to enhance the resilience of its interconnected smart infrastructure against future threats?
(4) How can the city balance innovation with robust cybersecurity measures?
(5) In what ways can Techville bridge the digital divide and ensure that all segments of the population, including the elderly and economically disadvantaged, benefit from the smart city initiative?
(6) What initiatives can be implemented to promote digital inclusion and address social inequalities?

Key Terms and Definitions

Connected Technology: Connected Technology refers to the integration of various devices, systems and services through digital networks, enabling them to communicate, share data and collaborate in real time.
Datafication: Datafication is the process of transforming various aspects of life, business and society into data that can be collected, analysed, and utilised for insights and decision-making.
Digital Vulnerability: Digital vulnerability refers to the susceptibility of individuals, organisations and systems to various risks and threats in the digital domain.
Digital Exclusion: Digital exclusion refers to the social and economic disparities that arise from unequal access to and use of digital technologies.

References

Braganza, A., Chen, W., Canhoto, A. I., & Sap, S. (2021). Productive employment and decent work: The impact of AI adoption on psychological contracts, job engagement and employee trust. *Journal of Business Research*, *131*, 485–494. https://doi.org/10.1016/j.jbusres.2020.08.018

Brodie, C., Karat, C. M., Karat, J., & Feng, J. (2005). Useable security and privacy: A case study of developing privacy management tools. In *Proceedings of the 2005 symposium on Useable privacy and security* (pp. 35–43). Association for Computing Machinery.

Canhoto, A. I., & Clear, F. (2020). Artificial Intelligence and Machine Learning as business tools: Factors influencing value creation and value destruction. *Business Horizons, 63*(1). https://doi.org/10.1016/j.bushor.2019.11.003

Canhoto, A. I., & Dibb, S. (2016). Unpacking the interplay between organisational factors and the economic environment in the creation of consumer vulnerability. *Journal of Marketing Management, 32*(3–4), 335–356. https://doi.org/10.1080/0267257X.2015.1123759

Canhoto, A. I., & Murphy, J. (2016). Learning from simulation design to develop better experiential learning initiatives – An integrative approach. *Journal of Marketing Education, 38*(2), 98–106. https://doi.org/10.1177/0273475316643746

Dey, B. L., Alwi, S. F. S., Babu, M. M., Roy, S. K., & Muhammad, S. S. (2023). Brexit or brand it? The effects of attitude towards Brexit and reshored brands on consumer purchase intention. *British Journal of Management, 34*(3), 1215–1237.

Gregory, R. W., Henfridsson, O., Kaganer, E., & Kyriakou, H. (2021). The role of artificial intelligence and data network effect for creating user value. *Academy of Management Review, 46*(3), 534–551. https://doi.org/10.5465/amr.2019.0178

Kynge, J. (2021). *Huawei suffers biggest-ever decline in revenue after US blacklisting*. Financial Times. https://www.ft.com/content/dc170be7-262e-4616-9ef9-2a49c61 1c26b. Last accessed 14 June 2022.

Mascheroni, G. (2020). Datafied childhoods: Contextualising datafication in everyday life. *Current Sociology, 68*(6), 798–813. https://doi.org/10.1177/0011392118807534

McIlwraith, A. (2021). *Information security and employee behaviour: how to reduce risk through employee education, training and awareness*. Routledge.

Paat, Y. F., & Markham, C. (2021). Digital crime, trauma, and abuse: Internet safety and cyber risks for adolescents and emerging adults in the 21st century. *Social Work in Mental Health, 19*(1), 18–40.

Stuart, R., Braganza, A., Charteris, V., & Jones, M. (2022). *Digital Poverty in Margate: A Study of Two Hyperlocal Communities* (p. 35). A report prepared by Brunel University London and funded by The British Academy. https://www.europarl.europa.eu/news/en/press-room/20220603IPR32196/deal-on-common-charger-reducing-hassle-for-consumers-and-curbing-e-waste. Last accessed 14 June 2022.

Tabaghdehi, A. (2022). COVID-19 and Digital Economy: The journey towards a digital transformation in new normal: How to prepare for the future. In *The Economics of COVID-19* (Vol. 296, pp. 95–104). Emerald Publishing Limited. 10: 180071694X. ISBN 13: 9781800716940.

Chapter 3

Innovation Ambidexterity Bibliometric Analysis: Is Technovation Ambidexterity a New Agenda in Future Study?

Alireza Aghakabiriha[a], Mohammad Reza Meigounpoory[a] and Pantea Foroudi[b]

[a]University of Tehran, Iran
[b]Brunel University London, UK

Abstract

Although many scholars have investigated different aspects of the notion of innovation ambidexterity, the conceptualization of examining this concept in a technological setting remained unclear, as no serious attempts have been made to figure out the core concept of innovation ambidexterity in a technological context, which is a critical concept for high-tech firms.

Keywords: Innovation ambidexterity; technovation ambidexterity; bibliometric study analysis; technology; environmental factors

Introduction

The concept of technovation ambidexterity is distinguished from other ambidexterity concepts as its origin is an emphasis on solving problems with high-tech firms or those in a technological setting with the aim of being ambidextrous amid technological turbulence in the environment (Hughes et al., 2020; Liao et al., 2018; Mahavarpour et al., 2023; Soto-Acosta et al., 2018). To survive in a fast-changing environment, firms should use their two wings simultaneously – innovative exploration and innovative exploitation (Acikgoz et al., 2021; Chen & Liu, 2020). Technovation ambidexterity refers to investigating the innovation ambidexterity concept in a technological setting. Innovation ambidexterity is defined as the capability of the firm to following exploratory and exploitative innovation simultaneously (Cabeza-Pullés et al., 2020; Chang & Hughes, 2012;

Business Strategies and Ethical Challenges in the Digital Ecosystem, 19–54
Copyright © 2025 Alireza Aghakabiriha, Mohammad Reza Meigounpoory and Pantea Foroudi
Published under exclusive licence by Emerald Publishing Limited
doi:10.1108/978-1-80455-069-420241003

Chen & Liu, 2020; Cho et al., 2019; Gupta et al., 2016; Hughes et al., 2020; Jansen et al., 2006; Simsek, 2009; Zang & Li, 2016). Those firms which are operating in a technological context are confronted with two basic challenges: exploiting current ideas and capabilities and exploring new ones. Doing much more exploration or exploitation means that the organization faces two types of trap: failure traps and success traps (Chen & Liu, 2020; Hughes et al., 2020; Zang & Li, 2016).

Exploratory innovation includes detecting new knowledge or skills, helping the firm to enter new markets or produce new ones, while exploitative innovation includes the ability of the firm to use current knowledge or capabilities satisfying customer needs (Balakrishnan & Foroudi, 2020; Chen & Liu, 2020; Foroudi et al., 2016; Liao et al., 2018; Ruiz-Alba et al., 2022). Ambidexterity is critical for doing these processes effectively (Hughes et al., 2020). Exploitation and exploration concepts are contradictory because they are competing on scarce resources in the firm and can lead to some challenges for firms being in technological or other contexts. For overcoming these challenges, two dimensions have been suggested: the balance dimension (BD) and the composed dimension (CD) (Chao et al., 2009; Zang & Li, 2016). These concepts are fundamentally different and completely dependent on the external resources and have synergistic effects. Despite the companies accessing adequate sources in order to pursue explorative and exploitative functions, organizations in the face of resource scarcity may gain from focusing on handling a trade-off encountered with these activities (Acikgoz et al., 2021; Chao et al., 2009).

Since detection of new things and operative duties need fundamentally various formations, methods, tactics, capacities and culture to be followed, this produces an effect on organizational adjustment and implementation (He & Wong, 2004; Liao et al., 2018), and the lack of rigorous investigation of the innovation ambidexterity concept in a technological setting, resulting in answering three important questions: (1) What subdivisions does innovation ambidexterity have?; (2) The extent to which innovations ambidexterity concept may be affected by technological factors; and (3) What are the possible future avenues for tech-novation ambidexterity? Different aspects of innovation ambidexterity have been published in international journals (Ardito et al., 2019; Bozic & Dimovski, 2019; Cabeza-Pullés et al., 2020; Wiratmadja et al., 2021; Zhang et al., 2022). However, no comprehensive review of innovation ambidexterity has been published based on bibliometric analysis (BR). Moreover, the lack of study on the innovation ambidexterity concept by scholars in a technological context is tangible. By using BR, the investigation aims to probe the innovation ambidexterity notion along different paths. Firstly, an overview of the innovation ambidexterity concept is presented. Secondly, according to the previous research frame extracted from WOS, by applying BR, the future structure model has been suggested. The WOS database presented 52 publications around the innovation ambidexterity concept published from 2010 to 2021 and the study contributes to show the most influential authors, top prominent countries studying the innovation ambidexterity concept, the best journal publications related to this concept, theoretical background and fundamentally different new future research structure.

In the next sections, an overview of technovation ambidexterity and innovation ambidexterity and the related theoretical concepts is presented. The methodology used in this indication and the results are then explained. Finally, after discussion about the core concepts, this chapter concludes with the arguments that offer directions for future researchers in the technovation ambidexterity concept.

Overview of Technovation Ambidexterity

Ambidextrous Innovation

Ambidextrous innovation refers to the ability of an organization to follow exploratory innovation together with exploitative innovation leading to superior sustainable performance (Acikgoz et al., 2021; Bozic & Dimovski, 2019; Cho et al., 2019; Hughes et al., 2020; Liao et al., 2018). Exploitative innovation is a learning activity referring to improvement of existing products, efficiency, refining execution and choice-inducing tasks along with using existing competencies, technologies and procedures implemented to satisfy the existing customers' needs and markets. Exploratory innovation is a learning activity referring to variance-inducing activities, discovery, experiments, proactive strategies for exploring new possibilities, satisfying the emerging customers' or markets' needs, expanding existing knowledge, skills and developing up-to-date products (Acikgoz et al., 2021; Cho et al., 2019; Hughes et al., 2010, 2020; Jin et al., 2018; Liao et al., 2018).

According to He and Wong (2004), innovative exploitation duties refer to the technical innovative functions aiming to improve existing product-market fields, and exploratory innovation is described as the technical innovative implementations aiming to penetrate new product-market areas (Gupta et al., 2006; Rezaei et al., 2022). Ambidextrous firms are proceeding with applying available sources in order to continue gradual innovation, while at the same time probing novel competencies and developing modern innovative functions (Soto-Acosta et al., 2018). Organizations which balance radical innovation activities against incremental innovation activities can perform competitively into existing and future marketplaces, improving their chances of survival. Although the functions related to the radical innovation are important factors for organizations to have a sustainable competitive advantage in the long-run, the incremental innovation activities are considered to help the company to be lucrative in the short-run (Ardito et al., 2019). Since exploratory innovation activities and exploitative innovation activities compete for scarce resources, firms face some challenges as these concepts are considered to be contrary functions (Ardito et al., 2019; Foroudi et al., 2021a, 2021b; Li et al., 2020; Sumrin et al., 2021).

Technovation Ambidexterity

Previous literature has offered various factors having critical impact on innovation ambidexterity consisting of environmental, technological, knowledge and market issues. For example, some of them have stated that knowledge plays a critical role following innovation ambidexterity. Cabeza-Pullés and his colleagues have found that there is a connection between intra-organizational networking and ambidextrous innovation and finally have concluded that knowledge absorption mediates this relation having a positive effect on ambidextrous innovation. Moreover, in their view intra-organizational networking has a positive impact on absorbing and transforming knowledge. In another study, Chang et al. (2011) have found that managers' intra-organizational mechanisms including centralization and inter-departmental connectedness in a highly turbulent environment provoke the emergence of innovation ambidexterity and that knowledge plays a crucial role in shaping centralization and inter-departmental connectedness. Acikgoz et al. (2021) have investigated the relation between unlearning processes and new product development, concluding that innovation ambidexterity mediates the relationship, while unlearning processes that occur in task-relevant knowledge promote NPD. Jin et al. (2018) have proposed that knowledge breadth and knowledge depth have a critical role in innovative performances. They mention that at low levels, the increasing of the former intensifies exploratory innovation performance quickly. In contrast, at high levels of the knowledge sources, the "ambidexterity balance" theory is more suitable to have an equivalence between knowledge depth and knowledge breadth, increasing in explorative innovation performances.

Additionally, this theory can be applied to exploitative innovation, which has a great equivalent. Lucena (2016) explored that technology alliances bring explorative and exploitative activities, related to R&D, into the equation. These alliances are related to mechanisms providing knowledge embedded in the firm's environment categorized into exploration and exploitation depending on using new knowledge or existing knowledge. According to Lucena (2016), the relation between the firm and external partners like universities or public research centers can generate and share new knowledge as a source of exploration with the organization. However, alliances between suppliers and clients as complementary partners' capabilities are perceived as a source of existing knowledge.

Other chapters have focused on issues related to market, technological and environmental fields. For example, Liao et al. (2018) have concentrated on examining the ambidextrous business model including two key elements (market-driven and driving-market). They probe that innovation ambidexterity in a technological context has some impacts on business model ambidexterity mediating the association with technological ambidextrous innovation ambidexterity and organizational implementation. Furthermore, they demonstrate that an ambidextrous business model has positive effects on organizational execution. In another study, Hughes et al. (2020) offer that in young technology-based firms entrepreneurial strategies involving behaviours referring to looking for opportunities and advantageous exploration play critical roles in innovation ambidexterity, and since these types of firms have some challenges with resource scarcity encountered with technological turbulences and environmental dynamisms, the importance of integrating these behaviours for generating innovation is palpable. They argue that entrepreneurial orientation and collaborative orientation as two critical factors are antecedents of innovation ambidexterity (Hughes et al., 2020; Sakhdari, 2016).

Hughes et al. (2010) in another study have shown the pivotal impact of innovation ambidexterity on risk of successful export of international high-tech companies. They suggest that according to resource based view (RBV) theory ambidextrous innovation covers different markets and the cost of lead advantages led to gain from performing risk of export. According to their perspective, market differentiation and cost leadership strategies together have positive impacts on differentiation and cost advantages, while market differentiation exclusively is a crucial factor in driving innovation ambidexterity. Zang and Li (2016) in their investigation mention that the technological capacities and the market competencies have an inverted connection with ambidextrous innovation in the U-shaped. In line with this, technology capabilities are described as the capabilities of the organization to engage and develop different technologies and performances including technological developments, product developments, improving manufacturing processes and the technology forecasting. The market capabilities are described as the competencies of an organization enabling them to be adaptive with customer changes by making an appropriate connection with customers and channel members. Along with this view, Kuo et al. (2018) mention that technological innovation capabilities and managerial innovation capabilities are identified as two crucial wings to achieve innovation ambidexterity. This means that the former improves exploration and the latter promotes exploitation. They also argue that dynamic capabilities and innovation capabilities can ease keeping balance between the two. Soto-Acosta et al. (2018) assess the relation between TOE theory agents (technology, organization and environment) and ambidextrous innovation. They suggest that technological information capabilities, managerial knowledge capacities and dynamic environment impact on innovation ambidexterity positively (Chang et al., 2011).

Method

Data was collected using bibliometric techniques and compiled from the ISI Web of Science database (WOS) which has been used by scholars (Dias, 2019; Foroudi et al., 2021a, 2021b; Martinez-Lopez et al., 2020, Zhao et al., 2018). The WOS database is among the most exact sources and entails documents from as far back as 1900 from over 12,000 journals and is a dominant database for academic research (Foroudi & Dennis, 2023; Martinez-Lopez et al., 2020; Zhao et al., 2018). The bibliometric technique, through its quantitative approach to prior literature, has obtained significant attention in fields of study and has been extensively used in different areas, such as marketing, engineering and mathematics (Foroudi et al., 2021a, 2021b; Van Raan, 2003). There are plenty of studies in diversity issues which have applied the method so far, for instance, food chemistry and innovation adoption (Kamdem et al., 2019; Van Oorschot et al., 2018), entrepreneurship education (Aparicio et al., 2019), innovation systems and climate change (Suominen et al., 2019; Wu et al., 2018). We have made an effort to extract different documents from WOS involving chapters, early access papers, review articles, data papers, editorial materials and the other documents available in WOS (Zha et al., 2023a, 2023b; Akarsu et al., 2022; Akbari et al., 2022a,

2022b). The research includes all documents with the "innovation ambidexterity" research term, using the "Topic" section of the database. The "All Year" time-frame to develop information about the journals has been chosen but the first records obtained from the database were from 2010 and included 69 documents, all of which have been published in the English language. The authors found 11 articles by changing the research terms ("innovation ambidexterity" and "tech-nology") to study innovation ambidexterity in a technological context. Moreover, articles which have been published in other fields have not been considered in this study and only articles related to fields of management, economics and business are included. Furthermore, the results showed that 52 documents were published in 38 journals based on the WOS database. Organization-Enhanced for studying innovation ambidexterity are "Chinese Academy of Science"(7), "University of Science and Technology of China CAS"(5), "Northeastern University"(4), "Telkom University"(4), "City University of Hong Kong"(3), "National Sun Yat Sen University"(3), "University of Nottingham"(3), "Brawijaya University"(2), "Cardiff University"(2) and "Central University of Finance Economics"(2). With VOSviewer software, which is a tool mapping are created, visualized and explored based on network data, we explored data and obtained particular relationships with networks and maps from the WOS database (Van Eck & Waltman, 2020). One of the current analysis methods to illustrate the graphical presentation of bibliometric analysis is network visualizing, allowing researchers to understand the research domain (Foroudi et al., 2021a, 2021b) (Fig. 3.1).

Results

This study recognizes 47 articles, four early access papers, two proceeding papers, two review papers and one item of editorial material. Furthermore, the results showed that 52 documents have been published by 130 authors in 38 journals and 26 countries. Then, these documents were classified into three clusters named as "Organizational ambidexterity", "Market ambidexterity" and "Environmental factors and ambidexterity". In order to identify the technological factors influ-encing innovation ambidexterity in the technological context, the terms "inno-vation ambidexterity" and "technology" were searched again in the WOS database, finding a new cluster named "Technovation ambidexterity" with 11 articles studying innovation ambidexterity with technological factors. As shown in Table 3.1, the number of studies assessing the innovation ambidexterity concept between 2010 and 2021 increased significantly.

Most Cited Studies

The publications with the most cited references have been extracted from the WOS database. The analysis demonstrated that the total citations of these publications were 1,007 and the average number of citations per year was 19.37 (see Table 3.2). "Managing the exploitation/exploration paradox: The role of a learning capability and innovation ambidexterity" (Lin et al., 2013) is the most cited paper, with 141

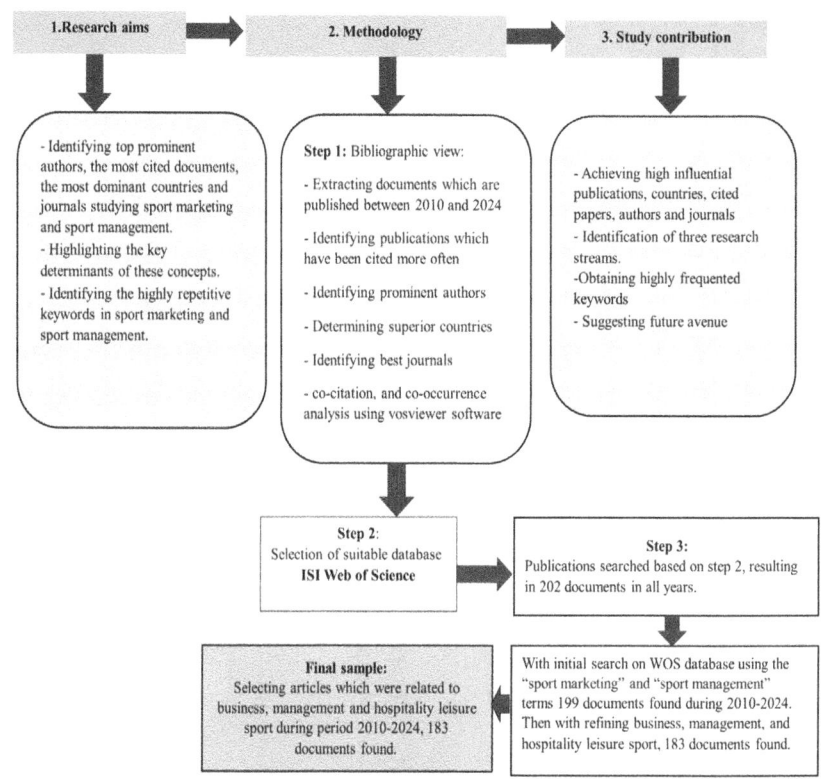

Fig. 3.1.   Research Approach.

Table 3.1. Total Studies in Innovation Ambidexterity per Year.

Publication Year	Number of Studies	Number of citations	h-Index
2021	8	2	1
2020	7	46	4
2019	8	62	5
2018	7	84	5
2017	5	56	4
2016	7	100	5
2015	3	96	2
2014	2	31	1
2013	1	140	1
2012	1	138	1
2011	2	170	2
2010	1	79	1

Table 3.2. Most Cited Studies in Innovation Ambidexterity.

Rank	Title	Authors	Journal	Year	Total Citation	Average Rate of Citations Yearly
1	Managing the exploration/ exploitation paradox: The role of a learning capability and innovation ambidexterity	Lin et al.	Journal of Product Innovation Management	2013	141	15.67
2	Drivers of innovation ambidexterity in small to medium-sized firms	Chang & Hughes	European Management Journal	2012	138	13.80
3	Internal and external antecedents of SME's innovation ambidexterity outcomes	Chang et al.	Management Decision	2011	98	8.91
4	Guest Editors' introduction: the role of human resources and organisational factors in ambidexterity	Junni et al.	Human Resource Management	2015	80	11.43
5	Realising product-market advantage in high-technology international new ventures: The mediating role of ambidextrous innovation	Hughes et al.	Journal of International Marketing	2010	79	6.58
6	Investigating the role of leadership and organisational culture in fostering innovation ambidexterity	Lin et al.	IEEE Transactions on Engineering Management	2011	72	6.55
7		Zhang et al.		2016	46	7.67

	Title	Author(s)	Journal	Year		
	The interactive effects of entrepreneurial orientation and capability-based HRM on firm performance: the mediating role of innovation ambidexterity		Industrial Marketing Management			
8	Information technology, knowledge management and environmental dynamism as drivers of innovation ambidexterity: a study in SMEs	Soto-Acosta et al.	Journal of Knowledge Management	2018	35	8.75
9	Cognitive frames, learning mechanisms, and innovation ambidexterity	Lin & McDonough	Journal of Product Innovation Management	2014	31	3.88
10	The influence of inbound open innovation on ambidexterity performance: Does it pay to source knowledge from supply chain stakeholders?	Ardito et al.	Journal of Business Research	2020	24	12
11	Flying or dying? Organisational change, customer participation, and innovation ambidexterity in emerging economies	Chen et al.	Asia Pacific Journal of Management	2018	22	5.5
12	Technology capabilities, marketing capabilities and innovation ambidexterity	Zang et al.	Technology Analysis & Strategic Management	2017	19	3.8

(Continued)

Table 3.2. (*Continued*)

Rank	Title	Authors	Journal	Year	Total Citation	Average Rate of Citations Yearly
13	Why does leader attention scope matter for innovation ambidexterity? The mediating role of transformational leadership	Zheng et al.	Leadership and Organisational Development Journal	2016	18	3
14	Innovation ambidexterity of open firms. The role of internal relational social capital	Lazzarotti et al.	Technology Analysis & Strategic Management	2017	17	3.4
15	How institutions influence SME innovation and networking practices: The case of Vietnamese Agribusiness	Minh & Hjortsø	Journal of Small Business Management	2015	15	2.14
16	Innovation ambidexterity: balancing exploitation and exploration for startup and established restaurants and impacts upon performance	Cho et al.	Industry and Innovation	2020	14	4.67
17	Business intelligence and analytics use, innovation ambidexterity, and firm performance: A dynamic capabilities perspective	Bozic & Dimovski	Journal of Strategic Information Systems	2019	13	4.33
18	Knowing what we know differently knowledge heterogeneity and dynamically ambidextrous innovation	Tsai	Journal of Organisational Change Management	2016	12	2

No.	Title	Authors	Journal	Year		
19	Effect of leadership styles on financial performance: Mediating roles of exploitative and exploratory innovations case of knowledge-intensive firms	Berraies & Bchini	International Journal of Innovation Management	2019	11	3.67
20	Is distributed leadership a driving factor of innovation ambidexterity? An empirical study with mediating and moderating effects	Fu et al.	Leadership & Organisation Development Journal	2018	11	2.75

citations. This study explains that the learning capabilities have been defined as the actions improving intra-organizational learning between employees and for contributing with other organizations in order to increase learning capabilities and build an open culture in the firm to enable them to promote shared knowledge. Moreover, the impacts of these capabilities on ambidextrous innovation and the effects of ambidextrous innovation on organizational implementation have been examined. The "Drivers of innovation ambidexterity" article title accounted for 138 citations (Chang & Hughes, 2012). This article investigates the top managers' features, intra-organizational structures characteristics and organizational contexts simplifying emergence of ambidextrous innovation into small- and medium-sized enterprises (SMEs). Furthermore, ambidextrous innovation mediates the relation between managerial, structural and contextual features and SMEs executions. The next article topic, "Internal and external antecedents of SMEs innovation ambidexterity outcomes", accounting for 98 citations (Chang et al., 2011), investigates the internal and external features which every SMEs must have for being ambidextrous.

The Most Influential Authors

This section presents the most influential authors cited by other researchers, their h-index and the number of publications which have been published by them. Overall, 130 authors have studied the innovation ambidexterity area and "Hughes M" with 320 citations and h-index 4 is the most dominant author with the most citations. Furthermore, "Lin he" and "Mcdonough EF" with 244 and "Chang YY" with 236 citations 'have been cited significantly more often' (See Table 3.3).

Table 3.3. Top Prominent Authors in Innovation Ambidexterity.

Raw	Author Names	Total Studies	Total Citations	h-index
1	LIU ZY	5	33	2
2	HUGHES M	4	320	4
3	LIAO SQ	3	13	2
4	LIN HE	3	244	3
5	MCDONOUGH EF	3	244	3
6	ARDITO L	2	32	2
7	CHANG YY	2	236	2
8	FU LH	2	11	1
9	MORGAN RE	2	84	2
10	ZHANG JA	2	56	2

Table 3.4. Top Prominent Countries in Innovation Ambidexterity.

Raw	Countries	Total Studies	Total Citations	h-index
1	PEOPLES R CHINA	16	189	7
2	The United States	11	437	7
3	TAIWAN	9	510	7
4	ENGLAND	7	401	5
5	ITALY	4	49	3
6	SPAIN	3	48	3
7	AUSTRIA	2	12	2
8	INDONESIA	2	5	1
9	JAPAN	2	3	1
10	NEW ZEALAND	2	56	2

The Most Dominant Countries

This section presents the most dominant countries studying the innovation ambidexterity concept. Table 3.4 shows the number of publications which have been studied in each country, the countries having the most cited publications and h-index (Fig. 3.2). In total, 26 countries have published articles related to the innovation ambidexterity concept and "Spain", "Italy", "England", "Taiwan", "the United States", "Peoples R China", "New Zealand", "Japan", "Indonesia" and "Austria" have the most cited publications. According to the ranking, China has the most major total studies, followed by the United States and Taiwan. Taiwan has the most cited publications, with 510, while the Unites States and England have 437 and 401, respectively. In addition, England is the country with the highest number of citations for the innovation ambidexterity concept, with

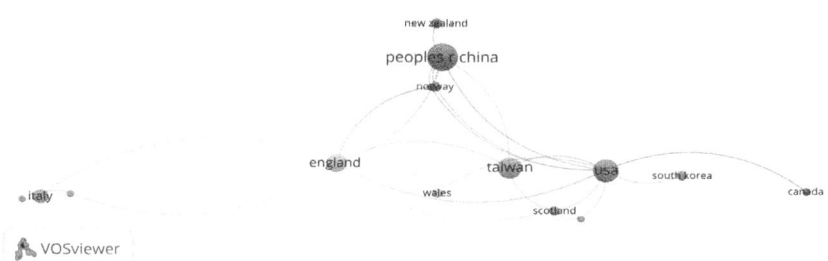

Fig. 3.2.   Mapping of Countries Have Published on the Innovation Ambidexterity Topic.

57.29 citations per document, while Taiwan has 56.67 citations per document and the United States has 39.73 citations per document.

The Most Prominent Journals Publishing on Innovation Ambidexterity

This section offers 52 documents published in 38 journals. Table 3.5 shows the total outstanding and the most cited journals in the innovation ambidexterity area. The statistical analysis showed the Journal of Product Innovation Management is the prominent journal, having 86.00 citations per document. The European Management Journal and the Journal of IEEE Transactions on Engineering Management have 73.00 and 36.00 citations per document, respectively. Moreover, the Journal of Technology Analysis Strategic Management has published five articles on innovation ambidexterity, the most of any journal.

Table 3.5. Top Prominent Journals in Innovation Ambidexterity.

Row	Journal Titles	Total Studies	Total Citations	h-index
1	TECHNOLOGY ANALYSIS STRATEGIC MANAGEMENT	5	49	4
2	EUROPEAN MANAGEMENT JOURNAL	2	146	2
3	IEEE TRANSACTIONS ON ENGINEERING MANAGEMENT	2	72	1
4	INDUSTRY AND INNOVATION	2	19	2
5	INTERNATIONAL BUSINESS REVIEW	2	3	1
6	INTERNATIONAL JOURNAL OF INNOVATION MANAGEMENT	2	21	2
7	JOURNAL OF BUSINESS RESEARCH	2	24	1
8	JOURNAL OF KNOWLEDGE MANAGEMENT	2	36	1
9	JOURNAL OF LEADERSHIP ORGANIZATIONAL STUDIES	2	18	2
10	JOURNAL OF PRODUCT INNOVATION MANAGEMENT	2	172	2

The Highest Cited Publications Studying the Notion of Innovation Ambidexterity

Document Co-citation Analysis

In order to investigate the conceptualization of the 52 publications, co-cited references have been studied. Generally, VOSviewer software by default illustrated 2,961 cited references of which the minimum number was 20, resulting in 13 papers. Then as the study authors wanted to assess more papers, nine citations of a cited reference were chosen, concluding in 34 papers (See Table 3.6). Fig. 3.3 displays networks of analysis obtained from VOSviewer co-citation analysis including three clusters. As shown in Fig. 3.4 innovation ambidexterity has three subdivisions, named "Organizational ambidexterity", "Market ambidexterity" and "Environmental factors and ambidexterity", which have been explained in the next sections.

Cluster A: Organizational Ambidexterity

Cluster A includes 16 articles named "Organizational ambidexterity". Generally, the cluster investigates approaches and tensions for implementing ambidexterity theory in the organization and the possible impacts that these challenges and approaches might have on the firm performance. Exploration and exploitation are identified as the two main wings for ambidextrous companies. These concepts are applied to other organizational topics such as technical organizational innovation, organizational design, organizational adaptation, organizational learning, competitive advantage, organizational surviving, innovation, strategic alliances, research and knowledge creating, issues for coming to market, strategic management, technological management, organizational theory and organizational behaviour, and were studied after the article by March (1991) (Gupta et al., 2006; Rothaermel & Alexandre, 2009; Simsek, 2009).

Among these studies emerged numerous challenges for managing these concepts. One of those is the conceptual differences between exploration and exploitation. Exploration refers to research, discovery, experiment, risk taking, learning and innovation. However, exploitative activities are the use of existing competencies, improvement, implementation, efficiency, manufacturing and choice (Chao et al., 2009; Gupta et al., 2006; He & Wong, 2004). Ambidextrous organizations are those which pursue the two wings simultaneously (O'Reilly & Tushman, 2013). Organizations paying more attention to adapting processes for exploitation rather than exploration have short-term efficiency while in the long-term they will fail (March, 1991). Additionally, organizations, particularly SMEs, find that it is more difficult to pursue exploration and exploitation simultaneously (Chang & Hughes, 2012; Gupta et al., 2006). To overcome these challenges and be ambidextrous, SMEs can rely on the features of the top managers and form suitable organizational structures and contexts (Chang & Hughes, 2012; Lubatkin et al., 2006).

Table 3.6. An Overview of the High-Cited Papers in Innovation Ambidexterity.

Authors Name	Findings	Key Definitions
Lin et al. (2013)	Investigating the effect of learning capabilities on innovation ambidexterity. Moreover, this paper examines the question of whether innovation ambidexterity has any impact on organizational performance.	Learning capability Innovation ambidexterity Performance Exploration Exploitation
Chang and Hughes (2012)	This paper studies the top manager features and the structural and contextual factors facilitating SMEs ambidexterity. In this study, ambidextrous innovation mediates the relation between these intra-organizational features and the top manager features.	SMEs Ambidexterity concept Innovation notion
Chang et al. (2011)	This study investigates the outputs of ambidexterity in SMEs and explains that internal structures of the firm and the environmental conditions have important impacts on pursuing ambidexterity.	Explorative innovation activities Exploitative innovation functions Ambidextrous innovation Intra-organizational structures Different environmental features SMEs Innovation concept
Junni et al. (2015)	In this study, the effects of employees and leadership features, intra-organizational structures, organizational culture issues, social relationship behaviours and impacts of different organizational environments on firm execution have been investigated.	Ambidextrous organizations Explorative activities Exploitative functions Human resource management Cultural issues Intra-organizational structures Social relationship behaviours

Hughes et al. (2010)	This study examines the relation between competitive strategies, innovation ambidexterity and the risks of export performance.	Innovation concept Strategies related to market Ambidextrous firms New international risks Functions related to export
Lin and McDonough (2011)	The key role of strategic managers is to have an equivalent in explorative activities and exploitative functions.	Ambidextrous innovation Exploration and exploitation Organization culture Strategic leadership Taiwan
Zhang et al. (2016)	This study examines the interactions of entrepreneurial orientation and human resource management and their impacts on innovation ambidexterity. In this paper, innovation ambidexterity was identified as a mechanism in which entrepreneurial orientation and human resource management working together to achieve high performance.	Entrepreneurial orientation Capability-based HRM Ambidextrous innovation Organizational execution
Soto-Acosta et al. (2018)	In this study, impacts of environmental characteristics, organizational features and technological elements on ambidextrous innovation have been examined. Moreover, the relation between ambidextrous innovation and SMEs implementations has been assessed. Furthermore, environmental dynamism is considered as a moderator in the relation.	Information technology capabilities Organizational implementation Ambidextrous innovation Dynamic environments Knowledge management capabilities

(Continued)

Table 3.6. (*Continued*)

Authors Name	Findings	Key Definitions
Lin et al. (2014)	This paper investigates that the conceptual paradigms of ambidexterity play a critical role in creating innovation ambidexterity.	–
Ardito et al. (2020)	This study reveals that the knowledge sourcing of the supply chain stakeholders has some impacts on ambidextrous innovation.	Ambidextrous innovation Stakeholders of supply chain Original innovation Continuous innovation Explorative activities Exploitative functions Open innovation External knowledge

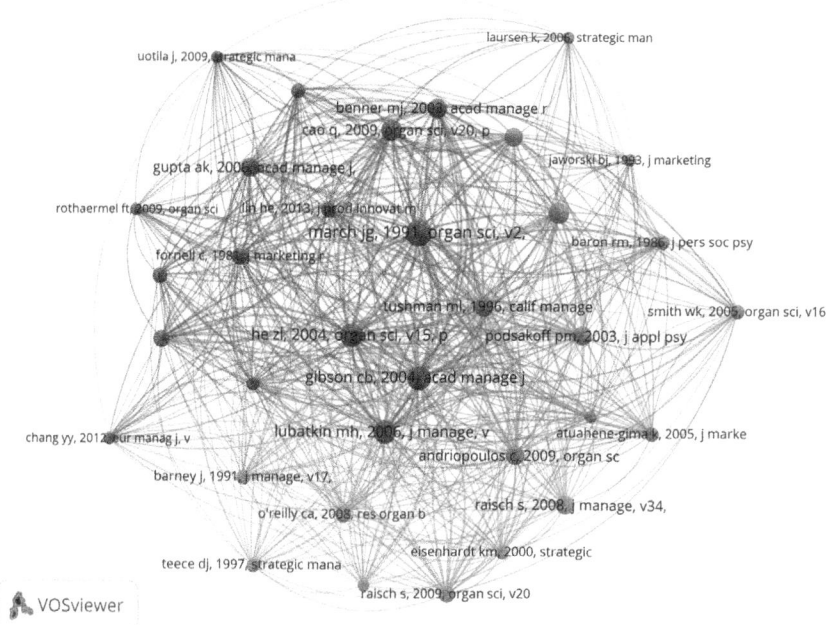

Fig. 3.3.   The Co-citation Network Analysis in Innovation
Ambidexterity Documents.

There are three main approaches for creating ambidexterity in firms: forming separated structures (structural ambidexterity), providing a suitable environment in the organization (contextual ambidexterity) and having a temporary change between explorative and exploitative functions (sequential ambidexterity). Structural ambidexterity is defined as the capability of an organization to pursue explorative activities and exploitative activities in separate units. Furthermore, these activities must be monitored and conducted by integrated strategic planning (Jenson et al., 2009; O'Reilly & Tushman, 2013). Another strategy is sequential ambidexterity, which involves a temporal change between exploration and exploitation during time. This strategy is inefficient, especially in dynamic environments. Contextual ambidexterity is identified as the organizational behavioural capacity that the performances related to adaptability and alignment will be pursued all through the unit (Gibson & Birkinshaw, 2004; Tushman & O'Reilly, 1996). Furthermore, crowdsourcing, human resource and team working activities and shared values related to contextual ambidexterity will be improved between employees encouraging them to think and act daily ambidextrously (Andriopoulos and Marianne, 2009). Two existing ambiguities for exploration and exploitation as two dimensions of ambidexterity are BD and CD. SMEs facing scarce resources must have a suitable balance between them, while

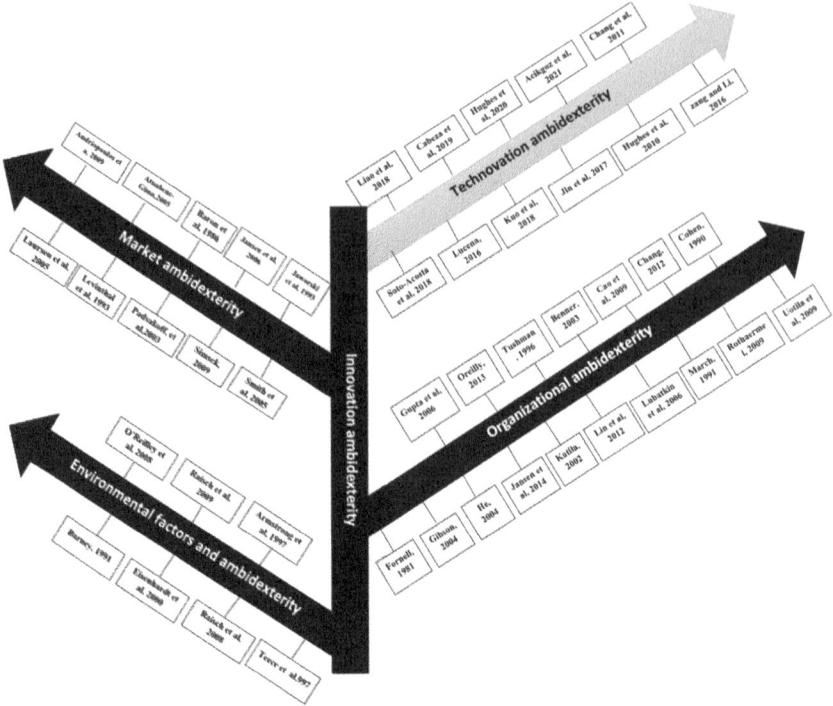

Fig. 3.4.   Innovation Ambidexterity Subdivisions, Resulting
Bibliometric Analysis.

big corporations having enough resources can use the combined dimensions for
being ambidextrous (Chao et al., 2009). Moreover, following exploitative and
explorative functions are completely dependent upon the environmental conditions and the technological dynamic situations of the firm. Those having
high-technologically changing environments must constantly explore new technologies as in the short term their existing resources and competencies might be
abolished. In contrast, firms located in the less technologically changing environments can gain from their basic technologies and concentrate more on
exploitation in the long term. Thus, the relation between tending to explore new
things properly and the financial performance is completely referred to the
research and development (R&D) processes (Uotila et al., 2009).

Regarding the size and resource availability of the firm, exploration and exploitation should be examined in other contexts. For instance, He and Wong (2004)
investigated ambidexterity theories in the particular context which aims to show how
firms in the technological innovation context focus on exploration and exploitation
strategically. In addition to having a good interactive strategy, exploitation and
exploration strategies have a significant impact on the sales growth of the firm.

The technology sourcing strategy can be critical for organizations, especially in recent decades in which the strict competition between firms has considerably increased and ambidextrous firms can finally be successful. In this way, exploration and exploitation are categorized into technological and organizational boundaries identified as internal and external sourcing and firms must keep a suitable balance between them in order to perform properly.

As a result, four strategies have been offered: known technology – internal sourcing; new technology – internal sourcing; known technology – external sourcing; and new technology-external sourcing (Rothaermel & Alexandre, 2009). In other studies, exploration and exploitation are defined differently; for example, Katila and Ahuja (2002) stated that the firm's research must be categorized in two ways: the research depth and the research scope. Research depth mentions that firms should use their current knowledge frequently, while research scope states that companies must explore new knowledge and ideas widely. As a result, the former is related to the exploitation and the latter is related to the exploration (Benner & Tushman, 2003). Another crucial way to follow exploration and exploitation simultaneously is facilitating learning and knowledge transfer in the firm with implementing learning capabilities in the organization (Lin et al., 2013). Learning capability is performed in the firm by following three functions: building an open culture in the firm in which shared knowledge will be promoted, improving intra-organizational learning between employees and contributing with other organizations helping to learn widely. All these activities must be done together as they have synergistic effects fostering ambidexterity in an organization (Lin et al., 2013).

Market Ambidexterity

This cluster has 11 articles which labelled as "Market ambidexterity" including market orientation, customer direction and competitor tendency as the subdivisions resulting in keeping a suitable balance between two market paradoxes, exploiting current product innovation and exploring new competencies, while different environmental features such as dynamic or static conditions will affect the firm to keep an appropriate balance between them (Andriopoulos and Marianne, 2009; Atuahene-Gima, 2005; Jansen et al., 2006; Fornell & Larcker, 1981). Innovation is identified as a challenging and critical managerial responsibility factor and has three paradoxes named as customer direction encompassing tight coupling and loose coupling learning cycles, employee intensives and profit-making. These paradoxes with applying differentiation ambidexterity and integration ambidexterity techniques can be managed and finally the ambidexterity strategy be implemented. Differentiation is described as the strength of an organization in order to separate existing product design activities and innovative ones, while the integration technique is described as the activities integrating the designs and strategies (Smith & Tushman, 2005). Managing these paradoxes not only needs the top manager's efforts but also needs whole organization contributions (Andriopoulos and Marianne, 2009). In addition, managers are dealing with an important strategic problem for product innovation which is exploiting current product innovation competencies helping to improve financial performance of the firm in competitive environments and at the same time preventing the effects like inflexibility and inefficiency at exploring new ones, especially in dynamic environments (Jansen et al., 2006). There are some factors helping the organization to conduct exploring new product innovation competencies and exploiting current ones simultaneously which are implementing the dual structures, behavioural contexts and the top management teams behavioural integration (Simsek, 2009). The firms which totally concentrate on exploiting current product innovation competencies might be successful in the short-run, while they might fail as not to gain from the benefits of creating new product innovation competencies in the long term. Innovative firms have changed their strategies to achieve new ideas and use open strategies including external actors and resources. The terms "searching widely" and "searching deeply" can be critical to have an equivalent in explorative product innovation and exploitative ones which former is concentrating on exploring knowledge and the latter is focusing on exploiting current knowledge (Laursen & Salter, 2005; Katila & Ahuja, 2002) and if the organization overcome the challenge, it will promote product innovation and create competitive advantage (Atuahene-Gima, 2005). Market orientation can be the main and crucial way for having the ability of keeping a suitable balance between exploring new product innovation and exploiting new ones solving the challenges in the face of the firm for being ambidextrous (Atuahene-Gima, 2005; Jaworski & Kohli, 1993). Likewise, customer orientation and competitor orientation can ensure exploring new product innovation competencies and exploiting current ones simultaneously. This means that the current knowledge of existing competitors and customers and the future ones can help the firm to allocate required resources for being ambidextrous (Atuahene-Gima, 2005; Andriopoulos and Marianne, 2009).

Market orientation is referred to the top manager teams having critical role in shaping the firm's values and orientations with giving clear signals about the importance of being responsiveness to customer needs, encouraging employees for tracking the market changes, sharing market intelligence with others in the organization and being responsible for the market needs (Jaworski & Kohli, 1993). Meanwhile, top manager teams can improve the trade-offs between exploration and exploitation and other factors like decisions related to organizational forms, cultures and the processes of resource allocation conducted by them which can help the organization to pursue exploration and exploitation simultaneously, being ambidextrous (Simsek, 2009). There are various coordination mechanisms in the firm known as formal and informal ones. Centralization mechanisms have negative effects on new innovation activities, while formalization mechanisms have positive impacts on exploitative innovation. However, the connectedness leads to a positive impact on explorative innovation functions and exploitative ones (Jansen et al., 2006). Moreover, learning is a key element for exploring new knowledge and exploiting current competencies specially when the firm is in the face of the dynamic environment and finally can overcome these problems through simplification and specialization improving exploration and exploitation (Levinthal & March, 1993). As mentioned above, market orientation is related to the features of the top manager team's policies and is the main way to pursue exploiting current innovative product competencies, while finding new ones leading to ambidextrous market and sustainable performance (Smith & Tushman, 2005). Market orientation is completely dependent on environmental factors such as market and technological turbulence and the level of the competition (Jaworski & Kohli, 1993). As a consequence, these factors can play a critical role in ambidextrous firms.

Environmental Factors and Ambidexterity. This cluster has seven articles, named "Environmental factors and ambidexterity". Environmental changes can have a crucial impact on an organization's survival. Organizational ecology has offered testimonies that organizations which are more stable will not be successful and ultimately fail. In contrast, firms improving learning processes and adapting themselves to environmental changes will succeed. Strategic researchers have stated that the dynamic capabilities are described as the capabilities of an organization in order to redesign available capabilities, product development, strategic decision-making and alliances, leading to long-run competitiveness. Nevertheless, since ambidexterity is a strategy performed in the firms to follow exploration and exploitation together, the top manager team's roles in shaping these capabilities are critical (Eisenhardt & Martin, 2000; O'Reilly & Tushman, 2008). The understanding of how competitive advantage will be achieved is a critical issue for industries located in high-technology contexts, such as semiconductors, information services and software. These firms prefer to follow the "Resource-based strategy" while this strategy is often not enough to provide significant competitive advantage. However, organizations which are flexible and timely in their responsiveness to constant changes can redeploy their interior and exterior capabilities and be innovative (Teece et al., 1997). Other studies have proved that companies gaining from sources which are worthwhile, scarce, unique and irreplaceable obtain tolerable competitiveness (Barney, 1991; Eisenhardt & Martin, 2000). In mildly environmental markets, dynamic abilities are identified as typical capabilities which are predictable, exact, analytical and constant processes which have predictable outputs. Moreover, encountered with high turbulence market conditions, these capabilities are defined as the processes which are simple and highly experiential which have unpredictable outcomes (Eisenhardt & Martin, 2000). Since ambidexterity needs both wings to be in alignment and adaptive with environmental changes, worthwhile. Furthermore, factors like organizational size, resource limitation, industrial context and the degree of environmental turbulence and competition have a critical impact on ambidexterity (Raisch & Birkinshaw, 2008; Raisch et al., 2009).

Technovation Ambidexterity. This cluster has 11 articles named "Technovation ambidexterity". Since in this article examining the innovation ambidexterity concept in a technological setting has a degree of importance, the research term has been changed from "Innovation ambidexterity" to "Innovation ambidexterity" and "Technology" in the WOS database and a new cluster with 11 papers examining the impacts of technological issues on innovation ambidexterity added as a new cluster. According to Teece et al. (1997) and Soto-Acosta (2018), managers encountering technological changes and competitive environments are obliged to have an equivalent in explorative and exploitative activities to be successfully ambidextrous in the technological setting. Therefore, "technological innovation ambidexterity" (technovation ambidexterity) can help them with the encountered challenges. Technological capabilities of organizations are defined as the capabilities which the firm can employ and develop various technologies helping the organization to implement executions like technological development improvement, developed production activities, improved operation processes and technological forecasting. These capabilities facilitate knowledge transfer to the organization, especially from universities and research institutions helping the firm to exploit current knowledge and technical resources and at the same time gain from explorative innovation through employing and developing organizational technological resources, being ambidextrous (Zang & Li, 2016; Cabeza-Pullés et al., 2020).

During the unlearning processes, organizational teams can improve their new product development performance, leading to explorative innovation functions and exploitative ones simultaneously (Acikgoz et al., 2021). Along with other technological factors, the knowledge management factor can be the main key to shape technology and in line with knowledge base view (KBV) theory the crucial resource of the firm is knowledge as the competitors cannot imitate it; and since organizations having worthy, scarce, unique and irreplaceable sources gain from sustainable competitive advantage, knowledge also leads to improved firm performance (Barney, 1991; Soto-Acosta et al., 2018).

Since ambidextrous organizations are dominant in exploiting current knowledge and experiences for improving incremental innovation and radical innovation, firms must encompass the knowledge management capabilities to response quickly against competitors and have an equivalent in probing innovative activities and using existing capabilities (Jin et al., 2018; Soto-Acosta et al., 2018). Technology alliances are recognized as the explorative and exploitative capabilities facilitating the access of the organization to up-to-date knowledge and improving the available knowledge usage. These associations commit partners to participating R&D implementations aiming to produce and share new knowledge as resources of exploration and to commercialize the existing knowledge aiming to exploit it further' (Lucena, 2016). However, the inter organizational structures like connectedness and centralization are the crucial factors to achieve new knowledge and ambidexterity. Connectedness can promote inter-organizational knowledge resources facilitating explorative innovation and exploitative innovation (Chang et al., 2011). Explorative and exploitative markets and technologies can simplify the challenges of the business models enabling organizations to reconfigure their innovation capabilities and finally achieve innovation ambidexterity and high performance which has positive impact on business model ambidexterity (Kuo et al., 2018; Liao et al., 2018). Young high-tech firms have some challenges to achieve innovation ambidexterity as their resources and knowledge are not enough and can obtain ambidexterity through behaviours related to looking for opportunities and benefits (Hughes et al., 2020). As a result, technological factors, such as technological capabilities and technology alliances, can help organizations to achieve innovation ambidexterity (Lucena, 2016; Zang & Li, 2016).

Discussion

In this study the prominent authors, journals and countries have been introduced. In addition, this chapter represents a bibliometric analysis of the innovation ambidexterity concept to identify the trend of the previous studies annually, highly cited papers and leading authors and journals. Moreover, co-citation analysis was done to recognize and categorize the previous research structures around the innovation ambidexterity concept and the related documents collected from the WOS database for English language documents (52 documents). The most dominant journal in the field of innovation ambidexterity is "Technology analysis strategic management" having the most documents (5); the "People R China" with 16 articles is the most influential country in the innovation ambidexterity field and "LIU ZY" with five articles is the most prominent author.

The investigation suggests three main contributions. Firstly, total innovation ambidexterity publications are presented annually and notable authors, outstanding journals, leading countries and highly cited articles around the innovation ambidexterity field were offered which can illustrate a detailed perspective for future studies. Secondly, using co-citation document analysis this chapter showed three main clusters offering subdivisions of the innovation ambidexterity concept named "Organizational ambidexterity", "Market ambidexterity" and "Environmental factors and ambidexterity". In general, the first cluster aims to discuss the tensions and challenges to keep a suitable balance between explorative and exploitative functions (Chao et al., 2009; Gupta et al., 2006; O'Reilly & Tushman, 2013) and argues that organizations in the face of rare resources can either have an equivalent in performing discovery duties and operational tasks or combine them (Chang & Hughes, 2012; Chao et al., 2009). In addition, the cluster suggests solutions for making firms ambidextrous and provides contexts such as flexibility, trust, discipline, support and learning capability having most focus on employees, leading to ambidexterity. Moreover, the absorptive capacity is an important factor in recognizing and assimilating new information, helping the firm to achieve their commercial goals (Chang & Hughes, 2012, Cohen & Levinthal, 1990; Gibson & Birkinshaw, 2004; Jansen et al., 2009; Katila & Ahuja, 2002; Lin et al., 2013; Lubtican et al., 2006; O'Reilly & Tushman, 2013).

There are three main ways to turn the firm into the ambidextrous firm, such as structural separation, in which innovative exploration functions and innovative exploitative activities are followed simultaneously in separate units, sequential ambidexterity, in which in a particular period of the time the company switches on exploration or exploitation in proportion to the environmental changes and, finally, contextual ambidexterity focusing on employees and the behavioural issues which are so crucial for firms to become ambidextrous (Jansen et al., 2009; O'Reilly & Tushman, 2013). Rothaermel and Alexandre (2009) debate the technology sourcing strategy and suggest that this strategy is related to technological and organizational boundaries of the firm and offer four dimensions for exploration and exploitation using ambidexterity theories. In their investigation, the more absorptive capacity the more ambidextrous effectiveness in technology sourcing (Cohen & Levinthal, 1990). The second cluster is related to market ambidexterity tensions defined as the functions of a firm in order to use available innovative productions and probing recent ones simultaneously (Andriopoulos and Marianne, 2009; Atuahene-Gima, 2005; Jaworski & Kohli, 1993). Moreover, factors like customer orientation, market orientation and competitor orientation play key roles to overcome exploratory product innovation and exploitative current product innovation competency tensions. Furthermore, market orientation is a critical key solution for overcoming the tensions and is directly related to the top management team performance to create an appropriate behavioural context in the organization in order to achieve ambidexterity (Atuahene-Gima, 2005; Andriopoulos and Marianne, 2009; Baron & Kenny, 1986; Jansen, 2006; Jaworski & Kohli, 1993; Laursen & Salter, 2006; Podsakoff et al., 2003; Simsek, 2009; Smith & Tushman, 2005; Tushman & O'Reilly, 1996). In the third cluster, the results show that dynamic capabilities have a great impact on ambidexterity and organizational performance (Teece, 1997). Since ambidextrous innovation has not been assessed in the technological context, the third critical contribution to previous literature is to offer a new cluster named "Technovation ambidexterity" and the possible impacts it has on ambidexterity and performance. We found that some technological factors, such as technology alliances, technology capabilities, technology acceptance, the technology readiness level (TRL) and technology adoption can influence the performance of innovation ambidexterity in technological settings. Since previous literature has not examined the impacts of these factors on innovation ambidexterity, we suggest that more investigation around this topic should be done to fulfil the research gap and offer three future research avenues, named "Techno-organizational ambidexterity", "Techno market ambidexterity" and "Techno environmental factors and ambidexterity".

Conclusion

This study investigates innovation ambidexterity concept articles published between 2010 and 2021 using the bibliometric analysis method. The results showed that the co-citation analysis of innovation ambidexterity publications illustrated three clusters, named "Organizational ambidexterity", "Market ambidexterity" and "Environmental factors and ambidexterity". The new cluster "Technovation ambidexterity" which studies the innovation ambidexterity concept in technological settings was added to the primary clusters. Zang and Li (2016) and Cabeza-Pullés et al. (2020) state in a technological context (especially high-tech), that innovation ambidexterity may differ from non-technological areas. In innovation processes, exploration is highly dependent on technology acquisition and development within the firm TRL management and manufacturing maturity level management (MLM) play an important role in innovation ambidexterity in technological firms, since it is not possible to exploit a new product without upgrading technology maturity and manufacturing maturity. Developing technological organizational resources is critical to gaining the firm from explorative innovation to ambidexterity (Cabeza-Pullés et al., 2020; Zang & Li, 2016).

During new product development (NPD) processes, technology development has a vital influence on the NPD team and interdisciplinary teams must improve the technology maturity level when they are conducting exploratory and exploitative innovation simultaneously (Ackigos et al., 2021). Soto-Acosta et al. (2018) and Jin et al. (2018) state that in technological areas, market pull and technology push force firms to be ready for being quickly responsive against competitors and have an equivalent in innovative exploration implementations and innovative exploitation activities. Technology alliances engage partners in research and development implementations aiming to produce and share up-to-date knowledge, which is a discovery resource, and to apply the partner's completed competencies in order to perform exploitative duties (Lucena, 2016). Market readiness level for high-tech products, technology acceptance by the users and technology adoption to the market, and according to Kuo et al. (2018) and Liao. (2018) exploitative and explorative technological markets, can simplify the achievement of technovation ambidexterity and high performance. There are many new research areas, especially in techno-startup firms and high-tech early-stage firms that have some difficulties for achieving technology innovation ambidexterity because their insufficient resources and knowledge (Hughes et al., 2020) and technological factors, such as technological capabilities and technology alliances, can help organizations to achieve innovation ambidexterity (Lucena, 2016; Zang & Li, 2016). The results showed that technovation ambidexterity is a new agenda in innovation ambidexterity research whereas all three clusters of innovation ambidexterity, that is organizational ambidexterity, market ambidexterity and environmental factors and ambidexterity, which have been found can be influenced in technology contexts, especially in high-technological areas, and shape future areas of research in the field of technovation ambidexterity. Since the customer and market behaviours in emerging and high-technology fields are different from non-technological contexts and marketing is dependent upon some features, such as technology adoption and technology acceptance, there would be serious research gaps in the market ambidexterity field. As a result, one of the suggested future avenues will be technological market ambidexterity. Due to increasingly tight global competitiveness and the need to acquire effective strategies for the survival and development of technology-based organizations (TBO) and the problems of high-technology-based organizations management (TBOM) compared to non-technology companies, the proposed branch for future research is technological organizational ambidexterity. As the factors that shape competition – technological push and market pull – affect the formation of the business environment and techno-entrepreneurship ecosystem, and due to the lack of theoretical research in this regard, according to the research results, one of the key areas for researchers and practitioners is how ambidexterity is affected by technological environmental factors. Finally, the future directions of innovation ambidexterity research in a technological context have been suggested in Fig. 3.5.

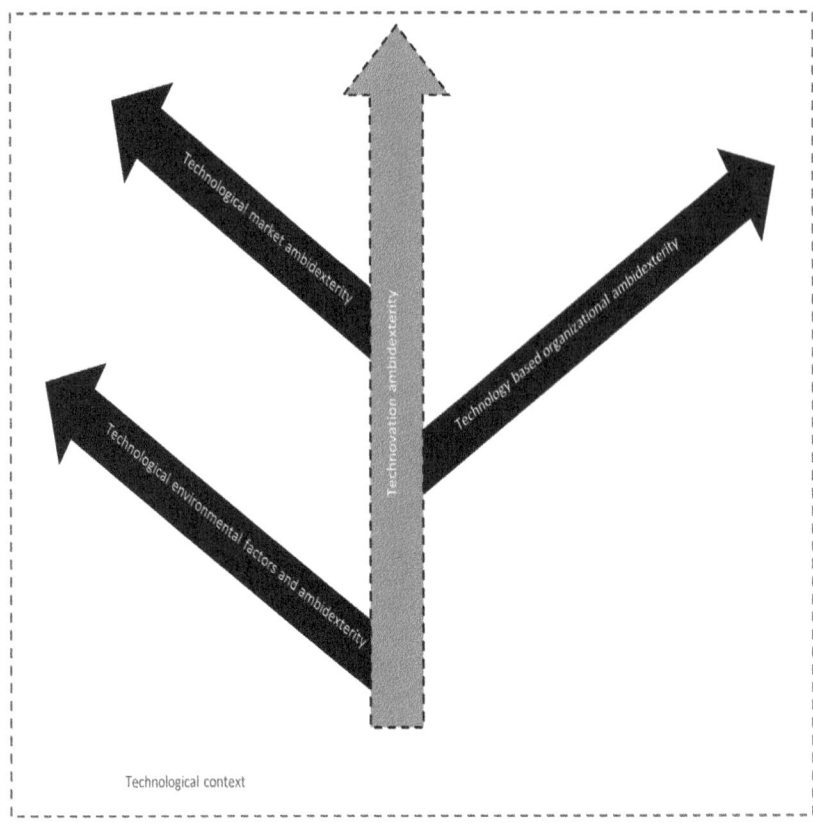

Fig. 3.5.   The Future Directions of Innovation Ambidexterity
Research in the Technological Context.

Case Study

Paragonetworks IT, established in 2009, is an IT company aiming to design refinement and product improvement supporting software related to surveying engineering. The company has designed and implemented various software in this field. Employing experts and experienced teams and implementing modern knowledge and technologies, Paragonetworks IT has completed various successful national projects in Iran and by doing so gained great market share. Pezhman Y, the founder of the company, is a successful entrepreneur who emphasizes the great importance of the innovation ambidexterity concept and the technological elements having a critical impact. The main strategy in the early stages of establishing the company was a profit-making strategy concentrated solely on exploitative strategies, without paying more attention to the market and technology turbulence of the environment and the new knowledge, ideas and technologies. By applying the strategy, this firm gained great profit from completely focusing on the exploitative strategies until 2013. However, after 2014, the firm revenues decreased dramatically and the circumstances forced Mr Y to transfer his business to the University incubator to find a solution.

From 2013 to 2015, revenue was reducing constantly and Mr Y concluded that by applying new technology or ideas he could save his business. Then he started to study and research Augmented Reality (AR) technology as a new knowledge and technology. Finally, he found that transferring such technology servers to the country was costly and the lack of experts to support the servers was a limitation. Eventually, he decided to use the reverse engineering method to reproduce the AR technology servers in the country and he succeeded. After implementing the servers, the governing body suggested many projects to Mr Y and the organization gained substantial profits from that until 2018. In 2018, the competition for using the software increased globally and industry leaders, firms which are known as powerful and dominant organizations, started to use AR software with low prices and higher support. Along with the high level of the competition in 2019, the coronavirus pandemic and the low rate of TRL of the environment caused revenue to constantly reduce. The company decided to change its structure to create an interactive context in the firm and connected with other partners like the University to share new knowledge and ideas. Finally, in 2021, this firm applied a new technology in the surveying engineering field, could become profitable again and became a successful firm. Mr Y mentioned that in addition to concentrating on profit-making strategies, firms must use new knowledge and technologies to be adaptive and responsive to environmental changes. Moreover, other technological factors, like the TRL and technology adoption, can play a critical role in applying new technologies. In addition, organizational structures can facilitate knowledge transfer in the firm and empower trust and innovation between employees.

Due to the fact that Paragonetworks IT develops new technologies using intelligent geospatial information technology, the market (mayoralty organizations) has not reached a suitable readiness level, and technology adoption has not begun, this project has barely penetrated the market. As a result, this issue confirms the fact that technological market ambidexterity can play a critical role in high-tech organizations. Moreover, for firms performing according to their business plan strategies indicators and considering the competitive advantage strategies, the technology acquisition strategies are critical. As a consequence, managing the companies based on technology is considerably different as the market and environment is fluctuating, bringing high-tech firms many problems and techno-organizational ambidexterity is a crucial issue for them. Other factors, like technology capabilities, intellectual property protection, technological asset protection and the possibility of maintaining these factors by technology alliances, which shape techno environmental factors, confirm the future research model of the study (Fig. 3.5) which is so vital for high-tech firms to follow.

Case Study Questions

(1) What are the key functions of Paragonetworks IT against the decreased income? How could Paragonetworks IT deal with the issue further?

(2) What do you think about the response of Paragonetworks IT to the environmental changes leading to decreased income? What are the impacts on Paragonetworks IT performance of using the new technology?

(3) What were the other challenges Paragonetworks IT was faced with in addition to the use of modern technology?

(4) What are the other market elements having a serious impact on business performance?

(5) What were the other environmental elements influencing firm performance? Can dynamic capabilities help organizations encountering technological turbulence?

Key Term and Definitions

Ambidextrous innovation: Ambidextrous innovation refers to an organizational ability to follow innovative detection activities and innovative operation functions simultaneously, leading to superior sustainable performance (Acikgoz et al., 2021; Bozic & Dimovski, 2019; Cho et al., 2019; Hughes et al., 2020; Liao et al., 2018).

Technovation ambidexterity: Technovation ambidexterity refers to applying innovative discovery executions and innovative utilization implementations to technological settings (Liao et al., 2018).

Bibliometric analysis: Bibliometric analysis was primarily offered and described as the use of statistical methods to analyze the bibliometric publications data, such as peer-reviewed journal articles, books, conference proceedings, periodicals, reviews, reports and related documents. It has been broadly used to present the relations of research domains with quantitative approaches (Dias, 2019).

References

Acikgoz, A., Demirkan, I., Latham, G. P., & Kuzey, C. (2021). The relationship between unlearning and innovation ambidexterity with the performance of new product development teams. *Group Decision and Negotiation, 30*(4), 945–982.

Akarsu, T. N., Marvi, R., & Foroudi, P. (2022). Forty-nine years of sensory research literature: A review on its development, foundation and future research directions. *European Journal of International Management, 1*(1).

Akbari, M., Foroudi, P., Fashami, R. Z., Mahavarpour, N., & Khodayari, M. (2022a). Let us talk about something: The evolution of e-WOM from the past to the future. *Journal of Business Research, 149*, 663–689.

Akbari, M., Foroudi, P., Khodayari, M., Fashami, R. Z., & Shahriari, E. (2022b). Sharing your assets: A holistic review of sharing economy. *Journal of Business Research, 140*, 604–625.

Andriopoulos, C., & Marianne, W. L. (2009). Exploitation-exploration tensions and organisational ambidexterity: Managing paradoxes of innovation. *Journal of Organisation Science, 20*(4), 696–717.

Aparicio, G., Iturralde, T., & Maseda, A. (2019). Conceptual structure and perspectives on entrepreneurship education research: A bibliometric review. *European Research on Management and Business Economics, 25*(3), 105–113.

Ardito, L., Peruffo, E., & Natalicchio, A. (2019). The relationships between the internationalisation of alliances portfolio diversity, individual incentives, and innovation ambidexterity: A microfoundational approach. *Technological Forecasting and Social Change, 148,* 119714.

Ardito, L., Petruzzelli, A. M., Dezi, L., & Castellano, S. (2020). The influence of inbound open innovation on ambidexterity performance: Does it pay to source knowledge from supply chain stakeholders?. *Journal of Business Research, 119,* 321–329.

Atuahene-Gima, K. (2005). Resolving the capability-rigidity paradox in new product innovation. *Journal of Marketing, 69*(4), 61–83.

Balakrishnan, J., & Foroudi, P. (2020). Does corporate reputation matter? Role of social media in consumer intention to purchase innovative food product. *Corporate Reputation Review, 23,* 181–200.

Barney, J. (1991). Firm resources and sustained competitive advantage. *Journal of Management, 17*(1), 99–120.

Baron, R. M., & Kenny, D. A. (1986). The moderator-mediator variable distinction in social psychological research: Conceptual, strategic, and statistical considerations. *Journal of Personality and Social Psychology, 51*(6), 1173–1182.

Benner, M. J., & Tushman, M. L. (2003). Exploitation, exploration, and process management: The productivity dilemma revisited. *Academy of Management Review, 28*(2), 238–256.

Berraies, S., & Bchini, B. (2019). Effect of leadership styles on financial performance: Mediating roles of exploitative and exploratory innovations case of knowledge-intensive firms. *International Journal of Innovation Management, 23*(3), 1950020.

Bozic, K., & Dimovski, V. (2019). Business intelligence and analytic use, innovation ambidexterity, and firm performance: A dynamic capabilities perspective. *The Journal of Strategic Information Systems, 28*(4), 101578.

Cabeza-Pullés, D., Fernández-Pérez, V., & Roldán-Bravo, M. I. (2020). Internal networking and innovation ambidexterity: The mediating role of knowledge management processes in university research. *European Management Journal, 38*(3), 450–461.

Chang, Y. Y., & Hughes, M. (2012). Drivers of innovation ambidexterity in small to medium-sized firms. *European Management Journal, 30*(1), 1–17.

Chang, Y. Y., Hughes, M., & Hotho, S. (2011). Internal and external antecedents of SMEs' innovation ambidexterity outcomes. *Management Decision, 49*(10), 1658–1676.

Chao, Q., Gedajlovic, E., & Zhang, H. (2009). Unpacking organisational ambidexterity: Dimensions, contingencies, and synergistic effects. *Organisation Science, 20*(4), 781–796.

Chen, J., & Liu, L. (2020). Reconciling temporal conflicts in innovation ambidexterity: The role of TMT temporal leadership. *Journal of Knowledge Management, 24*(8), 1899–1920.

Chen, M., Yang, Z., Dou, W., & Wang, F. (2018). Flying or dying? Organisational change, customer participation, and innovation ambidexterity in emerging economies. *Asia Pacific Journal of Management, 35*(1), 97–119.

Cho, M., Bonn, M. A., & Han, S. J. (2019). Innovation ambidexterity: Balancing exploitation and exploration for startup and established restaurants and impacts upon performance. *Industry & Innovation, 27*(4), 340–362.

Cohen, W. M., & Levinthal, D. A. (1990). Absorptive capacity: A new perspective on learning and innovation. *Administrative Science Quarterly, 35*(1), 128–152.

Dias, G. P. (2019). Fifteen years of e-government research in Ibero-America: A bibliometric analysis. *Government Information Quarterly, 36*(3), 400–411.

Eisenhardt, K. M., & Martin, J. A. (2000). Dynamic capabilities: What are they? *Management Journal, 21*(10/11), 1105–1121.

Fornell, C., & Larcker, D. F. (1981). Evaluating structural equation models with unobservable variables and measurement error. *Journal of Marketing Research, 18*(1), 39–50.

Foroudi, P., Akarsu, T. N., Marvi, R., & Balakrishnan, J. (2021a). Intellectual evolution of social innovation: A bibliometric analysis and avenues for future research trends. *Industrial Marketing Management, 93*, 446–465.

Foroudi, P., Akarsu, T. N., Marvi, R., & Balakrishnan, J. (2021b). Intellectual evolution of social innovation: A bibliometric analysis and avenues for future research trends. *Industrial Marketing Management, 93*(2), 446–465.

Foroudi, P., & Dennis, C. (2023). *Researching and analysing business: Research methods in practice.* Routledge.

Foroudi, P., Jin, Z., Gupta, S., Melewar, T., & Foroudi, M. M. (2016). Influence of innovation capability and customer experience on reputation and loyalty. *Journal of Business Research, 69*(11), 4882–4889.

Fu, L., Zhiying, L., & Suqin, L. (2018). Is distributed leadership a driving factor of innovation ambidexterity? An empirical study with mediating and moderating effects. *Leadership & Organisation Development Journal, 39*(3), 388–405.

Gibson, C. B., & Birkinshaw, J. (2004). The antecedents, consequences, and mediating role of organisational ambidexterity. *Academy of Management Journal, 47*(2), 209–226.

Gupta, S., Malhotra, N. K., Czinkota, M., & Foroudi, P. (2016). Marketing innovation: A consequence of competitiveness. *Journal of Business Research, 69*(12), 5671–5681.

Gupta, A. K., Smith, K. G., & Shalley, C. E. (2006). The interplay between exploration and exploitation. *Academy of Management Journal, 49*(4), 693–706.

He, Z. L., & Wong, P. K. (2004). Exploitation vs. exploitation: An empirical test of the ambidexterity hypothesis. *Organisation Science, 15*(4), 481–494.

Hughes, M., Hughes, P., Morgan, R. E., Hodgkinson, I. R., & Lee, Y. (2020). Strategic entrepreneurship behaviour and the innovation ambidexterity of young technology-based firms in incubators. *International Small Business Journal, 39*(3), 202–227.

Hughes, M., Martin, S. L., Morgan, R. E., & Robson, M. J. (2010). Realising product-market advantage in high-technology international new ventures: The mediating role of ambidextrous innovation. *Journal of International Marketing*, *18*(4), 1–21.

Jansen, J. J. P., Tempelaar, M. P., Van Den Bosch, F. A. J., & Volberda, H. W. (2009). Structural differentiation and ambidexterity: The mediating role of integration mechanisms. *Organisation Science*, *20*(4), 797–811.

Jansen, J. J. P., Van Den Bosch, F. A. J., & Volberda, H. W. (2006). Exploratory innovation, exploitative innovation, and performance: Effects of organisational antecedents and environmental moderators. *Management Science*, *52*(11), 1661–1674.

Jaworski, B. J., & Kohli, A. K. (1993). Market orientation: Antecedents and consequences. *Journal of Marketing*, *57*(3), 53–70.

Jin, X., Wang, J., Chu, T., & Xia, J. (2018). Knowledge source strategy and enterprise innovation performance: Dynamic analysis based on machine learning. *Technology Analysis and Strategic Management*, *30*(1), 1–13.

Junni, P., Sarala, R. M., Tarba, S. Y., Liu, Y., & Cooper, C. L. (2015). Guest editor's introduction: The role of human resources and organisational factors in ambidexterity. *Human Resource Management*, *54*(S1), s1–s28.

Kamdem, J. P., Duarte, A. E., Lima, K. R. R., Rocha, J. B. T., Hassan, W., Barros, L. M., & Tsompo, A. (2019). Research trends in food chemistry: A bibliometric review of its 40 years anniversary (1976–2016). *Food Chemistry*, *294*, 448–457.

Katila, R., & Ahuja, G. (2002). Something old, something new: A longitudinal study of search behaviour and new product introduction. *Academy of Management Journal*, *45*(6), 1183–1194.

Kuo, T. K., Lim, S. S., & Sonko, L. K. (2018). Catch-up strategy of latecomer firms in Asia: A case study of innovation ambidexterity in PC industry. *Technology Analysis & Strategic Management*, *30*(12), 1483–1497.

Laursen, K., & Salter, A. (2006). Open for innovation: The role of openness in explaining innovation performance among U.K. manufacturing firms. *Strategic Management Journal*, *27*(2), 131–150.

Lazzarotti, V., Manzini, R., Nosella, A., & Pellegrini, L. (2017). Innovation ambidexterity of open firms. The role of internal relational social capital. *Technology Analysis & Strategic Management*, *29*(1), 105–118.

Levinthal, D. A., & March, J. G. (1993). The myopia of learning. *Strategic Management Journal*, *14*(S2), 95–112.

Li, R., Fu, L., & Liu, Z. (2020). Does openness to innovation matter? The moderating role of open innovation between organisational ambidexterity and innovation performance. *Asian Journal of Technology Innovation*, *28*(2), 251–271.

Lin, H. E., & McDonough III, E. F. (2011). Investigating the role of leadership and organizational culture in fostering innovation ambidexterity. *IEEE Transactions on Engineering Management*, *58*(3), 497–509.

Liao, S., Liu, Z., & Zhang, S. (2018). Technology innovation ambidexterity, business model ambidexterity, and firm performance in Chinese high-tech firms. *Asian Journal of Technology Innovation*, *26*(3), 325–345.

Lin, H. E., & McDonough III, E. F. (2014). Cognitive frames, learning mechanisms, and innovation ambidexterity. *Journal of Product Innovation Management*, *31*, 170–188.

Lin, H. E., McDonough, E. F., Lin, S. J., & Lin, C. Y. Y. (2013). Managing the exploitation/exploration paradox: The role of a learning capability and innovation ambidexterity. *Journal of Product Innovation Management, 30*(2), 262–278.

Lubatkin, M. H., Simsek, Z., Ling, Y., & Veiga, J. F. (2006). Ambidexterity and performance in small- to medium-sized firms: The pivotal role of top management team behavioural integration. *Journal of Management, 32*(5), 646–672.

Lucena, A. (2016). The interaction mode and geographic scope of firm's technology alliances: Implications of balancing exploration and exploitation in R&D. *Industry & Innovation, 23*(7), 595–624.

Mahavarpour, N., Marvi, R., & Foroudi, P. (2023). A brief history of service innovation: The evolution of past, present, and future service innovation. *Journal of Business Research, 160*, 113795.

March, J. G. (1991). Exploration and exploitation in organisational learning. *Organisation Science, 2*(1), 71–87.

Martinez-Lopez, F. J., Merigo, J. M., Gazquez-Abad, J. C., & Ruiz-Real, J. L. (2020). Industrial marketing management: Bibliometric overview since its foundation. *Industrial Marketing Management, 84*, 19–38.

Minh, T. T., & Hjortsø, C. N. (2015). How institutions influence SME innovation and networking practices: The case of Vietnamese Agribusiness. *Journal of Small Business Management, 53*, 209–228.

O'Reilly, C. A., & Tushman, M. L. (2008). Ambidexterity as a dynamic capability: Resolving the innovator's dilemma. *Research in Organisational Behaviour, 28*, 185–206.

O'Reilly, C. A., & Tushman, M. L. (2013). Organisational ambidexterity: Past, present, and future. *Academy of Management Perspectives, 27*(4), 324–338.

Podsakoff, P. M., Mackenzie, S. B., Lee, J. Y., & Podsakoff, N. P. (2003). Common method biases in behavioural research: A critical review of the literature and recommended remedies. *Journal of Applied Psychology, 88*(5), 879–903.

Raisch, S., & Birkinshaw, J. (2008). Organisational ambidexterity: Antecedents, outcomes, and moderators. *Journal of Management, 34*(3), 375–409.

Raisch, S., Birkinshaw, J., Probst, G., & Tushman, M. L. (2009). Organisational ambidexterity: Balancing exploitation and exploration for sustained performance. *Organisation Science, 20*(4), 685–695.

Rezaei, H., Akbari, M., Karimi, A., & Foroudi, P. (2022). A bibliometric review of innovation networks: 30 years of study. *European Journal of International Management, 1*(1).

Rothaermel, F. T., & Alexandre, M. T. (2009). Ambidexterity in technology sourcing: The moderating role of absorptive capacity. *Organisation Science, 20*(4), 759–780.

Ruiz-Alba, J. L., Abou-Foul, M., Nazarian, A., & Foroudi, P. (2022). Digital platforms: Customer satisfaction, eWOM and the moderating role of perceived technological innovativeness. *Information Technology & People, 35*(7), 2470–2499.

Sakhdari, K. (2016). Corporate entrepreneurship: A review and future research agenda. *Technology Innovation Management Review, 6*(8), 5–18.

Simsek, Z. (2009). Organisational ambidexterity: Towards a multilevel understanding. *Journal of Management Studies, 46*(4), 597–624.

Smith, W. K., & Tushman, M. L. (2005). Managing strategic contradictions: A top management model for managing innovation streams. *Organisation Science, 16*(5), 522–536.

Soto-Acosta, P., Popa, S., & Martinez-Conesa, I. (2018). Information technology, knowledge management and environmental dynamism as drivers of innovation ambidexterity: A study in SMEs. *Journal of Knowledge Management, 22*(4), 824–849.

Sumrin, S., Gupta, S., Asaad, Y., Wang, Y., Bhattacharya, S., & Foroudi, P. (2021). Eco-innovation for environment and waste prevention. *Journal of Business Research, 122*, 627–639.

Suominen, A., Seppänen, M., & Dedehayir, O. (2019). A bibliometric review on innovation systems and ecosystems: A research agenda. *European Journal of Innovation Management*, (2), 335.

Teece, D. J., Pisano, G., & Shuen, A. (1997). Dynamic capabilities and strategic management. *Strategic Management Journal, 18*(7), 509–533.

Tsai, F. S. (2016). Knowing what we know differently: Knowledge heterogeneity and dynamically ambidextrous innovation. *Journal of Organisational Change Management, 29*(7), 1162–1188.

Tushman, M. L., & O'Reilly, C. A. (1996). Ambidextrous organisations: Managing evolutionary and revolutionary change. *California Management Review, 38*(4), 8–29.

Uotila, J., Maula, M., Keil, T., & Zahra, S. A. (2009). Exploration, exploitation, and financial performance: Analysis of S&P 500 corporations. *Strategic Management Journal, 30*(2), 221–231.

Van Eck, N. J., & Waltman, L. (2020). *VOSviewer Manual: Manual for VOSviewer version 1.6. 15.* Centre for Science and Technology Studies (CWTS) of Leiden University.

Van Oorschot, J. A., Hofman, E., & Halman, J. I. (2018). A bibliometric review of the innovation adoption literature. *Technological Forecasting and Social Change, 134*, 1–21.

Van Raan, A. (2003). The use of bibliometric analysis in research performance assessment and monitoring of interdisciplinary scientific developments. *TATuP-Zeitschrift für Technikfolgenabscätzung in Theorie und Praxis, 12*(1), 20–29.

Wiratmadja, I. I., Profityo, W. B., & Rumanti, A. A. (2021). Drivers of innovation ambidexterity on small medium enterprises (SMEs) performance. Drivers of innovation ambidexterity on small medium enterprises (SMEs) performance. *IEEE Access, 9*, 4423–4434.

Wu, F., Geng, Y., Tian, X., Zhong, S., Wu, W., Yu, S., & Xiao, S. (2018). Responding climate change: A bibliometric review on urban environmental governance. *Journal of Cleaner Production, 204*, 344–354.

Zang, J., & Li, Y. (2016). Technology capabilities, market capabilities and innovation ambidexterity. *Technology Analysis & Strategic Management, 29*(1), 23–37.

Zha, D., Marvi, R., & Foroudi, P. (2023a). Embracing the paradox of customer experiences in the hospitality and tourism industry. *International Journal of Management Reviews*.

Zha, D., Marvi, R., & Foroudi, P. (2023b). Synthesizing the customer experience concept: A multimodularity approach. *Journal of Business Research, 167*, 114185.

Zhang, J. A., Edgar, F., Geare, A., & O'Kane, C. (2016). The interactive effects of entrepreneurial orientation and capability-based HRM on firm performance: The mediating role of innovation ambidexterity. *Industrial Marketing Management, 59,* 131–143.

Zhang, Z., Wang, X., & Chun, D. (2022). The effect of knowledge sharing on ambidextrous innovation: Triadic intellectual capital as a mediator. *Journal of Open Innovation: Technology, Market, and Complexity, 8*(1), 1–21.

Zhao, H., Zhang, F., & Kwon, J. (2018). Corporate social responsibility research in international business journals: An author co-citation analysis. *International Business Review, 27*(2), 389–400.

Zheng, X., Liu, Z., & Gong, X. (2016). Why does leader attention scope matter for innovation ambidexterity? The mediating role of transformational leadership. *Leadership & Organisation Development Journal, 37*(7), 912–935.

Chapter 4

Perceived Product Innovation and Brand Loyalty: The Perceptions of Apple Product Users in the United Kingdom

Atta ur Rehman[a]*, Danae Manika*[a]*, Pantea Foroudi*[a] *and Maria Palazzo*[b]

[a]Brunel University London, UK
[b]Universitas Mercatorum, Italy

Abstract

This chapter explores how perceived product innovation influences brand loyalty among UK Apple users, extending the technology acceptance model. Using a quantitative approach, data were collected from 101 respondents via an online survey and analysed using SPSS. Objectives included examining the mediating role of perceived product usefulness and ease of use, exploring the relationship between product/brand attitudes and brand loyalty and assessing gender's impact on loyalty perceptions. Findings reveal a significant positive relationship among variables, with perceived product usefulness and ease of use jointly mediating the link between product innovation and attitude, affecting brand loyalty. Gender was found to have no moderating effect. The research contributes by highlighting these mediating effects and deepening understanding of product innovation's impact on loyalty. Managerially, prioritising innovation, usefulness and ease of use can enhance satisfaction and loyalty. Future research could explore additional variables to enrich understanding further.

Keywords: Perceived product innovation; technology acceptance model; perceived product usefulness; perceived product ease of use; product attitude; brand attitude; brand loyalty

Business Strategies and Ethical Challenges in the Digital Ecosystem, 55–77
Copyright © 2025 Atta ur Rehman, Danae Manika, Pantea Foroudi and Maria Palazzo
Published under exclusive licence by Emerald Publishing Limited
doi:10.1108/978-1-80455-069-420241004

Introduction

In the highly competitive technological environment of today, brand loyalty (BL) is an essential element for long-term business growth based on profitability as it leads to repeat purchases and positive word of mouth (Akbari et al., 2021; Foroudi et al., 2019, 2020; 2021a; Keller, 2013). It is the result of consumer satisfaction and perceived value which is derived from perceived product innovation (Khan et al., 2023). Companies need to constantly innovate and develop new products to meet the changing consumer needs and preferences. Product innovation is often viewed as a significant driver of BL since consumers are more inclined to remain loyal to a brand that offers them innovative products that satisfy their needs and wants (Li et al., 2020; Foroudi et al., 2018; 2016a, 2016b; Melewar et al., 2017).

Perceived product innovation refers to the extent to which consumers perceive a product to be innovative, which can influence their attitudes towards the product and the brand. It is defined as the consumer's perception of the degree of originality, uniqueness and intricacy of the product or service (Chang et al., 2020). It is an important driver of BL especially in technological industries where innovation is crucial in developing consumer preferences and purchase behaviours (Mavlanova et al., 2014).

The Technology Acceptance Model (TAM) (Davis, 1989) has been widely mentioned in the marketing literature to explain the concept of consumer behaviour in relation to new technological products adoption (Venkatesh et al., 2003). While utilising the TAM, this study aims to extend this model to investigate the impact of perceived product innovation in influencing customer attitudes and loyalty towards Apple products in the context of the UK market.

Main Focus of the Chapter

Perceived Product Innovation

Prior to a consumer interacting with a product to satisfy a need, want or a desire, being a high involvement technological product, they conduct research to try and understand what the products offer and how it is a unique offering in the market. This comes about due to constant product innovation. Perceived product innovativeness is therefore linked to how a new product is perceived in terms of unique attributes and features as compared to other products in a category from a consumer's perspective (Fu et al., 2008; Wu et al., 2004).

What may be thought of as innovative by an organisation's product development team may not be so by their target consumers (Calantone et al., 2006; Im et al., 2015; Langerak & Hultink, 2006; Lee & O'Connor, 2003; Sharma et al., 2016; Szymanski et al., 2007). Most of the current research on product innovation focuses on a firm's perspective and largely ignores the consumers' idea of innovation (Im et al., 2015). However, in the current age, it is imperative to place the needs of consumers at the forefront of product development and the way brands interact with their target audience. This suggests that consumers' perception of product innovativeness positively affects the customer lifetime value (Zhang et al., 2016) which is of immense significance to current organisations as customer retention is the key to be successful in the highly competitive technological sector. It is important for customers to observe that a brand is constantly being innovated, indicating that they actively listen to their target audience and are willing to provide products that satisfy them (Sharma et al., 2016).

Since the product life cycle tends to be short in the current times (Jamal et al., 2012), an organisation's market orientation involves being responsive to constantly changing customer needs through innovating marketing processes and strategies which lead to product and performance improvement (Boisvert & Khan, 2022). Perceived product innovation, mutually defined by the brand and the consumer, mediates the relationship between a firm's market orientation and the customer-based brand equity (Foroudi, 2023; 2022, 2021; Sarkar & Mishra, 2017).

The unique attributes embedded in a new product represent potential functional and symbolic values to many consumers and are the primary reasons consumers adopt new products (Castano et al., 2008). Since new innovative products claiming uniqueness elicit the feelings of anticipation and excitement among consumers, positive feelings are attributed towards adopting a new product. Perceived product innovativeness may therefore enhance consumers' motivation and facilitate the adoption process (Lafferty & Goldsmith, 2004).

While product innovation is needed, it does not guarantee success if a product is not perceived to be unique or easy to use (Goldenberg et al., 1999). For many consumers, attempting to understand the innovations is a challenge (Harmancioglu et al., 2009). Researchers argue that consumers tend to simplify the cognitive requirements of their decision-making process when facing a challenging task and rely on existing product knowledge to reach an informed decision (Abelson & Levi, 1985; Bettman et al., 1998). The study conducted by Lee and O'Connor (2003) discussed that although the technologically innovative computer chips speed up the work done, they may not necessarily affect the consumers' adoption of a new computer. Therefore, it is important for an organisation to portray their innovative product offering in a way that resonates with their target consumers and is easy to understand. This will enable consumers to have positive perceptions regarding the product innovation. Research shows that the concepts of appropriateness and novelty are included to measure the perception of innovativeness (Rubera et al., 2010) and perceived usefulness and ease of use are important dimensions on acceptance of new products (Davis, 1989; Kulviwat et al., 2007; Msaed et al., 2017; Zeithaml et al., 2002).

Prior research discusses the TAM and product innovation, and although interlinked, they are defined as separate dimensions. This suggests that perceived product innovation acts as a catalyst for perceived product usefulness (PPU) and perceived product ease of use (PPEU) – filling the gap to better explain the model and what drives a consumer towards adopting a certain technology.

Technology Acceptance Model (TAM)

The TAM (Davis et al., 1989) originated based on the gaps unanswered by the theory of planned behaviour and the theory of reasoned action (Ajzen & Fishbein, 1980). The goal of TAM is to clarify the determinants of consumers' adoptions of technology (Tsourela & Nerantzaki, 2020). TAM assumes that consumers' intention to adopt a particular technology is determined by their attitudes towards technology usage which is formed by two interlinked ideas – perceived usefulness and ease of use. Meaning, thereby, that one believes using the technology would enhance their performance and the technology usage will be free from effort (Negm, 2023). An individual's acceptance of technology is immediately influenced by their intention that is shaped by the attitude towards the usage which is formed through the simultaneous effects by perceived usefulness and ease of use.

The TAM ignores the influence of environmental variables and individual differences on technology acceptance (Bagozzi, 2007; Marangunić & Granić, 2015). Most current research revolves around the assumption of consumers' actions through cognition rather than their actions through affect which ignores the individualistic feelings, moods and beliefs one may have – whereas, in the current age, consumers highly emphasise their feelings, they may accept or reject a technology based on how they feel or think (Almomani et al., 2022).

Due to limited clarifications, further studies have been based on the foundations of TAM to better explain the phenomena of different variables influencing the level of technology adoption. The unified theory of attitude towards using technology (Venkatesh et al., 2003) extended the TAM by adding facilitating conditions as well as social influence. They suggested that access to a technology should be available. This means that if a consumer wants to use a smartphone application, they would need access to internet services. The significant contribution of the model was the social influence element of technology adoption – stating that it is not enough for the technology to be beneficial by itself, but also influencing consumers through the society around them. A second version of a similar extended model was published (Venkatesh et al., 2003) where the influence of further external variables was examined on technology adoption.

TAM is undoubtedly one of the most widely endorsed models with influential theories to understand end user acceptance of information systems technology use. The present research seeks to extend this model by adding certain constructs from a marketing and branding standpoint and including perceived product innovation.

Perceived Product Ease of Use (PPEU)

PPEU is one of the main constructs of the TAM. It is defined as how much an individual perceives a particular technology usage to be free of physical and mental effort (Davis, 1993). PPEU, as researched in previous studies, influences behaviours, either directly or indirectly, via PPU (Ramayah & Lo, 2007).

PPEU is also known to affect PPU. A technology which is deemed effortless to use should be regarded as more useful by the users (Selim, 2003; Shih, 2004;

Venkatesh, 2000; Venkatesh et al., 2003) although the validation results for this conclusion are mixed and many researchers claim that this effect is non-significant (Chau, 2002; Gentry, 2002; Yi & Hwang, 2003).

Even though the attitude towards usage spoke about its mediating effect, it was later dropped in the revised TAM model because, "...like many behavioural variables, it may be a necessary but not a sufficient condition for success" (Davis et al., 1989; Jackson et al., 1997). As an easy-to-use system, an individual will develop favourable beliefs regarding it and will therefore positively influence the product attitude (PA). Hence, the easier a technology usage is perceived to be, the higher the chance of a positive PA upon the use of that technology. Various literature has supported the idea that PPEU has a positive effect on PA (Venkatesh et al., 2003; Lee et al., 2003; Riemenschneider et al., 2003; Shih, 2004). Therefore, 'attitude toward usage' has not been included in the study, whereas 'PA' has been introduced – which is the stage that occurs after technology acceptance and product usage.

Perceived Product Usefulness (PPU)

PPU is another key indicator for the TAM which discusses the degree to which an individual believes whether a new technology makes systems and processes more efficient and improves the level of performance (Davis, 1989; Eriksson et al., 2005; Rahman et al., 2017). Perceived usefulness is significant in paving the way for a company's success, especially for businesses that are heavily reliant on technological products and innovation. Their success depends on whether their consumers deem their new product as a value addition in terms of its functions and usefulness.

The debate between 'the new technology or product will improve my performance and make processes easier for me' and 'the new technology does not provide any added benefit to the systems I already use' depends on the customers and their perceptions of the product's usefulness. If customers are unwilling to try a new technology as they do not see an added benefit, that may impede the business from innovating further as the company knows the product will not sell. Therefore, technologically reliant companies need to ensure their innovations are easy to use as well as provide an added benefit and value to what already exists through the use of their product (Tan & Teo, 2000; Rouibah et al., 2011). The extent to which the technology will enhance the user's performance will dictate whether or how much the user will engage with that technology – if a user ranks a product high in perceived usefulness, they must perceive a positive impact on the task completion through the use of that product (Davis, 1989).

PPU is crucial for pre and post stages of technology adoption. This idea is supported by numerous studies in information systems literature (Klopping & McKinney, 2004; Venkatesh & Morris, 2000). The decision to adopt a technology therefore depends on the user's perceptions based on the level of useful benefit(s) it offers. High levels of perceived usefulness would imply that the technology is beneficial – i.e. making the processes simpler and easier for the end user – eliciting positive emotions and attitude post product usage.

TAM as a Mediator Between Perceived Product Innovation and PA

The two constructs of the TAM – perceived product innovation and PPEU – are significant factors that influence consumers' attitudes towards a product. Although they have a direct correlation, they may also act as mediators between perceived product innovation and PAs.

A research by Lee and Koo (2015) identified that both perceived usefulness and perceived ease of use mediated the relationship between perceived product innovation and attitude towards mobile applications. The PAs were based on the perceptions on the ease of use and usefulness of those services. Similarly, another study concluded that consumers' positive attitudes towards online shopping were influenced by their perceptions of the ease of use and usefulness of the online shopping platforms (Park & Jun 2003). A third study investigated the effects of these variables on consumer attitudes towards new mobile communication devices and the authors concluded that the "…ease of use and usefulness of a new product are important determinants of consumer attitude, particularly when the product is also perceived as innovative" (Moon & Kim, 2001).

These findings suggest that in the current context, perceived product usefulness and ease of use are significant factors that influence how consumers evaluate innovative products which can lead to an increase in their technology adoption intention. As consumers perceive a product to be innovative, it will develop positive attitudes about the product, and this link would become stronger when consumers also perceive the product as useful and easy to use.

> H1a: Perceived Product Usefulness mediates the relationship between Perceived Product Innovation and Product Attitude (Such that the effect of Perceived Product Innovation on Product Attitude is stronger when consumers perceive the product as more useful).
> H1b: Perceived Product Ease of Use mediates the relationship between Perceived Product Innovation and Product Attitude (Such that the effect of Perceived Product Innovation on Product Attitude is stronger when consumers perceive the product is easier to use).
> H1c: Perceived Product Usefulness and Perceived Product Ease of Use collaboratively mediate the relationship between Perceived Product Innovation and Product Attitude.

PA, BA and BL

PA is defined as the consumer's overall judgement of the product performance, attributes (such as quality) and the benefits (Zafer Erdogan & Uzkurt, 2010). The attitude towards using a construct involves individuals' positive or negative feelings about performing the target behaviour (Davis et al., 1989). In terms of the

TAM, a technology that is easy to use and offers unique benefits that make the job easier for the end user will elicit positive feelings. In the case of Apple, an individual who uses one of their products (iPhones), when they find the usage that requires minimum to no effort and understand their interaction with the product while also completing their tasks more efficiently, they develop a positive PA. Davis et al. (1989) found that user's attitudes towards the product significantly affected their repurchase intention.

H2: Product Attitude has a significant relationship with Brand Attitude.

Another important factor for determining a brand's equity is one's attitude towards it. According to Mitchell and Olson (1981), BA refers to a person's overall assessment of a brand. This indicates that a consumer's attitude towards a brand is mostly determined by their own views of the brand, which are considered to be a trustworthy indicator of how customers will behave towards brands (Shimp, 2010). When considering a brand, consumers may also rely on the pre-existing attitudes towards that brand – which may change over time (Foroudi, 2019). Companies need to stand out, and a brand gives them a chance to stand out in a competitive market (Melewar et al., 2001).

In Apple's case, the product development and release stage is of great significance because it forms the basis for attitudes towards the products and therefore attitudes towards the brand. A product with embedded innovation in terms of features, design and attributes will push a consumer to consider it. If the said product is then easy to use and also provides useful benefits, it enables the consumer to purchase the product and form positive attitudes about the product itself. Consequently, this results in a positive BA.

Various studies (e.g. Aaker, 1996; Faircloth et al., 2001; Helgeson & Supphellen, 2004) view the brand image and BA as two different notions where the former aids in the formation of potential customers' attitude towards a brand.

The BL concept, which is closely related to user experience, denotes the level of attachment a customer has for a certain brand. According to previous literature, BL is attitudinal as well as behavioural (Dick & Basu, 1994; Neal & Strauss, 2008). While the behavioural dimension reflects a consumer's propensity to buy a specific brand frequently over time, the attitudinal dimension describes a consumer's overall level of pleasure based on the user experience. Therefore, if consumers have positive associations due to positive experiences with the brand's products (as the brand promise was maintained), it will drive consumer loyalty.

H3: Brand Attitude has a significant relationship with Brand Loyalty.

Influence of Gender on Product and Brand Perceptions

Recent research in technology usage and adoption has highlighted that men and women engage differently with technology, and also differ in their self-perception regarding technology, with women showing lower levels of interest in using a particular technology as compared to men (Hargittai & Shaw, 2015; Van Deursen et al., 2015). Venkatesh et al. (2003) identified that female consumers perceived technology differently – labelling it as more complex – than male consumers, which may influence their willingness to adopt or use new technology. The major reason for this difference stems from the socialisation processes that males and females go through that shape up their gender roles. According to gender roles, the technology usage is inherent for the men but not for the women (Morahan-Martin & Schumacher, 2007). According to the socialisation of men and women, females are likely to have more of an emotional inclination towards products, whereas males are more prone to be influenced by the perceived usefulness and the perceived ease of use (Shin et al., 2019; Park et al., 2017). Both genders have different preferences when it comes to product attributes with females placing design and style as their priority, whereas males value the functionality and technical features of a product (Jindal & Gogi, 2019).

Further research has shown that gender can influence overall consumer behaviour including the perceptions and attitudes towards a particular product or a brand and therefore impact the individual's decision-making process (Göksal & Turhan, 2020). In terms of BL, studies have reported mixed findings. Some studies have claimed females to be more brand loyal than men as the effect of perceived product innovation on BL was found to be stronger for female consumers than male consumers (Huang & Sarigöllü, 2014; Hu et al., 2021). Whereas other studies (Hussain et al., 2020) have found no significant differences.

The existing literature suggests that gender may have a significant impact on consumers' perceptions of products and brands including their willingness for technology adoption and usage. Therefore, it is important to consider gender differences in the perceptions of product innovation and BL for Apple product users in the United Kingdom. The survey responses provided by men and women would be analysed separately to identify the extent to which gender may moderate the relationship between perceived product innovation and BL in the context of the case study brand.

H4: The effect of perceived product innovation on brand loyalty is expected to be stronger for female consumers than male consumers.

Research Design

The study attempted to collect the data at a single point in time; therefore, it employed the cross-sectional survey design. This method greatly assisted the research as it provided insights on multiple variables (perceptions and attitudes) at a particular point in time making it an efficient way to understand consumer behaviour (Babin & Zikmund, 2016; Foroudi et al., 2021b, 2023). It became easier to distinguish respondents with similar characteristics which enabled identifying various customer segments (Foroudi & Foroudi, 2021; Kotler et al., 2017). Based on the context of this research, a cross-sectional research design generated insights regarding technology acceptance and brand perceptions by collecting data on consumer perceptions, brand attitude and loyalty – this facilitated a better understanding of how consumers perceive the brand (Keller, 2016). The survey method employed was useful for collecting data on attitudes, beliefs and behaviours of consumers (Foroudi, 2023; Foroudi & Dennis, 2023; Churchill, 2013).

Data Collection

The data for this study were collected using an online survey. The survey was designed using the Google Forms platform and was distributed through email and social media. The survey included close-ended questions and was divided into six sections: demographic information, perceived product innovation, PPU, PPEU, PA and BA and BL. The questions were adapted from existing scales used in previous studies (Choi & Kim, 2016). The responses were based on a five-point Likert scale (Strongly Disagree – Strongly Agree). This allowed for a standardised approach to data collection and an access to quantifiable data which could be analysed through statistical methods – which is also a key characteristic of the positivistic approach (Bryman, 2012; Foroudi et al., 2019). This further ensured that all respondents were asked the same questions, and their responses were measurable, consistent and reliable.

Sample

The target population for this study was Apple product users over the age of 18 in the United Kingdom. The sample was selected using a non-probability sampling technique – convenience sampling (Foroudi et al., 2022; 2020a, 2020b; Hair et al., 2019). This sampling method enabled easy access to and recruitment of participants and quick and efficient data collection from the target respondents (Saunders et al., 2019). A total of 101 authentic survey responses were collected during the study.

Results of the Quantitative Study

During this study, data were gathered through an online survey developed using Google Forms. The respondents included both genders, male and female. The responses were recorded on a five-point Likert scale for each variable being tested.

Descriptive Statistics

The first section of the survey required participants to enter their demographic data as part of the research which included their age group and gender. The data collected are summarised and interpreted below.

Most participants belonged to the age group of 25–34 accounting for 60% of the total responses. Based on the demographic profile of survey respondents, there was an approximately even distribution of responses between female and male where they accounted for 45.5% and 54.5% of the responses, respectively.

Data Preparation and Checking for Reliability

Data Coding and Editing

The survey data collected were downloaded through the Google Forms platform. Before initiating the analysis on SPSS, the data were filtered to ensure the data are reliable and accurate. "The results of statistical analysis are only as good as the data which is used to compute them" (Malhotra & Birks, 2016). As mentioned in Table 4.1, the codes for each construct were established for statistical analysis on SPSS.

No missing data were identified during the analysis which suggests that the survey questionnaire was easily understood by the respondents. Ensuring the confidentiality of data and having questions marked as required within each section also played a significant role in obtaining complete and accurate data.

It was important to identify consistency and accuracy within the data. Four survey question responses were therefore recorded before developing the combined variables. One question pertained to perceived product innovation, and three questions belonged to the PPEU section. As these questions were worded differently to the rest of the survey, inconsistencies could have arisen and compromised the quality and accuracy of data. Recoding the responses enabled uniformity and consistency, ensuring the data to highlight accurate and reliable results (Diamantopoulos et al., 2011).

Each survey section contained five to seven questions pertaining to a particular construct. Prior to the data analysis, combined variables were created for each construct to reduce the complexity of the dataset which made the analysis and interpretation easier (Grewal & Tansuhaj, 2001). This also improved the model fit (Hair et al., 2010) and the representativeness of the variables (Kline, 2011). As the responses were based on a five-point Likert scale, the average was taken for responses for each construct to compute the new combined variables.

Table 4.1. Demographic Profile of Respondents.

Sample Size (*N*) = 101		Frequency	Percentage
Gender	Female	46	45.5%
	Male	55	54.5%
	Total	101	100%
Age	18–24	21	21%
	25–34	61	60%
	35–44	11	11%
	45–54	4	4%
	55 and above	4	4%
	Total	101	100%

Measurement of Reliability of Scale

Cronbach's Alpha was calculated for each scale to ensure the reliability of the items within their respective constructs. This approach confirms that the items measure the same underlying construct and therefore can be reliably used to gauge constructs such as BL and perceived innovation (Bagozzi & Yi, 2012; Hair et al., 2019). The alpha values range from 0 to 1, with values above 0.7 generally considered acceptable, indicating good internal consistency and reliability of the scale.

Cronbach's Alpha was administered to identify whether individual items in the scale are reliable and measure the same construct. Therefore, this can be used as a measure of the scale's reliability (Bagozzi & Yi, 2012). It is particularly useful in the reliability of scales measuring constructs such as BL and perceived innovation (Hair et al., 2019). The value ranges from 0 to 1, with values greater than 0.7 indicating greater consistency and reliability.

Inferential Statistics

A total of six hypotheses were tested for this study to answer the research questions. The testing included a mediation analysis, a simple linear regression analysis and a moderation analysis. For the purposes of the mediation and moderation relationships between the variables, the PROCESS macro by Andrew-Hayes was downloaded and installed on SPSS as an add-on to conduct the analysis.

Mediation Analysis – H1(a), H1(b) and H1(c)

For the purposes of testing these three hypotheses, model four was selected in the PROCESS macro to run a simple mediation analysis.

For H1(a), the first part of the output shows PPU (mediator) as the outcome variable. The R-squared value is 0.4960 which suggests that PPI accounts for 49.6% of the variance in PPU. The regression coefficients for the constant ($B = 1.884$) and PPI ($B = 0.612$) are statistically significant with $p < 0.05$ (0.0000). The standardised coefficient for PPI is 0.7043, indicating a strong positive relationship between PPI and PPU. These results indicate that overall, there is a significant direct relationship between PPI and PPU.

$B = 0.612$, $t = 9.872$, $p = 0.000$, 95% CI (0.489, 0.735)

The second part of the output shows the outcome variable PA, with both PPI and PPU as the predictors. The R-squared value is 0.4574, which suggests that PPI and PPU together account for 45.7% of the variance of PA. The regression coefficients for the constant ($B = 1.6224$), PPI ($B = 0.1948$) and PPU ($B = 0.4544$) are statistically significant with p-values of less than 0.05. The standardised coefficients for PPI and PPU are 0.2395 and 0.4859, respectively. These results suggest that there is a direct significant relationship between PPI and PA and between PPU and PA.

(PPI) $B = 0.1948$, $t = 2.285$, $p = 0.0245$, 95% CI (0.256, 0.364)
(PPU) $B = 0.4544$, $t = 4.636$, $p = 0.0000$, 95% CI (0.260, 0.649)

The final part of the output shows the results of the total effect model indicating that PPI has a significant total effect on PA, with a coefficient of 0.4730 and *p*-value = 0.0000 and a standardised coefficient of 0.5817 implying a strong positive relationship between PPI and PA. As the total effect of PPI on PA is significant with a coefficient of 0.4730 of which 0.1948 is explained as the direct effect, there is a significant indirect effect of PPI on PA through PPU with a coefficient of 0.2782 and a complete standardised indirect effect of 0.3422. Therefore, the effect of PPI on PA is partially mediated through PPU, hence H1(a) is supported.

To test H1(b), a similar process was followed; however, the mediator variable changed to PPEU.

The first part of the output shows PPEU (mediator) as the outcome variable. The R-squared value is 0.0982 which suggests that PPI accounts for 9.82% of the variance in PPEU. The regression coefficients for the constant (B = 3.4425) and PPI (B = 0.2309) are statistically significant with a *p*-value of less than 0.05 (0.0014). The standardised coefficient for PPI is 0.3134, suggesting that PPI has a slight effect on PPEU.

B = 0.2309, t = 3.284, p = 0.0014, 95% CI (0.914, 0.3704)

The second part of the output shows the outcome variable PA, with both PPI and PPEU as the predictors. The R-squared value is 0.4040 which suggests that PPI and PPUE collectively explain 40.40% of variance in PA. Both PPI (B = 0.4043) and PPEU (B = 0.2976) are statistically significant coefficients with *p*-values of less than 0.05 indicating the significant impact on PA. The standardised coefficients for PPI and PPEU are 0.4972 and 0.2696, respectively. These results suggest that PPI has a stronger effect on PA than PPEU.

(PPI) B = 0.4043, t = 6.0547, p = 0.0000, 95% CI (0.2718, 0.5368)

(PPEU) B = 0.2976, t = 3.2834, p = 0.0014, 95% CI (0.1177, 0.4775)

The following section shows the total effect model, which indicates that PPI has a significant direct effect on PA with a coefficient of 0.4730, $p < 0.05$ and a standard coefficient of 0.5817. As the total effect of PPI on PA is significant with a coefficient of 0.4730 of which 0.4043 is explained by the direct effect, the indirect effect of PPI on PA through PPEU is significant at 0.0687 with $p < 0.05$ and a standard coefficient of 0.0845. Therefore, the effect of PPI on PA is partially mediated through PPEU and is statistically significant, hence H1(b) is supported.

For H1(c), the same analysis was followed; however, two mediators were selected together to run this model.

For PPU, the model summary shows that PPI is a significant predictor of PPU, and the standardised coefficient of 0.7043 implies a strong relationship between the two variables. A similar pattern was observed for PPEU, where PPI significantly predicts PPEU with a smaller standardised coefficient of 0.3134. For PA, the model summary highlights that all variables included in the model (PPI, PPU and PPEU) are significant and jointly predict PA. The standardised coefficients suggest that PPU has the strongest impact on PA with a value of 0.4336, followed by PPI (0.2108) and PPEU (0.2091).

The total effect model represents a significant value of 0.4730 ($p < 0.05$) when the mediators are not included in the model, and when controlling for the mediators, the direct effect of PPI on PA is still significant with a coefficient value of 0.1714 ($p = 0.0417$). The indirect effects show that the effect of PPI on PA is mediated jointly by PPU and PPEU. The total indirect effect has a coefficient value of 0.3016 which is also significant, with the indirect effect through PPU (0.2483) stronger than the indirect effect through PPEU (0.0533). The findings suggest that PPU and PPEU jointly mediate the relationship between PPI and PA, hence H1(c) is supported.

Linear Regression Analysis: H2 and H3

A simple regression analysis was conducted to test H2 and H3. For H2, the analysis shows that there is a significant relationship between PA and BA with a Pearson's correlation coefficient of 0.777. The adjusted R-squared value of 0.600 suggests that PA explains 60.0% of the variance in BA. The ANOVA results indicated that the regression model is significant, $F(1, 99) = 151.211$, $p < 0.05$, implying that PA significantly predicts BA. The unstandardised regression coefficient for PA is 0.942 meaning that for each one-unit increase in PA, BA is predicted to increase by 0.942 units, holding other variables constant. In terms of the residuals statistics, the mean of the predicted values is 4.2743 which is close to the actual mean of 4.2459, suggesting that the model is a good fit. The standard deviation of the residuals is relatively small (0.44026) indicating that the model has a good degree of precision to predict BA. H2 is supported.

Testing for H3, the results showed that there is a significant positive correlation between BA and BL, with a Pearson's correlation coefficient of 0.774 ($p < 0.05$). Regression analysis showed that the model is statistically significant, $F(1, 99) = 148.055$, $p < 0.05$, suggesting that BA significantly predicts BL. The model accounted for 59.5% of the variance in BL. H3 is supported.

Moderation Analysis – H4.

PROCESS macro on SPSS was used for a simple moderation analysis with model one selected. The first part of the output from linear regression suggested that PPI is positively associated with BL, as the coefficient is 0.8112 and is statistically significant at $p < 0.05$. However, the analysis also shows that gender does not have a significant effect on BL as the coefficient is 0.1690 and is not statistically significant at $p = 0.1695$. This means that gender does not moderate the relationship between PPI and BL. The interaction term between PPI and gender is also not significant at $p = 0.2289$, implying that the effect of PPI on BL does not vary significantly depending on gender. The results suggest that PPI is a significant predictor of BL; however, it is not influenced by gender, and therefore, gender does not appear to moderate that relationship. H4 is not supported.

Solutions and Recommendations

This research contributes to the literature pertaining to the TAM as well as consumer attitudes towards technological products and brands. Firstly, a new conceptual framework was developed based on previous studies, which aimed to examine the impact of perceived product innovation on BL among Apple users in the United Kingdom. The study found that perceived product innovation has a positive relationship with PA, leading to positive BAs and therefore BL.

The findings of this study support previous research on the role of perceived product innovation in shaping consumer attitudes and behaviour. Additionally, this study contributes to the literature by highlighting the significance of perceived product usefulness and ease of use as mediators between product innovation and attitude. The collaborative mediation effect on this relationship adds to the theoretical understanding of the complex interplay between these constructs.

The research also provides support for the TAM as a theoretical framework for understanding the relationships between perceived product innovation, product and BAs and BL among UK Apple product users. It confirms that overall, product and BA mediate the relationship between innovation and loyalty. These findings align with previous studies that have highlighted the usefulness of TAM in predicting technology adoption and usage.

The managerial implications are significant, particularly for technological companies such as Apple. Firstly, the findings highlight the importance of product innovation in creating positive product perceptions which is the basis of BL. Companies should constantly invest in innovation of their products to maintain a competitive advantage and appeal to customers who value innovation. The study also proves the mediation effect of perceived usefulness and ease of use on product innovation and attitude. Thus implying that companies should ensure the product's design and functionality meets the customers' desires and expectations. It is also important for organisations to provide excellent customer service and engaging marketing campaigns. By doing so, they can strengthen positive attitudes towards their products as well as their brand leading to strong BL.

Future Research Directions

This research followed a quantitative approach and utilised an online survey platform to collect data based on close-ended questions. As this survey was self-administered, it did not capture the in-depth data which could be obtained through qualitative research approaches such as interviews or focus groups. Since there was no direct interaction between the researcher and the respondent, there is a chance that the responses were not authentic, or the participants may have not fully understood some questions which could lead to response bias. Moreover, although participants were assured regarding the anonymity and confidentiality of the survey responses, they may have still provided responses that were socially desirable rather than their actual thoughts; this may create a social-desirability bias and therefore affect the reliability and validity of the results. To address this limitation, researchers may employ techniques such as pilot testing and consider using a mixed method research approach to mitigate the potential of social desirability bias (Foroudi & Dennis, 2023; Foroudi et al., 2021b; Foroudi & Foroudi, 2021). Additionally, online surveys are usually responded to by individuals who feel comfortable using technology in general, and there may be a pool of Apple product users within the United Kingdom that ignored responding to the survey as it was online.

While convenience sampling was administered to recruit participants that were easily accessible, one drawback was its lack of representativeness of the overall target population (Bryman, 2012). In this study, Apple product users in the UK were targeted for ease of availability which may not accurately represent the entire population of Apple product users in the region. Moreover, it is essential for participants to respond voluntarily, hence individuals who chose to respond to the survey may have different attitudes and behaviours towards Apple products than those who did not respond.

Conclusion

Based on the results, this research contributes key insights valuable to the brands and marketers. It examines 1) the perceptions of Apple users in the United Kingdom, 2) how the consumers generate product and brand perceptions and 3) how usefulness and ease of use mediate the relationship between product innovation and attitudes. This study provides empirical evidence for the importance of the TAM constructs as mediators between innovation and attitudes which result in BL.

While this study provides valuable insights into the attitudes and behaviours of Apple product users in the United Kingdom, the limitations of the research should be considered while interpreting the findings. Future research prospects could extend this study to address the limitations to further deepen the understanding of this phenomenon within the context of the technological UK market and beyond.

Case Study: Spiritronics Tech Mixing Innovation and Brand Loyalty During the COVID-19 Pandemic Crisis

From its birth year 30 years ago until today, thanks to the insight of its founder Mr B, who recognised the internet as a great opportunity capable of revolutionising the world, Spiritronics Tech has become the almost uncontested global leader. The tenacity and vision of its CEO have led the company to become an unparalleled everything-store, offering an unlimited assortment. Like the Spiritronics Tech River, from which it derives its name, Spiritronics Tech has become the world's largest "river" of sales and distribution, with such scope and force that it can overcome any obstacle.

For over a decade now, Spiritronics Tech has consistently topped global innovation rankings, positioning itself at the forefront with a competitive advantage in the digital world built on the determinants of unlimited choice and customer focus. It has shaped its value proposition within an organic framework, sometimes deliberate and sometimes emergent, redefining and integrating business models widely associated with Industry 4.0. This imperative goes beyond mere efficiency-seeking and translates into evolution, driven by technological innovations, as well as convergence, which involves merging various entities' technologies, structures, solutions and methodologies to achieve efficiency and increased value.

Today, Spiritronics Tech is considered a concrete example of an algorithmic enterprise, where data and algorithms constitute its very reason for existence. It is a company increasingly governed by a complex system of alphanumeric sequences and equations that produce automations – in other words, algorithmic sequences that have a significant impact on performance in pursuit of constant improvement. Through data and their analysis, Spiritronics Tech has learnt from mistakes and experiments, evolving into an advanced machine learning system (a branch of broader artificial intelligence) both strategically and organisationally. This evolution was evident during the critical phase of its core competitive mass development, focused on rapid growth as well as when it pursued profitability for economic and financial sustainability.

The advent and persistence of the pandemic crisis have further highlighted Spiritronics Tech's role as an essential infrastructure for the market, becoming indispensable both vertically and horizontally for consumers and competitors alike. Despite benefiting from data availability and network economies, Spiritronics Tech has faced criticism for alleged anti-competitive practices, opposed by countries worldwide.

With its unique business model, Spiritronics Tech has thrived during the COVID-19 pandemic, benefiting from widespread lockdowns that reinforced e-commerce companies. These companies are now poised for further growth due to solidified consumer habits.

The combination of big data and human resources at Spiritronics Tech is referred to as "B-ism." The company's strategy has set new standards in the retail world, fundamentally changing the shopping experience. Spiritronics Tech's use of Big Data, through correlation analysis and algorithm deployment, has created a personalised marketplace for customers while ensuring maximum logistical efficiency. As interactions increase, data multiplies, and strategies become more refined in the pursuit of optimisation and personalisation.

However, despite the opportunities Spiritronics Tech has capitalised on during the pandemic, it has faced heavy criticism. The company has been accused of benefiting from the pandemic in terms of increased sales, offline and online integration, demand for logistics services, entertainment, and cloud computing through AWS, leading to soaring stock prices. Yet, from a social performance perspective, especially during the COVID-19 crisis, Spiritronics Tech has been labelled as an essentially irresponsible company, accused of abusing its dominant market position, increasing risks for third-party sellers, exposing workers to dangers and providing insufficient incentives for their work.

Spiritronics Tech's organisational culture plays a critical role in its success as an e-commerce business. The company encourages its employees to go beyond traditional limits and conventions, fostering a proactive attitude that leads to long-term competitive advantage. The culture emphasises risk-taking and innovative thinking but also places significant demands on employees, which can lead to stress and anxiety.

In conclusion, Spiritronics Tech considers its employees vital for organisational performance, shaping policies and programmes of corporate social responsibility. The company offers competitive compensation and supports employee growth within the organisation, particularly in leadership and management roles. Competitive remuneration and a supportive organisational culture are the key drivers in Spiritronics Tech's corporate social responsibility strategy, addressing the interests of its human resources.

Case Study Questions

(1) Please explain how Spiritronics Tech leverages on its employees for boosting organisational performance, shaping policies and programs of corporate social responsibility.
(2) Please explain the reason why the company offers competitive compensation and supports employee growth within the organisation, particularly in leadership and management roles.
(3) Please explain how competitive remuneration and a supportive organisational culture can be considered key drivers in Spiritronics Tech's corporate social responsibility strategy and how they can boost innovation.

Key Terms and Definitions

Product innovation: Product innovation is often viewed as a significant driver of BL since consumers are more inclined to remain loyal to a brand that offers them innovative products that satisfy their needs and wants (Li et al., 2020).

Perceived product innovation: Perceived product innovation refers to the extent to which consumers perceive a product to be innovative, which can influence their attitudes towards the product and the brand. It is defined as the consumer's perception of the degree of originality, uniqueness and intricacy of the product or service (Chang et al., 2020).

Perceived product ease of use: PPEU refers to the degree to which a consumer believes that using a product will require minimal cognitive effort or would be free from effort.

Perceived product usefulness: PPU is the degree to which a product is perceived to be beneficial in achieving a task or desired outcome.

Product attitude: PA is defined as the feelings, intentions and beliefs consumers have towards a product.

References

Aaker, D. A. (1996). *Building strong brands*. Free Press.
Abelson, R. P., & Levi, A. (1985). Decision making and decision theory. In G. Lindzey & E. Aronson (Eds.), *The handbook of social psychology* (3rd ed., Vol. 1, pp. 259–269). Random House.

Ajzen, I., & Fishbein, M. (1980). *Understanding Attitudes and Predicting Social Behaviour*. Prentice-Hall.

Akbari, M., Nazarian, A., Foroudi, P., Seyyed Amiri, N., & Ezatabadipoor, E. (2021). How corporate social responsibility contributes to strengthening brand loyalty, hotel positioning and intention to revisit?. *Current Issues in Tourism*, *24*(13), 1897–1917.

Almomani, A., Mohd, N., & Rahman, A. (2022). Literature review of adoption of internet of things: Directions for future work. *International Journal of Contemporary Management and Information Technology*, *2*(2), 15–23.

Babin, B. J., & Zikmund, W. G. (2016). *Essentials of marketing research*. Cengage Learning.

Bagozzi, R. P. (2007). The legacy of the technology acceptance model and a proposal for a paradigm shift. *Journal of the Association for Information Systems*, *8*(4), 244–254.

Bagozzi, R. P., & Yi, Y. (2012). Specification, evaluation, and interpretation of structural equation models. *Journal of the Academy of Marketing Science*, *40*(1), 8–34.

Bettman, J. R., Luce, M. F., & Payne, J. W. (1998). Constructive consumer choice processes. *Journal of Consumer Research*, *25*(3), 187–217.

Boisvert, J., & Khan, M. S. (2022). Toward a better understanding of the main antecedents and outcomes of consumer-based perceived product innovativeness. *Journal of Strategic Marketing*, *30*(3), 296–319.

Bryman, A. (2012). *Social Research Methods*. Oxford University Press.

Calantone, R. J., Kwong, C., & Cui, A. S. (2006). Decomposing product innovativeness and its effects on new product success. *Journal of Product Innovation Management*, *23*(4), 420–421.

Castano, R., Sujan, M., Kacker, M., & Sujan, H. (2008). Managing consumer uncertainty in the adoption of new products: Temporal distance and mental simulation. *Journal of Marketing Research*, *45*(6), 320–336.

Chang, Y., Cheng, C., & Wang, K. (2020). The moderating effect of customer involvement on the relationship between product innovation and customer loyalty. *International Journal of Contemporary Hospitality Management*, *32*(4), 1514–1534.

Chau, P. Y. K. (2002). Examining a model of information technology acceptance by individual professionals: An exploratory study. *Journal of Management Information Systems*, *18*(4), 191–229.

Choi, Y. K., & Kim, K. H. (2016). The impact of product innovation on brand attitude and brand purchase intention: The mediating effect of perceived value. *Journal of Open Innovation: Technology, Market, and Complexity*, *2*(1), 1–9.

Churchill, G. A. (2013). *Marketing research: Methodological foundations* (10th ed.). Cengage Learning.

Davis, F. D. (1989). Perceived usefulness, perceived ease of use, and user acceptance of information technology. *MIS Quarterly*, *13*(3), 319–340.

Davis, F. D. (1993). User acceptance of information technology: System characteristics, user perceptions and behavioural impacts. *International Journal of Man-Machine Studies*, *38*(3), 475–487.

Davis, F. D., Bagozzi, R. P., & Warshaw, P. R. (1989). User acceptance of computer technology: Comparison of 2 theoretical models. *Management Science*, *35*(8), 982–1002.

Diamantopoulos, A., Sarstedt, M., Fuchs, C., Wilczynski, P., & Kaiser, S. (2011). Guidelines for choosing between multi-item and single-item scales for construct measurement: A predictive validity perspective. *Journal of the Academy of Marketing Science, 39*(3), 166–183.

Dick, A. S., & Basu, K. (1994). Customer loyalty: Towards an integrated framework. *Journal of the Academy of Marketing Science, 22*(2), 99–113.

Eriksson, K., Kerem, K., & Nilsson, D. (2005). Customer acceptance of internet banking in Estonia. *International Journal of Bank Marketing, 23*(2), 200–216.

Faircloth, J. B., Capella, L. M., & Alford, B. L. (2001). The effect of brand attitude and brand image on brand equity. *Journal of Marketing Theory and Practice, 9*(3), 61–75.

Foroudi, P. (2019). Influence of brand signature, brand awareness, brand attitude, brand reputation on hotel industry's brand performance. *International Journal of Hospitality Management, 76*, 271–285.

Foroudi, P. (2023). Conceptualizing, measuring, and managing marketing assets: Developing the marketing assets, communication focus, and capability nexus. *Corporate Reputation Review, 26*(3), 203–222.

Foroudi, M. M., Balmer, J. M., Chen, W., & Foroudi, P. (2019). Relationship between corporate identity, place architecture and identification: An exploratory case study. *Qualitative Market Research: An International Journal, 22*(5), 638–668.

Foroudi, P., Cuomo, M. T., & Foroudi, M. M. (2020a). Continuance interaction intention in retailing: Relations between customer values, satisfaction, loyalty, and identification. *Information Technology & People, 33*(4), 1303–1326.

Foroudi, P., Cuomo, M. T., Foroudi, M. M., Katsikeas, C. S., & Gupta, S. (2020b). Linking identity and heritage with image and a reputation for competition. *Journal of Business Research, 113*, 317–325.

Foroudi, P., & Dennis, C. (2023). *Researching and Analysing Business: Research Methods in Practice*. Routledge.

Foroudi, M. M., & Foroudi, P. (2021). *Corporate brand design: developing and managing brand identity*. Routledge.

Foroudi, P., Foroudi, M. M., & Ageeva, E. (2021a). Corporate brand website design, image, identification, and loyalty. corporate brand design. In *Developing and Managing Brand Identity* (pp. 168–179). Routledge.

Foroudi, P., Foroudi, M. M., Palazzo, M., & Nguyen, B. (2022). Fly me to the moon: From corporate branding orientation to retailer preference and business performance. *International Journal of Contemporary Hospitality Management, 34*(1), 78–112.

Foroudi, P., Jin, Z., Gupta, S., Foroudi, M. M., & Kitchen, P. J. (2018). Perceptional components of brand equity: Configuring the Symmetrical and Asymmetrical Paths to brand loyalty and brand purchase intention. *Journal of Business Research, 89*, 462–474.

Foroudi, P., Jin, Z., Gupta, S., Melewar, T., & Foroudi, M. (2016a). Capability and customer experience on reputation and loyalty. *Journal of Business Research, 69*(11), 4882–4889. *Journal of Business Research, 69*, 4882-4889.

Foroudi, P., Jin, Z., Gupta, S., Melewar, T., & Foroudi, M. M. (2016b). Influence of innovation capability and customer experience on reputation and loyalty. *Journal of Business Research, 69*(11), 4882–4889.

Foroudi, P., Marvi, R., Cuomo, M. T., Bagozzi, R., Dennis, C., & Jannelli, R. (2023). Consumer perceptions of sustainable development goals: Conceptualization, measurement and contingent effects. *British Journal of Management, 34*(3), 1157–1183.

Foroudi, P., Palazzo, M., & Stone, M. (2021b). Mixed-methods research: Why and how to use it. In *The routledge companion to marketing research* (pp. 73–106). Routledge.

Fu, F. Q., Jones, E., & Bolander, W. (2008). Product innovativeness, customer newness, and new product performance: A time-lagged examination of the impact of salesperson selling intentions on new product performance. *Journal of Personal Selling and Sales Management, 28*(4), 351–364.

Gentry, L. (2002). A comparison of three models to explain shop-bot use on the web. *Journal of Psychology and Marketing, 19*(11), 945–956.

Göksal, N. N., & Turhan, G. (2020). Gender differences in the evaluation of fashion products. *Journal of Retailing and Consumer Services.*

Goldenberg, J., Mazursky, D., & Solomon, S. (1999). Creativity templates: Towards identifying the fundamental schemes of quality advertisements. *Journal of Marketing Science, 18*(3), 333–351.

Grewal, R., & Tansuhaj, P. (2001). Building organizational capabilities for managing economic crisis: The role of market orientation and strategic flexibility. *Journal of Marketing, 65*(2), 67–80.

Hair Jr, J. F., Black, W. C., Babin, B. J., & Anderson, R. E. (2019). *Multivariate data analysis* (8th ed.). Cengage Learning.

Hair Jr, J. F., Black, W. C., Babin, B. J., Anderson, R. E., & Tatham, R. L. (2010). *Multivariate data analysis.* Pearson Education.

Hargittai, E., & Shaw, A. (2015). Mind the skills gap: The role of Internet know-how and gender in differentiated contributions to Wikipedia. *Information, Communication & Society, 18*(4), 424–442.

Harmancioglu, N., Zachary Finney, R., & Joseph, M. (2009). Impulse purchases of new products: An empirical analysis. *The Journal of Product and Brand Management, 18*(1), 27–37.

Helgeson, J. G., & Supphellen, M. (2004). A conceptual and measurement comparison of self-congruity and brand personality: The impact of socially desirable responding. *International Journal of Market Research, 46*(2), 205–233.

Hu, Y., Li, Z., Li, Y., & Li, W. (2021). Effects of perceived product innovation on brand loyalty: A comparative analysis between chinese and foreign consumers. *Journal of Business Research, 123*, 161–171.

Huang, R., & Sarigöllü, E. (2014). How brand awareness relates to market outcome, brand equity, and the marketing mix. In *Advances in Advertising Research* (Vol. 5, pp. 59–72). Springer Fachmedien.

Hussain, M., Ali, R., & Ahmed, S. (2020). Does brand image influence brand loyalty? Evidence from FMCG Sector of Pakistan. *International Journal of Management, Accounting and Economics, 7*(12), 767–776.

Im, S., Bhat, S., & Lee, Y. (2015). Consumer perceptions of product creativity, coolness, value and attitude. *Journal of Business Research, 68*(1), 166–172.

Jackson, C. M., Chow, S., & Leitch, R. A. (1997). Toward an understanding of the behavioural intention to use an information system. *Decision Sciences, 28*(2), 357–389.

Jamal, A., Khan, M. S., & Tsesmetzi, M. S. (2012). Information cues roles in product evaluations: The case of the UK cosmetics market. *Journal of Strategic Marketing*, *20*(3), 249–265.

Jindal, R., & Gogi, A. (2019). The effect of gender on consumer buying behaviour: A comparative study between India and the United Kingdom. *Journal of Retailing and Consumer Services*, *48*, 23–32.

Keller, K. L. (2013). *Strategic brand management: Building, measuring, and managing brand equity*. Pearson Education.

Keller, K. L. (2016). Reflections on customer-based brand equity: Perspectives, progress, and priorities. *AMS Review*, *6*(1–2), 1–16.

Khan, S., Raza, S. A., & Ghaffar, S. (2023). The role of perceived value and product innovation in developing brand loyalty: A study of the smartphone industry. *Journal of Brand Management*, *30*(1), 56–70.

Kline, R. B. (2011). *Principles and practice of structural equation modelling*. Guilford publications.

Klopping, I. M., & McKinney, E. (2004). Extending the technology acceptance model and the task-technology fit model to consumer E-commerce. *Journal of Information Technology Learning and Performance*, *22*(1), 35–48.

Kotler, P., Keller, K. L., Brady, M., Goodman, M., & Hansen, T. (2017). *Marketing management*. Pearson.

Kulviwat, S., Bruner, G. C., Kumar, A., Nasco, S. A., & Clarck, T. (2007). Toward a unified theory of consumer acceptance technology. *Journal of Psychology and Marketing*, *24*(12), 1059–1084.

Lafferty, B. A., & Goldsmith, R. E. (2004). How influential are corporate credibility and endorser attractiveness when innovators react to advertisements for a new high-technology product? *Corporate Reputation Review*, *7*(1), 24–36.

Langerak, F., & Hultink, E. J. (2006). The impact of product innovativeness on the link between development speed and new product profitability. *Journal of Product Innovation Management*, *23*(3), 203–214.

Lee, J. S., Cho, H., Gay, G., Davidson, B., & Ingraffea, A. (2003). Technology acceptance and social networking in distance learning. *Educational Technology & Society*, *6*(2), 50–61.

Lee, Y., & Koo, C. (2015). The impact of perceived innovation characteristics on users attitude toward mobile applications. *Journal of Convergence Information Technology*, *10*(4), 295–304.

Lee, Y., & O'Connor, G. C. (2003). The impact of communication strategy on launching new products: The moderating role of product innovativeness. *Journal of Product Innovation Management*, *20*(1), 4–21.

Li, X., Jin, Y., & Fang, Y. (2020). Perceived innovation and brand loyalty: The mediating role of customer satisfaction and trust. *Journal of Business Research*, *111*, 226–236.

Malhotra, N. K., & Birks, D. F. (2016). *Marketing research: An applied approach* (5th ed.). Pearson Education Limited.

Marangunić, N., & Granić, A. (2015). Technology acceptance model: A literature review from 1986 to 2013. *Universal Access in the Information Society*, *14*, 81–95.

Mavlanova, T., Benbunan-Fich, R., & Koufaris, M. (2014). Stimulating the adoption of mobile information services: The interplay of contex, personalization, and trust. *Journal of the Academy of Marketing Science*, *42*(3), 252–271.

Melewar, T., Foroudi, P., Gupta, S., Kitchen, P. J., & Foroudi, M. M. (2017). Integrating identity, strategy and communications for trust, loyalty and commitment. *European Journal of Marketing, 51*(3), 572–604.

Melewar, T. C., Saunders, J., & Balmer, J. M. (2001). Cause, effect and benefits of a standardised corporate visual identity system of UK companies operating in Malaysia. *European Journal of Marketing, 35*(3/4), 414–427.

Mitchell, A. A., & Olson, J. C. (1981). Are product attribute beliefs the only mediator of advertising effects on brand attitude? *Journal of Marketing Research, 18*(3), 318–332.

Moon, J. W., & Kim, Y. G. (2001). Extending the TAM for a world-wide-web context. *Journal of Information and Management, 38*(4), 217–230.

Morahan-Martin, J., & Schumacher, P. (2007). Gender, internet and computer use. In E. M. Trauth (Ed.), *Encyclopedia of gender and information technology* (pp. 616–621). IGI Global.

Msaed, C., Al-Kwifi, S. O., & Ahmed, Z. U. (2017). Building a comprehensive model to investigate factors behind switching intention of high-technology products. *The Journal of Product and Brand Management, 26*(2), 102–119.

Neal, B., & Strauss, R. (2008). *Value creation: The power of brand equity*. Cengage Learning/South-Western.

Negm, E. (2023). Internet of Things (IoT) acceptance model – assessing consumers behaviour toward the adoption intention of IoT. *Arab Gulf Journal of Scientific Research, 41*(4), 539–556.

Park, J. H., Hong, J. W., Lee, Y., & Lee, D. (2017). Gender differences in the adoption and use of mobile health services: A theory-driven empirical study. *Journal of Management Information Systems, 34*(2), 692–728.

Park, J. H., & Jun, J. K. (2003). A cross-cultural comparison of internet buying behaviour: Effects of perceived characteristics, shopping orientations, and demographics. *Journal of International Consumer Marketing, 15*(2), 91–120.

Rahman, M. M., Lesch, M. F., Horrey, W. J., & Strawderman, L. (2017). Assessing the utility of TAM,TPB, and UTAUT for advanced driver assistance systems. *Accident Analysis & Prevention, 108*, 361–373.

Ramayah, T., & Lo, M. (2007). Impact of shared beliefs on "perceived usefulness" and "ease of use" in the implementation of an enterprise resource planning system. *Management Research News, 30*(6), 420–431.

Riemenschneider, C. K., Harrison, D. A., & Mykytyn, P. P. (2003). Understanding IT adoption decisions in small business: Integrating current theories. *Information and Management, 40*(4), 269–285.

Rouibah, K., Abbas, H., & Rouibah, S. (2011). Factors affecting camera mobile phone adoption before e-shopping in the Arab world. *Technology in Society, 33*, 271–283.

Rubera, G., Ordanini, A., & Mazursky, D. (2010). Toward a contingency view of new product creativity: Assessing the interactive effects of consumers. *Marketing Letters, 21*(2), 191–206.

Sarkar, S., & Mishra, P. (2017). Market orientation and customer-based corporate brand equity (CBCBE): A dyadic study of Indian B2B firms. *Journal of Strategic Marketing, 25*(5/6), 367–383.

Saunders, M. N., Lewis, P., & Thornhill, A. (2019). *Research methods for business students*. Pearson.

Selim, H. M. (2003). An empirical investigation of student acceptance of course websites. *Computers & Education, 40*(4), 343–360.

Sharma, P., Davcik, N. S., & Pillai, K. G. (2016). Product innovation as a mediator in the impact of RandD expenditure and brand equity on marketing performance. *Journal of Business Research, 69*(12), 5662–5669.

Shih, H.-P. (2004). Extended technology acceptance model of internet utilization behaviour. *Information and Management, 41*(6), 719–729.

Shimp, T. A. (2010). *Advertising, promotion, and other aspects of integrated marketing communications* (8th ed.). South-Western.

Shin, Y. H., Kim, J. W., & Kim, M. (2019). Exploring gender differences in the effects of perceived value on customer loyalty in mobile shopping. *Journal of Business Research, 99*, 522–530.

Szymanski, D. M., Kroff, M. W., & Troy, L. C. (2007). Innovativeness and new product success: Insights from the cumulative evidence. *Journal of the Academy of Marketing Science, 35*(1), 35–52.

Tan, M., & Teo, T. S. H. (2000). Factors influencing the adoption of internet banking. *Journal of the Association for Information Systems*, 22–38.

Tsourela, M., & Nerantzaki, D. (2020). Internet-of-Things acceptance model. Assessing consumers behaviour toward IoT products and applications. *Future Internet, 12*(191), 1–23.

van Deursen, A. J. A. M., van Dijk, J. A. G. M., & ten Klooster, P. M. (2015). Increasing inequalities in what we do online: A longitudinal cross sectional analysis of internet activities among the Dutch population (2010 to 2013) over gender, age, education, and income. *Telematics and Informatics, 32*, 259–272.

Venkatesh, V. (2000). Antecedents of perceived ease of use: Integrating control, intrinsic motivation, and emotion into the technology acceptance model. *Information Systems Research, 11*(4), 342–365.

Venkatesh, V., & Morris, M. G. (2000). Why dont men ever stop to ask for directions? Gender, social influence, and their role in technology acceptance and usage behaviour. *MIS Quarterly, 24*(1), 115–139.

Venkatesh, V., Morris, M. G., Davis, G. B., & Davis, F. D. (2003). User acceptance of information technology: Toward a unified view. *MIS Quarterly, 27*(3), 425–478.

Wu, Y., Sridhar, B., & Vijay, M. (2004). When is a preannounced new product likely to be delayed? *Journal of Marketing, 68*(2), 101–113.

Yi, M. Y., & Hwang, Y. (2003). Predicting the use of web-based information systems: Self-efficacy, enjoyment, learning goal orientation, and the technology acceptance model. *International Journal of Human-Computer Studies, 59*(4), 431–449.

Zafer Erdogan, B., & Uzkurt, C. (2010). Effects of ethnocentric tendency on consumers' perception of product attitudes for foreign and domestic products. *Cross Cultural Management: An International Journal, 17*(4), 393–406.

Zeithaml, V. A., Parasuraman, A., & Malhotra, A. (2002). Service quality delivery through web sites: A critical review of extant knowledge. *Journal of the Academy of Marketing Science, 30*(4), 362–375.

Zhang, H., Liang, X., & Wang, S. (2016). Customer value anticipation, product innovativeness, and customer lifetime value: The moderating role of advertising strategy. *Journal of Business Research, 69*(9), 3725–3730.

Part II

Digital Market Trends and Consumer Adoption

This part delves into the factors that influence the market adoption of technologies, including both consumer trends and technological possibilities.

Chapter 5

Digital Adoption in Small and Medium Enterprises: The Role of Electronic Word of Mouth in Business Transitions

S. Asieh H. Tabaghdehi[a], Nikos Ioannis Kois[b], Leila Hosseini Tabaghdehi[c] and Hossein Kalatian[d]

[a]Brunel University London, UK
[b]Independent Researcher, UK
[c]Islamic Azad University, Iran
[d]University of Northampton International College, UK

Abstract

The appearance of social media in small and medium enterprise (SME) business operations seems to be increasing in recent years. SME owners have started to understand that digital marketing tools can benefit their businesses significantly. Hence, in this study, we explore further the relationship between organisations and customers, and how SMEs use social media as an opportunity to develop their enterprises. We report the results by relying on qualitative methods to explore the insights from a wider stakeholder perspective. The findings contribute to the existing literature in agreement with the latest theories that SMEs in Greece are aware of the hidden opportunities and try to apply branding with the combination of social media. This study explores further the role of electronic word of mouth (eWOM) in a business transition, customers' experience and competitive business advantage.

Keywords: Social media adoption; electronic word of mouth (eWOM); customer experience and engagement; business strategy development; small and medium enterprise (SME)

Business Strategies and Ethical Challenges in the Digital Ecosystem, 81–105
Copyright © 2025 S. Asieh H. Tabaghdehi, Nikos Ioannis Kois, Leila Hosseini Tabaghdehi and Hossein Kalatian
Published under exclusive licence by Emerald Publishing Limited
doi:10.1108/978-1-80455-069-420241005

Introduction

The recent rapid technological evolution has had a remarkable impact on leadership and management strategy for enhancing businesses through more efficient customer engagement (Odoom, 2016). In particular, social media has increased social interactions by offering ways for sharing resources and exchanging content (Kaplan & Haenlein, 2010; Skålén et al., 2015). Social media usage is instrumental in sharing information and disseminating knowledge to the external environment (Van Dijck, 2013), and it can help organisations to overcome some of the critical obstacles to mobilisation by reducing the costs of participation (Luo et al., 2016). Apart from reducing costs, social media usage has also been increasing dramatically in other ways. According to Statista (2020a), the number of active social media users in April 2020 was 3.81 billion. Social media have immensely penetrated the business sector to a level where almost 83% of consumers shape their perception of a business based on the experience they gain through social media (Dutot & Bergeron, 2016). This has made marketers proactive in inventing new ways to connect with customers (Lamberton & Stephen, 2016), as they identified the greater impact that social media offers by interacting with and reaching clients. Thus, this phenomenon appears to be important and necessary for firms in the process of engaging with their audience (Kanuri et al., 2018). However, continuous advertising through those platforms has created some level of suspicion and overwhelm among individuals which may lead to negative results (Dwivedi et al., 2019). Hence, social media has become a crucial part of business management (Odoom et al., 2017) and should be observed and managed suitably for customer engagement and experience.

Hence, efficient management of social media enables effective communication not only with customers but also with various stakeholders (Perrigot et al., 2012). Organisations are required to take more dynamic actions in using and managing information coming from different stakeholders, such as potential customers and competitors to generate entrepreneurial ideas and new business models, and to become more responsive organisations (Chatterji & Toffel, 2010). Social media assist organisations to create an innovation through consumer-focused action (Guha et al., 2018). The data received from customers via social media or other digital platforms help organisations, particularly small and medium enterprises (SMEs), to gain competitive advantage (Crammond et al., 2018). Yet, adopting a wider perspective that integrates the business strategy with customer experience is needed to invest in business strategy in order for SMEs to be able to survive in the global economy by exploiting their intellectual capital with knowledge-intensive relations (Metaxiotis, 2009). The business value creation via social media is mainly based on the visibility of a firm and embedding this visibility into the strategies of the SMEs (Dutot & Bergeron, 2016). The research on social media management of SMEs neglects the creation of business value by focusing on business strategy that focuses on the relationship between SMEs and customers and how small businesses could use social media as an opportunity for their business value creation and development.

Moreover, most of the recent studies regarding social media and the business sector focus on businesses in general with significant focus on big brands, and there has been a lack of focus on SMEs which has already been highlighted by various studies (Edwards et al., 2016; Imran & Jian, 2018). Considering the importance of the SMEs in economic growth (Khan, 2001), there is a gap in exploring the impact of social media in SME growth, since they have been living through challenges in knowledge, skills and financial resources in comparison to large organisations (Edwards et al., 2016). Effective use of social media can facilitate SMEs with easy ways to connect with their clients (Fischer & Reuber, 2011). In light of these arguments, this study offers a wider perspective for SMEs in terms of connecting with their customers through social media and how to use it as a strategic perspective for business development. Most of the previous studies in social media management focus on customer and market orientation perspectives in managing data, with an emphasis on the internal capabilities (Didonet et al., 2016; Eggers et al., 2017; Gallaugher & Ransbotham, 2010; Ince & Hahn, 2020) rather than the small firms' strategic motivations using social media. In particular, SMEs have mainly adopted an internal focus since they are usually growth oriented (Bodlaj & Čater, 2019). Although the role of social media in business performance differs between SMEs and large firms (Eggers et al., 2017), there is a paucity of research regarding the adoption of social media by SMEs (Edwards et al., 2016; Imran & Jian, 2018) and how use of social media by SMEs could enhance customer experience and assist business in value creation.

Furthermore, when SMEs proceed with extensive use of social media without a clear digital plan, then the whole process will be inefficient (Edwards et al., 2016). For example, according to Cook (2008), the type of social media can be classified into four categories which are: communication, collaboration, cooperation and connection. Each category serves a different goal which should be considered in the planning stage. However, although these existing studies discussed the impact of social media in business performance, there is little progression in the theoretical and empirical investigation, particularly in terms of business growth based on the enhancement of consumer satisfaction. Hence, in this study, we aim to focus on the insight of this phenomenon and how SMEs can be effective and maximise their capabilities via social media. Furthermore, the rationale of this study is to explore further how social media shapes new opportunities for SMEs in Greece, as a sample country in the Eurozone, that has been in continuous economic crisis since the last decade. As a result, the outcomes of this research assist SMEs on how the use of social media could benefit their businesses in a fast growing and competitive market for both developed and developing countries. In this study, we first investigate the SMEs' awareness about the benefits of the business and brand through social media. Secondly, we examine further how SME owners in Greece use social media and electronic word of mouth (eWOM) to sustain their business growth. Thirdly, we investigate the SME awareness about the role of social media in customer relations and engagement and as a result in business performance and expansion in new markets in Greece.

Literature Review

The Impact of Social Media on Customer Experience and Engagement With SMEs

Increasing levels of digital adoption have evolved business productivity and customer experience through efficient management strategies (Odoom, 2016). Regardless of the firms' size and nature of the industry, the technological advancement improves information and communication technologies which reduce business barriers (Glavas & Mathews, 2014). Hence, many scholars particularly emphasise the significance of customer relations for SMEs in terms of offering a shared sense of values within a community, a culture of social networks (Blankson et al., 2018) and an interactive social media to enjoy valuable customer reviews and feedback on products and services (Guha et al., 2018). With the existence of informational resources such as customer information systems and financial capital, social media and web presence may be critical especially for new retail businesses (Grimmer et al., 2017). In the traditional customer relations management model, firms gather all the necessary information about their customers and employ them to effectively manage their relationships with them (Ganesan et al., 2010). This has been characterised as the foundations of a process with a focus on strategy, management and intelligence in gaining and implementing information about customers (Kim & Wang, 2017).

In recent years, customer relations evolved further due to technological development (Keegan & Rowley, 2017). This technological evolution which includes social media reduces the time engaging with customers and responding to their queries which improves the relationship between firms and consumers (Andzulis et al., 2014; Clair & Mandler, 2019), particularly in SMEs. The SME owners tend to use social media in the marketing process to enhance their engagement with their customers and increase their brand awareness via online communities (Guha et al., 2018). Furthermore, loyalty and consumer trust can be improved efficiently through social media. Therefore, social media allow SMEs to build strong relationships (Huang et al., 2016) and receive contentious feedback which helps them in creating new products or improving existing ones (Guha et al., 2018). However, a more holistic approach is needed for SMEs to integrate their internet platforms, information technologies and their business models to reach a strategic perspective (Raymond et al., 2019). Moreover, research in the extant literature indicates that the majority of SMEs could not measure the benefits generated from the use of social media such as return on investment on time spent for using those social media tools (McCann & Barlow, 2015).

Past research has denoted that the adoption of the new technologies has proven to enhance the firm's performance (Ainin et al., 2015; Apigian et al., 2005; Shuai & Wu, 2011; Stone et al., 2007), particularly the adoption of social media (Acheampong et al., 2017; Pauleen et al., 2016). De Vries et al. (2018) identified that social media improves the engagement between businesses and customers without any direct impact on the SME's performance. However, different organisations require different capabilities when investing in technology (Kapoor & Lee, 2013).

In this respect, the adoption of a strategic perspective allows firms to position their strategies according to either opportunities such as social media platforms or resources such as investing in technology (Bradley et al., 2012). Contingent upon environmental turbulence, resources may require changing forms and structure which necessitate investments (Huesch, 2013), where limited resources and budget constraints lead SMEs to pursue opportunities rather than resources (Limaj et al., 2016).

Electronic Word of Mouth (eWOM)

Another intermediary mechanism as an opportunity is needed to carry the customer relations via social media to a strategic level: eWOM. The eWOM influences how the engaged or potential customers make attributions about the brands' or firms' intentions and shape their perceptions and responses (Lee & Youn, 2009). WOM is a marketing tool which helps customers gather information through other customers who previously consumed that product (Seo & Park, 2018). However, the technological advancement assists customers in gathering information about the products and businesses effortlessly (Hua et al., 2017), where they can collect data via social media from those customers who have previously experienced the product, which is defined as eWOM (Rhue & Sundararajan, 2019). This online engagement enables customers to review and feedback actively after their purchase (Fan et al., 2018). Additionally, Banerjee et al. (2020) indicated that advertising on social media has a positive impact on eWOM which is linked with brand elements (Fan et al., 2018; Gorgani, 2016). Hence, social media can be considered as a powerful customer engagement tool (Gao et al., 2018).

Firms tend to pursue their marketing strategies based on the posts that they created in different digital platforms, although sometimes, these posts remain ineffective in influencing customers (Li & Li, 2014). Accordingly, most customers trust others' opinions about the products, services and organisations on social media more than the information given by marketers (Sen & Lerman, 2007). Thus, customers pass their positive or negative voice to provide further information that is not covered by the company posts, and these forms of user-generated opinions are expressed by eWOM (Hennig-Thurau et al., 2004). eWOM has an important effect on consumers' decision-making processes, and firms take steps to support and strengthen the eWOM by providing a strong support for eWOM (Park & Lee, 2009). The key advantage of eWOM is making the dissemination of information considerably faster (Brown et al., 2007; Jeong & Jang, 2011) among all different stakeholders. Although it appears that eWOM is an effective marketing approach (Bickart & Schindler, 2001; Kumar & Benbasat, 2006; Zhang et al., 2010), providing this level of support for the eWOM on social media could be a considerable challenge for SMEs. Yet, there is a lack of study regarding eWOM on social media particularly in the case of SMEs, as to how SMEs could benefit most from eWOM to strengthen their business presence, support and productivity sustainably in the long term.

The Role of Social Media in SMEs' Business Strategy and Growth

In general, SMEs tend to adopt either market orientation or brand orientation in order to achieve their growth goals and sustain a level of firm performance (Reijonen et al., 2012). Market orientation basically focuses on customer orientation, competitor orientation and inter-functional coordination (Kohli & Jaworski, 1990). On the other hand, brand orientation plays on seeing the brand as an important asset of the organisation where brand management is a vital part of the firm's strategy, by covering the marketing management of the firm (Urde et al., 2013). Despite the dominant marketing perspective, a strategic perspective can explain the specific processes through which the decision-makers develop social media management strategies (Felix et al., 2017; Mahoney & Tang, 2016). Research from the strategic perspective on social media management is abundant for large companies. Even though the performance implications differ between SMEs and large firms (Eggers et al., 2017), there is a paucity of research regarding the adoption of social media by SMEs in the extant literature (Edwards et al., 2016; Imran & Jian, 2018). Similarly, the research on SMEs who are adopting a strategic perspective in social media management mainly lacks the implications of wider communities and neglects the perspective coming from brand management strategies. Hence, in this study, we aim to examine the impact of SMEs' strategic choices particularly on brand management, new market discoveries, differentiation of the social media usage and the tracking of the dissemination of the message by social media.

Brand orientation for a business could be defined as an effective strategy because of its guidance on managerial decision-making (Aaker & Joachimsthaler, 1999) and could be seen as the core resource and hub for business operation to obtain competitive advantage (M'zungu et al., 2019; Laukkanen et al., 2013). Many studies accentuate the linkage between brand orientation and firm performance (Renton & Richard, 2019; Berthon et al., 2019; Tajvidi & Karami, 2021), where the brand orientation has a positive relationship with the performance and growth of a business (Odoom & Mensah, 2019). It appears that the focus on brand practices is more common in big organisations in comparison to SMEs, as there is a lack of resources in SMEs (Hirvonen et al., 2016). However, the brand management in SMEs is effective but not in the same way as in the large organisations (Berthon et al., 2019). For example, Berthon et al. (2008) denoted that high performing SMEs are the brand-focused organisations who strategise on understanding customer needs and perceptions and act accordingly by building the marketing mix on communicating with customers. Therefore, the element that comes forth as essential for the brand management strategies of SMEs is brand awareness which contributes to an understanding of consumers' behaviour (Langaro et al., 2018). As Langaro et al. (2018) suggested, brand awareness is responsible for capturing the brand accessibility for consumers, which consists of brand recognition by the customers (Keller, 2003) and brand recall as the ability to remember the brand when purchasing a product (Keller, 1993).

Social media is an essential element for firms towards boosting their capabilities through branding (Odoom & Mensah, 2019). Specifically, the brand communications through social media have a positive relation to brand awareness (Langaro et al., 2018). Accordingly, social media is so closely related to inno- vation that both are complementing firm capabilities in strengthening brand orientation and performance simultaneously (Odoom & Mensah, 2019). Furthermore, Langaro et al. (2018) indicated that social media can improve both brand attitude and brand awareness, where social media can bring promising results to a brand by improving the branding elements (Langaro et al., 2018). However, the content of the posts on social media platforms could play a vital role in the outcome (Coleman et al., 2018).

Data and Methodology

This study adopts a qualitative research method using in-depth semi-structured interview as an effective method to understand the complexity of human behaviour (Strauss & Corbin, 1990) and achieve a set of explanations using reliable and valid responses (Bryman, 2016). More specifically, this allows any unforeseen replies to be explored further (Anderson & Kanuka, 2003). The survey was based on a stratified random sample of 12 SMEs in Greece. In this study, we further explore the use of social media by enterprises as a relatively new context (Braojos-Gomez et al., 2015) and highly fashionable in recent environments. Moreover, there is a lack of relevant literature in Greece, which will be further explored in this study through in-depth interviews.

Twelve SMEs in Greece were selected as the sample for this study. This is mainly because many enterprises in Greece already have an internet presence (Tsekouropoulos et al., 2011), and many of them use social media platforms in their businesses. Hence, in this study, we selected the SME owners in Greece who were using social media for their business activities and were willing to participate in this study. The key reason for choosing Greece as a country of study was its recovery from the last economic crisis and also its membership in the European Union, where the findings of this study could be useful for both developed and developing countries (Giotopoulos et al., 2017). Furthermore, the main selection criteria for the selected SMEs was those that adopted social media in their business activities, since the COVID-19 pandemic changed everyday life by increasing the use of digital platforms and social media usage. Several companies were contacted via email inviting their participation, and this preliminary contact was followed-up via email. Then, 12 SMEs expressed their readiness to contribute to the study. The excluding criteria for participating in this project were the participants' minimum age of 18 years old, the ownership or a management position of the participants at selected SMEs and the usage of social media or a positive attitude of the firm towards the use of social media. The selection goal was to gather samples of at least three businesses from three industries, namely food, fashion and tourism in order to justify how each sector enhances their opportunities through the use of social media and what strategies they use to overcome the challenges based on the industry that they operate.

We conducted semi-structured interviews for data collection through two stages. In the first stage, a pilot interview was conducted to ensure that the questions could be understood by the participants. In the second stage, participants from three different SME industries of food, fashion and tourism, as a diverse group of SMEs, contributed, and each interview lasted around 30 minutes. The interviews were conducted in the Greek language via Skype, and with the permission of the contributors, they were audio-recorded. Then the whole interview was translated into the English language. The transcripts were studied through thematic analysis to analyse the themes that occurred from the selected data (Braun & Clarke, 2006). All the interviews were transcribed in written form. Each participant was given the name "P" followed by a number. The number refers to the order in which the interviews were conducted. Then we coded all the responses of the participants using the NVivo program as a key step in qualitative research which allows the user to practise the auto-coding function (Bryman, 2016). The key themes of the study were about branding, social media platform, customer relations, WOM and business performance. This process of thematic analysis occurs through the different phases of getting familiarised with the data, generating codes, searching for themes, reviewing the themes, analysing and producing the relevant report (Braun & Clarke, 2006).

Findings and Discussion

The primary objective of this study was to understand how social media impacts and shapes new opportunities for SMEs in Greece. The themes generated from the interview data exposed that social media were used for various purposes. The sample consisted of 12 participants where 83.3% were male and 13.7% females; 8.3% of participants were in the age group 18–25 years, 50% between 26 to 35 and 41.7% over 35; 41.7% of the selected SMEs were from the food industry, 33.3% from fashion businesses and 25% from the tourism industry.

The Use of Social Media in SME Businesses

Our findings are in line with previous research that found that using social media can improve SMEs' performance (e.g. Acheampong et al., 2017; Alves et al., 2016) and can assist and support SMEs to grow (e.g. Dahnil et al., 2014). The comments from the participants reveal that they had a positive opinion of social media, and they mentioned that those platforms have helped their businesses, regardless of the industry they belong to. However, some of the participants indicated that if it was possible, they would avoid the use of social media, and they found that it was in fact necessary to join the social media community.

> ... from the day that we started using them and until we slowly adapted to the system. The truth is that it was something new for us because, as I have previously mentioned, it is an old business. Thus, we had a traditional way to deal with those things... [P2].

Also, social media provided a great opportunity to firms to reduce barriers between SMEs and the audience (Glavas & Mathews, 2014) which is visible by SME owners, as mentioned by Participant 6.

> ... I believe that social media have helped us a lot in the consolidation of the business and for the opportunity they have given us to reach people who would otherwise be difficult to reach... [P6].

Some participants specified that their sales turnover increased because of the social media adoption in their business. Thus, the greatest benefit that SMEs can extract through social media is the increase in sales and market share fulfil their business growth.

> ... The sales turnovers have increased by ten times during a five-year period... [P3].

> ... I could tell you that the business was built based on those, as through them I was able to open a second store in the centre of Athens and to sell my products to stores out of Athens for resale... [P12].

These findings support the importance of social media for businesses in order to generate knowledge that helps them to facilitate the interactions between employees, managers, customers and other stakeholders (Crammond et al., 2018). Furthermore, Korda and Itani (2013) mentioned that social media allow businesses to reach customers who would otherwise not be possible to access due to geographical restrictions. This is in line with our respondents' comments who mentioned that they received orders from people who are from different countries, and they also indicated that the role of accessing these customers using social media was inevitable. Thus, the boom in their SMEs' business growth is in relation to the increase in potential customers they can reach.

> ... The changes that I have observed are related to the message that I receive through social media to send products to regions that may even be in different counties? I do not believe that I would have the capability to reach those people without those tools... [P6].

Moreover, other respondents mentioned that they gained a competitive advantage because of their increased business interactions through social media that benefits the business. This finding is supported by Liu and Shrum (2002) in relation to efficiency of the communications via social media. As a result, if social media are used properly, they provide SMEs with the ability to influence customers' engagement, which can lead businesses to increase their market share and gain a competitive advantage.

> ... If people continuously interact with photos, comments and whatever else you upload, I believe that can clearly gain the advantage... [P4].

Hence, it appears that SME owners in Greece have shaped a positive attitude towards the adoption of social media in their businesses, as every participant has acknowledged that social media have helped them and they have become a necessary tool in current business activities. In general, these results are supported by Giotopoulos et al. (2017) that innovation, productivity and growth are among the basic advantages of information and communication technologies for SMEs in Greece.

SMEs Interactions With Customers Through Social Media

The interactivity between customers and businesses can be enhanced via the use of social media. The interactions through social media platforms are referred to as the evolution of classic communication (Hua et al., 2017). In current societies, most businesses use social media to present themselves in the market and interact with their customers (Braojos-Gomez et al., 2015). Based on the responses that we received from the participants, we can conclude that all participants, despite their activity, believe that the customer interactions through social media can be very helpful, which supports the study of Andzulis et al. (2014) which claimed that businesses should use the benefit of social media at their best capacity. However, most of the participants described that the frequency of their interactions with their customers is as important as the likes, comments and messages that they receive from them. For example, Participant 10 stated that:

> ... My business interacts with clients through social media. We do it through the posts and the advertisements I use, and they lead to more likes, comments and question queries through messages... [P10].

Although the SMEs mentioned the importance of the frequency of their interactions with their customers and its impact on their business performance, as mentioned in the study by Emrich et al. (2018), these effects depend on the nature of the brand. Similarly, Participant 6 believes that:

> ... I could characterise the performance of my business as good. However, there are some ups and downs... [P6].

Hence, social media provide a platform for businesses to have instant access to their customers' feedback and to meet customers' expectations capably, and the ways that businesses would respond to customers' feedback and requests could encourage customer loyalty.

SMEs and Customer Relations Management Through Social Media

Even though SMEs are mainly aware of customer actions, they are also aware of the advantages of adopting a strategy that integrates customer experience and engagement to build a sounder business strategy. In particular, the customers are among the most important stakeholders in the current digital market where SMEs need to effectively monitor their social media platform for various purposes from managing the negative comments to improving customer engagement. Today's customers have very sophisticated tastes and preferences where they choose how to engage with the companies with high expectations for better experiences (Hennig-Thurau et al., 2010). Hence, companies need to improve their social media pages frequently and efficiently, as stated by Participant 1:

> ... I have already used paid ads but did not get the results that we were expecting. The truth is that there is space for improvement. However, there are interactions on the pages and positive comments... [P1].

Many of the participants mentioned that they would need someone to manage their social media page to improve their effectiveness.

> ... If there was a social media manager, I believe that the situation would be better... [P7].

These findings are supported by Edwards et al. (2016) who indicated that SMEs do not have the same resources and knowledge as the large companies. Hence, SMEs must gain all advantages that social media can offer to improve their presence and business activities in the market. Furthermore, a group of participants revealed that they are willing to practise customer relations management through social media. They emphasised that managing customer relations in their businesses through social media has helped their businesses to perform optimally, as they are available to answer their customers' queries even when the business is closed. This is an advantage which has already been identified by Clair and Mandler (2019) where they indicated that new ways in managing customer relations have led to the SME owners responding quickly to their clients.

> ... Through social media, you can be available to the customers beyond the opening hours of the business and as a result, you can provide them with your services faster... [P6].

On the other hand, a participant mentioned that he would not choose social media to manage customer relations as he believes that face-to-face interactions appear to build stronger and direct connections with his customers. This has already been indicated by Guha et al. (2018).

... No, they would not improve the relationship I have with the
client ... The connection I have through face-to-face interactions is
the best you could ever have... [P2].

In this regard, other participants stated that customer relation management
through a combination of both the classic approach and through social media can
give businesses the ideal outcomes.

... I believe that both ways can help a business... [P1].

Consequently, it appears that SME owners in Greece are well informed about
the digital evolution that has occurred in customer relations management.
However, this does not mean they are only adopting digital interaction via social
media and forgetting about the traditional method. They may try to take
advantage of social media, follow the classic way or even combine them according
to their needs.

Brand Acknowledgement and Promotion Through Social Media

Social media helps businesses to benefit from a low-cost brand presence and
orientation (Singh & Sonnenburg, 2012). It appears that SME owners have an
interest and try to experiment when it comes to branding, but they are restricted
because of their limited resources. (Furthermore, Laukkanen et al. (2013) indicated that those enterprises which tend to be brand-oriented have a priority to
satisfy their customers' needs, and social media could improve the elements of
branding (Langaro et al., 2018), particularly in SMEs with limited resources.) For
example, Participant 11 stated that they practise their branding activities using
social media, as they are aware of its benefits.

... Specifically, the application is being done through social media
as we already knew the power those tools are hiding... [P11].

Furthermore, another respondent (Participant 12) indicated that his business
had grown because of their brand presence through social media. This was also
indicated by existing literature that branding through social media can improve
brand presence and lead to business growth (Langaro et al., 2018; Odoom &
Mensah, 2019).

... in this way, we have become the first choice of young people
when it comes to buying clothes. As I said before, in that way we
managed to reach this position by building our name through use
of social media... [P12].

Similarly, Participant 3 believes that social media is necessary when it comes to branding because of their popularity in providing the SME owners with the best way to connect with the audience.

> ... Facebook and Instagram have the greatest impact on the audience we are addressing. They are a basic part in the progression of the sales and the branding... [P3].

Thus, SMEs' owners in Greece have acknowledged the benefits of branding particularly when it is combined with social media. However, few participants may know the benefits but would not adopt this strategy in their businesses. This could be because they want their businesses to remain stable as they are satisfied with their current results.

> ... I do not think that I would apply brand practices through social media... [P2].

The response received from the participants indicates that social media enhances brand awareness, better marketing of the products and the improvement of their business interactions with customers. Hence, social media could assist businesses to influence their customers by revealing recommendations and likes to everyone transparently.

The Impact of eWOM Through Social Media on Customers' Interaction and SME Business Performance

The eWOM is the evolved version of WOM and takes place through social media (Fan et al., 2018; Hua et al., 2017). eWOM is the same as WOM in being able to influence more customers (Prendergast et al., 2010). According to our findings, most participants had a positive opinion of the role of eWOM in business activities, particularly in SMEs. The response from Participant 10 agrees with the observations of Blankson et al. (2018) that WOM is essential for SMEs.

> ... The effect of eWOM is decisive... [P10].

However, another participant claimed that the combination of both eWOM and WOM is most beneficial for them due to their business location. They believe that WOM is a more essential factor for business survival and growth in less populated locations.

> ... as I said before it is a tourist destination. So, it should not be ignored that if someone sees positive reviews or comments it will lead to positive outcomes... [P1].

> ... The truth is that we also try to use the classic form and the electronic one. Regarding the traditional way as I have already

said, population here is limited and locals are influenced by friendships and what is said... [P1].

As indicated by participants, the SME owners are willing to act as marketing tools and at the same time engage with the audience through social media on their way to success.

eWOM consists of several aspects such as online reviews, which can be used as a measure for the eWOM for SMEs (Fan et al., 2018), where most participants indicated that both positive and negative reviews are acceptable. The positive feedback illustrates that they satisfy their clients, and the negative reviews can help them to improve. However, some participants stated that there are occasions when negative reviews that appear on their profile are fake and were made just to harm their businesses. On the other hand, in some cases, they observed that business owners 'beg' their customers to give them positive reviews. Thus, through the participants' answers, it is observed that online reviews may not ethically measure the eWOM which can be considered in contrast to the findings of Fan et al. (2018).

> ... I know a lot of businesses which 'beg' their clients, especially in the food industry, to give them a positive review, forexample on Instagram or TripAdvisor ... [P2].

> ... Positive or negative reviews can benefit a business. Through positives we can be approached by more customers easier and through negatives we can improve the services we offer in case it is needed... [P11].

The result indicates that, SMEs in Greece believe that eWOM can be helpful. However, in several circumstances, they may choose to take advantage of both WOM and eWOM. Lastly, SME owners may have a positive attitude towards online reviews, but they are afraid that fake reviews could harm their businesses.

SMEs Market Expansion Opportunities Through Social Media

Social media can be a crucial marketing tool when used for business expansion (Gao et al., 2018). Participant 3 indicated that he would use social media to expand into a new market and found this the best approach when you have not gathered enough information about the particular customer's culture, preference and market structure.

> ... I would use them. It is the ideal tool, especially when you try to develop in a new market in which you do not know the customer needs... [P3].

Moreover, another way to expand into new markets is through export nationally or internationally. This supports the study developed by Imran and Jian (2018) that shows that when business visibility and sales are at a good level, this could lead the business to increase performance through export. Participant 1 managed to increase the number of people that are following his business social media page, that could help him to increase the visibility of his business and enhance his competitive business advantage by planning to export his products to a new market in the same or foreign country in the future.

> ... The truth is that something like that could be achieved. However, to rely mostly on social media, the business social media page had to have more likes on Facebook, to achieve improved visibility to the audience... [P1].

Conclusion

This research contributes to the existing literature about SMEs and social media usage and aims to fill the gap that was mentioned by Imran and Jian (2018). Through qualitative methodology, the aspects of this phenomenon, that have already been researched by other authors, are observed. It appears that SME owners in Greece are aware of the social media benefits, as they use them for their everyday business activities to engage with their customers. Moreover, they are also aware that wider engagement that goes beyond customers and integrates the business strategy and growth is necessary to gain a competitive advantage.

The research questions of this study are addressed through the findings related to the research objectives. Regarding the first objective which is related to the SMEs' practices through social media, it seems that SME owners in Greece have acknowledged that social media have become part of their businesses, and they use them to interact with their customers. However, it appears that some of them must increase their expenses on social media to gain a competitive advantage. The second objective was regarding social media and branding practices on SMEs. According to the findings, SMEs in Greece are aware of the hidden opportunities that exist and try to apply branding with the combination of social media. In several cases, it was stated that businesses had grown because of this combination. Also, the WOM and the eWOM in SMEs were studied as part of the third objective as it was necessary to discover which type is more commonly adopted by business owners in Greece. The findings illustrate that most of them would choose eWOM as they are aware of all capabilities. Despite that, some of them are willing to take advantage of both WOM and eWOM to maximise the outcome, as they are afraid that individuals may give them reviews that do not reflect their businesses. This raises the SMEs' concern around the information transparency issue in social media platforms. In the same vein, it was observed whether SMEs try to manage their relationships with customers through social media. Results show that they try to handle their customers either through face to face or through social media communication, as each method provides them with different benefits. It was an expected result, which was previously found by Kim and Wang (2017). In addition, it was identified that businesses can increase their number of customers through social media adoption, which also results in increased sales. Finally, SME owners would use social media to expand or to export products in new markets. However, it was observed that they would expand without gathering information about the targeted markets, which is opposed to the findings of Glavas et al. (2019).

Theoretical Implications

The extant literature on the social media adoption of SMEs previously suggested the role of customer orientation (e.g. Cheng & Shiu, 2019; Guha et al., 2018), customer engagement (Hardwick & Anderson, 2019) or promotional activities like marketing campaigns through social media (e.g. Odoom et al., 2017), which are the driving forces of the market orientation. However, these notably remain limited in touching the strategic motives for social media adoption in SMEs. Our study attempts to fill this gap by integrating the isolated contributions of customer experience and engagement with business strategy perspective by asserting the essential roles of branding, business productivity, growth and competitive advantage. The holistic view of strategic perspective, instead of customer orientation, has been demonstrated for large and multinational firms. One possible reason might be the resource allocation of large and multinational firms and the strategic planning that comes from the headquarters regardless of their market conditions. Even though the strategic perspective represents a long-term focus where SMEs need to deploy the resources immediately to survive, the motives for adopting strategic perspectives have comparable impacts on SMEs as a way to strengthen their position. This finding implies that conceptual relationships formed through empirical studies conducted for large and multinational firms could also be considered for SMEs where their visibility could be sustained by eWOM. These discussions, therefore, remind researchers that adopting a strategic perspective is as important for the SMEs and must be regarded as a complimentary factor while considering the customer engagement and experience in reaching competitive advantage over other SMEs. Hence, the theories related to the use of resources for social media in terms of resource-based view and resource dependency (Casciaro & Piskorski, 2005) and dynamic capabilities (Garrido-Moreno et al., 2020) designed in the context of large and multinational firms should serve as a guide for expanding the knowledge on the research of SMEs. Accordingly, the extant literature generated studies that have similar results (Felix et al., 2017; Rimkuniene & Zinkeviciute, 2014). We explained our findings with the theoretical insights of strategic perspective that conceptualise the social media usage of SMEs as the outcomes of strategic choices, representing a holistic view as opposed to narrower approaches that focus solely on customer experience and engagement. By doing so, our chapter has the potential to open up new research avenues that integrate insights coming from a strategic perspective with the existing market orientation perspectives. These results could also be used for other SMEs in different countries as our study points out the potential aspects of the strategic perspective for SMEs while using social media, the types of social media and social media platforms. Future research streams may provide the relevancy and the validity for these strategic focal aspects.

Practical Implications

This research also has implications for business management. First, the SME owners should be continuously informed about any new abilities that appear through social media use. Also, they should know about the popularity of social media platforms as they may change through time. Furthermore, business owners should try to take advantage of all social media, even if their business performance is currently at a reasonable level, as their market position can change all of a sudden, by competitors who are aware of social media opportunities. In some cases, hiring social media specialists could be characterised as an investment for any business, as it will benefit them greatly. Moreover, business owners should invest in branding through social media as it could assist their businesses. However, it seems that the outcome takes years to achieve because of the limited resources that SMEs have. Despite that, SMEs should pay attention to traditional customer relations management, as well as to its electronic version, as their combination could maximise their benefits. Finally, social media offers the opportunity for SMEs expansion, as through them, they can reach audiences from different markets, which means increases in sales.

Limitations and Recommendations

It should be mentioned that this study was undertaken with several limitations. First, the sample for this research was gathered from only one country. The same country may be part of the European Union, but it cannot be claimed that SMEs throughout Europe use social media in the same way. Thus, similar research in different countries would be ideal to validate the results. Second, the sample may have been gathered from the same country, but there were participants who did not belong to the same geographical location. Some of them had businesses in the capital city of the country, whereas others we found in smaller towns. As a result, studies should be conducted regarding the fact that social media applications differ according to SMEs' location and population. Third, this research aimed to classify results regarding different industries that SMEs had and, at the same time, regarding whether they sell products or services to understand if there are any differences. However, the great number of SME owners that did not respond to the invitation in combination with the limited time that was given to conduct this study led to a lack of attention to detail as there were not enough participants. Therefore, it would be wise to have more research that meets those criteria. Finally, the study was undertaken during the COVID-19 period which resulted in an increase of active social media members. Also, it led businesses to use social media to interact with their customers, as during this period, individuals had to keep their distance. Hence, it should be explored whether the changes that appeared during this period have influenced the way that people engage with businesses, in general and from a social media perspective.

Case Study: Navigating Growth Through Social Media Adoption in SMEs

- In the ever-evolving landscape of SMEs, the impact of social media adoption on business strategy, customer experience and engagement is profound. This case study delves into the journey of XYZ Boutique, an emerging SME in the fashion retail sector, as it strategically integrates social media, harnesses eWOM and transforms customer engagement to propel business growth.
- XYZ Boutique recognised the potential of social media to amplify its brand presence and engage with its customer base. With limited resources typical of an SME, the company aimed to leverage social platforms for organic growth, strengthen customer relationships and inform its business strategy. They embarked on a deliberate social media adoption strategy, selecting platforms aligned with its target demographic. Regular posts featuring new arrivals, behind-the-scenes glimpses and customer testimonials were curated to create a cohesive online presence.
- Engaging content prompted customers to share their experiences on social media, generating positive eWOM. The company strategically encouraged and responded to customer reviews, turning them into powerful endorsements that resonated within the online community. Social media became a dynamic channel for XYZ Boutique to enhance customer experiences. Interactive features, such as live Q&A sessions, polls for product preferences and exclusive promotions, contributed to a sense of community and loyalty. Insights derived from social media analytics guided XYZ Boutique in shaping its business strategy. Data on customer preferences, popular products and engagement patterns informed inventory decisions, marketing campaigns and expansion plans.

Case Study Questions

- How can XYZ Ltd. strategically integrate social media into its business operations to enhance customer experience and engagement?
- What specific social media platforms and features align best with XYZ Ltd.'s business goals, considering its SME status?
- In what ways can XYZ Ltd. effectively harness eWOM from social media platforms to influence customer perceptions and preferences?
- How can the company turn positive eWOM into a tangible advantage for brand building and customer loyalty?
- How should XYZ Ltd. align its overall business strategy with the insights gained from social media analytics and customer engagement data?
- What steps can the company take to monitor and adapt its strategy based on real-time feedback and market trends gathered through social media channels?

Key Terms and Definitions

Social Media Adoption: Social media adoption refers to the process by which individuals, businesses and organisations integrate social media platforms into their daily activities and operations.

eWOM Amplification: eWOM amplification refers to the process of enhancing the reach, impact and visibility of eWOM messages through various digital channels and mechanisms.

Business Strategy Development: Business strategy development is the systematic process of formulating and implementing plans and actions to achieve a company's long-term goals and objectives.

References

Aaker, D. A., & Joachimsthaler, E. (1999). The lure of global branding. *Harvard Business Review, 77,* 137–146.

Acheampong, G., Anning-Dorson, T., & Odoom, R. (2017). Antecedents of social media usage and performance benefits in small-and medium-sized enterprises (SMEs). *Journal of Enterprise Information Management, 30*(3), 383–399.

Ainin, S., Parveen, F., Moghavvemi, S., Jaafar, N. I., & Mohd Shuib, N. L. (2015). Factors influencing the use of social media by SMEs and its performance outcomes. *Industrial Management & Data Systems, 115*(3), 570–588.

Alves, H., Fernandes, C., & Raposo, M. (2016). Social media marketing: A literature review and implications. *Psychology and Marketing, 33*(12), 1029–1038.

Anderson, T., & Kanuka, H. (2003). *E-Research: Methods, Strategies and Issues.* Pearson Education Inc.

Andzulis, J. M., Agnihotri, R., Rapp, A., & Trainor, K. J. (2014). Social media technology usage and customer relationship performance: A capabilities-based examination of social CRM. *Journal of Business Research, 67*(6), 1201–1208.

Apigian, C. H., Ragu-Nathan, B. S., Ragu-Nathan, T., & Kunnathur, A. (2005). Internet technology: The strategic imperative. *Journal of Electronic Commerce Research, 6*(2), 123–145.

Banerjee, S., Jenamani, M., & Pratihar, D. K. (2020). A survey on influence maximization in a social network. *Knowledge and Information Systems, 62*(9), 3417–3455.

Berthon, P., Ewing, M. T., & Napoli, J. (2008). Brand management in small to medium-sized enterprises. *Journal of Small Business Management, 46*(1), 27–45.

Berthon, P., Ewing, M., & Napoli, J. (2019). Brand management in small to medium-sized enterprises. *Journal of Small Business Management, 46*(1), 27–45.

Bickart, B., & Schindler, R. M. (2001). Internet forums as influential sources of consumer information. *Journal of Interactive Marketing, 15*(3), 31–40.

Blankson, C., Cowan, K., & Darley, W. K. (2018). Marketing practices of rural micro and small businesses in Ghana: The role of public policy. *Journal of Macromarketing, 38*(1), 29–56.

Bodlaj, M., & Čater, B. (2019). The impact of environmental turbulence on the perceived importance of innovation and innovativeness in SMEs. *Journal of Small Business Management, 57,* 417–435.

Bradley, S. W., McMullen, J. S., Artz, K., & Simiyu, E. M. (2012). Capital is not enough: Innovation in developing economies. *Journal of Management Studies, 49*(4), 684–717.

Braojos-Gomez, J., Benitez-Amado, J., & Llorens-Montes, F. J. (2015). How do small firms learn to develop a social media competence?. *International Journal of Information Management, 35*(4), 443–458.

Braun, V., & Clarke, V. (2006). Using thematic analysis in psychology. *Qualitative Research in Psychology, 3*(2), 77–101.

Brown, J., Broderick, A. J., & Lee, N. (2007). Word of mouth communication within online communities: Conceptualizing the online social network. *Journal of Interactive Marketing, 21*(3), 2–20.

Bryman, A. (2016). *Social Research Methods* (5th ed.). Oxford University Press.

Casciaro, T., & Piskorski, M. J. (2005). Power imbalance, mutual dependence, and constraint absorption: A closer look at resource dependence theory. *Administrative Science Quarterly, 50*(2), 167–199.

Chatterji, A. K., & Toffel, M. W. (2010). How firms respond to being rated. *Strategic Management Journal, 31*(9), 917–945.

Cheng, C. C., & Shiu, E. C. (2019). How to enhance SMEs customer involvement using social media: The role of Social CRM. *International Small Business Journal, 37*(1), 22–42.

Clair, A., & Mandler, J. (2019). Building relationships with the new media in a cyber landscape. *Journal of Business Strategy, 40*(6), 49–54.

Coleman, P. T., Kugler, K. G., Vallacher, R., & Kim, R. (2018). Hoping for the best, preparing for the worst: Regulatory focus optimality in high and low-intensity conflict. *International Journal of Conflict Management, 30*(1), 45–64.

Cook, N. (2008). *Enterprise 2: How social software will change the future of work.* Gower Pub.

Crammond, R., Omeihe, K. O., Murray, A., & Ledger, K. (2018). Managing knowledge through social media: Modelling an entrepreneurial approach for Scottish SMEs and beyond. *Baltic Journal of Management, 13*(3), 303–328.

Dahnil, M. I., Marzuki, K. M., Langgat, J., & Fabeil, N. F. (2014). Factors influencing SMEs adoption of social media marketing. *Procedia-social and behavioral sciences, 148*, 119–126.

De Vries, H. P., De Vries, K. V., & Veer, E. (2018). An examination of SME social media use in the food industry. *Small Enterprise Research, 25*(3), 227–238.

Didonet, S. R., Simmons, G., Díaz-Villavicencio, G., & Palmer, M. (2016). Market orientation's boundary-spanning role to support innovation in SMEs. *Journal of Small Business Management, 54*, 216–233.

Dutot, V., & Bergeron, F. (2016). From strategic orientation to social media orientation: Improving SMEs' performance on social media. *Journal of Small Business and Enterprise Development, 23*(4), 1165–1190.

Dwivedi, Y. K., Islam, R., Mukerji, B., Rana, N. P., & Shareef, M. A. (2019). Social media marketing: Comparative effect of advertisement sources. *Journal of Retailing and Consumer Services, 46*, 58–69.

Edwards, C., Josimvski, S., & Stankovska, I. (2016). Digital channels diminish SME barriers: The case of the UK. *Economic Research-Ekonomska Istraživanja, 29*(1), 217–232.

Eggers, F., Hatak, I., Kraus, S., & Niemand, T. (2017). Technologies that support marketing and market development in SMEs—Evidence from social networks. *Journal of Small Business Management*, 55(2), 270–302.

Emrich, A., Klein, S., Frey, M., Fettke, P., & Loos, P. (2018). A platform for data-driven self-consulting to enable business transformation and technology innovation. In *MKWI* (pp. 1309–1315).

Fan, S., Wu, J., & Zhao, J. L. (2018). Community engagement and online word of mouth: An empirical investigation. *Information and Management*, 55(2), 258–270.

Felix, R., Rauschnabel, P. A., & Hinsch, C. (2017). Elements of strategic social media marketing: A holistic framework. *Journal of Business Research*, 70, 118–126.

Fischer, E., & Reuber, A. R. (2011). Social interaction via new social media: (how) can interactions on Twitter affect effectual thinking and behaviour?. *Journal of Business Venturing*, 26(1), 1–18.

Gallaugher, J., & Ransbotham, S. (2010). Social media and customer dialog management at Starbucks. *MIS Quarterly Executive*, 9(4).

Ganesan, S., Krafft, M., Malthouse, E. C., McAlister, L., Venkatesan, R., & Verhoef, P. C. (2010). CRM in datarich multichannel retailing environments: A review and future research directions. *Journal of Interactive Marketing*, 24(2), 121–137.

Gao, H., Tate, M., Zhang, H., Chen, S., & Liang, B. (2018). Social media ties strategy in international branding: An application of resource-based theory. *Journal of International Marketing*, 26(3), 45–69.

Garrido-Moreno, A., García-Morales, V., King, S., & Lockett, N. (2020). Social Media use and value creation in the digital landscape: A dynamic-capabilities perspective. *Journal of Service Management*, 31(3), 313–343.

Giotopoulos, I., Kontolaimou, A., Korra, E., & Tsakanikas, A. (2017). What drives ICT adoption by SMEs? Evidence from a large-scale survey in Greece. *Journal of Business Research*, 81, 60–69.

Glavas, C., & Mathews, S. (2014). How international entrepreneurship characteristics influence internet capabilities for the international business processes of the firm. *International Business Review*, 23(1), 228–245.

Glavas, C., Mathews, S., & Russell-Bennett, R. (2019). Knowledge acquisition via internet-enabled platforms. *International Marketing Review*, 36(1), 74–107.

Gorgani, M. R. N. (2016). The impact of social network media on brand equity in SMEs. *European Journal of Sustainable Development*, 5(3), 239.

Grimmer, L., Miles, M. P., Byrom, J., & Grimmer, M. (2017). The impact of resources and strategic orientation on small retail firm performance. *Journal of Small Business Management*, 55, 7–26.

Guha, S., Harrigan, P., & Soutar, G. (2018). Linking social media to customer relationship management (CRM): A qualitative study on SMEs. *Journal of Small Business and Entrepreneurship*, 30(3), 193–214.

Hardwick, J., & Anderson, A. R. (2019). Supplier-customer engagement for collaborative innovation using video conferencing: A study of SMEs. *Industrial Marketing Management*, 80, 43–57.

Hennig-Thurau, T., Gwinner, K. P., Walsh, G., & Gremler, D. D. (2004). Electronic word-of-mouth via consumer-opinion platforms: What motivates consumers to articulate themselves on the internet?. *Journal of Interactive Marketing*, 18(1), 38–52.

Hirvonen, S., Laukkanen, T., & Salo, J. (2016). Does brand orientation help B2B SMEs in gaining business growth?. *Journal of Business & Industrial Marketing, 31*(4), 472–487.

Hua, L. Y., Ramayah, T., Ping, T. A., & Jun-Hwa, C. (2017). Social media as a tool to help select tourism destinations: The case of Malaysia. *Information Systems Management, 34*(3), 265–279.

Huang, L., Hudson, S., Roth, M. S., & Madden, T. J. (2016). The influence of social media interactions on consumer–brand relationships: A three-country study of brand perceptions and marketing behaviors. *International Journal of Research in Marketing, 33*(1), 27–41.

Huesch, M. (2013). Are there always synergies between productive resources and resource deployment capabilities?. *Strategic Management Journal, 34,* 1288–1313.

Imran, M., & Jian, Z. (2018). Social media orientation and SME export performance: A conceptual framework. *International Journal of Management, Accounting and Economics, 5*(6), 473–481.

Ince, I., & Hahn, R. (2020). How dynamic capabilities facilitate the survivability of social enterprises: A qualitative analysis of sensing and seizing capacities. *Journal of Small Business Management, 58*(6), 1256–1290.

Jeong, E., & Jang, S. S. (2011). Restaurant experiences triggering positive electronic word-of-mouth (eWOM) motivations. *International Journal of Hospitality Management, 30*(2), 356–366.

Kanuri, V. K., Chen, Y., & Sridhar, S. (2018). Scheduling content on social media: Theory, evidence, and application. *Journal of Marketing, 82*(6), 89–108.

Kaplan, A. M., & Haenlein, M. (2010). Users of the world, unite! The challenges and opportunities of Social Media. *Business Horizons, 53*(1), 59–68.

Kapoor, R., & Lee, J. M. (2013). Coordinating and competing in ecosystems: How organizational forms shape new technology investments. *Strategic Management Journal, 34*(3), 274–296.

Keegan, B. J., & Rowley, J. (2017). Evaluation and decision making in social media marketing. *Management Decision, 55*(1), 15–31.

Keller, K. L. (1993). Conceptualizing, measuring, and managing customer-based brand equity. *Journal of Marketing, 57*(1), 1–22.

Keller, K. L. (2003). *Strategic brand management: Building, measuring, and managing brand equity.* Pearson Education International.

Khan, H. (2001). Rural poverty in developing countries – Implications for public policy. *Economic Series, 26,* 15–31.

Kim, H. G., & Wang, Z. (2017). Can social media marketing improve customer relationship capabilities and firm performance? Dynamic capability perspective. *Journal of Interactive Marketing, 39,* 15–26.

Kohli, A. K., & Jaworski, B. J. (1990). Market orientation: The construct, research propositions, and managerial implications. *Journal of Marketing, 54*(2), 1–18.

Korda, H., & Itani, Z. (2013). Harnessing social media for health promotion and behavior change. *Health Promotion Practice, 14*(1), 15–23.

Kumar, N., & Benbasat, I. (2006). Research note: The influence of recommendations and consumer reviews on evaluations of websites. *Information Systems Research, 17*(4), 425–439.

Lamberton, C., & Stephen, A. T. (2016). A thematic exploration of digital, social media, and mobile marketing: Research evolution from 2000 to 2015 and an agenda for future inquiry. *Journal of Marketing, 80*(6), 146–172.

Langaro, D., Rita, P., & de Fátima Salgueiro, M. (2018). Do social networking sites contribute for building brands? Evaluating the impact of users' participation on brand awareness and brand attitude. *Journal of Marketing Communications, 24*(2), 146–168.

Laukkanen, T., Nagy, G., Hirvonen, S., Reijonen, H., & Pasanen, M. (2013). The effect of strategic orientations on business performance in SMEs: A multigroup analysis comparing Hungary and Finland. *International Marketing Review, 30*(6), 510–535.

Lee, M., & Youn, S. (2009). Electronic word of mouth (eWOM) How eWOM platforms influence consumer product judgement. *International Journal of Advertising, 28*(3), 473–499.

Li, Z., & Li, C. (2014). Tweet or "re-tweet"? An experiment of message strategy and interactivity on Twitter. *Internet Research, 24*(5), 648–667.

Limaj, E., Bernroider, E. W., & Choudrie, J. (2016). The impact of social information system governance, utilization, and capabilities on absorptive capacity and innovation: A case of Austrian SMEs. *Information and Management, 53*(3), 380–397.

Liu, Y., & Shrum, L. J. (2002). What is interactivity and is it always such a good thing? Implications of definition, person, and situation for the influence of interactivity on advertising effectiveness. *Journal of Advertising, 31*(4), 53–64.

Luo, X. R., Zhang, J., & Marquis, C. (2016). Mobilization in the internet age: Internet activism and corporate response. *Academy of Management Journal, 59*(6), 2045–2068.

M'zungu, S., Merrilees, B., & Miller, D. (2019). Strategic and operational perspectives of SME brand management: A typology. *Journal of Small Business Management, 57*(3), 943–965.

Mahoney, L. M., & Tang, T. (2016). *Strategic social media: From marketing to social change*. John Wiley and Sons.

McCann, M., & Barlow, A. (2015). Use and measurement of social media for SMEs. *Journal of Small Business and Enterprise Development, 22*(2), 273–287.

Metaxiotis, K. (2009). Exploring the rationales for ERP and knowledge management integration in SMEs. *Journal of Enterprise Information Management, 22*(1/2), 51–62.

Odoom, R. (2016). Brand-building efforts in high- and low-performing small- and medium-sized enterprises (SMEs). *Journal of Small Business and Enterprise Development, 23*(4), 1229–1246.

Odoom, R., Anning-Dorson, T., & Acheampong, G. (2017). Antecedents of social media usage and performance benefits in small-and medium-sized enterprises (SMEs). *Journal of Enterprise Information Management, 30*(3), 383–399.

Odoom, R., & Mensah, P. (2019). Brand orientation and brand performance in SMEs. *Management Research Review, 42*(1), 155–171.

Park, C., & Lee, T. M. (2009). Information direction, website reputation and eWOM effect: A moderating role of product type. *Journal of Business Research, 62*(1), 61–67.

Pauleen, D. J., Wang, W. Y., & Zhang, T. (2016). How social media applications affect B2B communication and improve business performance in SMEs. *Industrial Marketing Management, 54*, 4–14.

Perrigot, R., Kacker, M., Basset, G., & Cliquet, G. (2012). Antecedents of early adoption and use of social media networks for stakeholder communications: Evidence from franchising. *Journal of Small Business Management, 50*(4), 539–565.

Prendergast, G., Ko, D., & Siu Yin, V. Y. (2010). Online word of mouth and consumer purchase intentions. *International Journal of Advertising, 29*(5), 687–708.

Raymond, L., Bergeron, F., Croteau, A. M., & Uwizeyemungu, S. (2019). Determinants and outcomes of IT governance in manufacturing SMEs: A strategic IT management perspective. *International Journal of Accounting Information Systems, 35*, 100422.

Reijonen, H., Laukkanen, T., Komppula, R., & Tuominen, S. (2012). Are growing SMEs more market-oriented and brand-oriented?. *Journal of Small Business Management, 50*(4), 699–716.

Renton, M., & Richard, J. E. (2019). Exploring brand governance in SMEs: Does socialisation provide a means to value creation?. *Journal of Brand Management, 26*(4), 461–472.

Rhue, L., & Sundararajan, A. (2019, May). Playing to the crowd? Digital visibility and the social dynamics of purchase disclosure. *MIS Quarterly (Forthcoming), NYU Stern School of Business.* SSRN: http://dx.doi.org/10.2139/ssrn.3384357

Rimkuniene, D., & Zinkeviciute, V. (2014). Social media in communication of temporary organisations: Role, needs, strategic perspective. *Journal of Business Economics and Management, 15*(5), 899–914.

Sen, S., & Lerman, D. (2007). Why are you telling me this? An examination into negative consumer reviews on the web. *Journal of Interactive Marketing, 21*(4), 76–94.

Seo, E. J., & Park, J. W. (2018). A study on the effects of social media marketing activities on brand equity and customer response in the airline industry. *Journal of Air Transport Management, 66*, 36–41.

Shuai, J. J., & Wu, W. W. (2011). Evaluating the influence of E-marketing on hotel performance by DEA and grey entropy. *Expert Systems with Applications, 38*(7), 8763–8769.

Singh, S., & Sonnenburg, S. (2012). Brand performances in social media. *Journal of Interactive Marketing, 26*(4), 189–197.

Skålén, P., Pace, S., & Cova, B. (2015). Firm-brand community value co-creation as alignment of practices. *European Journal of Marketing, 49*(3/4), 596–620.

Statista. (2020a). Worldwide digital population as of April 2020. Available at: https://www.statista.com/statistics/617136/digital-population-worldwide/. Accessed 4 May, 2020.

Stone, R. W., Good, D. J., & Baker-Eveleth, L. (2007). The impact of information technology on individual and firm marketing performance. *Behaviour and Information Technology, 26*(6), 465–482.

Strauss, A., & Corbin, J. (1990). *Basics of Qualitative Research.* Sage.

Tajvidi, R., & Karami, A. (2021). The effect of social media on firm performance. *Computers in Human Behavior, 115*, 105174.

Tsekouropoulos, G., Andreopoulou, Z. S., Koliouska, C., Stavroula, I., Koutroumanidis, T., & Batzios, C. (2011, September). e-Marketing and internet functions of agricultural products in SME in Greece. CEUR workshop proceedings (CEUR-WS.org). In *HAICTA* (pp. 213–224).

Urde, M., Baumgarth, C., & Merrilees, B. (2013). Brand orientation and market orientation—From alternatives to synergy. *Journal of Business Research*, *66*(1), 13–20.

Van Dijck, J. (2013). *The Culture of Connectivity: A Critical History of Social Media.* Oxford University Press.

Zhang, J. Q., Craciun, G., & Shin, D. (2010). When does electronic word-of-mouth matter? A study of consumer product reviews. *Journal of Business Research*, *63*(12), 1336–1341.

Chapter 6

Green Purchase Intention Antecedents and Consequences

Fahimeh Dousthosseini[a], *Manijeh Haghighinasab*[a] *and Pantea Foroudi*[b]

[a]Alzahra University, Iran
[b]Brunel University London, UK

Abstract

In this article, the authors try to determine why and under what conditions consumers intend to buy green and what the consequences are. Relying on theories of reasoned action and theory of planned behaviour (TPB), the authors offer that the green purchase intention (GPI) is impressed by environmental and personality components. Provide statements about the determinants and key implications of such market identification.

Keywords: Green purchase; purchase intention; environmental; personality components; perceived value

Introduction

Green purchase intention (GPI) is the attitude, and the value received by today's marketing mantras. More companies are striving to be sustainable in today's turbulent market by offering products that are both attractive to consumers and have a competitive advantage, thereby 'attracting customers' attention. Activities in the field of selling environmentally friendly products and services are developing, and retailers have turned to selling environmentally friendly goods in order to sell more, promote products and services and present a favourable image to customers (Hou & Sarigöllü, 2022). Green products are items that have less impact on the environment and have fewer risks to the environment and use fewer resources, and also prevent the production of waste (Sdrolia & Zarotiadis, 2019). It is important that customers consider the interests of the community alongside their own interests in order to purchase the product. Therefore, in order to inform

Business Strategies and Ethical Challenges in the Digital Ecosystem, 107–137
Copyright © 2025 Fahimeh Dousthosseini, Manijeh Haghighinasab and Pantea Foroudi
Published under exclusive licence by Emerald Publishing Limited
doi:10.1108/978-1-80455-069-420241006

consumers and customers about the positive features of green products, information should be provided.

In this study, the researcher examines the factors affecting the GPI, and also seeks to answer the question, what is the important result of GPI? What social factors can moderate between GPI and technology adoption? What social factors can moderate between system beliefs and technology acceptance? What social factors can moderate between technology adoption and attitude towards green products? Extensive research has been conducted in various areas of GPI (Zhuang et al., 2021), organic shopping (Wojciechowska-Solis & Barska, 2021), attitudes (Cheung & To, 2019) and identifying factors effective on green product selection (Toklu & Kucuk, 2017). It should be noted that a lot of research has been done on GPI and attitude (Jan et al., 2019; Majhi, 2022; Mehta & Chahal, 2021; Rroy & Nayak, 2022); However, no explanatory research has been conducted on customer attitudes and GPI (Zaremohzzabieh et al., 2021).

In the studies conducted in the past, although the selected sample size was appropriate, it can be said that this amount is not enough compared to some researches (Roh et al., 2022). Also, lack of research on behaviour of buying an environmentally friendly product by integrating different environmentally friendly products (Roh et al., 2022). Past researches have also investigated the effect of numerical factors in increasing the price of normal items with regard to their effect on the buying behaviour of green products (Chou, 2019; Fecher et al., 2019, 2020).

While the ultimate goal of green shopping behaviour is to reduce the destructive effects of the environment and destructive effects, the problem of environmental degradation can be examined on a large scale and social dimensions and can be reduced with the participation of individuals and collective and group behaviours. Various research studies have confirmed the effect of environmental attitude on the intention to purchase products. It is also said that environmental concern is caused by attitude (Adnan et al., 2018; Alzahrani et al., 2019; Dhir et al., 2021). However, this finding has been rejected in other studies (Chen & Zhang, 2021; Choi & Johnson, 2019). The connection among environmental concerns and environmental behaviours is not always empirically proven and in most cases causes a gap or attitude-behaviour concern. The results of the previous research showed that consumers who are concerned about the environment, when they have a positive attitude towards a green product, tend to buy it because the feeling is conveyed to them that their purchase of green products has an impact on the environment (Choi & Johnson, 2019).

These academic gaps expressed in the theoretical literature show that the understanding of GPI in various fields has not yet been developed and more study and research is needed to examine them. In order to solve the gaps identified in this research from the theory of planned behaviour (TPB) (Sharma et al., 2020; Sreen et al., 2018), and another theory called reasoned action (Sharma et al., 2020; Sreen et al., 2018), has been used and seeks to investigate the factors affecting the intention to buy green products with the help of these two theories. Past research (Kang, 2014; Maichum et al., 2016; Nguyen et al., 2017) indicate that psychological variables such as concern about the environment, responsibility, perceived communication and environmental attitudes and sensitivities can affect the purchase intention and determine it. However, so far, the role of social and technological factors in GPI has not been specifically checked. The purpose of this research is to explore the nature of GPI, its antecedents and determine how GPI positively contributes to life satisfaction and Willingness to Pay More (WPM). By expressing the concept of identifying the factors affecting the GPI, this research helps to create deep relationships with consumers, creating commitment that marketers are increasingly looking for.

To date, identification research has focused primarily on identifying behavioural factors on green purchasing intent, but in this study we seek to examine impact of behavioural factors as well as social and technological agents on green purchasing intent (Vahdat et al., 2021). In the following sections, we use marketing research to describe the nature of identifying the intention to buy a green product and to define the conceptual framework of our consumer level, which provides statements about the determinants and key implications of such identification in the market. We then present possible methods for testing these propositions. We conclude by discussing the theoretical importance of identifying green buying intentions and their implications for companies looking for consumer heroes.

Literature Review

Green Purchase Intention (GPI)

GPI is a main and necessary dimension of client's actual green purchase behaviour (Al-Gasawneh & Al-Adamat, 2020; Beckford et al., 2010; Klabi & Binzafrah, 2022; Lasuin & Ng, 2014; Liao et al., 2021; Zhuang et al., 2021). GPI includes the client's desire to buy green items to support the environment (Akehurst et al., 2012; Ali & Ahmad, 2016; Brooker, 1976; Chekima & Chekima, 2019; Esmaeilpour & Bahmiary, 2017; Juliana et al., 2020; Kinnear et al., 1974; Paul et al., 2016; Rashid et al., 2009; Shen et al., 2012; Zhang et al., 2018). Green purchasing is an important issue because it plays a great role in reducing the negative effects on the environment caused by production, consumption and recycling processes (Dubey et al., 2013). It also promotes societal health through a clean environment, reduces the expenses and costs related to health and ultimately protects sustainability (Green et al., 1998; Winds, 2007). Consumers' GPI includes the desire to buy and consume green and environmentally conducive items in the framework of this study (Yii et al., 2020).

In addition, green purchasing improves dynamic and functional capabilities and has a favourable effect on environmental and economic efficiency (Yook et al., 2018). This issue leads to the achievement of global sustainable development goals (Al Amosh & Khatib, 2021) and promotes the trust of stakeholders in different areas. Examining various studies in recent years has shown that research in the field of green shopping has increased (Al-Swidi & Saleh, 2021; Visser & Dlamini, 2021). However, many areas regarding this issue need more and more detailed research due to various effects that result green purchasing in various environments (Mutum et al., 2021).

In particular, it can be said that the motivation that the consumer has when making a decision or planning to buy a green product is called the intention to buy a green product (Chan & Lau, 2002; Lee et al., 2015). In addition, based on previous research results, consumer trust and attitude towards green products can determine the intention to buy green products (Amallia et al., 2021).

The results of Manget et al. (2009) research showed that the number of consumers who buy and consume green products has increased to more than 50% (Manget et al., 2009). Also, in recent years, environmentally friendly customers have changed the markets to a great extent (Sonnenberg et al., 2014). In response to this change, both manufacturers and retailers have turned to selling environmentally friendly products to improve their company's competitiveness and become a priority for customers (Soyez, 2012). Therefore, considering these things, it is very important to check the intention to buy environmentally friendly products.

Attitude Towards Green Products

The attitude variable of behavioural intention refers to the degree of appropriate or inappropriate assessment of a person of a specific behaviour (Ajzen, 1991; Bonne et al., 2007; Varah et al., 2021). Attitude has two dimensions and judgemental people have a tendency to perform or not perform the behaviour regarding the consequences of behaviour as appropriate or inappropriate. Therefore, we conclude that the beliefs about the behaviours and also the examination of the resulting consequences form a person's attitude (Varah et al., 2021). Positive-negative-pleasant-unpleasant-harmful-bad changes are among the attitude factors regarding the consumer's intentions. Based on the TPB and the issues raised, one of the predictors of people's behavioural intention is attitude (Dwivedy & Mittal, 2013; Wang & Liao, 2008). The evaluation of the intention to buy environmentally friendly products is called the attitude towards the green product (Amallia et al., 2021). According to the literature, it can be said that the customer's attitude about environmentally friendly products is the result of knowledge and awareness of health and attention to environmental issues (Kardoyo et al., 2020).

Green Perceived Value (GPV)

GPV includes all the actions customers take to obtain net benefits from consuming green products (Chen & Chang, 2012; Rizwan et al., 2014). In addition to this, previous studies showed that the intention to buy green and long-term relationships with customers is greatly influenced by the perceived value of the consumer (Zhuang et al., 2010). The comprehensive assessment and review of the product or service is defined by the buyer's perceived value, which is done in order to purchase that product and service and all items received from them (Patterson & Spreng, 1997; Zeithaml, 1988; Zulfanizy & Wahyono, 2019). In general, it is a mental, general idea that depends on different dimensions and also defines the different characteristics of different goods (Lin et al., 2017; Sangroya & Nayak, 2017). The customer's behaviour at the time of purchase is examined from two point of views, i.e. the economic point of view and the psychological point of view (de Medeiros et al., 2016). These cases are especially significant when examining and measuring customer behaviour when buying and consuming products, especially environmentally friendly products and the quality and values that these products offer.

An important factor for investigating consumer satisfaction and post-purchase behaviour is consumer perceived value (Teng & Wu, 2019). Consumers' general assessment of the profit received is a market recommendation according to their wishes. The GPV includes perspectives and needs that are environmentally sustainable (Juliana et al., 2020). Patterson and Spreng (1997) define the GPV of consumers' classification of green goods and state that consumers consume by comparing the benefits of what they accept to sacrifice to acquire the product, which includes their needs for green products. Since customers' interest in consuming and buying depends on the GPV, this component is very important for the company (Steenkamp & Geyskens, 2006). According to Grimmer and Woolley (2014), the customer makes a purchase when the value he receives is maximum and also adjusts the cost to the perceived value and seeks to buy products that have a higher perceived value.

Beliefs of System

Beliefs about the basic system include attitudes (Muk & Chung, 2015) and behaviour (Agarwal & Karahanna, 2000) about technology. To form a belief about a system, we need to understand how to use the system's capabilities, such as the level of system quality and the quality of system information. Therefore, this issue can affect the behavioural intention to use a system (Zheng et al., 2013). Having a common belief about the value of a system allows consumers to have common areas and a sense of aim (Ramayah & Lo, 2007). As it is clear that the benefits of systems, especially information systems, are complex and uncertain at different levels (Kamhawi, 2008), therefore, people in this field believe in unique advantages and benefits. Users of intricate data systems express their opinion with others and managers. This argument shows that managers in the field of business can influence the beliefs about the system by means of its characteristics and the flow of information gathering to make decisions (Verma et al., 2018).

Technology Acceptance

Based on previous research, two components related to the attitude towards technology are called perceived ease of use (PEOU) and perceived usefulness (PU) of technology adoption (Al-Qaysi et al., 2020; Muk & Chung, 2015; Taherdoost, 2018;

Venkatesh et al., 2003). Also, previous research showed that the attitude of people who accept technology originates from the perceived usefulness and ease of use of that technology, which causes its acceptance (Abdellateef & Foroudi, 2022; Davis, 1989; Foroudi et al., 2017, 2018, 2020). In fact, the main nature of technology acceptance is to predict the behavioural intention of clients (Hafeez et al., 2018, 2019; Muk & Chung, 2015; Nazemi et al., 2022; Ruiz-Alba et al., 2022). In general, technology acceptance means a person's voluntary choice to accept new technology (Kamal et al., 2020). The willingness of clients to use technology and also the successful implementation of technology is an important issue (Aggelidis & Chatzoglou, 2009). The basic objective of the technology acceptance model (TAM) is to predict the acceptance of new technology among users and to highlight information system design problems before its use becomes common among people (Mun et al., 2006).

Social Factors

Components that are related to the client's interplay with other individuals and influence their customer choices are social factors (Akbari et al., 2021; Alqayed et al., 2021; Foroudi et al., 2023; Gbadamosi, 2019; Pandey, 2018). Social factors, such as the factors that result in the beginning of a person's life and lead to gaining experience, such as the care and maintenance that parents do, have a great impact on the health of a person's body, mind and nerves. It should be noted that brain development is influenced by genetic and natural factors (McGowan et al., 2014). Well-being can be greatly weakened or strengthened by social factors (Fish et al., 2011). In this research, social factors are considered by the two dimensions of social influence and peer influence. The limit to which customers change and modify their behaviour under the influence of other people is called social influence (Hew et al., 2015; Peng et al., 2017). Social factors are considered by the two dimensions of social influence and peer influence. Social impact includes two dimensions of subjective norm and descriptive norm. The subjective norm of person's perception of other population is (compliance) and the descriptive norm is the perception and understanding of the attitudes of others' behaviour (internalisation) (Wang & Lin, 2011). The peer influence construct has several dimensions (Thompson et al., 2007); these dimensions include teasing, talking and negotiating with peers about appearance status (Jones et al., 2004) and peer attributions regarding the importance of weight to reputation (Lieberman et al., 2001).

Life Satisfaction

Life satisfaction alludes to one's acknowledgement of the condition of life as well as the rating to which an individual can fulfil what he/she needs completely (Bernarto et al., 2020; Sousa & Lyubomirsky, 2001). It is exceptionally subjective since each person incorporates a level of life fulfilment that is exceptionally distinctive from others' point of view (Berlemann, 2016; Bernarto et al., 2020;

Camfield & Skevington, 2008; O'Sullivan, 2011). Life satisfaction is characterised as the worldwide assessment of an individual's life in its entirety and the cognisant cognitive judgemental part of subjective well-being (Crooker & Near, 1998; Diener et al., 1985; Veenhoven, 1996). People should consider their life satisfaction as a whole (Diener, 2009). Life satisfaction is the evaluation of the level of satisfaction and satisfaction with life performance according to people's feelings and mental state (Diener et al., 2003).

It states that life satisfaction is related to kinship, hereditary and social cognitive dimensions that these dimensions are appropriate to the goals of a person's life, and also life satisfaction is related to other factors, including well-being, riches, mental well-being and social connections (Ye et al., 2012). Also, life satisfaction can be related to personal matters in life and self-esteem (Rode, 2004).

Willingness to Pay More (WPM)

The tendency of people to pay more money for a product or an advantage is called WPM (Finkelman, 1993; Homburg et al., 2005; Koschate-Fischer et al., 2012; Reichheld & Sasser, 1990) and also includes the consumer's willingness to buy goods and services again if the price increases (Srinivasan et al., 2002). Based on the surveys, demographic characteristics such as income, age, education and training are related to willingness to pay (WTP) and it was shown that people with higher income and more education will tend to pay more (Gargallo et al., 2020; Grösche & Schröder, 2011; Ilie et al., 2007; Štreimikienė, 2015). WTP refers to the maximum price a consumer is willing to pay for a certain amount of a product or service (Wertenbroch & Skiera, 2002).

The Theory of Reasoned Action and the Theory of Planned Behaviour

According to the research literature, the TPB first originated from the theory of reasoned action and sought to expand it. This model is a superior model compared to psychological models for investigating people's behaviour (Ajzen, 1991), which is used to predict and evaluate a person's behaviour (Dean et al., 2012). According to Ajzen and Fishbein (1975), people's attitudes about the products and services offered and the subjective norms about these products create the intention to use the product and purchase behaviour, which is expressed in the form of the theory of rational action (TRA). This model has mental standards for behavioural control in predicting the intention to buy a product or service (Ajzen, 1991) and it states that when a person acquires a positive attitude and behaviour towards the product or service and social approval, the probability of performing that behaviour in the person increases (Ajzen, 1991).

Conceptual Framework

The designed framework articulates (i) What factors affect the GPI? (ii) What are the main outcomes of GPI? (iii) The moderating role of the social factors between GPV and technology acceptance; (iv) The moderating role of the social factors between beliefs of system and technology acceptance; (v) The moderating role of the social factors between technology acceptance and attitude towards green products (Fig. 6.1).

Beliefs of System Technology Acceptance

Beliefs are the basis of the formation of attitudes about a technology (Muk & Chung, 2015). In order to understand how to use the features of a technology system, such as the quality of the system and the level of information quality, it is important to understand the belief and the process of belief formation about that technology system. Therefore, it can be stated that the understanding of system belief can affect the behavioural intention and then play a role in using an information system (Zheng et al., 2013). Having the same beliefs for a system and technology allows users to have a common sense about it (Ramayah & Lo, 2007).

Therefore, the subscribers of these systems express their personal beliefs with colleagues and managers. This issue indicates that managers and peers can play a role in the amount and type of beliefs about the system through the features of the system and available information. Users' intentions regarding the use of the system are influenced by the beliefs about that system (Shin & Choi, 2015). The perceived usefulness and benefit of belief is identified based on how a system improves job performance and the performance of system users (Palacios-Marques et al., 2013). With this explanation, it can be said that beliefs about a system must be shared with others, including colleagues and managers, to understand the value of a system. There is a point that if the users' understanding and acceptance of the system is similar, the perceived usefulness will improve, and the complexity of a system can affect the perceived ease according to people's beliefs about that system (Chen et al., 2015). Research has shown that the activity of people and the statements and beliefs of peers and managers have an effect on the perceived ease of using a system and its acceptance (Gangwar et al., 2015; Wu et al., 2011). Therefore, there is an opinion that accepting the usefulness of the system and frameworks has an effect on the perceived ease of people. In this manner, the hypothesis below is proposed:

H1. The presence of beliefs of the system has a positive effect on technology acceptance.

Green Perceived Value Technology Acceptance

The comprehensive review of products and services by the consumer based on what the buyer paid and what he got in return for his payment is called perceived value (Zeithaml, 1988). The perceived value of a person is a mental and intellectual issue that expresses the characteristics of different goods in different environments (Sangroya & Nayak, 2017). Two financial and mental dimensions guide the buyer's behaviour. The financial dimension includes utilitarianism and price, and the mental dimension includes the knowledge and emotions of the

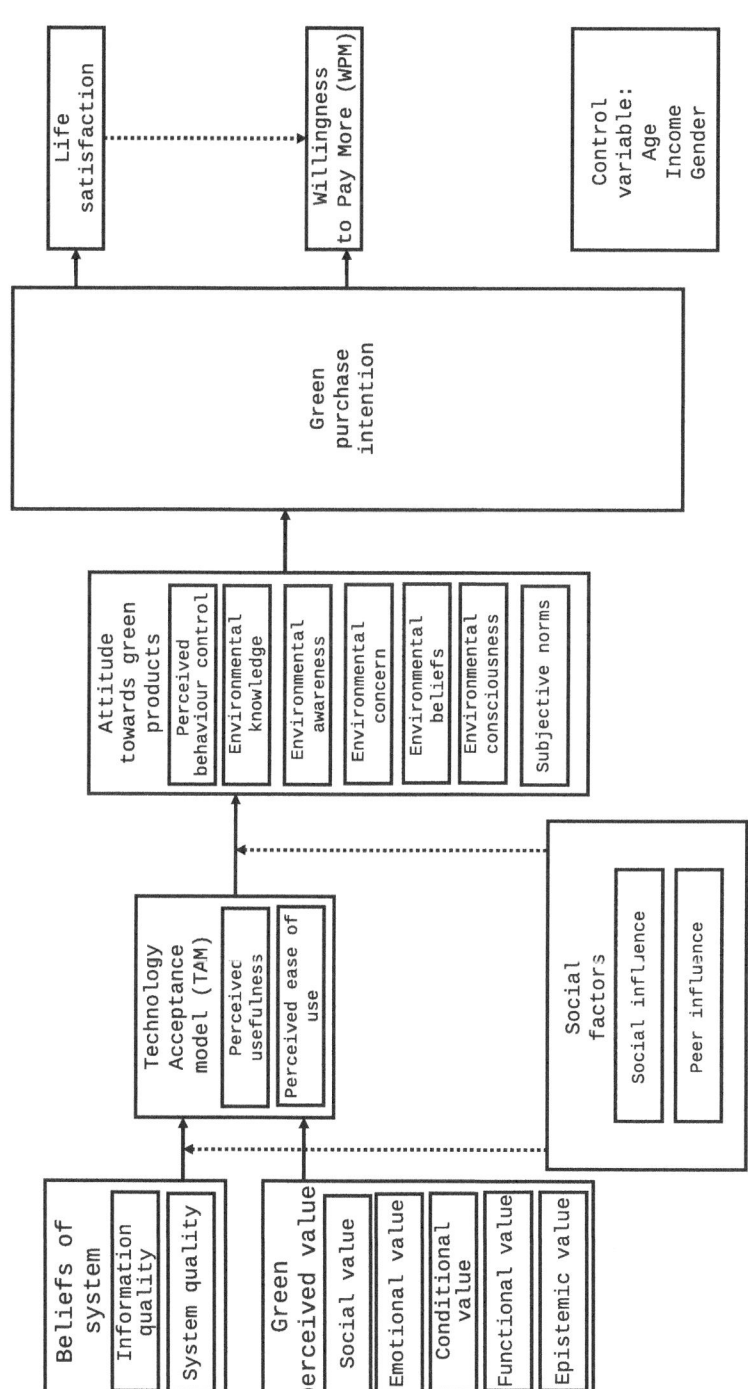

Fig. 6.1. The Research Conceptual Framework. *Source:* Developed by the Researcher.

individual (de Medeiros et al., 2016). These dimensions are significant when examining and predicting consumer behaviour and characteristics, especially when using environmentally friendly products (Danish et al., 2019).

It was stated in theoretical literature that the perceived value of a green product is the result of a comprehensive examination of the desirability of the product or service that is compatible with the environment and the resulting knowledge (Zeithaml, 1988). At the time of application and consumption of a product, the perceived green value plays a role (Steenkamp & Geyskens, 2006). As the issues related to the environment have become very important today, the perceived green value has also attracted a lot of attention, and based on surveys the perceived green value can affect the intention to use environmentally friendly products (Dodds et al., 1991) The TAM model has been proposed to understand people's behavioural intentions as well as acceptance of information frames (Davis, 1989; Davis et al., 1989). According to Ajzen and Fishbein (1975), the model (TAM) can be an introduction to the activity (TRA) which provides a background regarding the beliefs and mental state and behavioural intentions according to the available information. According to the TAM model, perceived ease and usefulness during the use of the system and technology form the individual's attitude, and the attitude predicts the individual's behavioural intention and the application of that technology and system (Davis, 1989). Therefore, according to this issue, the TAM model can predict the behavioural intention of people. Based on the previous studies, this study proposes:

H2. The presence of green perceived value has a positive effect on technology acceptance.

Attitude Towards Green Products Green Purchase Intention

One of the mental factors that affects people's satisfaction or dissatisfaction with an issue and decision-making is attitude (Eagly & Chaiken, 2007). The theory proposed in the form of planned behaviour states that a positive mindset about a behaviour improves the chance of performing the behaviour (Ajzen, 1991). Based on the research done in the past, it can be claimed that there is a positive relationship between people's attitude and their purchase intention (Bredahl, 2001; Chen, 2007; Lane & Potter, 2007; Michaelidou & Hassan, 2010; Sheppard et al., 1988; Tang & Medhekar, 2010). Also, the results of the research showed that according to the TPB framework, people's GPI is most influenced by attitude (Paul et al., 2016; Varshneya et al., 2017; Yadav & Pathak, 2017). Based on the previous studies, this study proposes:

H3. The presence of an attitude towards green products has a positive effect on green purchase intention.

Technology Acceptance Attitude Towards Green Products

As previously stated, technology acceptance is influenced by the two dimensions of perceived ease of use (PEOU) and perceived usefulness (PU) (Al-Qaysi et al., 2020) and it is claimed that people, when the usefulness and ease in the process of using technology occurs, tend to use it (Kim et al., 2016). On the other hand, attitude determines how much people want and how much they try to do an activity and is a cognitive response to action (Baek, 2013). Also, the results of the research by Laforet and Li (2005) state that the less effort people make to use mobile applications, the more they like and tend towards it. Therefore, a hypothesis is proposed as follows:

H4. The presence of technology acceptance has a positive effect on attitude towards green products.

As mentioned earlier, the components that are related to the interaction of people with each other and can affect their purchasing decisions are considered social factors (Gbadamosi, 2019; Pandey, 2018). Economic conditions, religion, literacy and the number of family members are social factors that play a role in a person's lifestyle. Social influence indicates the degree of influence of people from others, based on which they replace the previous behaviour with new behaviours (Hew et al., 2015; Peng et al., 2017). It is recommended that when people decide to buy a product, they should exchange information with others about this decision, because consumers usually follow the opinion of the majority and the approval of others is important to them (Qin et al., 2011). Following and conforming to other people can change the customer's attitude and acceptance is formed (Book et al., 2018). This adaptation is called normative adaptation in the field of norms and social factors. Based on the normative compliance, the consumer makes decisions regarding the expected and accepted behaviours in social activities (Knoll et al., 2015). Therefore, if an individual's desire is accompanied by the norms and expectations of the society, and the person understands this compliance from important social authorities, it will have a greater impact (Talukder & Quazi, 2011). Also, the results of Kang's research (2014) showed that people's attitudes about a technology are influenced by people's thoughts. On the other hand, when people see technology used by others, they are encouraged to think positively about that technology (Graf-Vlachy et al., 2018). Therefore, when people see others, especially those in the social groups they are interested in, using that technology or programme, they change their attitude (Carter & Yeo, 2016).

In the fields related to services, social influence is clear and the reason is that the inherent intangibility and variability in the field of services leads to the formation of problems in decision-making and selection (Argo & Main, 2008; Mourali et al., 2005; Xu et al., 2017). Because a new technology is ambiguous, people may be hesitant to adopt it; so they seek advice from others about their choice (Abrahamson & Rosenkopf, 1993; Burkhardt & Brass, 1990). The investigations carried out in the research conducted in this field showed that the perceived pleasure, TAM model and the influence of social factors provide theoretical grounds for the investigation and development of the research model and it also shows that the perceived pleasure, social factors such as community impact, ease of use and understanding of usefulness are among the things that are effective in customer decision-making. It should be noted that cognitive processes determine the TAM model, but this is not the only factor because customers are also involved with other factors such as the pleasantness of the new technology and it affects their motivation (Davis et al., 1989).

Based on the findings of past studies people are looking for technology to improve and improve their work, and they also tend to enjoy the technology used (Venkatesh et al., 2012). Moreover, Koenig-Lewis et al. (2015) claim that enjoyment in receiving a technology can diminish inquietude, in turn bringing down perceived risk. Also, the perceived pleasure when using technology reduces the perceived risk and reduces a person's fear (Koenig-Lewis et al., 2015). Likewise, when a person enjoys a technology, they are stimulated, and thus improving their belief in that technology (Davis et al., 1992; Kaushik et al., 2015; Van der Heijden, 2004). The TAM model shows the significant impact of PU and PEOU on consumer behaviour, especially when a person seeks to choose a technology (Agrebi & Jallais, 2015; Okumus & Bilgihan, 2014; Ozturk et al., 2016). Finally, based on past studies, it was found that PU and PEOU can influence people's intention to use green products and people behave accordingly. (Davis et al., 1989; Ko, 2017). Consequently, we hypothesise the following:

> *H1a.* The social factor moderates the relationship between beliefs of system and technology acceptance.
>
> *H1b.* The social factor moderates the relationship between green perceived value and technology acceptance.

Green Purchase Intention Life Satisfaction

According to the studies conducted on this issue, it is clear that there are factors that affect people's behaviour but are not under our control, including those factors related to individual, social and mental factors. One of the individual factors that influence a person's buying behaviour is the judgement about the product, so it is very important to check the customer's judgement (Puth et al., 1999; Schiffman & Kanuk, 1991).

A person's judgement and evaluation of the quality of life is defined as satisfaction (Diener et al., 1985; Pavot et al., 1991; Shin & Johnson, 1978). It has also been stated that life satisfaction is a subjective judgement about the quality of life (Diener et al., 1985) and in order to check life satisfaction, a person compares his situation and life conditions with his desired standards (Pavot & Diener, 2009). Therefore, on this basis, it can be said that a person's inability to buy can cause negative judgement and dissatisfaction with his life. Based on previous research and the above arguments, there is a hypothesis that:

H5. The presence of green purchase intentions has a positive effect on life satisfaction.

Green Purchase Intention WPM

Based on previous research, consumers who are concerned about environmental factors are looking to buy from companies that put environmental responsibilities and social responsibility on the agenda, so it can be claimed that the company's behaviour in the case of the environment can determine the purchase intention of customers (Rahbar & Wahid, 2011). People may be willing to pay the highest amount to get a service or product, which is called WPM. Also, people are looking to buy hot products that are compatible with their attitudes and on the other hand, create a lot of profit for them (Homburg et al., 2005). Regarding green and environmentally friendly products, previous research showed that people tend to pay more for green products than other products (Ayadi & Lapeyre, 2016). In this way, the last stage of investigation and measurement to investigate the intention to buy green is the WPM and its impact can be checked from the responses of people in the research. Therefore, the following hypothesis is developed.

H6. The presence of green purchase intention has a positive effect on Willingness to Pay More (WPM).

The behaviour of people who are looking for technology can be analysed and predicted with the help of the model (TAM), which according to Davis (1986) is a cognitive model (Legris et al., 2003). The model (TAM) plays a significant role in identifying and accepting technology, as well as recognising external variables that affect people's beliefs, attitudes and behaviours (King & He, 2006). The model (TAM) consists of two components under the title of usefulness and ease of use of technology. Perceived usefulness and ease of use of technology affect the consumer's choice and intention, and ease of use of technology makes the person's attitude about technology positive (Kallweit et al., 2014). Also, PEOU has a positive effect on customer usage intention and is a determining factor (e.g. Lucas & Spitler, 1999; Okumus & Bilgihan, 2014; Subramanian, 1994). Ellis and Fisher (1975) posited that roles and norms are common standards for behaviour. Role is the basic unit of socialisation. When people participate in a social system, they identify with and assume a role in it. In addition, they usually behave as expected by other members. Through group action, they develop a perception of membership in a group. A norm is considered to influence an individual's behaviour. In the theory (TPB) introduced by Ajzen (1991), theoretical discussions are presented for social factors and people's behaviour.

Social norms have a positive effect on behaviour (Teo & Pok, 2003; Venkatesh et al., 2003). Also, by using TAM, it is possible to evaluate the level of technology usage and examine the type of impact (positive or negative) on the intention and attitude of the consumer. Technology acceptance considering TAM has been extensively investigated in past studies. Saadé et al. proposed that in order for the e-learning framework to be effective, it is vital to evaluate the college students' cooperation and association based on their acceptance behaviour and TAM was utilised as a strong theoretical model. According to the mentioned literature, the following hypothesis is created:

> *H1c.* The social factors moderates the relationship between technology acceptance and attitude towards green products.

Conclusion

The main purpose of this research was to evaluate and investigate consumers' understanding of green purchasing intentions and the influencing factors, after which people's satisfaction with life and their WPM for environmentally friendly products were investigated. Based on the research of Beckford et al. (2010) and Chan and Lau (2002), it cannot be definitely claimed that the WPM for a product or service or satisfaction with one's life is strongly related to the intention to buy environmentally friendly products. It has an effect because according to the results of their research, the behaviour of buying environmentally friendly products can also affect the purchase intention. Therefore, a person's decision to buy environmentally friendly items is influenced by the purchase intention. GPI is mainly a behavioural phenomenon and also because other environmental factors may explain the effects of purchase intention. Current research supports the existence of additional features for the GPI, which leads to life satisfaction and the desire to buy.

Theoretical Contribution

In our research, the theoretical concepts are as follows. At first, the role of GPV as a multidimensional structure was investigated from top to bottom, and emotional, social and commercial values were presented based on the TPB. Based on past research, there are various factors in decision-making and the intention to buy green, which is one of the most important factors to solve the unsatisfying curiosity about environmentally friendly products (Biswas & Roy, 2015; Gonçalves et al., 2016). In order to solve consumers' doubts, this study answered the limitations of past studies by comprehensively examining GPV. Also, this research identified a comprehensive structure for the relationship between GPV and purchase intention in order to strengthen the theoretical literature in the field of intention to purchase green products and services. Also, the distinguishing feature of this research with other researches is the application of the theory of reasoned action in the field of purchasing environmentally friendly products. This theory was used in other studies for environmentally friendly behaviours such as material recycling (Wang & Liao, 2008), energy (Ha & Janda, 2012) and clothing (Rausch & Kopplin, 2021).

But in general, in the field of environmentally friendly products, the comprehensive use of the TRA has been limited (Vermeir & Verbeke, 2008). On the other hand, in the field of buying green products and services, the concept of GPV based on the theory of consumption value in the TRA has been investigated. For this reason, our research using this theory provides a new insight in the field of environmentally friendly products and services. In this research, we evaluated previous studies in the field of norms, concerns, awareness, knowledge of the environment and people's beliefs on the consumer's attitude and intention, but the unique goal of this research was in the field of relationship between people's attitude and intention. Although past studies have shown the effect of customer attitude towards environmentally friendly products and GPI, this research has several theoretical implications for the literature.

Also, based on previous research, it is clear that perceived ease and usefulness when using technology is influenced by the user's attitude. In this regard, it is possible to improve the programs and technologies with proper design and facilitate the use of this technology by using the guidelines and educating the users (Qin et al., 2011). On the other hand, considering the effect of age and gender on the relationship between TAM factors and user's attitude, it is recommended that operators consider programs to improve the usefulness and ease perceived by the user and adjust the programs in a way that is in line with the user's expectations (Vahdat et al., 2021). Also, social factors, including social influence, can affect the user's attitude; so it is recommended that curators receive people's opinions and requests. To get people's opinions, they can be motivated by considering a reward (Hsu & Lin, 2016). Also, by using social media, you can communicate directly with consumers and receive their opinions and increase the volume of sales (Seitz & Aldebasi, 2016). Another way to influence the attitude of people is to get the opinion of the intellectual leaders of a society (Hsu & Lu, 2004). Also, the use of word-of-mouth (WoM) marketing plays a significant role in social variables and people's intention to use (Hsu & Lu, 2004) and is a practical technique to gain the attention of customers. The use of electronic coupons that can be published on social networks with a mobile phone can influence people's attitudes (Tseng & Lee, 2013). One of the encouraging factors for WoM marketing by people is the existence of hedonistic perception, which ultimately leads to the creation of social value and the use of technology, so it is recommended that marketers and curators consider this factor (Chang, 1998).

And finally, using behaviour and self-concept structures, this study investigated the factors affecting GPI in the field of environmentally friendly products and identified its predictive criteria. Also, in new economies, this unique model, which has been studied by few researchers, was investigated. The relationship between the self-concept and the behavioural dimensions of customers of green products and services has been limited in research, so this research showed that the consumption of green products is significant and expanding in developing and emerging economies.

Managerial Contribution

Considering several cultures, the understanding of GPI can be investigated in new and developing economies such as Iran. The findings of this research explain the behaviour of buyers of green products and the influencing factors on green buying behaviour. These results will be useful for marketing and advertising service companies and other researchers and managers and operators of non-profit companies (Albino et al., 2009). Consumers support the use of environmentally friendly products and services; so it can be said that people in developing economies are purposefully seeking to buy environmentally friendly products and services, but it is noteworthy that marketers must know the attitude of customers in the field of different social functions of these products and services are not the same. This study provides the basis for retailers to create new strategies and plans for Iranian markets. Also, this research investigates the factors that hinder the purchase, such as social effects and awareness of the product and values. This research measures the relationship of metrics with the intention to buy green and shows that people who buy green products become environmentally friendly because they recognise their identity as a person who is responsible for the environment. In addition, the intention to buy green affects the tendency to pay more and life satisfaction. Therefore, the company should direct its programs to focus on customers as people who support the environment. It is also necessary for the company or its subsidiary retail stores to offer affordable green items to customers and eliminate middlemen as much as possible. Based on the theoretical literature, it can be said that the intention to buy green is a collectivist behaviour, so the marketer should consider a suitable combination of green products for the market segment.

The managerial implications of this study are as follows. In the first place, it was found that GPV is directly and indirectly related to several variables, including attitude and value. Therefore, marketers should seek to implement programs that promote value and positive attitude. For example, advertisements should state that consumption of green products leads to health benefits, or show the appropriate social status for people who consume green products. Advertisements that encourage people to buy green products by stimulating values can create a positive attitude towards GPV.

Second, in this study, it was found that customers' attitudes about green products and services are influenced by people's knowledge. In this regard, there should be training in the field of environmentally friendly products and services and programs to identify these products and services by operators and marketers. If people do not have enough knowledge and awareness in the field of environmentally friendly products, they cannot distinguish between green and non-green products and may make mistakes. Therefore, it is necessary for companies that operate in the field of green products to consider strategies to increase the awareness and knowledge of consumers so that people can choose products consciously. To develop the customer's information and knowledge in this regard, it is possible to act through government guidelines for the public or training by the company itself, and hence show the suitability of these products and services in the target market. Customers of green products are increasing in developed countries, so training in the field of environmentally friendly products and services can be done online and have a great impact on choosing people and improving the company's profitability.

Future Research Direction

Based on the investigations carried out in the past research, it is clear that there are important directions for future research, which will be discussed in the following section. Based on the surveys that were conducted, the intention to buy green and the WPM were identified as the final factors in previous research, and the intention to buy green of the customers was investigated in general, while various factors affect the green purchase and can affect the intention. Buying leads to many factors. Customers of environmentally friendly products may improve their knowledge in this area to achieve peace of mind, or they may exaggerate their attention and awareness about the environment and think that they have the necessary awareness. It is also possible that people who have already used green products and services answer the questionnaire, which affects the results of the research.

The data of this research is cross-sectional in terms of collection time, and also this research can show the psychological activities of people at a specific time. Environmental factors such as politics and government have not been investigated in this model. Considering the rapid changes that are happening today and considering the speed of technological progress and transformation, it should be kept in mind that the preferences of consumers will also change, so it is difficult to collect data in this turbulent environment. Therefore, the researcher must continuously track and evaluate the buyer's behaviour and also closely measure the impact of changes in the external and internal environment on the behaviour of customers of green products.

Currently, the number of research articles compiled in the field of our research in developed and developing countries does not differ much, but cultural studies in the field of green shopping are few. Cultural, economic and customs conditions are different between developed countries and developing countries like Iran. Therefore, by comparing the research conducted in these countries, it is possible to obtain appropriate marketing strategies to encourage green purchasing behaviour.

Case Study

Spiritronics Tech is one of the most popular online retailers in the world. This company started its business by selling books, which earned good income. After that, this company also entered the field of e-commerce, cloud processing and artificial intelligence. This company offers various services and products such as clothes, precious stones, food, pet items, home appliances, etc. The headquarters of this company is in the United States and it has several centres related to profit, programme development, information centre and website.

Spiritronics Tech has faced strong reactions from many sources over the years. There is a concern and claim that Spiritronics Tech has encountered over time that their carbon footprint is huge. According to environmental activists, Spiritronics Tech has played a significant role in carbon production in the last 20 years. Based on this, it is clear that sending products to customers with vehicles is based on burning oil, and since this company has to deliver the sold goods, it needs a large transportation system, which produces carbon. On the other hand, this company has produced electronic waste due to its actions, including the destruction of electronic products that remain unused for any reason, and has created a crisis in this field. Among these products are telephones, computers and televisions, the electronic waste resulting from their destruction is dangerous for the environment and animals. Spiritronics Tech has discharged its 2020 Maintainability Report to diagram the continuous commitment to building feasible commerce for clients and the planet. The report highlights Spiritronics Tech's work in bolster of The Planet Promise, a commitment made by Spiritronics Tech that calls on signatories to reach zero carbon emanations by 2040. Spiritronics Tech's most recent sustainability report traces our progressing way to decarbonisation by progressing our commitment to The Planet Promise. Here are a few key pointers in moving forward:

Spiritronics Tech became the largest buyer of a renewable energy company in the world. Spiritronics Tech said that by 2020, it would have reached 65% of renewable energy across the business, up from 42% in 2019. Spiritronics Tech is on a fast track to power global operations with 100% renewable energy by 2025, 5 years ahead of its original target of 2030. As of June 2021, Spiritronics Tech has a total of 232 wind and solar projects worldwide and with a capacity of 10 GW it generates enough electricity to power 2.5 million homes in the United States. This company electrifies its transportation vehicles and has delivered more than 20 million orders to customers with electric delivery vehicles.

So far, 100 companies have joined this commitment and celebrated it. Spiritronics Tech reduced its carbon footprint from 2019 to 2020. Spiritronics Tech created (i) a $2 billion investment fund in 2020 that will provide services and technologies that reduce carbon emissions; (ii) a web service; (iii) planet integrity mission; (iv) the Climate Friendly programme. This programme aims to protect the environment. The company has allocated a billion-dollar sustainable bond to create sustainable projects for environmental protection and sustainability. It proposed new solutions to reduce the energy consumption of their devices and plans to advance climate and clean energy solutions. The CEO has announced that Spiritronics Tech's mission as the most customer-centric company in the world is to provide sustainable business for employees, consumers and society. Spiritronics Tech is looking to achieve a carbon-free future. Spiritronics Tech's 2020 sustainability report shows the progress of the sustainability programme.

Case Study Questions

(1) What do you think about Spiritronics Tech's response to sustainability? How can Spiritronics Tech improve on this even more?
(2) What are Spiritronics Tech's key steps in creating a green buying intention for customers?
(3) What are some ways to increase your green buying intentions? What do you recommend for Spiritronics Tech executives?
(4) What are Spiritronics Tech's possible/viable marketing strategies to encourage eco-friendly behaviour and green shopping?

Key Terms and Definitions

Green purchase intention (GPI): GPI is a person's likelihood and willingness to purchase environmentally friendly products and services to support the environment.

Attitude towards green products: Beliefs and preparation of the mind about green products and services that affect the individual's reaction to that green product or service and predict people's GPI.

Green perceived value: Perceived green value includes the evaluation of the net benefit obtained from an environmentally friendly product or service based on the customer's judgement.

Beliefs of system: Beliefs of a system is a network of people's attitudes and opinions towards the capabilities and quality of the system.

Technology acceptance: Technology acceptance shows that perceived usefulness (PU), which expresses the individual's belief about the increase in job performance due to the use of a particular system, and perceived ease of use (PEOU), which expresses the use of a system without effort, influence the individual's decision about how and when. The use of that technology affects.

Social factors: Social factors include things that are related to other people in society and can affect a person's behaviour, choice and attitude.

Life satisfaction: Life satisfaction is a measure for the overall evaluation of life and the way of functioning in which people show their emotions, feelings and moods.

Willingness to pay more (WPM): Willingness to pay more (WPM) is a person's willingness to buy from the seller despite the price increase to receive the desired benefits.

References

Abdellateef, M., & Foroudi, P. (2022). Impact of motivation, technology and social interaction on teaching using blended learning. In *The Emerald handbook of multi-stakeholder communication* (pp. 191–211). Emerald Publishing Limited.

Abrahamson, E., & Rosenkopf, L. (1993). Institutional and competitive bandwagons: Using mathematical modeling as a tool to explore innovation diffusion. *Academy of Management Review*, *18*(3), 487–517.

Adnan, N., Nordin, S. M., Amini, M. H., & Langove, N. (2018). What make consumer sign up to PHEVs? Predicting Malaysian consumer behavior in adoption of PHEVs. *Transportation Research Part A: Policy and Practice*, *113*(1), 259–278.

Agarwal, R., & Karahanna, E. (2000). Time flies when you're having fun: Cognitive absorption and beliefs about information technology usage. *MIS Quarterly*, *24*(4), 665–694.

Aggelidis, V. P., & Chatzoglou, P. D. (2009). Using a modified technology acceptance model in hospitals. *International Journal of Medical Informatics*, *78*(2), 115–126.

Agrebi, S., & Jallais, J. (2015). Explain the intention to use smartphones for mobile shopping. *Journal of Retailing and Consumer Services*, *22*, 16–23.

Ajzen, I. (1991). The theory of planned behavior. *Organizational Behavior and Human Decision Processes*, *50*(2), 179–211.

Ajzen, I., & Fishbein, M. (1975). A Bayesian analysis of attribution processes. *Psychological Bulletin*, *82*(2), 261–277.

Akbari, M., Nazarian, A., Foroudi, P., Seyyed Amiri, N., & Ezatabadipoor, E. (2021). How corporate social responsibility contributes to strengthening brand loyalty, hotel positioning and intention to revisit? *Current Issues in Tourism*, *24*(13), 1897–1917.

Akehurst, G., Afonso, C., & Gonçalves, H. M. (2012). Re-examining green purchase behaviour and the green consumer profile: New evidences. *Management Decision*, *50*(5), 972–988.

Al Amosh, H., & Khatib, S. F. (2021). Corporate governance and voluntary disclosure of sustainability performance: The case of Jordan. *SN Business & Economics*, *1*(12), 1–22.

Al-Gasawneh, J., & Al-Adamat, A. (2020). The mediating role of e-word of mouth on the relationship between content marketing and green purchase intention. *Management Science Letters*, *10*(8), 1701–1708.

Al-Qaysi, N., Mohamad-Nordin, N., & Al-Emran, M. (2020). A systematic review of social media acceptance from the perspective of educational and information systems theories and models. *Journal of Educational Computing Research*, *57*(8), 2085–2109.

Al-Swidi, A., & Saleh, R. M. (2021). How green our future would be? An investigation of the determinants of green purchasing behavior of young citizens in a developing country. *Environment, Development and Sustainability*, *23*(9), 13436–13468.

Albino, V., Balice, A., & Dangelico, R. M. (2009). Environmental strategies and green product development: An overview on sustainability-driven companies. *Business Strategy and the Environment*, *18*(2), 83–96.

Ali, A., & Ahmad, I. (2016). Environment friendly products: Factors that influence the green purchase intentions of Pakistani consumers. *Pakistan Journal of Engineering, Technology & Science*, *2*(1), 84–117.

Alqayed, Y., Foroudi, P., Kooli, K., Foroudi, M., & Ferri, M. A. (2021). Exploring value co-creation concept. In *Sustainable branding: Ethical, social, and environmental cases and perspectives*. Routledge.

Alzahrani, K., Hall-Phillips, A., & Zeng, A. Z. (2019). Applying the theory of reasoned action to understanding consumers' intention to adopt hybrid electric vehicles in Saudi Arabia. *Transportation, 46*(1), 199–215.

Amallia, B. A., Effendi, M. I., & Ghofar, A. (2021). The effect of green advertising, trust, and attitude on green purchase intention: An evidence from Jogjakarta, Indonesia. *International Journal of Commerce and Business Management, 1*(1), 66–79.

Argo, J. J., & Main, K. J. (2008). Stigma by association in coupon redemption: Looking cheap because of others. *Journal of Consumer Research, 35*(4), 559–572.

Ayadi, N., & Lapeyre, A. (2016). Consumer purchase intentions for green products: Mediating role of WTP and moderating effects of framing. *Journal of Marketing Communications, 22*(4), 367–384.

Baek, Y. (2013). Analysis of user's attitude toward apps, intention to use and continual consuming intention-focused on mobile commerce. *International Journal of Contents, 9*(4), 35–44.

Beckford, C. L., Jacobs, C., Williams, N., & Nahdee, R. (2010). Aboriginal environmental wisdom, stewardship, and sustainability: Lessons from the Walpole Island First Nations, Ontario, Canada. *The Journal of Environmental Education, 41*(4), 239–248.

Berlemann, M. (2016). Does hurricane risk affect individual well-being? Empirical evidence on the indirect effects of natural disasters. *Ecological Economics, 124*(1), 99–113.

Bernarto, I., Bachtiar, D., Sudibjo, N., Suryawan, I. N., Purwanto, A., & Asbari, M. (2020). Effect of transformational leadership, perceived organizational support, job satisfaction toward life satisfaction: Evidences from Indonesian teachers. *International Journal of Advanced Science and Technology, 29*(3), 5495–5503.

Biswas, A., & Roy, M. (2015). Green products: An exploratory study on the consumer behaviour in emerging economies of the East. *Journal of Cleaner Production, 87*, 463–468.

Bonne, K., Vermeir, I., Bergeaud-Blackler, F., & Verbeke, W. (2007). Determinants of halal meat consumption in France. *British Food Journal, 109*(5), 367–386.

Book, L. A., Tanford, S., Montgomery, R., & Love, C. (2018). Online traveler reviews as social influence: Price is no longer king. *Journal of Hospitality & Tourism Research, 42*(3), 445–475.

Bredahl, L. (2001). Determinants of consumer attitudes and purchase intentions with regard to genetically modified food–results of a cross-national survey. *Journal of Consumer Policy, 24*(1), 23–61.

Brooker, G. (1976). The self-actualizing socially conscious consumer. *Journal of Consumer Research, 3*(2), 107–112.

Burkhardt, M. E., & Brass, D. J. (1990). Changing patterns or patterns of change: The effects of a change in technology on social network structure and power. *Administrative Science Quarterly, 35*(1), 104–127.

Camfield, L., & Skevington, S. M. (2008). On subjective well-being and quality of life. *Journal of Health Psychology, 13*(6), 764–775.

Carter, S., & Yeo, A. C. M. (2016). Mobile apps usage by Malaysian business undergraduates and postgraduates: Implications for consumer behaviour theory and marketing practice. *Internet Research, 26*(3), 733–757.

Chan, R. Y., & Lau, L. B. (2002). Explaining green purchasing behavior: A cross-cultural study on American and Chinese consumers. *Journal of International Consumer Marketing, 14*(2–3), 9–40.

Chang, M. K. (1998). Predicting unethical behavior: A comparison of the theory of reasoned action and the theory of planned behavior. *Journal of Business Ethics, 17*(16), 1825–1834.

Chekima, B., & Chekima, K. (2019). The impact of human values and knowledge on green products purchase intention. In A. Gbadamosi (Ed.), *Exploring the dynamics of consumerism in developing nations* (pp. 266–283). IGI Global.

Chen, M. F. (2007). Consumer attitudes and purchase intentions in relation to organic foods in Taiwan: Moderating effects of food-related personality traits. *Food Quality and Preference, 18*(7), 1008–1021.

Chen, Y. S., & Chang, C. H. (2012). Enhance green purchase intentions: The roles of green perceived value, green perceived risk, and green trust. *Management Decision, 50*(3), 502–520.

Chen, D. Q., Preston, D. S., & Swink, M. (2015). How the use of big data analytics affects value creation in supply chain management. *Journal of Management Information Systems, 32*(4), 4–39.

Chen, M., & Zhang, W. H. (2021). Purchase intention for hydrogen automobile among Chinese citizens: The influence of environmental concern and perceived social value. *International Journal of Hydrogen Energy, 46*(34), 18000–18010.

Cheung, M. F., & To, W. M. (2019). An extended model of value-attitude-behavior to explain Chinese consumers' green purchase behavior. *Journal of Retailing and Consumer Services, 50*(1), 145–153.

Choi, D., & Johnson, K. K. (2019). Influences of environmental and hedonic motivations on intention to purchase green products: An extension of the theory of planned behavior. *Sustainable Production and Consumption, 18*(1), 145–155.

Chou, H. Y. (2019). Units of time do matter: How countdown time units affect consumers' intentions to participate in group-buying offers. *Electronic Commerce Research and Applications, 35*, 100839.

Crooker, K. J., & Near, J. P. (1998). Happiness and satisfaction: Measures of affect and cognition? *Social Indicators Research, 44*(2), 195–224.

Danish, M., Ali, S., Ahmad, M. A., & Zahid, H. (2019). The influencing factors on choice behavior regarding green electronic products: Based on the green perceived value model. *Economies, 7*(4), 1–18.

Davis, G. (1986). Advances in biomedical sensor technology: A review of the 1985 patent literature. *Biosensors, 2*(2), 101–124.

Davis, F. D. (1989). Perceived usefulness, perceived ease of use, and user acceptance of information technology. *MIS Quarterly, 13*(3), 319–340.

Davis, F. D., Bagozzi, R. P., & Warshaw, P. R. (1989). User acceptance of computer technology: A comparison of two theoretical models. *Management Science, 35*(8), 982–1003.

Davis, F. D., Bagozzi, R. P., & Warshaw, P. R. (1992). Extrinsic and intrinsic motivation to use computers in the workplace 1. *Journal of Applied Social Psychology, 22*(14), 1111–1132.

de Medeiros, J. F., Ribeiro, J. L. D., & Cortimiglia, M. N. (2016). Influence of perceived value on purchasing decisions of green products in Brazil. *Journal of Cleaner Production, 110*(100), 158–169.

Dean, M., Raats, M. M., & Shepherd, R. (2012). The role of self-identity, past behavior, and their interaction in predicting intention to purchase fresh and processed organic food 1. *Journal of Applied Social Psychology*, *42*(3), 669–688.

Dhir, A., Sadiq, M., Talwar, S., Sakashita, M., & Kaur, P. (2021). Why do retail consumers buy green apparel? A knowledge-attitude-behaviour-context perspective. *Journal of Retailing and Consumer Services*, *59*, 102398.

Diener, E. (2009). Subjective well-being. In E. Diener (Ed.), *The science of well-being. Social indicators research series* (Vol. 37, pp. 11–58). Springer.

Diener, E. D., Emmons, R. A., Larsen, R. J., & Griffin, S. (1985). The satisfaction with life scale. *Journal of Personality Assessment*, *49*(1), 71–75.

Diener, E., Oishi, S., & Lucas, R. E. (2003). Personality, culture, and subjective well-being: Emotional and cognitive evaluations of life. *Annual Review of Psychology*, *54*(1), 403–425.

Dodds, W. B., Monroe, K. B., & Grewal, D. (1991). Effects of price, brand, and store information on buyers' product evaluations. *Journal of Marketing Research*, *28*(3), 307–319.

Dubey, R., Bag, S., Ali, S. S., & Venkatesh, V. G. (2013). Green purchasing is key to superior performance: An empirical study. *International Journal of Procurement Management*, *6*(2), 187–210.

Dwivedy, M., & Mittal, R. K. (2013). Willingness of residents to participate in e-waste recycling in India. *Environmental Development*, *6*(1), 48–68.

Eagly, A. H., & Chaiken, S. (2007). The advantages of an inclusive definition of attitude. *Social Cognition*, *25*(5), 582–602.

Ellis, D. G., & Fisher, B. A. (1975). Phases of conflict in small group development: A Markov analysis. *Human Communication Research*, *1*(3), 195–212.

Esmaeilpour, M., & Bahmiary, E. (2017). Investigating the impact of environmental attitude on the decision to purchase a green product with the mediating role of environmental concern and care for green products. *Management & Marketing*, *12*(2), 297–315.

Fecher, A., Robbert, T., & Roth, S. (2019). Same price, different perception: Measurement-unit effects on price-level perceptions and purchase intentions. *Journal of Retailing and Consumer Services*, *49*(17), 129–142.

Fecher, A., Robbert, T., & Roth, S. (2020). Per piece or per kilogram? Default-unit effects in retailing. *Journal of Retailing and Consumer Services*, *53*, 101956.

Finkelman, D. P. (1993). Crossing the "zone of indifference". *Marketing Management*, *2*(3), 22–32.

Fish, R., Danneman, P. J., Brown, M., & Karas, A. (Eds.). (2011). *Anesthesia and analgesia in laboratory animals*. Academic Press.

Foroudi, P., Cuomo, M. T., & Foroudi, M. M. (2020). Continuance interaction intention in retailing: Relations between customer values, satisfaction, loyalty, and identification. *Information Technology & People*, *33*(4), 1303–1326.

Foroudi, P., Gupta, S., Nazarian, A., & Duda, M. (2017). Digital technology and marketing management capability: Achieving growth in SMEs. *Qualitative Market Research: An International Journal*, *20*(2), 230–246.

Foroudi, P., Gupta, S., Sivarajah, U., & Broderick, A. (2018). Investigating the effects of smart technology on customer dynamics and customer experience. *Computers in Human Behavior*, *80*, 271–282.

Foroudi, P., Marvi, R., Cuomo, M. T., Bagozzi, R., Dennis, C., & Jannelli, R. (2023). Consumer perceptions of sustainable development goals: Conceptualization, measurement and contingent effects. *British Journal of Management, 34*(3), 1157–1183.

Gangwar, H., Date, H., & Ramaswamy, R. (2015). Understanding determinants of cloud computing adoption using an integrated TAM-TOE model. *Journal of Enterprise Information Management, 28*(1), 107–130.

Gargallo, P., García-Casarejos, N., & Salvador, M. (2020). Perceptions of local population on the impacts of substitution of fossil energies by renewables: A case study applied to a Spanish rural area. *Energy Reports, 6*(1), 436–441.

Gbadamosi, A. (2019). A conceptual overview of consumer behavior in the contemporary developing nations. In A. Gbadamosi (Ed.), *Exploring the dynamics of consumerism in developing nations* (pp. 1–30). IGI Global.

Gonçalves, H. M., Lourenço, T. F., & Silva, G. M. (2016). Green buying behavior and the theory of consumption values: A fuzzy-set approach. *Journal of Business Research, 69*(4), 1484–1491.

Graf-Vlachy, L., Buhtz, K., & König, A. (2018). Social influence in technology adoption: Taking stock and moving forward. *Management Review Quarterly, 68*(1), 37–76.

Green, K., Morton, B., & New, S. (1998). Green purchasing and supply policies: Do they improve companies' environmental performance? *Supply Chain Management: International Journal, 3*(2), 89–95.

Grimmer, M., & Woolley, M. (2014). Green marketing messages and consumers' purchase intentions: Promoting personal versus environmental benefits. *Journal of Marketing Communications, 20*(4), 231–250.

Grösche, P., & Schröder, C. (2011). Eliciting public support for greening the electricity mix using random parameter techniques. *Energy Economics, 33*(2), 363–370.

Ha, H. Y., & Janda, S. (2012). Predicting consumer intentions to purchase energy-efficient products. *Journal of Consumer Marketing, 29*(7), 461–469.

Hafeez, K., Alghatas, F. M., Foroudi, P., Nguyen, B., & Gupta, S. (2019). Knowledge sharing by entrepreneurs in a virtual community of practice (VCoP). *Information Technology & People, 32*(2), 405–429.

Hafeez, K., Foroudi, P., Nguyen, B., Gupta, S., & Alghatas, F. (2018). How do entrepreneurs learn and engage in an online community-of-practice? A case study approach. *Behaviour & Information Technology, 37*(7), 714–735.

Hew, J. J., Lee, V. H., Ooi, K. B., & Wei, J. (2015). What catalyses mobile apps usage intention: An empirical analysis. *Industrial Management & Data Systems, 115*(7), 1269–1291.

Homburg, C., Koschate, N., & Hoyer, W. D. (2005). Do satisfied customers really pay more? A study of the relationship between customer satisfaction and willingness to pay. *Journal of Marketing, 69*(2), 84–96.

Hou, C., & Sarigöllü, E. (2022). Is bigger better? How the scale effect influences green purchase intention: The case of washing machine. *Journal of Retailing and Consumer Services, 65*, 102894.

Hsu, C. L., & Lin, J. C. C. (2016). Effect of perceived value and social influences on mobile app stickiness and in-app purchase intention. *Technological Forecasting and Social Change, 108*(1), 42–53.

Hsu, C. L., & Lu, H. P. (2004). Why do people play on-line games? An extended TAM with social influences and flow experience. *Information & Management, 41*(7), 853–868.

Ilie, L., Horobet, A., & Popescu, C. (2007). *Liberalization and regulation in the EU energy market.* MPRA Paper 6419, University Library of Munich.

Jan, I. U., Ji, S., & Yeo, C. (2019). Values and green product purchase behavior: The moderating effects of the role of government and media exposure. *Sustainability, 11*(23), 6642.

Jones, D. C., Vigfusdottir, T. H., & Lee, Y. (2004). Body image and the appearance culture among adolescent girls and boys: An examination of friend conversations, peer criticism, appearance magazines, and the internalization of appearance ideals. *Journal of Adolescent Research, 19*(3), 323–339.

Juliana, J., Djakasaputra, A., & Pramono, R. (2020). Green perceived risk, green viral communication, green perceived value against green purchase intention through green satisfaction. *Journal of Industrial Engineering & Management Research, 1*(2), 124–139.

Kallweit, K., Spreer, P., & Toporowski, W. (2014). Why do customers use self-service information technologies in retail? The mediating effect of perceived service quality. *Journal of Retailing and Consumer Services, 21*(3), 268–276.

Kamal, S. A., Shafiq, M., & Kakria, P. (2020). Investigating acceptance of telemedicine services through an extended technology acceptance model (TAM). *Technology in Society, 60,* 101212.

Kamhawi, E. M. (2008). System characteristics, perceived benefits, individual differences and use intentions: A survey of decision support tools of ERP systems. *Information Resources Management Journal, 21*(4), 66–83.

Kang, S. (2014). Factors influencing intention of mobile application use. *International Journal of Mobile Communications, 12*(4), 360–379.

Kardoyo, K., Feriady, M., Farliana, N., & Nurkhin, A. (2020). Influence of the green leadership toward environmental policies support. *The Journal of Asian Finance, Economics, and Business, 7*(11), 459–467.

Kaushik, A. K., Agrawal, A. K., & Rahman, Z. (2015). Tourist behaviour towards self-service hotel technology adoption: Trust and subjective norm as key antecedents. *Tourism Management Perspectives, 16,* 278–289.

Kim, S., Baek, T. H., Kim, Y. K., & Yoo, K. (2016). Factors affecting stickiness and word of mouth in mobile applications. *The Journal of Research in Indian Medicine, 10*(3), 177–192.

King, W. R., & He, J. (2006). A meta-analysis of the technology acceptance model. *Information & Management, 43*(6), 740–755.

Kinnear, T. C., Taylor, J. R., & Ahmed, S. A. (1974). Ecologically concerned consumers: Who are they? Ecologically concerned consumers can be identified. *Journal of Marketing, 38*(2), 20–24.

Klabi, F., & Binzafrah, F. (2022). The mechanisms for influencing green purchase intention by environmental concern: The roles of self-green image congruence and green brand trust. *South Asian Journal of Management, 16*(1), 76–101.

Knoll, L. J., Magis-Weinberg, L., Speekenbrink, M., & Blakemore, S. J. (2015). Social influence on risk perception during adolescence. *Psychological Science, 26*(5), 583–592.

Ko, C. H. (2017). Exploring how hotel guests choose self-service technologies over service staff. *The International Journal of Oral Implantology, 9*(3), 16–27.

Koenig-Lewis, N., Marquet, M., Palmer, A., & Zhao, A. L. (2015). Enjoyment and social influence: Predicting mobile payment adoption. *Service Industries Journal, 35*(10), 537–554.

Koschate-Fischer, N., Stefan, I. V., & Hoyer, W. D. (2012). Willingness to pay for cause-related marketing: The impact of donation amount and moderating effects. *Journal of Marketing Research, 49*(6), 910–927.

Laforet, S., & Li, X. (2005). Consumers' attitudes towards online and mobile banking in China. *International Journal of Bank Marketing, 23*(5), 362–380.

Lane, B., & Potter, S. (2007). The adoption of cleaner vehicles in the UK: Exploring the consumer attitude–action gap. *Journal of Cleaner Production, 15*(11–12), 1085–1092.

Lasuin, C. A., & Ng, Y. C. (2014). Factors influencing green purchase intention among university students. *Malaysian Journal of Business and Economics (MJBE), 1*(2), 1–14.

Lee, S. H. N., Kim, H., & Yang, K. (2015). Impacts of sustainable value and business stewardship on lifestyle practices in clothing consumption. *Fashion and Textiles, 2*(1), 1–18.

Legris, P., Ingham, J., & Collerette, P. (2003). Why do people use information technology? A critical review of the technology acceptance model. *Information & Management, 40*(3), 191–204.

Liao, S. H., Hu, D. C., Chung, Y. C., & Huang, A. P. (2021). Risk and opportunity for online purchase intention – A moderated mediation model investigation. *Telematics and Informatics, 62*, 101621.

Lieberman, M., Gauvin, L., Bukowski, W. M., & White, D. R. (2001). Interpersonal influence and disordered eating behaviors in adolescent girls: The role of peer modeling, social reinforcement, and body-related teasing. *Eating Behaviors, 2*(3), 215–236.

Lin, J., Lobo, A., & Leckie, C. (2017). The role of benefits and transparency in shaping consumers' green perceived value, self-brand connection and brand loyalty. *Journal of Retailing and Consumer Services, 35*, 133–141.

Lucas Jr, H. C., & Spitler, V. K. (1999). Technology use and performance: A field study of broker workstations. *Decision Sciences, 30*(2), 291–311.

Maichum, K., Parichatnon, S., & Peng, K. C. (2016). Application of the extended theory of planned behavior model to investigate purchase intention of green products among Thai consumers. *Sustainability, 8*(10), 1077.

Majhi, R. (2022). Behavior and perception of younger generation towards green products. *Journal of Public Affairs, 22*(1), e2288.

Manget, J., Roche, C., & Münnich, F. (2009). Capturing the green advantage for consumer companies. *The Boston Consulting Group, 13*.

McGowan, P. O., Sasaki, A., & Roth, T. L. (2014). The social environment and epigenetics in psychiatry. In J. Peedicayil, D. R. Grayson, & D. Avramopoulos (Eds.), *Epigenetics in psychiatry* (pp. 547–562). Academic Press.

Mehta, P., & Chahal, H. S. (2021). Consumer attitude towards green products: Revisiting the profile of green consumers using segmentation approach. *Management of Environmental Quality: An International Journal, 32*(5), 902–928.

Michaelidou, N., & Hassan, L. M. (2010). Modeling the factors affecting rural consumers' purchase of organic and free-range produce: A case study of consumers' from the Island of Arran in Scotland, UK. *Food Policy, 35*(2), 130–139.

Mourali, M., Laroche, M., & Pons, F. (2005). Individualistic orientation and consumer susceptibility to interpersonal influence. *Journal of Services Marketing, 19*(3), 164–173.

Muk, A., & Chung, C. (2015). Applying the technology acceptance model in a two-country study of SMS advertising. *Journal of Business Research, 68*(1), 1–6.

Mun, Y. Y., Jackson, J. D., Park, J. S., & Probst, J. C. (2006). Understanding information technology acceptance by individual professionals: Toward an integrative view. *Information & Management, 43*(3), 350–363.

Mutum, D. S., Ghazali, E. M., & Wei-Pin, W. (2021). Parallel mediation effect of consumption values and the moderation effect of innovativeness, in predicting the influence of identity on green purchasing behavior. *Journal of Consumer Behaviour, 20*(3), 827–844.

Nazemi, A., Haghighinasab, M., & Foroudi, P. (2022). Proposing self-service technology model in a service ecosystem playground. In *The Emerald handbook of multi-stakeholder communication* (pp. 501–519). Emerald Publishing Limited.

Nguyen, T. N., Lobo, A., & Greenland, S. (2017). Energy efficient household appliances in emerging markets: The influence of consumers' values and knowledge on their attitudes and purchase behaviour. *International Journal of Consumer Studies, 41*(2), 167–177.

Okumus, B., & Bilgihan, A. (2014). Proposing a model to test smartphone users' intention to use smart applications when ordering food in restaurants. *Journal of Hospitality and Tourism Technology, 5*(1), 31–49.

O'Sullivan, G. (2011). The relationship between hope, eustress, self-efficacy, and life satisfaction among undergraduates. *Social Indicators Research, 101*(1), 155–172.

Ozturk, A. B., Bilgihan, A., Nusair, K., & Okumus, F. (2016). What keeps the mobile hotel booking users loyal? Investigating the roles of self-efficacy, compatibility, perceived ease of use, and perceived convenience. *International Journal of Information Management, 36*(6), 1350–1359.

Palacios-Marques, D., Cortés-Grao, R., & Carral, C. L. (2013). Outstanding knowledge competences and web 2.0 practices for developing successful e-learning project management. *International Journal of Project Management, 31*(1), 14–21.

Pandey, J. (2018). Factors affecting job performance: An integrative review of literature. *Management Research Review, 42*(2), 263–289.

Patterson, P. G., & Spreng, R. A. (1997). Modelling the relationship between perceived value, satisfaction and repurchase intentions in a business-to-business, services context: An empirical examination. *International Journal of Service Industry Management, 8*(5), 414–434.

Paul, J., Modi, A., & Patel, J. (2016). Predicting green product consumption using theory of planned behavior and reasoned action. *Journal of Retailing and Consumer Services, 29*, 123–134.

Pavot, W., & Diener, E. (2009). Review of the satisfaction with life scale. In E. Diener (Ed.), *Assessing well-being. Social indicators research series* (Vol. 39, pp. 101–117). Springer.

Pavot, W., Diener, E. D., Colvin, C. R., & Sandvik, E. (1991). Further validation of the satisfaction with life scale: Evidence for the cross-method convergence of well-being measures. *Journal of Personality Assessment, 57*(1), 149–161.

Peng, S., Yang, A., Cao, L., Yu, S., & Xie, D. (2017). Social influence modeling using information theory in mobile social networks. *Information Sciences, 379*, 146–159.

Puth, G., Mostert, P., & Ewing, M. (1999). Consumer perceptions of mentioned product and brand attributes in magazine advertising. *The Journal of Product and Brand Management, 8*(1), 38–50.

Qin, L., Kim, Y., Hsu, J., & Tan, X. (2011). The effects of social influence on user acceptance of online social networks. *International Journal of Human-Computer Interaction, 27*(9), 885–899.

Rahbar, E., & Wahid, N. A. (2011). Investigation of green marketing tools' effect on consumers' purchase behavior. *Business Strategy Series, 12*(2), 73–83.

Ramayah, T., & Lo, M. C. (2007). Impact of shared beliefs on "perceived usefulness" and "ease of use" in the implementation of an enterprise resource planning system. *Management Research News, 30*(6), 420–431.

Rashid, N. R. N. A., Jusoff, K., & Kassim, K. M. (2009). Eco-labeling perspectives amongst Malaysian consumers. *Canadian Social Science, 5*(2), 1–10.

Rausch, T. M., & Kopplin, C. S. (2021). Bridge the gap: Consumers' purchase intention and behavior regarding sustainable clothing. *Journal of Cleaner Production, 278*, 123882.

Reichheld, F. F., & Sasser, W. E. (1990). Zero defections: Quality comes to services. *Harvard Business Review, 68*(5), 105–111. http://www.fivewinds.com

Rizwan, M., Mahmood, U., Siddiqui, H., & Tahir, A. (2014). An empirical study about green purchase intentions. *Journal of Sociological Research, 5*(1), 290–305.

Rode, J. C. (2004). Job satisfaction and life satisfaction revisited: A longitudinal test of an integrated model. *Human Relations, 57*(9), 1205–1230.

Roh, T., Seok, J., & Kim, Y. (2022). Unveiling ways to reach organic purchase: Green perceived value, perceived knowledge, attitude, subjective norm, and trust. *Journal of Retailing and Consumer Services, 67*, 102988.

Rroy, A. D., & Nayak, P. (2022). A study on consumers perception towards green products consumption in the post pandemic scenario in Kamrup district of Assam. *Academy of Marketing Studies Journal, 26*(1), 1–8.

Ruiz-Alba, J. L., Abou-Foul, M., Nazarian, A., & Foroudi, P. (2022). Digital platforms: Customer satisfaction, eWOM and the moderating role of perceived technological innovativeness. *Information Technology & People, 35*(7), 2470–2499.

Sangroya, D., & Nayak, J. K. (2017). Factors influencing buying behaviour of green energy consumer. *Journal of Cleaner Production, 151*, 393–405.

Schiffman, L. G., & Kanuk, L. L. (1991). *Consumer behavior*. Prentice-Hall.

Sdrolia, E., & Zarotiadis, G. (2019). A comprehensive review for green product term: From definition to evaluation. *Journal of Economic Surveys, 33*(1), 150–178.

Seitz, V. A., & Aldebasi, N. M. (2016). The effectiveness of branded mobile apps on user's brand attitudes and purchase intentions. *Review of Economic and Business Studies, 9*(1), 141–154.

Sharma, N., Saha, R., Sreedharan, V. R., & Paul, J. (2020). Relating the role of green self-concepts and identity on green purchasing behaviour: An empirical analysis. *Business Strategy and the Environment, 29*(8), 3203–3219.

Shen, B., Wang, Y., Lo, C. K., & Shum, M. (2012). The impact of ethical fashion on consumer purchase behavior. *Journal of Fashion Marketing and Management: International Journal, 16*(2), 234–245.

Sheppard, B. H., Hartwick, J., & Warshaw, P. R. (1988). The theory of reasoned action: A meta-analysis of past research with recommendations for modifications and future research. *Journal of Consumer Research, 15*(3), 325–343.

Shin, D. H., & Choi, M. J. (2015). Ecological views of big data: Perspectives and issues. *Telematics and Informatics, 32*(2), 311–320.

Shin, D. C., & Johnson, D. M. (1978). Avowed happiness as an overall assessment of the quality of life. *Social Indicators Research, 5*(1), 475–492.

Sonnenberg, N. C., Erasmus, A. C., & Schreuder, A. (2014). Consumers' preferences for eco-friendly appliances in an emerging market context. *International Journal of Consumer Studies, 38*(5), 559–569.

Sousa, L., & Lyubomirsky, S. (2001). Life satisfaction. In J. Worell (Ed.), *Encylopedia of women and gender: Sex similarities and differences and the impact of society on gender* (Vol. 2, pp. 667–676). Academic Press.

Soyez, K. (2012). How national cultural values affect pro-environmental consumer behavior. *International Marketing Review, 29*(6), 623–646.

Sreen, N., Purbey, S., & Sadarangani, P. (2018). Impact of culture, behavior and gender on green purchase intention. *Journal of Retailing and Consumer Services, 41*, 177–189.

Srinivasan, S. S., Anderson, R., & Ponnavolu, K. (2002). Customer loyalty in e-commerce: An exploration of its antecedents and consequences. *Journal of Retailing, 78*(1), 41–50.

Steenkamp, J. B. E., & Geyskens, I. (2006). How country characteristics affect the perceived value of web sites. *Journal of Marketing, 70*(3), 136–150.

Štreimikienė, D. (2015). The main drivers of environmentally responsible behaviour in Lithuanian households. *Amfiteatru Economic, 17*(2015), 1023–1035.

Subramanian, G. H. (1994). A replication of perceived usefulness and perceived ease of use measurement. *Decision Sciences, 25*(5–6), 863–874.

Taherdoost, H. (2018). A review of technology acceptance and adoption models and theories. *Procedia Manufacturing, 22*, 960–967.

Talukder, M., & Quazi, A. (2011). The impact of social influence on individuals' adoption of innovation. *Journal of Organizational Computing & Electronic Commerce, 21*(2), 111–135.

Tang, Y., & Medhekar, M. (2010). Drivers of green power electricity purchase in Australia. *Asian Journal of Business Research, 1*(1), 80–96.

Teng, Y. M., & Wu, K. S. (2019). Sustainability development in hospitality: The effect of perceived value on customers' green restaurant behavioral intention. *Sustainability, 11*(7), 1987.

Teo, T. S., & Pok, S. H. (2003). Adoption of WAP-enabled mobile phones among internet users. *Omega, 31*(6), 483–498.

Thompson, J. K., Shroff, H., Herbozo, S., Cafri, G., Rodriguez, J., & Rodriguez, M. (2007). Relations among multiple peer influences, body dissatisfaction, eating disturbance, and self-esteem: A comparison of average weight, at risk of overweight, and overweight adolescent girls. *Journal of Pediatric Psychology, 32*(1), 24–29.

Toklu, I. T., & Kucuk, H. O. (2017). The impact of brand crisis on consumers' green purchase intention and willingness to pay more. *International Business Research*, *10*(1), 22–33.

Tseng, L. Y., & Lee, T. S. (2013). Investigating the factors influence tweens' purchase intention through peer conformity in Taiwan. *Advances in Management and Applied Economics*, *3*(3), 259.

Vahdat, A., Alizadeh, A., Quach, S., & Hamelin, N. (2021). Would you like to shop via mobile app technology? The technology acceptance model, social factors and purchase intention. *Australasian Marketing Journal*, *29*(2), 187–197.

Van der Heijden, H. (2004). User acceptance of hedonic information systems. *MIS Quarterly*, *28*(4), 695–704.

Varah, F., Mahongnao, M., Pani, B., & Khamrang, S. (2021). Exploring young consumers' intention toward green products: Applying an extended theory of planned behavior. *Environment, Development and Sustainability*, *23*(6), 9181–9195.

Varshneya, G., Pandey, S. K., & Das, G. (2017). Impact of social influence and green consumption values on purchase intention of organic clothing: A study on collectivist developing economy. *Global Business Review*, *18*(2), 478–492.

Veenhoven, R. (1996). Developments in satisfaction-research. *Social Indicators Research*, *37*(1), 1–46.

Venkatesh, V., Morris, M. G., Davis, G. B., & Davis, F. D. (2003). User acceptance of information technology: Toward a unified view. *MIS Quarterly*, *27*(3), 425–478.

Venkatesh, V., Thong, J. Y., & Xu, X. (2012). Consumer acceptance and use of information technology: Extending the unified theory of acceptance and use of technology. *MIS Quarterly*, *27*(3), 157–178.

Verma, S., Bhattacharyya, S. S., & Kumar, S. (2018). An extension of the technology acceptance model in the big data analytics system implementation environment. *Information Processing & Management*, *54*(5), 791–806.

Vermeir, I., & Verbeke, W. (2008). Sustainable food consumption among young adults in Belgium: Theory of planned behaviour and the role of confidence and values. *Ecological Economics*, *64*(3), 542–553.

Visser, R., & Dlamini, S. (2021). Green purchasing behaviour towards compostable coffee pods. *Sustainability*, *13*(12), 6558.

Wang, Y. S., & Liao, Y. W. (2008). Assessing eGovernment systems success: A validation of the DeLone and McLean model of information systems success. *Government Information Quarterly*, *25*(4), 717–733.

Wang, S. M., & Lin, J. C. C. (2011). The effect of social influence on bloggers' usage intention. *Online Information Review*, *35*(1), 50–65.

Wertenbroch, K., & Skiera, B. (2002). Measuring consumers' willingness to pay at the point of purchase. *Journal of Marketing Research*, *39*(2), 228–241.

Winds, F. (2007, March). *Green procurement. Good environmental stories for North Americans*. Five Winds International.

Wojciechowska-Solis, J., & Barska, A. (2021). Exploring the preferences of consumers' organic products in aspects of sustainable consumption: The case of the Polish consumer. *Agriculture*, *11*(2), 138.

Wu, C. S., Cheng, F. F., Yen, D. C., & Huang, Y. W. (2011). User acceptance of wireless technology in organizations: A comparison of alternative models. *Computer Standards & Interfaces*, *33*(1), 50–58.

Xu, X., Li, Q., Peng, L., Hsia, T. L., Huang, C. J., & Wu, J. H. (2017). The impact of informational incentives and social influence on consumer behavior during Alibaba's online shopping carnival. *Computers in Human Behavior, 76*, 245–254.

Yadav, R., & Pathak, G. S. (2017). Determinants of consumers' green purchase behavior in a developing nation: Applying and extending the theory of planned behavior. *Ecological Economics, 134*, 114–122.

Ye, S., Yu, L., & Li, K. K. (2012). A cross-lagged model of self-esteem and life satisfaction: Gender differences among Chinese university students. *Personality and Individual Differences, 52*(4), 546–551.

Yii, J., Shein, H., & Poh Ming, W. (2020). Green products purchase intention: A study of Sibu Sarawak. *e-BANGI, 17*(1), 62–79.

Yook, K. H., Choi, J. H., & Suresh, N. C. (2018). Linking green purchasing capabilities to environmental and economic performance: The moderating role of firm size. *Journal of Purchasing and Supply Management, 24*(4), 326–337.

Zaremohzzabieh, Z., Ismail, N., Ahrari, S., & Samah, A. A. (2021). The effects of consumer attitude on green purchase intention: A meta-analytic path analysis. *Journal of Business Research, 132*, 732–743.

Zeithaml, V. A. (1988). Consumer perceptions of price, quality, and value: A means-end model and synthesis of evidence. *Journal of Marketing, 52*(3), 2–22.

Zhang, B., Fu, Z., Huang, J., Wang, J., Xu, S., & Zhang, L. (2018). Consumers' perceptions, purchase intention, and willingness to pay a premium price for safe vegetables: A case study of Beijing, China. *Journal of Cleaner Production, 197*, 1498–1507.

Zheng, Y., Zhao, K., & Stylianou, A. (2013). The impacts of information quality and system quality on users' continuance intention in information-exchange virtual communities: An empirical investigation. *Decision Support Systems, 56*, 513–524.

Zhuang, W., Cumiskey, K. J., Xiao, Q., & Alford, B. L. (2010). The impact of perceived value on behavior intention: An empirical study. *Journal of Global Business Management, 6*(2), 1–7.

Zhuang, W., Luo, X., & Riaz, M. U. (2021). On the factors influencing green purchase intention: A meta-analysis approach. *Frontiers in Psychology, 12*, 644020.

Zulfanizy, K., & Wahyono, W. (2019). The influence of green perceived value, risk and quality toward green purchase intention through green trust. *Management Analysis Journal, 8*(1), 79–89.

Chapter 7

IoT Adoption in Agriculture, Manufacturing, Logistics, and Supply Chain Management: A Bibliometric Analysis

Mostafa Oboudi, Ayatolah Momayez, Nader Seyyedamiri and Morteza Akbari

University of Tehran, Iran

Abstract

This chapter reviews Internet of Things (IoT) as a concept with bibliometric analysis using data selected from the Scopus database. The cited references included two clusters. Also, co-occurrence keyword analysis found four groups. The first cluster shows IoT adoption in agriculture, manufacturing, logistics, and supply chain management. The second cluster includes behavioral models of IoT technology acceptance. The third cluster refers to the adoption of IoT and automation technology in intelligent buildings, smart homes, smart cities, and health care. Finally, the fourth cluster contains information management.

Keywords: Internet of Things; technology adoption; acceptance of IoT; technology acceptance; supply chain management

Introduction

The increasing prosperity of technology has revolutionized the methods of production or processing of products and has covered almost all aspects of life (Clim et al., 2020; Sivathanu, 2019b). Many researchers have discussed the importance and necessity of technology in different fields and also its relationship with business growth and performance (Garcia-Morales et al., 2018; Lohmuller & Petrikhin, 2018; Resch & Kaminski, 2019). Therefore, the decision to accept or

---

Business Strategies and Ethical Challenges in the Digital Ecosystem, 139–161

Copyright © 2025 Mostafa Oboudi, Ayatolah Momayez, Nader Seyyedamiri and Morteza Akbari

Published under exclusive licence by Emerald Publishing Limited

doi:10.1108/978-1-80455-069-420241007

reject it has been raised as a fundamental question (Cozzolino et al., 2018; Marangunić & Granić, 2015; Wu & Chen, 2017). To answer this question, researchers have used different theories and models. which can be mentioned: Theory of Planned Behavior (TPB) (Al-Emran et al., 2020; Lee et al., 2020), Technology Acceptance Model (TAM) (Chen & Wu, 2020; Singh et al., 2020), unified theory of acceptance and use of technology (UTAUT) (Singh et al., 2020; Sohn & Kwon, 2020), Expectation-Confirmation Model Technology (Malik & Rao, 2019; Park, 2020), Flow Theory (Liu et al., 2016; Naglis & Bhatiasevi, 2019), Technology Readiness and Acceptance Model (Buyle et al., 2018; Martens et al., 2017), Diffusion of Innovation Theory (Rogers, 1983; Mensah, 2019; Sardjono et al., 2019), etc.

One of the technologies that recently, as a new paradigm, has attracted the attention of individuals and companies is the Internet of Things (IoT); this technology has been recognized as one of the main fields of technology to meliorate efficiency and help improve business processes, as well as the positive effects it has on various aspects of users' lives (Lee, 2019; Lohmuller & Petrikhin, 2018; Metallo et al., 2018; Zaminkar et al., 2021). The ways of using IoT to serve humanity are different and have consequences for various dimensions of life, involving health care, tourism, education, food production, traffic, agriculture, and smart government (Khan et al., 2021); but to benefit from these consequences, it is important to examine the issues facing the adoption of this technology. Therefore, the adoption of IoT as one of the research areas has been the focus of researchers; considering the increase of publications in the field of IoT technology adoption, it seems necessary to evaluate the research in this field.

One of the research methods that has received attention in the field of the IoT is a bibliometric review, which examines and reviews the IoT research in different dimensions and fields, including supply chain management and logistics (Rejeb et al., 2020), food safety (Bouzembrak et al., 2019), blockchain (Kamran et al., 2020), smart home (Choi et al., 2021), marketing (Miskiewicz, 2020), circular economy (Nobre & Tavares, 2017). However, during our literature review, no research on "IoT adoption" has been done with a bibliometric review method. Therefore, our study aims to review and evaluate the research about the adoption of the IoT with the bibliometric method and using VOSviewer software. In other words, we are the pursuit of answers to the following questions:

- What is the trend of publishing research in the field of IoT adoption?
- What are the most cited researches in the field of IoT adoption?
- What is the co-citation status of research in the field of IoT adoption?
- What is the status of the co-occurrence keyword in research in the field of IoT adoption?

IoT Technology: Definition and Trend

Various conceptualizations have been proposed for the IoT. Kevin Ashton first used the term IoT in early 1999 (Nawi et al., 2021; Szentesi et al., 2021). In the last few years, the IoT has revolutionized all areas of human–machine interaction (Qadri et al., 2020). IoT is considered a concept and paradigm, where all kinds of smart appliances and operating objects can relate to other devices through wired and wireless connections and addressing schemes (Albăstroiu, 2021; Atzori et al., 2010). In the Oxford dictionary, the definition of IoT is the connection of devices within everyday objects via the internet, enabling them to share data (Berte, 2018; Hays, 2020).

The concept of the IoT has received a lot of attention in the past few years (Farrokhi et al., 2021; Jaiswal et al., 2022). IoT is an interconnected collection of intelligent objects. It is clear that the conventional internet connects people, but IoT technologies connect things using integrated sensors (Atzori et al., 2014). Researchers call IoT the Fourth Industrial Revolution; this technology connects things such as physical devices, smart meters, and smart vehicles so that every object can obtain and convey data (Kalsoom et al., 2021; Majid et al., 2022; Zaminkar et al., 2021). IoT provides modern, creative, and intelligent products to users and thus facilitates the lives of consumers (Gil et al., 2016; Szentesi et al., 2021).

Although IoT technologies have been noticed and used in fields such as insurance, transportation, automobiles, military industries, smart homes, health, logistics, retail, etc., at the user level, it is in the beginning. (Al-Momani et al., 2019; Haddud et al., 2017; Karahoca et al., 2018); anyway, the number of IoT-based devices is increasing, for example, the number of these devices will reach 75 billion by 2025 (Nguyen et al., 2019). The increase in the number of devices based on the IoT and the development of this technology provides a rich market for investment (Ghanbari et al., 2017). Because of this, IoT will affect their daily lifestyle and behavior through the new ways and opportunities it provides. Consumers and organizations using the IoT can capture 90% of the value that IoT applications create. This technology provides many opportunities for an organization such as cost savings, product and service improvement, and risk reduction (Bakhitjaafreh, 2018).

Considering the benefits of IoT and its profound effects, the issue of accepting and using this technology has been raised. In other words, although the expansion of technologies such as the IoT is important and should be considered, it is also necessary to accept consumers who are going to use this technology (Park & Jeong, 2021). However, the adoption of IoT is expanding, and the outlook shows that this technology will have a great impact on users, businesses, and human societies as a whole (Haddud et al., 2017). Adaptation or acceptance of technology is defined in the form of acceptance, integration, and usage of new technologies by persons, organizations, public and private associations, or any active actor in society (Ghobakhloo & Ching, 2019). In the field of IoT, it should be noted that the impact of the adoption of this technology in various industries is significant, and this impact will increase in the future because part of the survival of companies to develop a sustainable competitive advantage and meet the growing demands and expectations of consumers requires the use of this technology (Ghobakhloo & Ching, 2019). Technology acceptance in the field of IoT infrastructure takes place at different levels, including individuals, companies, governments, localities, and nations (AlHogail, 2018; Straub, 2009). At the macro level, it should be noted that although the speed of technology adoption is one of the components of increasing productivity and thus achieving economic development, in developing countries due to reasons such as poverty, lack of public infrastructure, and little expertise, people are facing countless problems to achieve technologies like IoT (Thyagaraj & Narayanan, 2021). In the case of organizations, it should be noted that their level of competence is directly related to the speed at which technology is adopted; how companies react to digital technology changes (including the IoT) to accomplish a competitive advantage may require management processes and organizational dynamics (Sivathanu, 2019a).

Methodology

Database

The initial stage of bibliometric review involves identifying the databases that are most suitable for research (Akbari et al., 2020). To carry out this research, Scopus database data have been used. A review of the Scopus database displays that this database contains around 23,452 journal titles, 206,000 books from more than 5,000 publishers, and 120,000 conferences (Singh et al., 2021). The reason for choosing the Scopus database was the number of documents, i.e., a higher sample that it provided to us compared to other databases.

Search Strategy and Data

In the present research, we searched for the words *"IoT adoption*"* or *"Internet of things adoption*"* or *"acceptance of IoT*"* or *"acceptance of Internet of things*"* or *"IoT acceptance*"* or *"Internet of things acceptance*"* in the title, abstract, and keywords of Scopus database studies. The search results included 327 items; it contains 147 articles, 132 conference papers, 24 book chapters, 15 reviews, and 9 conference reviews. According to our goal in this research (which requires the review of research related to the adoption of IoT technology) and with a more detailed review of 327 research indexed by two independent researchers to reach the limit of bias, finally, 156 documents were selected, including 83 articles, 58 conference articles, 8 book chapters, and 7 reviews.

Analytical Methods

Synthesizing previous research findings in a specific field can determine the research direction of that field. Researchers can use three methods to understand previous findings: a meta-analysis, meta-synthesis, and scientific mapping based on bibliometric methods (Zupic & Čater, 2015). In the present study, we have chosen the bibliometric method. Compared to the other two methods of examining past research, the advantage of the bibliometric method is having an unbiased approach to the literature (Foroudi et al., 2021).

Results

In this section, we present the findings. This section includes the results of publication trends, citation analysis, co-citation analysis, and co-occurrence keyword analysis.

Publication Trends

Fig. 7.1 shows the publication trend of IoT adoption documents. As it is clear in the figure, the trend of publishing articles in this field is exponential.

Examining the results shows that between the years 2011 and 2014, one research has been conducted in this field every year, and the number of researchers has been increasing, and since 2018, this issue has received more attention from researchers. The number of researchers in 2021 is 50, which is the highest number of research conducted per year.

Citation Analysis

Forty-nine articles with more than 10 citations were identified among 156 articles. The highest number of citations is related to Gao and Bai's article. Janssen M, Brous P, and Guerrero C.D have the most articles on IoT adoption with four documents. The total number of citations of Janssen M documents is 167.

The journal *Technological Forecasting and Social Change* has the largest number of articles in the field of IoT adoption. Table 7.1 shows the most articles in journals along with their citations.

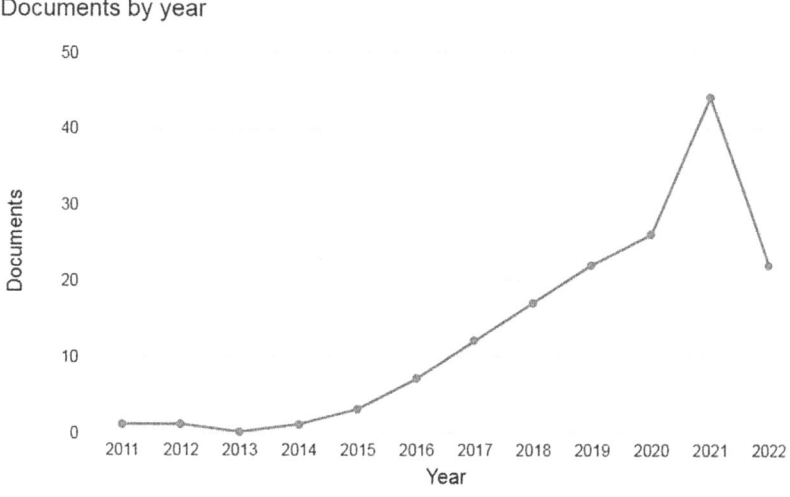

Fig. 7.1.   The Trend of Publishing Articles on the IoT Adoption.

Table 7.1. The Highest Number of Documents of a Source.

Rank	Source	Documents	Citations
1	*Technological Forecasting and Social Change*	5	192
2	*IEEE Access*	3	49
3	*Journal of Business Research*	3	39
4	*Lecture Notes in Computer Science*	3	18
5	*Journal of Theoretical and Applied Information Technology*	3	17

Also, most documents are related to Malaysia with 25, India with 23, and the United States with 13. Also, India with 520, Italy with 450, and America with 248 has the highest number of citation documents. South and Southeast Asian countries have the largest share of articles in the field of IoT adoption (See Table 7.2).

Co-citation Analysis

In co-citation analysis, several items (authors, documents, journals, etc.) are chosen to demonstrate a research area. Then, the relationships between these cases have been analyzed using citation counting as an analytical tool to inquire into the intellectual structure of this research field and to derive some specifications of the relevant scientific society. In other words, two items are considered co-citations when they emerge together in the reference list of a subsequent article (Zhao, 2006). In this chapter, we considered the cited reference as the unit of analysis.

Cited References

Fig. 7.2 shows the cited references to IoT adoption for cited reference; we considered the minimum number of citations to be five. The output of co-citation analysis led us to two clusters.

Cluster A: Examining documents of cluster A, using VOSviewer, showed that most of them are review studies that have examined different dimensions of IoT, including vision, programs, elements of IoT, and its challenges.

The importance of the IoT and its role in various aspects of life is mentioned in the article of Atzori et al. They also point out that the operationalization of IoT requires the integration of technologies such as middleware, recognition, and sensing and communication (Atzori et al., 2010). Similarly, Lee and Lee (2015) refer to essential IoT technologies in their research. According to their opinion, five technologies: radio frequency identification (RFID), wireless sensor networks (WSNs), cloud computing, middleware, and application software should be

Table 7.2. The Most Highly Cited IoT Adoption Publications.

Ranke	Source	Author	CF
1	*Asia Pacific Journal of Marketing and Logistics*	Gao and Bai (2014)	250
2	*Journal of Cleaner Production*	Shrouf and MiraglIoTta (2015)	221
3	*International Journal of Logistics Management*	Tu (2018)	126
4	*Journal of Retailing and Consumer Services*	Kamble et al. (2019)	119
5	*IEEE IoT Journal*	Park et al. (2017)	117
6	*Technological Forecasting and Social Change*	Mital et al. (2018)	101
7	*International Journal of Information Management*	Brous et al. (2020)	82
8	*Journal of Business and Industrial Marketing*	Jayashankar et al. (2018)	79
9	*Journal of Computer Information Systems*	Hsu and Lin (2018)	78
10	*Technology Analysis and Strategic Management*	Hsu & Yeh (2017)	73
11	*Journal of Cleaner Production*	Sharma et al. (2020)	70
12	*Procedia Computer Science*	Luthra et al. (2018)	56
13	*Journal of Organizational and End User Computing*	Al-Momani et al. (2018)	48
14	*Internet Research*	Janssen et al. (2019)	45
15	*Journal of Computer Information Systems*	Aldossari and Sidorova (2020)	40
16	*Journal of Internet Services and Applications*	Brambilla et al. (2017)	38
17	*IEEE International Conference on Industrial Engineering and Engineering Management*	Lin et al. (2016)	37
18	*Security and Communication Networks*	Trnka et al. (2018)	33
19	*International Journal of Innovation Management*	Alansari et al. (2018)	29
20	*Technological Forecasting and Social Change*	Arfi et al. (2021)	28

(Continued)

Table 7.2. *(Continued)*

Ranke	Source	Author	CF
21	*Technological Forecasting and Social Change*	Ben Arfi et al. (2021)	26
22	*IEEE Access*	Alkawsi and Ali (2018)	26
23	*International Journal of Information Systems in the Service Sector*	Al-Momani et al. (2019)	24
24	*Proceedings - 2012 IEEE Int. Conf. on Green Computing and Communications, Green.Com*	Coughlan et al. (2012)	24
25	*IEEE Security and Privacy*	Jalali et al. (2019)	23
26	*International Conference on Computing, Analytics and Security Trends, CAST 2016*	Patil (2016)	23
27	*International Journal of Innovation and Technology Management*	Arnold and Voigt (2019)	21
28	*Journal of Business Research*	Pappas et al. (2021)	20
29	*Telematics and Informatics*	Lee (2020)	20
30	*European Journal of Innovation Management*	Ammirato et al. (2019)	20
31	*IEEE Access*	Siddiqa et al. (2018)	20

considered to deploy IoT-based products and services. In addition, Gubbi et al. consider IoT factors such as RFID, WSN, addressing schemes, data storage and analysis, and visualization (Gubbi et al., 2013).

In the articles of cluster A, the applications of IoT are also discussed. Table 7.3 shows the classification of these applications according to the researchers' point of view. Another issue that has been considered in the research of this cluster is the challenges and open issues around the IoT. Regarding the challenges of the IoT, Lee and Lee refer to data management challenges, data mining challenges, privacy challenges, security challenges, and chaos challenges (Lee & Lee, 2015). Atzori et al. (2010) mentioned standardization activity, addressing and networking issues, and security and privacy as open issues in IoT technology. Miorandi et al. (2012) also acknowledge security as one of the challenges of the IoT and consider it to include data confidentiality, privacy, and trust. Gubbi et al. emphasized things such as energy efficient sensing, secure networks that can be reprogrammed, privacy, data mining, architecture, quality of service, new protocols, collaborative sensing, data mining, GIS-based visualization, cloud computing, and international operations under the title of open challenges and

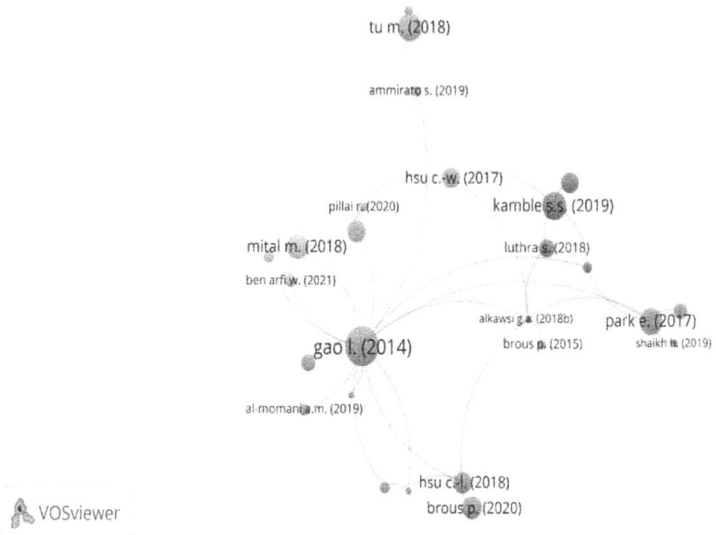

Fig. 7.2.   The Most Highly Cited Publications on IoT Adoption.

future directions (Gubbi et al., 2013). In the research of Gao and Bai (2014), trust is included as one of the variables of their model. They seek to develop and test an integrated model of the determinants of consumer acceptance of IoT technology. They have emphasized RFID application to logistics. Park et al. (2017) have paid attention to the use of IoT in the smart home environment and have developed and tested a model to accept this technology. While emphasizing the importance of security in the IoT following previous literature, they have included the technology acceptance model and the variables of perceived enjoyment, perceived connectedness compatibility, perceived control, and perceived cost in their proposed model (Table 7.4).

Table 7.3. Clusters From Cited References.

Clusters	Authors/References	Citations	Total Link Strength
Cluster A	Gubbi et al. (2013)	14	20
	Atzori et al. (2010)	11	15
	Gao and Bai (2014)	9	16
	Lee and Lee (2015)	7	7
	Park et al. (2017)	5	14
	Miorandi et al. (2012)	5	7
Cluster B	Venkatesh and Davis (2000)	5	16
	Davis et al. (1989)	5	11
	Davis (1989)	5	11
	Ha and Stoel (2009)	5	9

Table 7.4. Application Domains of the IoT.

Authors	Application
(Atzori et al., 2010)	• Transportation and logistics domain: Logistics Assisted driving Mobile ticketing Monitoring environmental parameters Augmented maps • Healthcare domain: Tracking Identification and authentication Data collection Sensing • Smart environment (home, office, plant) domain: Comfortable homes and offices Industrial plants Smart museum and gym • Personal and social domain: Social networking Historical queries Losses Thefts • Futuristic applications domain: Robot taxi City information model Enhanced game room
(Lee & Lee, 2015)	• IoT applications to enhance customer value: Monitoring and control Big data and business analytics Information sharing and collaboration
Gubbi et al. (2013)	• Personal and Home • Enterprise • Utilities • Mobile
(Miorandi et al., 2012)	• Smart homes/smart buildings • Smart cities • Environmental monitoring • Health care • Smart business/inventory and product management • Security and surveillance

Cluster B: The research of this cluster includes the basic theories of user acceptance. In Davis' research, scales for two specific variables, perceived usefulness and perceived ease of use, which are assumed to be fundamental determinants of user acceptance, are developed and validated (Davis, 1989). Also, in another study, Davis et al. compared and integrated two theoretical models for user acceptance of computer technology. These models are the Theory of Reasoned Action (TRA) which includes variables of attitudes and subjective norms and the TAM which includes variables of perceived usefulness, perceived ease of use, and related variables (Davis et al., 1989). Venkatesh and Davis (2000) developed and tested the TAM. This developed model, known as TAM 2, explains perceived usefulness and usage intentions in terms of social influence and cognitive instrumental processes. The fourth research in cluster B belongs to Ha and Stoel (2009). To understand consumer acceptance of e-shopping, they have integrated the quality, enjoyment, and trust of e-shopping into the TAM.

Co-occurrence Keyword Analysis

In this section, we analyze the co-occurrence of words using VOSviewer software. By using the co-occurrence approach, a conceptual structure can be presented using the most common keywords of the document (Akbari et al., 2020). The main structure of the keyword co-occurrence network, cases with at least five keyword occurrences, is shown in Fig. 7.3. The keywords, which include a total of 29 items, were grouped into four clusters (Table 7.5).

The first cluster contains 10 items. This cluster shows IoT adoption in agriculture, manufacturing, logistics, and supply chain management. The second

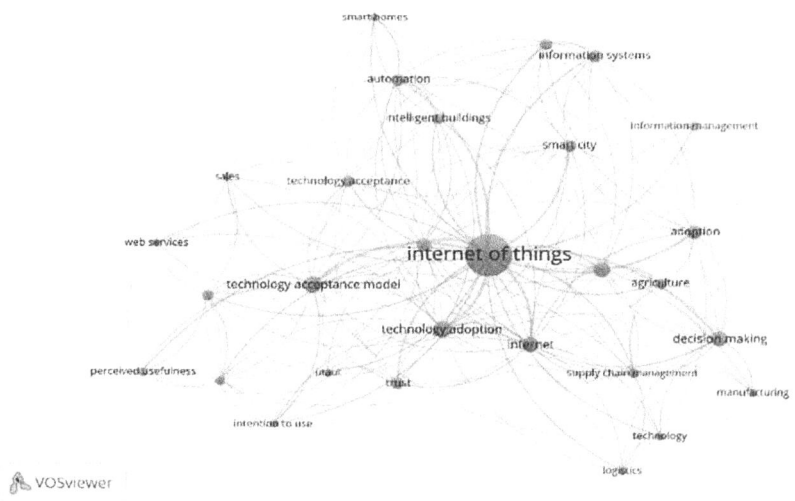

Fig. 7.3.   Network of Cited Keyword Co-occurrence.

Table 7.5. Extracted Keywords.

Cluster	Keyword	Occurrences	Total Link Strength
Cluster A (10 items)	adoption	13	35
	agriculture	8	15
	decision-making	15	39
	internet	15	59
	IoT	121	233
	IoT adoption	16	27
	logistics	5	15
	manufacturing	5	11
	supply chain management	7	28
	technology	5	15
Cluster B (10 items)	behavioral intention	8	33
	intention to use	5	21
	perceived usefulness	6	21
	sales	5	19
	structural equation modeling	6	24
	technology acceptance model	20	62
	technology adoption	19	59
	trust	9	24
	UTAUT	5	17
	web services	5	16
Cluster C (8 items)	automation	11	46
	health care	12	43
	information systems	11	36
	information use	10	36
	intelligent buildings	8	38
	smart city	11	37
	smart homes	5	19
	technology acceptance	9	25
Cluster D (1 item)	information management	7	17

cluster includes behavioral models of IoT technology acceptance. In this cluster, TAM, UTAUT, and the trust variable are located. The third cluster refers to the adoption of IoT and automation technology in intelligent buildings, smart homes, smart cities, and health care. The fourth cluster contains one item. It includes information management (See Table 7.5).

Conclusion

The goal of reviewing documents in the field of IoT adoption is to show the current state of knowledge in this field. For this purpose, the present research has categorized the documents using the bibliometric method and briefly discussed the content of the articles in this field. This research aims to examine the research trends in the field of "IoT adoption" from the beginning until the compilation of the current research in the Scopus database. The review of research shows that the first research was published in 2011. The trend of publishing research is completely upward, which shows the growing importance of IoT technology and the increasing attention of researchers and industrialists to this technology. It should be noted that we selected 156 studies that matched our goals. In the following, we discuss some of the results obtained from the analysis of the co-citation network of cited references and network of cited keyword co-occurrence. The results of the citation network analysis show two clusters. The articles of the first cluster mostly include review studies that examine IoT technology from different dimensions. These dimensions include the vision of IoT, its applications, IoT elements, and challenges facing IoT.

Various categories have been provided for the technologies or elements of the Internet of Things that are used to deploy successful products and services based on this technology: RFID, WSNs, middleware, cloud computing, and IoT application software (Lee & Lee, 2015). In addition to RFID and WSN, Gubbi et al. also mention addressing schemes, data storage and analytics, and visualization as IoT elements (Gubbi et al., 2013). Also Atzori et al. point out that realizing the concept of IoT in the real world is possible through the integration of several enabling technologies. They consider these technologies to include identification, sensing and communication technologies and middleware (applications, service composition, service management, object abstraction, trust, privacy, and security management) (Atzori et al., 2010). RFID is the main development in the embedded communication paradigm (Gubbi et al., 2013). RFID provides automatic identification and data recording using radio waves, a tag, and a reader. This tag can store more data than traditional barcodes (Lee & Lee, 2015). WSNs fulfill spatial measurements, such as field measurements in IoT scenarios (Miorandi et al., 2012). In other words, WSNs are locally distributed autonomous sensor devices for monitoring physical or environmental status. These devices can work with RFID systems to better track the status of things such as their location, temperature, and movements (Lee & Lee, 2015). WSN and RFID can be considered as a subset of identification, sensing, and communication technologies (Atzori et al., 2010). Middleware, which has been proposed by researchers as another element or technology related to IoT, is a software layer or a set of sub-layers that are placed between the technology and application levels (Atzori et al., 2010; Lee & Lee, 2015; Miorandi et al., 2012).

The second topic that has been considered in the articles of the first cluster of citation network analysis is the applications of IoT. In Table 7.4, the scope of IoT applications is categorized. Research studies show that IoT is used in a wide range of sectors and at the individual, organizational, micro, and macro levels. Among the applications of IoT in businesses, we can mention the collection of data related to the performance of equipment and tools, production status, energy consumption, issues related to repairs and maintenance, inventory management, supply chain, and all possible elements affecting the production line, which helps managers to continuously and uninterruptedly check the performance of the business (Atzori et al., 2010; Gubbi et al., 2013; Lee & Lee, 2015; Miorandi et al., 2012). Another application of IoT is helping managers to identify and solve business problems, including changing customer behavior and market conditions. In fact, big data and business analytics are the basis for making key business decisions. Also, IoT technology can prevent delay and distortion of information through information sharing and cooperation (Lee & Lee, 2015). In the field of IoT applications at the individual level, for example, we can refer to various mobile applications that measure various parameters. Also, controlling home equipment such as air conditioning, refrigerator, washing machine, etc., allows people to better manage their home and energy (Atzori et al., 2010; Gubbi et al., 2013).

Another problem that can be seen in the articles of the first cluster is citation network analysis. In the results section, the challenges emphasized by the researchers were mentioned. The challenge that almost all researchers unanimously pointed out is security and privacy (Atzori et al., 2010; Gao & Bai, 2014; Gubbi et al., 2013; Lee & Lee, 2015; Miorandi et al., 2012; Park et al., 2017). Security and privacy issues are the main challenges to consumer acceptance of user-centric IoT applications (Gao & Bai, 2014).

The second cluster of citation network analysis includes articles related to technology adoption. Davies' article includes a TAM. TAM is one of the adapted forms of the theory of rational action, whose purpose is to predict the acceptance of information technology by the user. This model describes users' motivation based on three factors: perceived usefulness, ease of use, and attitude toward use. This model is well confirmed empirically. Of course, TAM has ignored the influence of social factors on technology acceptance; it faces limitations in its application. Also, internal motivations are not mentioned in this model (Davis, 1989; Davis et al., 1989). Another model in this cluster is the developed model of technology acceptance, also known as TAM2 in the literature. In this model, to improve the power of predicting the perceived benefit, two groups of construct have been added to the basic TAM model. These constructs include the social influence construct (image, subject norms, and voluntariness) and the cognitive construct (result demonstrability, job relevance, and output quality) (Venkatesh & Davis, 2000).

According to the literature in the field of technology acceptance and also the concepts, elements, and application areas of IoT technology, it can be concluded that the keywords of cluster A represent the areas in which the adoption of IoT has been discussed and the attention of researchers. These sectors include production, agriculture, logistics, and supply chain management. It also points out the importance and role of IoT technology in decision-making, as one of the duties of managers. Cluster B represents the models and variables used to investigate behavioral intention, intention to use, and IoT adoption technology. In this cluster, TAM, UTAUT, and the trust variable can be seen. The occurrence of the keyword structural equation modeling shows that the models presented to check the adoption of IoT technology are often causal. And according to this point, the research method in this field is often few. Cluster C also refers to the areas of application and acceptance of IoT technology in these areas. Unlike the areas mentioned in cluster A, which can be categorized in the form of business, the areas mentioned in this cluster can be categorized in the form of welfare services. These areas include health care, intelligent buildings, smart cities, and smart homes. Information management is the only item of cluster D.

Limitations

The current research has limitations; in this research, the studied samples were selected from the Scopus database. And we have not checked the documents of other scientific databases. Future researchers can select and examine documents from other databases. Another limitation of this research is that we only examined documents that are in English. Researchers can examine the research of other languages in future research. Another limitation of this research is that it only used the bibliometric method, and in the analysis of this method, it was limited to co-citation analysis and co-occurrence keyword analysis. In future studies, researchers can perform other bibliometric analyzes and also use other research methods.

Case Study

Examining the strategies of countries in the field of IoT can lead to the creation of a perspective. For this reason, we examine Iran's strategy and position as a developing country in the field of IoT. IoT technology in Iran has been noticed both in the public sector and in the private sector. So far, the government's focus has been on drafting legal approvals and adopting supportive policies. And the private sector has also invested in the development of smart solutions in some industries. The fields of application affected by IoT technology in Iran are smart agriculture, smart city, smart house and building, environment, and smart transportation. In 2018, a government decree dealt with the requirements and needs of IoT development in four articles according to the three pillars of big data, smartness, and machine-type communication (MTC). According to the surveys, the ecosystem of IoT in Iran includes 104 companies and startups active in this field, 14 IoT and smart labs, 39 training centers in the field of smart and IoT training, and 16 accelerators and innovation centers to support IoT teams. Some of the projects in the field of Internet of Things in Iran are: 1. Implementation of the national plan for intelligent energy measurement and management, intelligent load control and energy management using Internet-based meters. 2. Implementation of the intelligent traffic navigation system of the country's road transport. 3. The project of intelligentization of agricultural fields in line with the use of soil and air data in tillage, planting and harvesting operations. 4. Fire monitoring project in Golestan National Park. 5. Smart fire alarm operator project. In general, in the field of IoT, the Islamic Republic of Iran pursues the following goals and perspectives: Using intelligent systems for economic prosperity, adopting policies to support startup and knowledge-based businesses based on new technologies and IoT, development of native systems and platforms, and using IoT to conserve natural resources and energy.

Case Study Questions

(1) Has government policy helped the adoption of IoT?
(2) Is Iran's infrastructure suitable for accepting IoT technology?
(3) In which sector (government or private) is the speed of adoption of IoT technology faster?
(4) What factors affect the adoption of IoT technology?

Key Terms and Definitions

Smart city: A smart city uses information and communication technology (ICT) to improve operational efficiency, share information with the public, and provide a better quality of government service and citizen welfare.

Smart agriculture: The term smart agriculture refers to the usage of technologies like IoT, sensors, location systems, robots, and artificial intelligence on your farm.

Smart home: A smart home refers to a convenient home setup where appliances and devices can be automatically controlled remotely from anywhere with an internet connection using a mobile or other networked device.

Smart transportation: Smart transportation refers to the integrated application of modern technology and management strategies into transportation systems.

Machine-Type Communication: MTC describes data communication between two entities without the involvement of a human. MTC involves many devices such as computers, embedded systems, sensors, meters, mobile devices, etc.

Big data: Big data is a collection of data that is huge in volume, yet growing exponentially with time. It is data with so large size and complexity that none of the traditional data management tools can store it or process it efficiently.

References

Akbari, M., Khodayari, M., Khaleghi, A., Danesh, M., & Padash, H. (2020). Technological innovation research in the last six decades: A bibliometric analysis. *European Journal of Innovation Management.* https://doi.org/10.1108/EJIM-05-2020-0166

Al-Emran, M., Arpaci, I., & Salloum, S. A. (2020). An empirical examination of continuous intention to use m-learning: An integrated model. *Education and Information Technologies.* https://doi.org/10.1007/s10639-019-10094-2

Al-Momani, A. M., Mahmoud, M. A., & Ahmad, M. S. (2018). Factors that influence the acceptance of internet of things services by customers of telecommunication companies in Jordan. *Journal of Organizational and End User Computing, 30*(4), 51–63. https://doi.org/10.4018/JOEUC.2018100104

Al-Momani, A. M., Mahmoud, M. A., & Ahmad, M. S. (2019). A review of factors influencing customer acceptance of internet of things services. *International Journal of Information Systems in the Service Sector, 11*(1), 54–67. https://doi.org/10.4018/IJISSS.2019010104

Alansari, Z., Anuar, N. B., Kamsin, A., Soomro, S., & Belgaum, M. R. (2018). The Internet of Things adoption in healthcare applications. In *2017 IEEE 3rd International Conference on Engineering Technologies and Social Sciences* (Vol. 5, pp. 1–5). 2018, January. https://doi.org/10.1109/ICETSS.2017.8324138

Aldossari, M. Q., & Sidorova, A. (2020). Consumer acceptance of Internet of Things (IoT): Smart home context. *Journal of Computer Information Systems, 60*(6), 507–517. https://doi.org/10.1080/08874417.2018.1543000

AlHogail, A. (2018). Improving IoT technology adoption through improving consumer trust. *Technologies, 6*(3), 64. https://doi.org/10.3390/technologies6030064

Alkawsi, G. A., & Ali, N. B. (2018). A systematic review of individuals' acceptance of IOT-based technologies. *International Journal of Engineering and Technology (UAE), 7*(4), 136–142. https://doi.org/10.14419/ijet.v7i4.35.22342

Ammirato, S., Sofo, F., Felicetti, A. M., & Raso, C. (2019). A methodology to support the adoption of IoT innovation and its application to the Italian bank branch security context. *European Journal of Innovation Management, 22*(1), 146–174. https://doi.org/10.1108/EJIM-03-2018-0058

Arfi, W. B., Nasr, I. B., Kondrateva, G., & Hikkerova, L. (2021). The role of trust in intention to use the IoT in eHealth: Application of the modified UTAUT in a consumer context. *Technological Forecasting and Social Change, 167.* https://doi.org/10.1016/j.techfore.2021.120688

Arnold, C., & Voigt, K. I. (2019). Determinants of industrial Internet of Things adoption in German manufacturing companies. *International Journal of Innovation and Technology Management, 16*(6). https://doi.org/10.1142/S021987701950038X

Atzori, L., Iera, A., & Morabito, G. (2010). The Internet of Things: A survey. *Computer Networks, 54*(15), 2787–2805. https://doi.org/10.1016/j.comnet.2010.05.010

Atzori, L., Iera, A., & Morabito, G. (2014). From "smart objects" to "social objects": The next evolutionary step of the internet of things. *IEEE Communications Magazine, 52*(1), 97–105. https://doi.org/10.1109/MCOM.2014.6710070

Bakhitjaafreh, A. (2018). The effect factors in the adoption of Internet of Things (IoT) technology in the SME in KSA: An empirical study. *International Review of Management and Business Research, 7*(1), 135–148. https://doi.org/10.30543/7-1(2018)-13

Ben Arfi, W., Ben Nasr, I., Khvatova, T., & Ben Zaied, Y. (2021). Understanding acceptance of eHealthcare by IoT natives and IoT immigrants: An integrated model of UTAUT, perceived risk, and financial cost. *Technological Forecasting and Social Change, 163*(October), 120437. https://doi.org/10.1016/j.techfore.2020.120437

Berte, D.-R. (2018). Defining the IoT. *Proceedings of the International Conference on Business Excellence, 12*(1), 118–128. https://doi.org/10.2478/picbe-2018-0013

Bouzembrak, Y., Klüche, M., Gavai, A., & Marvin, H. J. P. (2019). Internet of Things in food safety: Literature review and a bibliometric analysis. *Trends in Food Science and Technology, 94*, 54–64. https://doi.org/10.1016/j.tifs.2019.11.002

Brambilla, M., Umuhoza, E., & Acerbis, R. (2017). Model-driven development of user interfaces for IoT systems via domain-specific components and patterns. *Journal of Internet Services and Applications, 8*(1), 14. https://doi.org/10.1186/s13174-017-0064-1

Brous, P., Janssen, M., & Herder, P. (2020). The dual effects of the Internet of Things (IoT): A systematic review of the benefits and risks of IoT adoption by organizations. *International Journal of Information Management, 51*. https://doi.org/10.1016/j.ijinfomgt.2019.05.008

Buyle, R., Van Compernolle, M., Vlassenroot, E., Vanlishout, Z., Mechant, P., & Mannens, E. (2018). "Technology readiness and acceptance model" as a predictor for the use intention of data standards in smart cities. *Media and Communication, 6*(4), 127–139. Theoretical Reflections and Case Studies. https://doi.org/10.17645/mac.v6i4.1679

Chen, C. L., & Wu, C. C. (2020). Students' behavioral intention to use and achievements in ICT-Integrated mathematics remedial instruction: Case study of a calculus course. *Computers and Education, 145*. https://doi.org/10.1016/j.compedu.2019.103740

Choi, W., Kim, J., Lee, S., & Park, E. (2021). Smart home and internet of things: A bibliometric study. *Journal of Cleaner Production, 301*, 126908. https://doi.org/10.1016/j.jclepro.2021.126908

Clim, A., Zota, R., Constantinescu, R., & Ilie-Nemedi, I. (2020). Health services in smart cities: Choosing the big data mining based decision support. *International Journal of Healthcare Management, 13*(1), 79–87. https://doi.org/10.1080/20479700.2019.1650478

Coughlan, T., Brown, M., Mortier, R., Houghton, R. J., Goulden, M., & Lawson, G. (2012). Exploring acceptance and consequences of the Internet of Things in the home. In *Proceedings – 2012 IEEE IEEE Int'l Conference on & Int'l Conference on Cyber, Physical and Social Computing (CPSCom) Green Computing and Communications (GreenCom)* (pp. 148–155). https://doi.org/10.1109/GreenCom.2012.32

Cozzolino, A., Verona, G., & Rothaermel, F. T. (2018). Unpacking the disruption process: New technology, business models, and incumbent adaptation. *Journal of Management Studies, 55*(7), 1166–1202. https://doi.org/10.1111/joms.12352

Davis, F. D. (1989). Perceived usefulness, perceived ease of use, and user acceptance of information technology. *MIS Quarterly: Management Information Systems, 13*(3), 319–339. https://doi.org/10.2307/249008

Davis, F. D., Bagozzi, R. P., & Warshaw, P. R. (1989). User acceptance of computer technology: A comparison of two theoretical models. *Management Science, 35*(8), 982–1003. https://doi.org/10.1287/mnsc.35.8.982

Farrokhi, A., Farahbakhsh, R., Rezazadeh, J., & Minerva, R. (2021). Application of Internet of Things and artificial intelligence for smart fitness: A survey. *Computer Networks, 189*, 107859. https://doi.org/10.1016/j.comnet.2021.107859

Foroudi, P., Akarsu, T. N., Marvi, R., & Balakrishnan, J. (2021). Intellectual evolution of social innovation: A bibliometric analysis and avenues for future research trends. *Industrial Marketing Management*, *93*, 446–465. https://doi.org/10.1016/j.indmarman.2020.03.026

Gao, L., & Bai, X. (2014). A unified perspective on the factors influencing consumer acceptance of internet of things technology. *Asia Pacific Journal of Marketing and Logistics*, *26*(2), 211–231. https://doi.org/10.1108/APJML-06-2013-0061

Garcia-Morales, V. J., Martín-Rojas, R., & Lardón-López, M. E. (2018). Influence of social media technologies on organizational performance through knowledge and innovation. *Baltic Journal of Management*, *13*(3), 345–367. https://doi.org/10.1108/BJM-04-2017-0123

Ghanbari, A., Laya, A., Alonso-Zarate, J., & Markendahl, J. (2017). Business Development in the Internet of Things: A Matter of Vertical Cooperation. *IEEE Communications Magazine*, *55*(2), 135–141. https://doi.org/10.1109/MCOM.2017.1600596CM

Ghobakhloo, M., & Ching, N. T. (2019). Adoption of digital technologies of smart manufacturing in SMEs. *Journal of Industrial Information Integration*, *16*, 100107. https://doi.org/10.1016/j.jii.2019.100107

Gil, D., Ferrández, A., Mora-Mora, H., & Peral, J. (2016). Internet of Things: A review of surveys based on context aware intelligent services. *Sensors*, *16*(7), 1069. https://doi.org/10.3390/s16071069

Gubbi, J., Buyya, R., Marusic, S., & Palaniswami, M. (2013). Internet of Things (IoT): A vision, architectural elements, and future directions. *Future Generation Computer Systems*, *29*(7), 1645–1660. https://doi.org/10.1016/j.future.2013.01.010

Ha, S., & Stoel, L. (2009). Consumer e-shopping acceptance: Antecedents in a technology acceptance model. *Journal of Business Research*, *62*(5), 565–571. https://doi.org/10.1016/j.jbusres.2008.06.016

Haddud, A., DeSouza, A., Khare, A., & Lee, H. (2017). Examining potential benefits and challenges associated with the Internet of Things integration in supply chains. *Journal of Manufacturing Technology Management*, *28*(8), 1055–1085. https://doi.org/10.1108/JMTM-05-2017-0094

Hays, J. P. (2020). The internet of things for combatting antimicrobial resistance. *Biotechniques*, *69*(5), 330–332. https://doi.org/10.2144/btn-2020-0104

Hsu, C.-L., & Lin, J. C.-C. (2018). Exploring factors affecting the adoption of Internet of Things services. *Journal of Computer Information Systems*, *58*(1), 49–57. https://doi.org/10.1080/08874417.2016.1186524

Hsu, C. W., & Yeh, C. C. (2017). Understanding the factors affecting the adoption of the Internet of Things. *Technology Analysis and Strategic Management*, *29*(9), 1089–1102. https://doi.org/10.1080/09537325.2016.1269160

Jaiswal, T., Pandey, M., & Tripathi, P. (2022). Real Time Multiple-Object Detection Based on Enhanced SSD. In *ICPC2T 2022 - 2nd International Conference on Power, Control and Computing Technologies, Proceedings* (pp. 1–5). https://doi.org/10.1109/ICPC2T53885.2022.9776899

Jalali, M. S., Kaiser, J. P., Siegel, M., & Madnick, S. (2019). The Internet of Things promises new benefits and risks: A systematic analysis of adoption dynamics of IoT products. *IEEE Security & Privacy*, *17*(2), 39–48. https://doi.org/10.1109/MSEC.2018.2888780

Janssen, M., Luthra, S., Mangla, S., Rana, N. P., & Dwivedi, Y. K. (2019). Challenges for adopting and implementing IoT in smart cities: An integrated MICMAC-ISM approach. *Internet Research, 29*(6), 1589–1616. https://doi.org/10. 1108/INTR-06-2018-0252

Jayashankar, P., Nilakanta, S., Johnston, W. J., Gill, P., & Burres, R. (2018). IoT adoption in agriculture: The role of trust, perceived value and risk. *Journal of Business and Industrial Marketing, 33*(6), 804–821. https://doi.org/10.1108/JBIM-01-2018-0023

Kalsoom, T., Ahmed, S., Rafi-Ul-shan, P. M., Azmat, M., Akhtar, P., Pervez, Z., Imran, M. A., & Ur-Rehman, M. (2021). Impact of IoT on manufacturing industry 4.0: A new triangular systematic review. *Sustainability, 13*(22). https://doi.org/10. 3390/su132212506

Kamble, S. S., Gunasekaran, A., Parekh, H., & Joshi, S. (2019). Modeling the internet of things adoption barriers in food retail supply chains. *Journal of Retailing and Consumer Services, 48*, 154–168. https://doi.org/10.1016/j.jretconser.2019.02.020

Kamran, M., Khan, H. U., Nisar, W., Farooq, M., & Rehman, S.-U. (2020). Blockchain and Internet of Things: A bibliometric study. *Computers and Electrical Engineering, 81*, 106525. https://doi.org/10.1016/j.compeleceng.2019.106525

Karahoca, A., Karahoca, D., & Aksöz, M. (2018). Examining intention to adopt to internet of things in healthcare technology products. *Kybernetes, 47*(4), 742–770. https://doi.org/10.1108/K-02-2017-0045

Khan, A. U., Zhang, Z., Chohan, S. R., & Rafique, W. (2021). Factors fostering the success of IoT services in academic libraries: A study built to enhance the library performance. *Library Hi Tech.* https://doi.org/10.1108/LHT-06-2021-0179

Lee, I. (2019). The Internet of Things for enterprises: An ecosystem, architecture, and IoT service business model. *Internet of Things, 7*, 100078. https://doi.org/10.1016/j. IoT.2019.100078

Lee, H. (2020). Home IoT resistance: Extended privacy and vulnerability perspective. *Telematics and Informatics, 49*, 101377. https://doi.org/10.1016/j.tele.2020.101377

Lee, I., & Lee, K. (2015). The Internet of Things (IoT): Applications, investments, and challenges for enterprises. *Business Horizons, 58*(4), 431–440. https://doi.org/10. 1016/j.bushor.2015.03.008

Lee, C. K., Lee, M. S., & Thurasamy, R. (2020). Using mediation in project disputes based on theory of planned behavior and technology acceptance model. *Journal of Legal Affairs and Dispute Resolution in Engineering and Construction, 12*(1). https:// doi.org/10.1061/(asce)la.1943-4170.0000361

Lin, D., Lee, C. K. M., & Lin, K. (2016, December). Research on effect factors evaluation of internet of things (IOT) adoption in Chinese agricultural supply chain. In *IEEE International Conference on Industrial Engineering and Engineering Management* (pp. 612–615). https://doi.org/10.1109/IEEM.2016.7797948

Liu, C. C., Wang, P. C., & Tai, S. J. D. (2016). An analysis of student engagement patterns in language learning facilitated by Web 2.0 technologies. *ReCALL, 28*(2), 104–122. https://doi.org/10.1017/S095834401600001X

Lohmuller, B., & Petrikhin, A. (2018). The Growing importance of technology executives/Hidden chief technology officers and their organizational roles. In *2018 IEEE International Conference on Engineering, Technology and Innovation, ICE/ ITMC 2018 - Proceedings.* https://doi.org/10.1109/ICE.2018.8436317

Luthra, S., Garg, D., Mangla, S. K., & Singh Berwal, Y. P. (2018). Analyzing challenges to Internet of Things (IoT) adoption and diffusion: An Indian context. *Procedia Computer Science*, *125*, 733–739. https://doi.org/10.1016/j.procs.2017.12.094

Majid, M., Habib, S., Javed, A. R., Rizwan, M., Srivastava, G., Gadekallu, T. R., & Lin, J. C. W. (2022). Applications of wireless sensor networks and Internet of Things Frameworks in the Industry Revolution 4.0: A systematic literature review. *Sensors*, *22*(6), 2087. https://doi.org/10.3390/s22062087

Malik, G., & Rao, A. S. (2019). Extended expectation-confirmation model to predict continued usage of ODR/ride hailing apps: Role of perceived value and self-efficacy. *Information Technology & Tourism*, *21*(4), 461–482. https://doi.org/10.1007/s40558-019-00152-3

Marangunić, N., & Granić, A. (2015). Descriptors of social media use in higher education. *Universal Access in the Information Society*, *14*(1), 81–95. https://doi.org/10.1007/s10209-014-0348-1

Martens, M., Roll, O., & ElIIoTt, R. (2017). Testing the Technology readiness and acceptance model for mobile payments across Germany and South Africa. *International Journal of Innovation and Technology Management*, *14*(6). https://doi.org/10.1142/S021987701750033X

Mensah, I. K. (2019). Predictors of the continued adoption of Wechat mobile payment. *International Journal of E-Business Research*, *15*(4), 1–23. https://doi.org/10.4018/IJEBR.2019100101

Metallo, C., Agrifoglio, R., Schiavone, F., & Mueller, J. (2018). Understanding business model in the Internet of Things industry. *Technological Forecasting and Social Change*, *136*(January), 298–306. https://doi.org/10.1016/j.techfore.2018.01.020

Miorandi, D., Sicari, S., De Pellegrini, F., & Chlamtac, I. (2012). Internet of things: Vision, applications and research challenges. *Ad Hoc Networks*, *10*(7), 1497–1516. https://doi.org/10.1016/j.adhoc.2012.02.016

Miskiewicz, R. (2020). Internet of Things in marketing: Bibliometric analysis. *Marketing and Management of Innovations*, *3*(3), 371–381. http://doi.org/10.21272/mmi.2020.3-27

Mital, M., Chang, V., Choudhary, P., Papa, A., & Pani, A. K. (2018). Adoption of Internet of Things in India: A test of competing models using a structured equation modeling approach. *Technological Forecasting and Social Change*, *136*, 339–346. https://doi.org/10.1016/j.techfore.2017.03.001

Naglis, M., & Bhatiasevi, V. (2019). Why do people use fitness tracking devices in Thailand? An integrated model approach. *Technology in Society*, *58*(May 2018), 101146. https://doi.org/10.1016/j.techsoc.2019.101146

Nawi, N. B. C., Mamun, A. Al, Isa Yusoff, Y. Z. M., Salameh, A. A., Muhammad, M. Z., & Hayat, N. (2021). Motivation towards adoption of internet of things (IoT) services in retailing among Malaysian youth. *Malaysian Journal of Consumer and Family Economics*, *26*, 158–180.

Nguyen, B. M., Binh, H. T. T., Anh, T. T., & Son, D. B. (2019). Evolutionary algorithms to optimize task scheduling problem for the IoT based Bag-of-Tasks application in Cloud-Fog computing environment. *Applied Sciences*, *9*(9). https://doi.org/10.3390/app9091730

Nobre, G. C., & Tavares, E. (2017). Scientific literature analysis on big data and internet of things applications on circular economy: A bibliometric study. *Scientometrics, 111*(1), 463–492. https://doi.org/10.1007/s11192-017-2281-6

Pappas, N., Caputo, A., Pellegrini, M. M., Marzi, G., & Michopoulou, E. (2021). The complexity of decision-making processes and IoT adoption in accommodation SMEs. *Journal of Business Research, 131*, 573–583. https://doi.org/10.1016/j.jbusres.2021.01.010

Park, E. (2020). User acceptance of smart wearable devices: An appexpectation-confirmation modelroach. *Telematics and Informatics, 47*(November 2019). https://doi.org/10.1016/j.tele.2019.101318

Park, E., Cho, Y., Han, J., & Kwon, S. J. (2017). Comprehensive approaches to user acceptance of Internet of Things in a smart home environment. *IEEE Internet of Things Journal, 4*(6), 2342–2350. https://doi.org/10.1109/JIOT.2017.2750765

Park, C., & Jeong, M. (2021). A study of factors influencing on passive and active acceptance of home energy management services with internet of things. *Energies, 14*(12). https://doi.org/10.3390/en14123631

Patil, K. (2016). Retail adoption of Internet of Things: Applying TAM model. In *2016 International Conference on Computing, Analytics and Security Trends (CAST)* (pp. 404–409). https://doi.org/10.1109/CAST.2016.7915003

Rejeb, A., Simske, S., Rejeb, K., Treiblmaier, H., & Zailani, S. (2020). Internet of Things research in supply chain management and logistics: A bibliometric analysis. *Internet of Things, 12*, 100318. https://doi.org/10.1016/j.IoT.2020.100318

Resch, M., & Kaminski, A. (2019). The epistemic importance of technology in computer simulation and machine learning. *Minds and Machines, 29*(1), 9–17. https://doi.org/10.1007/s11023-019-09496-5

Sardjono, W., Mulianto, P., & Perdana, W. G. (2019). Effect of ease of use, usefullness, cost effectiveness, and compatibility towards cloud computing usage in manufacturing company. *International Journal of Recent Technology and Engineering, 8*(3), 49–53. https://doi.org/10.35940/ijrte.C3872.098319

Sharma, M., Joshi, S., Kannan, D., Govindan, K., Singh, R., & Purohit, H. C. (2020). Internet of Things (IoT) adoption barriers of smart cities' waste management: An Indian context. *Journal of Cleaner Production, 270*. https://doi.org/10.1016/j.jclepro.2020.122047

Shrouf, F., & Miragliotta, G. (2015). Energy management based on Internet of Things: Practices and framework for adoption in production management. *Journal of Cleaner Production, 100*, 235–246. https://doi.org/10.1016/j.jclepro.2015.03.055

Siddiqa, A., Shah, M. A., Khattak, H. A., Akhunzada, A., Ali, I., Bin Razak, Z., & Gani, A. (2018). Social Internet of Vehicles: Complexity, adaptivity, issues and beyond. *IEEE Access, 6*, 62089–62106. https://doi.org/10.1109/ACCESS.2018.2872928

Singh, V. K., Singh, P., Karmakar, M., Leta, J., & Mayr, P. (2021). The journal coverage of Web of Science, Scopus and Dimensions: A comparative analysis. *Scientometrics, 126*(6), 5113–5142. https://doi.org/10.1007/s11192-021-03948-5

Singh, N., Sinha, N., & Liébana-Cabanillas, F. J. (2020). Determining factors in the adoption and recommendation of mobile wallet services in India: Analysis of the effect of innovativeness, stress to use and social influence. *International Journal of Information Management, 50*(May 2019), 191–205. https://doi.org/10.1016/j.ijinfomgt.2019.05.022

Sivathanu, B. (2019a). Adoption of Industrial IoT (IIoT) in Auto-Component Manufacturing SMEs in India. *Information Resources Management Journal*, *32*(2), 52–75. https://doi.org/10.4018/irmj.2019040103

Sivathanu, B. (2019b). An Empirical Study on the Intention to Use Open Banking in India. *32*(3), 27–47. https://doi.org/10.4018/IRMJ.2019070102

Sohn, K., & Kwon, O. (2020). Technology acceptance theories and factors influencing artificial Intelligence-based intelligent products. *Telematics and Informatics*, *47*, 101324. https://doi.org/10.1016/j.tele.2019.101324

Straub, E. T. (2009). Understanding technology adoption: Theory and future directions for informal learning. *Review of Educational Research*, *79*(2), 625–649. https://doi.org/10.3102/0034654308325896

Szentesi, S.-G., Lavinia Denisia, C., Ramona, L., & Cuc, P. N. (2021). Internet of Things (IoT), challenges and perspectives in Romania: A qualitative research. *Www.Amfiteatrueconomic.Ro*, *23*(57), 448. https://doi.org/10.24818/EA/2021/57/448

Thyagaraj, A., & Narayanan, K. (2021). *Internet of Things (IoT) adoption in Indian Healthcare Industry-A case study from a hospital.*

Trnka, M., Cerny, T., & Stickney, N. (2018). Survey of Authentication and Authorization for the Internet of Things. *Security and Communication Networks*, *2018*. https://doi.org/10.1155/2018/4351603

Tu, M. (2018). An exploratory study of internet of things (IoT) adoption intention in logistics and supply chain management a mixed research approach. *International Journal of Logistics Management*, *29*(1), 131–151. https://doi.org/10.1108/IJLM-11-2016-0274

Venkatesh, V., & Davis, F. D. (2000). Theoretical extension of the Technology Acceptance Model: Four longitudinal field studies. *Management Science*, *46*(2), 186–204. https://doi.org/10.1287/mnsc.46.2.186.11926

Wu, B., & Chen, X. (2017). Continuance intention to use MOOCs: Integrating the technology acceptance model (TAM) and task technology fit (TTF) model. *Computers in Human Behavior*, *67*, 221–232. https://doi.org/10.1016/j.chb.2016.10.028

Zaminkar, M., Sarkohaki, F., & Fotohi, R. (2021). A method based on encryption and node rating for securing the RPL protocol communications in the IoT ecosystem. *International Journal of Communication Systems*, *34*(3). https://doi.org/10.1002/dac.4693

Zhao, D. (2006). Towards all-author co-citation analysis. *Information Processing & Management*, *42*(6), 1578–1591. https://doi.org/10.1016/j.ipm.2006.03.022

Zupic, I., & Čater, T. (2015). Bibliometric methods in management and organization. *Organizational Research Methods*, *18*(3), 429–472. https://doi.org/10.1177/1094428114562629

Chapter 8

The Role of Technology in Customer Purchase Intention in the UK Market

Mehdi Rahmani, Pantea Foroudi, S. Asieh H. Tabaghdehi and Ramin Behbehani

Brunel University London, UK

Abstract

With the global market for advanced technology-driven customer service set to soar, understanding the complicated relationship between advanced technology and customer purchase behaviour is paramount. While prior research has touched upon the impact of technology on purchase processes in some aspects, this study investigates the specific features of advanced technology that shape customer purchase intention in greater depth. By investigating when and under what conditions customers choose advanced technology-based purchases, this research sheds light on the evolving landscape of consumer decision-making and it seeks to quantify the transformative power of advanced technology in driving customer purchase intentions.

Keywords: Advanced technology; customer purchase intention; customer behaviour theory; online buying behaviour; broaden-and-build theory

Introduction

The use of advanced technology has emerged as a pivotal factor influencing customer purchase intentions (Acquila-Natale & Iglesias-Pradas, 2021). However, the integration of advanced technology into the customer purchasing process is not merely about incorporating it at one stage. Rather, it involves a profound transformation of customer behaviour and a reshaping of the dynamics within the purchase process (Akarsu et al., 2018; Balakrishnan & Dwivedi, 2021; Balakrishnan & Foroudi, 2020; Jeon, 2022; Rodgers & Nguyen, 2022; Wen Wan et al., 2017) and needs to be investigated on how and what extent the use of

Business Strategies and Ethical Challenges in the Digital Ecosystem, 163–195

Copyright © 2025 Mehdi Rahmani, Pantea Foroudi, S. Asieh H. Tabaghdehi and Ramin Behbehani

Published under exclusive licence by Emerald Publishing Limited

doi:10.1108/978-1-80455-069-420241008

advanced technology influences on the customer purchase intention. Statista's forecast indicates a rapid expansion in the worldwide market for advanced technology, particularly artificial intelligence (AI), in customer service. They predict this market to surge at a rate seven times faster than traditional manual customer service, with a projected market revenue of $126 billion by 2025 (Statista, 2022). According to studies, intelligent customer service has the potential to solve 80% of common problems, which could reduce the $1.3 trillion annual cost of customer service inquiries for businesses worldwide by 30% (Prentice et al., 2020).

The use of advanced technology in customer purchase processes has been extensively studied and proven to simplify it (Bhagat et al., 2023; Fakhreddin & Foroudi, 2022; Foroudi, Jin, et al., 2018; Foroudi & Marvi, 2019; Huang & Rust, 2021; Mustak et al., 2021; Wu, Chen, & Chiu, 2016). Through its innovative application in problem-solving and logical decision-making, advanced technology, particularly in the form of machine learning (ML) and language processing, has emerged as a valuable tool. By harnessing these capabilities, customers can find their purchase journey more effectively. Customers who embrace advanced technology during their purchase process have experienced positive outcomes, achieving profitability by having their demand met efficiently within optimal time and financial constraints (Kim et al., 2017; Zha et al., 2022a, 2022b, 2022c, 2023, 2024). This transformational power of advanced technology has enabled the attainment of goals that were once considered unrealistic (Weber & Schütte, 2019). This research aims to understand to what extent the intention to use advanced technology brings about a change in customer purchase intention and customer behavioural intention and whether customers are more willing to repurchase from those that use advanced technology (Bhagat et al., 2023; Kalsoom et al., 2023; Luo et al., 2019; Mehmannavazan et al., 2023). Despite the significant and positive view of the use of advanced technology in the purchase process, little systematic research and less emphasis addressed the characteristics of advanced technology that influence purchase and behavioural intention (Hsieh et al., 2023; Nazir et al., 2023; Park et al., 2022). Hence, this study attempts to fill this theoretical gap by examining the effect of advanced technology features (Acquila-Natale & Iglesias-Pradas, 2021; Kautish et al., 2023; Pillai et al., 2020) on the purchase intention of customers.

To date, numerous endeavours have been dedicated to predicting customer purchasing behaviour that is influenced by advanced technology in specific fields like anthropomorphism (Jang et al., 2022; Maeng & Aggarwal, 2018; Wen Wan et al., 2017; Yuan & Dennis, 2019), Shopbot (Montgomery et al., 2004), conversational commerce (Aw et al., 2022; Balakrishnan & Dwivedi, 2021; Hsu & Lin, 2021) and virtual reality (VR) (Leung et al., 2022). Furthermore, a substantial body of research has utilised advanced technology techniques and methods to generate insights and practical outcomes in the field of customer purchase intention and behaviour (He et al., 2021; Kar et al., 2022; Park et al., 2022; Rodgers et al., 2021; Xia et al., 2022).

Various factors contributing to the realisation of purchase intention and behaviour have been explored, including impulse purchase behaviour (Katakam et al., 2021;

Wu, Chen, & Chiu, 2016), shelf space allocation (Chen et al., 2006; Tsai & Huang, 2015) and market basket analysis (Omar et al., 2023; Solnet et al., 2016). Furthermore, advanced technology has been extensively utilised in various domains that are closely associated with customer purchase intention. These areas have been investigated from the perspective of purchase intention, including marketing (Cheng & Sun, 2012; Jeon, 2022), customer relationship management (CRM) (Ha et al., 2002), optimal pricing strategies (Li et al., 2020), advertising (Rodgers & Nguyen, 2022; Shumanov et al., 2022), demand forecasting (Kharfan et al., 2021; Papanagnou & Matthews-Amune, 2018), the intention to use online delivery services (Ray & Bala, 2021), customisation and personalisation services (Kim et al., 2001) and customer segmentation (Wu & Chou, 2011). These studies delve into the impact of advanced technology on customer purchase intention within these specific contexts, contributing to a comprehensive understanding of its effects in diverse areas such as marketing, customer relationship management and advertising.

Prior literature has shown broad factors related to advanced technology and purchase intention (Balakrishnan & Dwivedi, 2021; Bhagat et al., 2023; Jain & Gandhi, 2021; Jang et al., 2022). For most business owners and marketers, however, these relationships may not be clearly defined without a thorough understanding of advanced technology and customer purchase intention relationships, as well as a thorough understanding of the circumstances and timing under which customers intend to make purchase decisions using advanced technology. This research aims to fill knowledge gaps in the field of discourse by investigating when, under what circumstances and why customers make advanced technology-based intentions and purchases. This study seeks to address the contribution of advanced technology and customer purchase intention with the aim of investigating the development of customer purchase behaviour and consumer response to the use of advanced technology through valuable insights into the role of advanced technology in the customer decision-making processes. Particularly, this study evaluates the impact of the intention to use advanced technology on customer purchase intention.

This study focuses on understanding the impact of the intention to use advanced technology on customer purchase intention. The objective is to explore how consumers' perceptions and utilisation of advanced technology influence their purchase decisions. Specifically, this study aims to investigate the internal drivers that shape consumers' attitudes and purchase intentions towards adopting advanced technology in their purchasing process. To address the key objective of this study, a combination of customer behaviour theory and broaden-and-build theory is well-suited for exploring the impact of the intention to use advanced technology on customer purchase intentions. These theories provide a framework for understanding how customers intend to use advanced technology in their purchasing decisions.

The broaden-and-build theory also plays a significant role in this research. This theory focuses on positive emotions, motivation and their impact on individual well-being and personal growth. It suggests that positive emotions and motivation broaden an individual's thought–action repertoire, leading to increased resilience and the building of resources over time. Both positivist and interpretivist paradigms can incorporate the broaden-and-build theory. By conducting this research, valuable insights will be gained by marketing managers, data analysts and firms to comprehend the relationship between advanced technology and customer purchase intentions in the online markets and industry. The primary goal is to empirically test hypotheses related to the antecedents and consequences of customers' intention to use advanced technology in their purchasing decisions. This study contributes to the fields of business management, marketing and innovation, providing a deeper understanding of how advanced technology influences consumer behaviour.

The findings from this research offer practical tools to drive advancements in online markets and industries through the adoption of advanced technology. By emphasising the significance of advanced technology in the online markets and industry, this study supports marketers, data analysts and firms in leveraging its potential. The results obtained will illustrate the relationships between different dimensions of advanced technology utilisation and positive customer purchase intentions. Furthermore, the data collected and the research elements provide insights relevant to customers in various contexts, including the British market. As part of this study, a conceptual framework (Fig. 8.1) is proposed that examines the relationship between advanced technology usage and customer behavioural intentions within the online marketplace and industry in order to advance the current understanding of the impact of the intention to use advanced technology on customer purchase intentions. A deeper examination of the factors that influence customers' inclination to adopt advanced technology is then conducted by addressing the following research questions:

- What are the key factors that positively influence customers' intention to use advanced technology?
- Question 2: What are the main influences of customers' intention to use advanced technology on purchase intentions?

By examining the above, this study aims to extend the existing literature on the influence of advanced technology on customer purchase intention. The conceptual framework proposed in Fig. 8.1 provides valuable insights into understanding the role of advanced technology in shaping consumer behaviour and decision-making.

Propositional Framework

This propositional model (Fig. 8.1) has been developed based on previous research (Balakrishnan & Dwivedi, 2021; Kautish et al., 2023) to provide a comprehensive understanding of the relationship between advanced technology and consumer purchase intention, including its antecedents and consequences. Kautish et al. (2023) suggest three theoretical pathways through which visual and auditory characteristics of advanced technology can influence purchase intentions: an emotional pathway, a

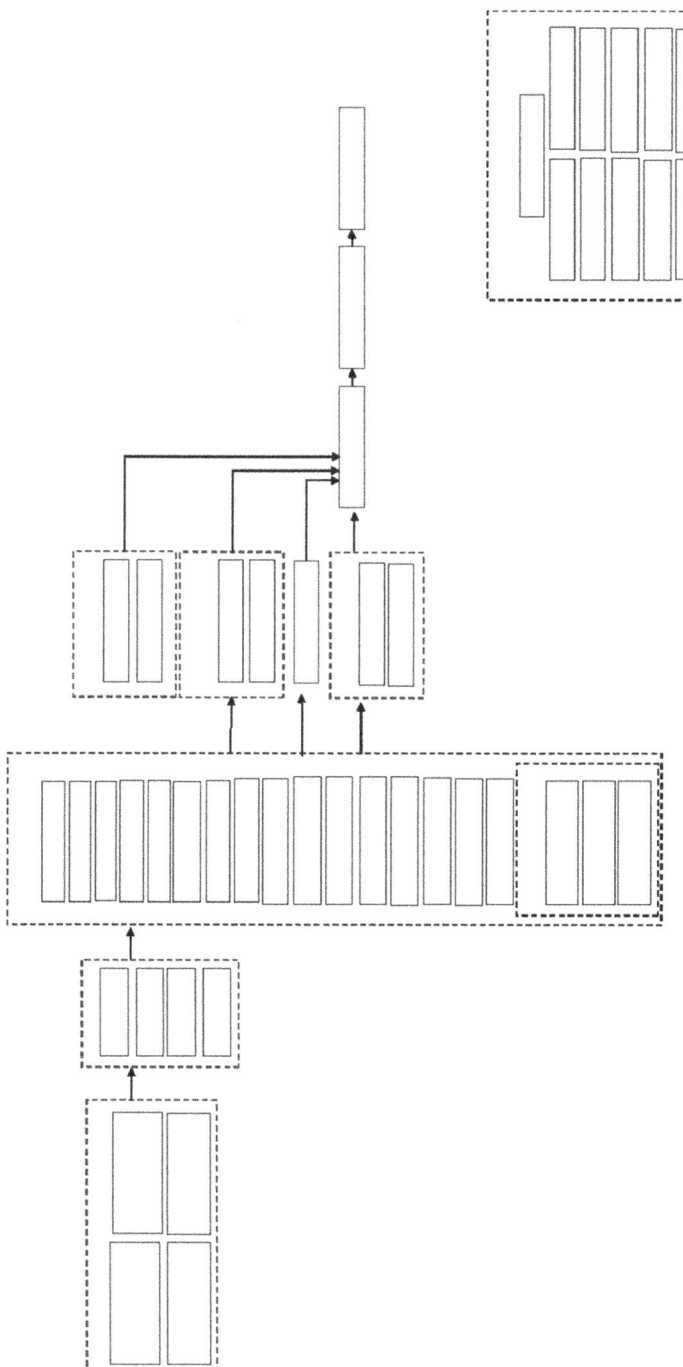

Fig. 8.1. Conceptual Research Model. *Source:* Developed by the researchers.

product attachment pathway and a perceived quality pathway. Balakrishnan and Dwivedi (2021) support the notion that advanced technology creates animacy perceptions among users and highlights the influence of advanced technology attributes on purchase intention. Additionally, Hu et al. (2008) suggest that advanced technology components encompass both cognitive and affective elements. Building upon this foundation, Yuan and Dennis (2019) and Park et al. (2022) demonstrate the impact of customer consumer motivation through advanced technology on customer purchase intention. Other researchers, such as Hasan et al. (2021), Brakus et al. (2009), Lemon and Verhoef (2016), Leung et al. (2022) and Ray and Bala (2021) explore the relationship between customer experience and the intention to use advanced technology. Brakus et al. (2009) and Zha et al. (2020, 2022) define the concept of 'experience' as the way customers react subjectively, considering sensory, emotional, intellectual and behavioural aspects. This multifaceted experience has an impact on customers' intentions to use a product or service. In contrast, the studies conducted by Goli et al. (2023) and Pillai et al. (2020) focus on various factors like customisation, perceived usefulness, perceived ease of use and perceived enjoyment, all of which have a direct influence on customers' intentions to use advanced technology. However, it is worth noting that Pillai et al. (2020) introduce the interactivity factor in addition to the four factors mentioned above, emphasising its significance in relation to the intention to use advanced technology. On the other hand, Goli et al. (2023) expand upon this by introducing two additional factors, namely, perceived information quality and innovativeness which further influence the intention to use advanced technology.

Furthermore, Hsieh et al. (2023) identify three antecedents (consumer competitive arousal, gift design aesthetics and broadcaster's image) that may lead to continuous purchase intention. Authors (Akarsu et al., 2018, 2020; Barta Sergio & Carlos, 2019; Cuomo et al., 2021; Foroudi, Gupta, et al., 2018; Foroudi & Marvi, 2019) investigate perceived risk, decision consequences, satisfaction and engagement which influence user evaluation of the shopping experience through advanced technology. To comprehensively address the aim of this study, a combination of customer behaviour theory and the broaden-and-build theory is employed to examine the influence of the intention to use advanced technology on customer purchase intentions. These theories provide a robust conceptual framework for understanding how customers intend to incorporate advanced technology into their decision-making processes. Customer behaviour theory offers valuable insights into the factors that drive customer actions and choices. By exploring the intention to use advanced technology, this theory can shed light on the underlying motivations and drivers that influence customer purchase intentions. It provides a comprehensive understanding of the cognitive and behavioural aspects that shape customer behaviour in the context of advanced technology adoption.

In addition, the broaden-and-build theory plays a significant role in this research. This theory emphasises the significance of positive emotions and motivation in enhancing individual well-being and personal growth. It posits that positive emotions and motivation broaden an individual's range of thoughts and actions, leading to increased resilience and the accumulation of resources over time. By incorporating the broaden-and-build theory, this study aims to uncover how positive emotions and motivation related to advanced technology usage can positively impact customer purchase intentions. Both the positivist and interpretivist paradigms can effectively incorporate the broaden-and-build theory into their respective frameworks. This allows for a comprehensive analysis of the intentions and behaviours of customers using advanced technology, considering the various factors that shape their decision-making processes. By integrating these theories into the conceptual framework, this study seeks to provide a nuanced understanding of how the intention to use advanced technology influences customer purchase intentions by drawing on both cognitive and emotional perspectives. Considering these factors and their implications, the propositional framework here considers various elements related to the intention to purchase and use advanced technology, as well as their antecedents and consequences.

Literature Review

Motivation and Experience

Scholars have identified two main streams of motivation: hedonic values and utilitarian values (Babin et al., 1994; Scarpi et al., 2014; Wagner & Rudolph, 2010). Additionally, hedonic and socialisation motivations have been recognised as critical factors in the field of motivation (Kautish et al., 2023; Park et al., 2022). Kautish et al. (2023) introduce two additional motivations: functional and cognitive. Functional motivation involves practical benefits like enhanced performance, greater productivity and a sense of reduced risk (Foroudi et al., 2023; Vandecasteele & Geuens, 2010). These factors encourage customers to make use of advanced technology (Venkatraman & Price, 1990). On the flip side, cognitive motivation pertains to the longing for new experiences that engage the mind (Venkatraman & Price, 1990). Social motivation entails consumers driven by a need for social differentiation, using advanced technology-based products/services to enhance their social status or impress others (Brown & Venkatesh, 2005; Vandecasteele & Geuens, 2010).

Advanced technology provides valuable insights into the diverse drivers of customer motivation, encompassing functional, hedonic and utilitarian factors, as well as emotions, social influences and service situations (Vitezić & Perić, 2021). Motivations play a crucial role in shaping purchase intentions, and shopping behaviour is influenced by a range of factors that stimulate the intention to make purchases (Atalay & Meloy, 2011; Babin et al., 1994; Rick et al., 2014). However, existing literature does not adequately explain the motivations behind the use of advanced technology that triggers purchase intentions (Kautish et al., 2023). Therefore, it is essential to study motivations within the context of advanced technology, as emphasised in the psychological literature (Lin & Filieri, 2015).

Importantly, customer experiences with advanced technology products/ services have a significant impact on motivation, leading to higher customer retention and repurchasing, provided there are consistent experiences and perceived value (Pansari & Kumar, 2017; Park et al., 2022). Recognising and leveraging customer motivations throughout the purchase journey, facilitated by advanced technology, have the potential to greatly enhance the overall customer experience (Lemon & Verhoef, 2016). It is noteworthy that experiences and motivation work in synergy (Kautish et al., 2023). Hence, we propose the following hypothesis:

H1. Motivation to use advanced technology significantly consumer experience.

Experience and Intention to Use Advanced Technology

The customer experience involves a wide range of elements, including how customers think, feel and react on cognitive, emotional, social and physical levels to businesses, products and services (Pansari & Kumar, 2017; Verhoef et al., 2009). It occurs during the search for products, the shopping process, the receipt of service and the consumption of goods (Arnould & Price, 1993; Brakus et al., 2009; Holbrook, 2000). In the context of advanced technology, 'experience' involves the sensations, emotions, thoughts and actions triggered by interactions with advanced technology (adapted from Brakus et al., 2009). Previous research has employed the term 'experience' to define various reactions that occur either before or after using services or products (Brakus et al., 2009).

Experiences can arise in various settings, such as exposure to advertising, advanced technology and marketing communications, and the pattern of extended experiences, whether increasing or decreasing in intensity, can influence how they are evaluated (Ariely, 1998; Ariely & Zauberman, 2003; Brakus et al., 2009). The use of advanced technology allows for significant improvements in products and services, ultimately enhancing the consumer experience (Cukier, 2021). However, to gain a more comprehensive understanding, it is necessary to reframe the issue by examining what advanced technology truly entails and identifying the unique attributes that impact the customer experience. Furthermore, it is vital to highlight the connection between technology and customers as a give-and-take relationship, emphasising value exchange (Cukier, 2021). By examining these factors, we can acquire a better grasp of how advanced technology and customer experience interact (Cukier, 2021). This leads us to the following hypothesis:

H2. Experience significantly influences the intention to use advanced technology.

Intention to Use Advanced Technology and Post Content on Social Media

When customers evaluate the advantages of advanced technology (Kautish et al., 2023), they are more likely to engage with others, recommend its use and share their experiences on social media (Huang & Rust, 2018; Patel et al., 2024; Perez-Vega et al., 2021). This sharing of experiences can take the form of visual or non-visual posts (Ray & Bala, 2021). These interactions help raise awareness and encourage wider adoption of advanced technology (Esfahani & Reynolds, 2021; Patel et al., 2024).

Consequentially, the content shared by previous customers plays a crucial role in building confidence among current and potential customers when it comes to utilising advanced technology for their purchases. Positive posts on social media act as a catalyst, directing attention towards both favourable and unfavourable experiences with the offered products or services. This, in turn, significantly influences purchase decisions (Chung et al., 2020; Filieri, 2015; Patel et al., 2024; Wang et al., 2018) and further reinforces the intention to continue using advanced technology (Vlačić et al., 2021). Therefore, we propose the following hypothesis:

> *H3*. The intention to use advanced technology significantly influences posting content on social media.

Intention to Use Advanced Technology and Perceived Service/Product Value

The precision, valuable insights and interactive encounters provided by advanced technology significantly enhance customers' perceived value, subsequently affecting their intent to make a purchase (Yin & Qiu, 2021). When customers perceive that a company provides value-added services or products, this increases the likelihood of repurchase (Finn, 2012). Customer perceived value refers to the evaluation of the differences between what consumers pay and what they receive during the shopping process (Zeithaml, 1988), with an emphasis on value-for-money (Kim et al., 2017; Monroe, 1990; Sweeney & Soutar, 2001).

According to reports released by the Capgemini Digital Transformation Research Institute titled 'Secrets of Artificial Intelligence Winning Consumers: Enabling Human Intelligence' and 'Why consumers love generative AI', 38% of consumers have had positive experiences with advanced technology, leading to a significant increase in their purchase volume. Moreover, there is a great opportunity for businesses to incorporate advanced technology into their purchase processes, as 70% of consumers already rely on advanced technology tools for seeking recommendations on new products and services. Additionally, a majority of consumers (64%) are open to making purchases based on these recommendations. Hence, this directs us to the following hypothesis:

> *H4*. The intention to use advanced technology significantly influences perceived service/product value.

Intention to Use Advanced Technology and Reduce Risk of Online Buying

Research has shown that trust plays a vital role in determining the success or failure of an organisation. In the context of online shopping, where there is increased risk and uncertainty (Alqayed et al., 2022), maintaining high levels of information quality becomes crucial for establishing trust and reducing risk (Nicolaou & McKnight, 2006). Perceived information quality, characterised by the accuracy, reliability and appropriate level of detail of the data, is a key aspect in building trust (Barta et al., 2023). Advanced technology, such as Augmented Reality (AR) and Virtual Technology (Nazir et al., 2012), possesses these attributes and thus contributes to risk reduction and enhances the overall buying experience for customers (Barta et al., 2023). Hence, we propose the following hypothesis:

> *H5.* The intention to use advanced technology significantly influences the reduction of risk in online buying.

Intention to Use Advanced Technology and Decision Consequences

Advanced technology plays a significant role in shaping consumer behaviour as customers increasingly rely on various websites for their purchasing decisions (Duan et al., 2019). By offering speed, efficiency and a lack of judgemental bias compared to human decision-making processes, advanced technology instils decision confidence (Chattaraman et al., 2024). This is achievable by gathering extensive digital data, often referred to as Big Data, from various origins like chatbots, social media, emails, location-based ads and websites (Bag et al., 2021).

Companies have the opportunity to harness the influence of advanced technology by utilising it to predict customer behaviour (Duan et al., 2019). Additionally, engaging customers on social media platforms enables businesses to make more informed decisions through the analytical capabilities of advanced technology (Majeed et al., 2022). Through the gathering and analysis of data related to products or services, advanced technology reshapes the online shopping experience and fosters closer connections between customers and businesses (Dwivedi et al., 2021). Consequently, it is evident that advanced technology provides the means for customers to consider electronic word-of-mouth (eWOM) before making their final purchase decisions, which is highly valued by 90% of consumers (Akhtar et al., 2019; Rita et al., 2022). Hence, we propose the following hypothesis:

> *H6.* The intention to use advanced technology significantly influences decision consequences.

Post Content on Social Media and Satisfaction

Customers increasingly rely on social media platforms as a valuable source of information about products and services (Ma & Wang, 2021; Nazir et al., 2023). Among the various forms of content available on social media, customer reviews in the form of posts hold particular significance in providing crucial insights to customers (e.g. Chen & Xie, 2008; Shin et al., 2021). In comparison to information provided by marketers, customer reviews on social media are perceived as more credible (Bickart & Schindler, 2001; Chatterjee, 2001), have a greater influence on consumer choices (Huang & Chen, 2006) and play a pivotal role in reducing perceived uncertainty among consumers (Hu et al., 2008; Weathers et al., 2007).

Posting positive content on social media serves as an expression of customer satisfaction and can be regarded as an affective aspect of their overall contentment (Brakus et al., 2009; Oliver et al., 1997). Thus, customers who actively engage on social media platforms and share positive content are more likely to demonstrate higher levels of satisfaction with a particular product or service (Majeed et al., 2022; Mogaji et al., 2021). Therefore, we propose the following hypothesis:

H7. The act of posting content on social media significantly influences customer satisfaction.

Perceived Service/Product Value and Satisfaction

Perceived service/product value is a crucial determinant of customer decision-making, encompassing the evaluation of benefits received relative to the associated costs or sacrifices incurred when acquiring a product or service (Samudro & Sumarwan, 2020; Wu & Cheng, 2018). Customers' perceptions of receiving good value for their money leads to heightened satisfaction with their choices (Foroudi et al., 2023; Jin et al., 2013). In the advanced technology services, customers' overall satisfaction is significantly impacted by both experience quality and perceived value (Alqayed et al., 2021, 2022; Lei et al., 2023). Among the various dimensions of perceived value, functional aspects play a pivotal role in shaping customer satisfaction and influencing their behavioural intentions (Foroudi, Marvi, et al., 2020, 2022; Gupta et al., 2018; Ozdemir et al., 2020; Xu et al., 2022). Understanding and effectively managing perceived value is crucial for businesses aiming to enhance customer satisfaction and foster long-term loyalty in the competitive marketplace. This leads us to propose the following hypothesis:

H8. The perceived service/product value significantly influences customer satisfaction.

Reduced Risk of Online Buying and Satisfaction

Advanced technology has emerged as a key factor in mitigating the risks associated with online purchasing and enhancing overall customer satisfaction (Bhagat et al., 2023; Foroudi, Marvi, et al., 2019; Foroudi, Yu, et al., 2019; Foroudi, Cuomo, et al., 2020; Haenlein et al., 2019; Nazarian et al., 2021; Ruiz-Alba et al., 2022). Through the use of advanced technology in their purchasing processes, buyers can efficiently oversee and address a wide range of supplier-related risks in real time. These risks encompass ethical, climatic, logistical, environmental, geopolitical, financial and qualitative factors (Yang et al., 2017). The integration of advanced technology-based information systems also incorporates algorithms that analyse the market environment and provide buyers with valuable insights for decision-making. These algorithms assess proposed solutions, establish potential scenarios and offer suggestions that optimise performance while minimising risks (Allal-Chérif et al., 2021). Drawing from the existing literatures, we propose the following hypothesis:

H9. The reduced risk of online buying significantly influences customer satisfaction.

Decision Consequences and Satisfaction

When customers are trying to decide what to purchase, they often have thoughts and preferences about the choices available to them. These thoughts act as guides, making the decision process smoother by narrowing down the options to a smaller, more manageable group that they think about more carefully (Alba et al., 1997).

In today's world, the advanced technology integrated into online shopping websites plays a remarkable role in boosting people's confidence and comfort when they are making purchase decisions (Haenlein et al., 2019). Imagine having an extra dose of creativity and brainpower while deciding – this is what the technology offers. It is like having a helpful assistant that takes away some of the mental effort, allowing people to think more creatively and come up with new ideas (Heller et al., 2019). This added boost of creativity through technology makes people feel more assured about their choices, providing them with a sense of trust in the decisions that they are making (Jessen et al., 2020). Based on the existing literature, we propose the following hypothesis:

H10. The decision consequences significantly influence customer satisfaction.

Satisfaction and Engagement

In considering the concept of satisfaction as a whole, customer satisfaction can be seen as a multifaceted construct. It involves a response, which can be emotional or cognitive in nature, and this response is tied to various aspects, including expectations, the product itself, or the overall consumption experience. Additionally, the timing of this response varies, occurring after consumption, choice-making or based on cumulative experiences (Giese & Cote, 2000; Marvi et al., 2022; Nankali et al., 2022; Soltani et al., 2023). Advanced technology has been found to have a positive impact on customer satisfaction (Kautish et al., 2023; Kumar et al., 2016; Nica et al., 2022). This satisfaction, in turn, plays a significant role in shaping the relationship between a company and its customers (Barry et al., 2008, p. 155). The quality of this relationship is determined by the level of satisfaction derived from the interaction and the emotional connection that customers feel towards the relationship (Alqayed et al., 2022). When a firm successfully establishes trust and commitment and fosters a satisfied and emotionally connected relationship with customers, this leads to increased engagement between the firm and the customer (Pansari & Kumar, 2017). Following the existing literature, we propose the following hypothesis:

H11. Satisfaction significantly influences customer engagement.

Engagement and Repurchase Intention

Customer engagement (CE) can be defined as a psychological state arising from dynamic concretive interactions between customers and a central entity, often a brand, within specific service relationships. This state manifests itself in varying degrees of intensity based on context-specific factors. Importantly, it represents an ongoing cyclical process within these service relationships, where both parties collaboratively generate value (Maslowska et al., 2016). Firms place significant emphasis on customer engagement as a key focus area (Pansari & Kumar, 2017). A study conducted by Gallup, which involved 438 marketing managers, revealed the substantial impact of engagement on repurchasing intention. The research uncovered significant findings across various industries. In the consumer electronics sector, it was noted that highly engaged shoppers make 44% more visits to their preferred retailer each year compared to those who are not engaged. Moreover, engaged consumers typically spend an average of $373 per shopping trip, while those who are actively disengaged spend $289 per trip. Similarly, in casual restaurants, fully engaged customers visit 56% more often per month compared to actively disengaged customers. In fast-food restaurants, fully engaged customers make 28% more visits per month. In the hospitality sector, fully engaged hotel guests spend 46% more money per year compared to actively disengaged guests. Furthermore, in the insurance sector, fully engaged policy-holders purchase 22% more types of insurance products than actively disengaged policyholders (Pansari & Kumar, 2017). Drawing from the existing literature, we propose the following hypothesis:

H12. Engagement has a significant influence on repurchasing intention.

Research Approach

Hence, in this study the research design incorporates elements of both positivism and interpretivism, recognising the value of qualitative and quantitative approaches (Foroudi & Dennis, 2023; Foroudi & Foroudi, 2021). From a positivist perspective, behaviour theory is employed to develop and test the hypotheses through empirical observation and measurement of behaviour (Bandura & Walters, 1963; Ellis, 1962). Qualitative research methods, such as interviews or observations, are employed to gain a deeper understanding of the underlying factors influencing customer intentions and behaviours. Quantitative research methods, such as surveys or experiments, are utilised to investigate the relationships between variables and predict customer purchase intentions. On the other hand, from an interpretive perspective, behaviour theory is used to delve into the subjective meanings, motivations and interpretations that individuals assign to their behaviours.

The broaden-and-build theory also plays a significant role in this research. This theory focuses on positive emotions, motivation and their impact on individual well-being and personal growth. It suggests that positive emotions and motivation broaden an individual's thought–action repertoire, leading to increased resilience and the building of resources over time. From an interpretive perspective, qualitative research methods are employed to explore individuals' subjective experiences of positive emotions, their interpretations and their influence on intentions and behaviours. In-depth interviews capture the richness and nuances of these experiences. Both positivist and interpretivist paradigms can incorporate broaden-and-build theory. From a positivist perspective, quantitative research methods are used to measure and analyse positive emotions, well-being and their effects on customer purchase intentions. Surveys are conducted to examine the relationships between positive emotions, customer experiences and behavioural outcomes. For conducting a comprehensive level of analysis, we employ two-stage approach. The first stage utilises qualitative research methods, drawing from established methodologies such as Churchill (1979). This stage aims to explore the phenomenon in depth and develop a conceptual framework based on the qualitative findings and existing literature. The stage employs a quantitative research method to examine and validate the proposed theories and their relationships. By combining qualitative and quantitative approaches and integrating behaviour theory and broaden-and-build theory, this research aims to provide a comprehensive understanding of the impact of the intention to use advanced technology on customer purchase intention.

Churchill (1979) proposes specific approaches for developing and measuring constructs, which include the impact of advanced technology on customer purchase intention, literature examination, interviews and focus groups. In line with this recommendation, this study utilises a combination of methods to measure the customer purchase construct, which is the focal construct of this research. To gather comprehensive and insightful data, in-depth interviews and group discussions are conducted. This approach aligns with the work of Ritchie et al. (2003) and highlights the effectiveness of combining these methods to integrate existing knowledge with new perspectives. By engaging participants in focused discussions and interviews, this study gains valuable information and insights that may not have been captured through the literature review alone.

The use of qualitative data, primarily in the form of questionnaires, serves to complement the quantitative aspects of this study. This approach, as recommended by Churchill (1979), helps to mitigate any potential weaknesses in the development of a purely quantitative study. By incorporating qualitative data, the research can gather rich context-specific information that enhances the understanding and validity of the subsequent quantitative analysis. By employing a combination of in-depth interviews, focus groups and qualitative questionnaires, this study aims to collect comprehensive and diverse data that will enrich the exploration and measurement of the customer purchase construct. These methods go beyond the limitations of a purely quantitative study and contribute valuable insights to the research, ensuring a more robust and comprehensive understanding of the subject matter.

Data Collection and Data Analyses

This study aims to gather valuable insights into the intention to use advanced technology for purchase in the United Kingdom by conducting a survey of 750 respondents who actively engage with advanced technology in their purchasing process. The size of the sample is designed to ensure a comprehensive overview of individuals' activities and to achieve a deep understanding of the research goal (Kautish et al., 2023).

To analyse the data effectively, a rigorous approach is taken. The collected data, including interviews, are thoroughly reviewed multiple times to identify emerging patterns and themes. The information obtained is classified systematically to enable a comprehensive and objective analysis. Through dynamic analysis, the researchers compare and contrast the explanations found in the data to uncover meaningful insights.

The reliability and validity of the data are critical considerations in this study. Churchill (1979) emphasises the importance of ensuring the reliability and validity of the collected data, as they form the foundation for designing, analysing and assessing the research. To maintain reliability, the data are carefully reviewed and cross-checked to ensure consistency and accuracy. Validity is addressed by employing robust research methods, adhering to ethical standards and critically evaluating the data to ensure their relevance and representativeness. By employing a sample size of 750 respondents and conducting thorough data analysis with a focus on reliability and validity, this study aims to provide a comprehensive understanding of the intention to use advanced technology for purchase. The dynamic analysis approach helps to uncover patterns and insights, contributing to the overall research goal.

Furthermore, as defined by Anderson and Gerbing (1988), quantitative research involves explaining phenomena through the collection and analysis of numerical data using mathematically based methods, particularly statistics. In this phase, the focus is on collecting statistical data to gain a clearer understanding of the phenomenon under investigation and to address specific research problems using a quantitative approach. The second phase of this study utilises the conceptual model developed earlier to explore the impact of using advanced technology on customer purchase intentions. A sample size of 750 respondents has been selected to facilitate multivariate analysis of the data. This larger sample allows for a more comprehensive examination of the relationships between variables. The research employs various statistical and ML techniques to ensure the validity and reliability of the measures used. Exploratory factor analysis (EFA) is employed to explore the underlying factors and dimensions within the data. Cronbach's alpha is calculated to assess the internal consistency and reliability of the scales developed and adapted for the study. Confirmatory factor analysis (CFA) is conducted to validate the measurement model and ensure its robustness. To examine the hypothesised relationships between constructs, structural equation modelling (SEM) is applied. This statistical technique allows for a comprehensive analysis of the interrelationships between variables and provides insights into the overall fit of the model to the data (Foroudi et al., 2014). The model is assessed based on criteria such as good fit indices, convergent and discriminant validity, nomological validity and stable reliability. By employing a quantitative approach and utilising statistical techniques such as EFA, Cronbach's alpha, CFA and SEM, this phase of the study aims to provide a rigorous examination of the impact of advanced technology on customer purchase intentions. The application of these methods ensures the development of valid and reliable measures, as well as the comprehensive evaluation of the proposed model.

Sampling and Procedures

The research employs a deductive research approach, which is commonly associated with the survey method (Hyde, 2000). This approach is suitable for gathering specific data from respondents within a targeted population (Lefever et al., 2007). The sample for this study consists of customers in the United Kingdom, assess their intention to use advanced technology and its impact on purchase intention. The sampling procedure for data collection was purposive sampling (Kautish et al., 2023; Sharma, Dwivedi, et al., 2022) as it is considered to be cost effective and provides a homogenous sample for better managerial insights (Sharma, Fadahunsi, et al., 2022). The sample is selected based on entities that are accessible and can provide relevant answers (Foroudi et al., 2014). A total of 750 questionnaires are developed, aiming to achieve an appropriate ratio for structural equation modelling (Foroudi et al., 2014).

The respondents selected were those individuals who were adequately conversant with the use of advanced technology for purchase intention (Jain et al., 2022) and have previous experience using advanced technology for purchases. It is believed that this group will provide insights into the larger population. Self-administered questionnaires are developed and distributed among the participants. Before conducting the main survey, the questionnaire underwent a thorough review to assess reliability and validity, ensuring that the measures are free from error and will yield consistent results (Peter, 1979). The measures used in the survey are developed and examined for reliability to ensure their suitability for the study. By adopting a deductive research approach and utilising self-administered questionnaires, this study aims to collect data from a representative sample of customers in the United Kingdom. The research design, including the sample selection and questionnaire development, has been carefully planned to ensure reliability, validity and consistency in measuring the variables of interest.

Analysis

This phase of the study aims to provide a rigorous examination of the impact of advanced technology on customer purchase intentions by employing a quantitative methodology. Employing statistical methods including EFA, Cronbach's alpha, CFA and SEM enables a thorough evaluation of the proposed model. EFA facilitates the investigation of underlying factor structures and the identification of patterns and relationships between variables (Churchill, 1979). Using Cronbach's alpha, the internal consistency and reliability of the measurement scales can be evaluated, ensuring that the items measure the same construct in a consistent manner. Confirmatory Factor Analysis CFA is applied to test the hypothesised factor structure and determine whether the observed variables correlate to the anticipated latent factors. This method enables this study to confirm or refute their initial hypotheses and validate the underlying construct measurements (Balakrishnan & Dwivedi, 2021). In addition, SEM combines factor analysis and multiple regression analysis in order to evaluate both the measurement model and the structural relationships among latent variables (Fornell & Larcker, 1981; Gefen et al., 2000; MacCallum & Austin, 2000; Steenkamp & Baumgartner, 2000). SEM provides an exhaustive evaluation of the proposed theoretical model, ensuring an in-depth comprehension of the impact of advanced technology on customer purchase intentions. Using these statistical techniques, this study is designed to develop valid and reliable measures while conducting a thorough examination of the complex links between advanced technology and customer purchase intentions.

A two-step approach is taken using the Anderson and Gerbing (1988) two-stage procedure. First, the CFA is conducted to allow a stricter assessment of construct unidimensionality; the examination of each subset of items is internally consistent and validated the constructs on the basis of the measurement models (Anderson & Gerbing, 1988; Balakrishnan & Dwivedi, 2021). Following that step, the structural model fit is tested through goodness-of-fit indices and simultaneously estimated the paths between the constructs to assess the study hypotheses.

Conclusion

Hence, it is crucial to investigate how advanced technology contributes to fostering a positive attitude and purchase intention. This study identifies that advanced technology plays a dominant role in creating a more favourable attitude and increasing the intention to make a purchase. To gain a detailed understanding of the factors that influence individuals' intention to use advanced technology, the research proposes a number of hypotheses related to different aspects of motivation and experience. These include functional, hedonic, social and cognitive motivations, as well as affective, intellectual, sensory and behavioural experiences. By examining these specific elements, the study aims to provide a comprehensive understanding of the factors that shape individuals' willingness to adopt and utilise advanced technology. Furthermore, the findings of this study can be extended to apply to emerging advanced technologies that involve interaction between humans and machines. As technology continues to progress, it becomes crucial to comprehend the dynamics between individuals and new forms of advanced technology. Therefore, the results of this research have broader implications and can guide the future development of human–machine interaction, thus ensuring the design of advanced technological systems that are user-friendly and well-informed.

Theoretical Contributions

This study has important theoretical contributions. Firstly, it addresses the need for research that explores the intersection of advanced technology and marketing, as suggested by Vlačić et al. (2021). By examining various outcomes such as purchase intention, social media post content, the perceived value of service/product, risk reduction in online buying, decision consequences, satisfaction, engagement and repurchase intention resulting from the intention to use advanced technology, this study provides valuable theoretical insights for the fields of marketing and customer behaviour. Second, this study applies customer behaviour theory and the broaden-and-build theory to the intention of using advanced technology. It advances the current understanding of customer motivations for adopting advanced technology, as proposed by Vandecasteele and Geuens (2010). While a few studies have explored customer motivations for using AI-enabled technologies (e.g. Kautish et al., 2023; Lalicic & Weismayer, 2021), their effects on purchase intention were not known, and the focus was limited to specific market fields. Previous studies on advanced technology's impact on purchase intention (e.g. Kautish et al., 2023; Morotti et al., 2022; Speicher, 2018) did not identify the antecedents and consequences of the intention to use advanced technology that affects purchase intentions.

Scholars have acknowledged the importance of advanced technology use for purchase intention in certain fields (Chung et al., 2020; Kautish & Khare, 2022) as well as the motivations behind its usage (Rodgers, 2003). Thus, this study makes a significant theoretical contribution to the existing literature. Furthermore, this study examines, for the first time, the impact of motivational and experiential factors on purchase intention within the context of advanced technology. Based on the customer behaviour theory and the broaden-and-build theory, the proposed framework explains the relationship between motivation, experience with advanced technology and various outcomes, including purchase intention, social media post content, the perceived value of service/product, risk reduction in online buying, decision consequences, satisfaction, engagement and repurchase intention. Consequently, this study advances the customer behaviour theory and the broaden-and-build theory in the context of advanced technology and its influence on purchase intention. It demonstrates that different facets of motivation (functional, hedonic, social, and cognitive) and experience factors (affective, intellectual, sensory and behavioural) shape purchase intention based on advanced technology, along with its consequences. These constructs warrant further investigation.

Managerial Contributions

According to Bhagat et al. (2023), Kumar et al. (2016) and Nazir et al. (2023), advanced technology-enabled intelligent agents have the potential to offer customised products and services, providing valuable insights into purchase behaviour, the customer journey, experience and satisfaction. This study suggests that motivation, experience and other important factors related to the intention to use advanced technology influence purchase intention and its outcomes. Therefore, companies can emphasise the social acceptance of utilising advanced technology. Furthermore, empirical evidence from this research indicates that advanced technology enhances the purchase experience and customer satisfaction. The findings also reveal that experience plays a crucial role in driving engagement and repurchase intentions. As a result, firms should focus on improving the purchase experience through advanced technology. For example, incorporating human-like features into advanced technology can create a pristine experience and enhance customer satisfaction.

When customers share their experiences and interact with e-commerce platforms through user-generated content on social media, these interactions can be noticed by other social networks, thereby enhancing credibility and customer engagement. Therefore, using advanced technology in purchase processes can encourage customers to share their experiences on various platforms. This approach allows for mutually engaging in communication and greater integration of customers in firms' activities, ultimately benefiting companies. By utilising advanced technology in purchase processes, companies can provide customers with access to credible information, convenient purchasing options, decision consequences and a reduced risk of online buying. The use of advanced technology in purchase processes also stimulates interest, encourages repurchase intentions and fosters favourable attitudes, strong attachments and higher purchase intentions. Additionally, the data obtained and the research elements provide insights into the purchase behaviour of British customers to a certain extent.

Case Study: The Importance of the Impact of Intention to Use Advanced Technology on Customer Purchase Intention in the Retail Sector in the United Kingdom

The use of advanced technology significantly influences customer purchase intentions (Acquila-Natale & Iglesias-Pradas, 2021). It is worth noting that advanced technology is not just changing customer behaviour and purchase intentions but also reshaping customer landscape and purchasing process (Balakrishnan & Dwivedi, 2021; Jeon, 2022; Rodgers & Nguyen, 2022; Wen Wan et al., 2017). Customers are now more confident and have more convenient ways to interact with businesses and make purchases by using advanced technology. It has made the process smoother and more efficient for customers. Additionally, there's a growing trend towards online purchases that utilise advanced technology, and this trend is expected to keep growing and improving in the future. Using advanced technology in the buying process benefits not only customers and companies but also the broader economy. A study by the Centre for Economics and Business Research (CEBR) (2021) suggests that continuous investment in advanced technology could lead to a significant transformation in the retail industry and contribute to the growth of the UK economy. In fact, it is estimated that this investment could boost the UK's Gross Domestic Product (GDP) by as much as £232 billion by the year 2040. Furthermore, the study by CEBR (2021) also mentions that the retail sector itself stands to gain substantially from advanced technology adoption, with a forecasting increase of 6%, equivalent to £21 billion, in its total revenue by 2040. This demonstrates how advanced technology has the potential to drive economic growth and prosperity at both the industrial and national levels. Although advanced technology is still in its early stages of development, its vast potential benefits are already quite evident. Nowhere is this more apparent than in the retail and consumer products, which has already experienced substantial changes due to technological advancements. The influence of advanced technology on the retail sector can be outlined as follows:

Personalisation: Previously, personalising experiences relied on basic rules. However, with the growth of ML, one of the advanced technology techniques, it is now possible to analyse vast and seemingly unrelated datasets rapidly and thoroughly. This enables real-time actions based on the analysis, elevating personalisation to a whole new level.

Product recommendations: Among the widely recognised applications of advanced technology today is the automated recommendation of products and services to shoppers. These recommendation engines, powered by advanced technology, come in various levels of sophistication. Advanced algorithms can seamlessly connect diverse data points like purchasing patterns, viewed images, social media activity, location, basket analysis, shelf allocation analysis, or even weather conditions, in real time.

Chatbots, virtual assistants, self-service kiosks and in-store robots: Advanced technology finds its most established applications in chatbots, which mimic human conversations through text or speech. They often handle customer service inquiries, FAQs, delivery updates and product recommendations. Virtual assistants, like smart speakers, respond to verbal commands using natural language systems. They are always accessible, eliminating the need to visit a webpage and are increasingly integrated into devices like phones or smart homes. *Checkout-less payment:* Retailers, especially grocery stores, have long used cashier-less payment systems. The next evolution is checkout-less payment, where embedded sensors, deep learning and computer vision automate the process. Shoppers can now select their products and exit the store with minimal friction. Some companies like British groceries retailer 'Tesco' have established some branches in the United Kingdom, with customers benefiting from the checkout payments. *Dynamic pricing:* This practice involves adjusting item prices based on a customer's perceived willingness to pay. A well-known example is airlines changing flight costs depending on factors like destination, time of day, or time of year. The next step involves determining prices based on a customer's search history, buying habits or even their voice tone. Advanced technology enables real-time, personalised price adjustments, benefiting customers with more competitive pricing and better deals. *Drones:* Advanced technology-powered drones offer the potential for online order fulfilment. Commercial drones are estimated to have revenue from parcel drone delivery totalling US $113 billion by 2030 (ARK Investment Management LLC, 2020). This makes drone deliveries appealing to both retailers and consumers. Although tech giants are exploring drone delivery systems, consumer adoption remains a work in progress. Recently, the Royal Mail initiated parcel shipments via drones in some UK areas. *Service and support:* Outstanding or poor customer service can determine whether a customer remains loyal or abandons a brand (Foroudi, 2019, 2020, 2023). Many elements that constitute effective human service-such as consistency, personalisation, accurate product information and clear communication, can now be replicated or improved through advanced technology applications. As consumers become increasingly accustomed to non-human interactions for customer service matters, the use of advanced technology applications is expected to grow. Despite the numerous benefits that advanced technology has brought to the UK retail industry, it also raises privacy concerns. Research conducted by Retail Economics in 2023 reveals that only 17% of customers trust retailers and customer companies to handle sensitive data properly, while 85% of organisations believe that customers will be receptive to advanced technology-powered solutions.

Case Study Questions

(1) In your opinion, which aspects of advanced technology do you find most beneficial in the purchase process?
(2) Besides privacy, are there any other concerns that customers have about using advanced technology in their purchase processes?
(3) What are the main challenges that the retail sector faces when implementing advanced technology in their operations?

Key Terms and Definitions

Functional motivation: It reflects the utilitarian benefits, such as improved performance, increased productivity and perceived risk, which prompt the customer to use a product or service.

Hedonic motivation: It reflects the affective or sensory stimulation and gratification that prompt the customer to use a product or service.

Social motivation: It reflects a self-assertive social need to elevate social status or make an impression, prompting the customer to use a product or service.

Cognitive motivation: It reflects the desire for new experiences to stimulate the mind, prompting the customer to use a product or service.

Affective experience: It reflects the feelings induced due to the emotional interaction of the customer with a product or service.

Intellectual experience: It reflects the excitement that arises within a customer due to the creativity of a product or service.

Sensory experience: It reflects an individual's perception of a product or service, which stimulates his/her senses or mind.

Behavioural experience: It reflects various lifestyles and interactions with a product and service.

Post visual content on social media: It refers to the sharing of experiences in the form of visual posts on social media and forums.

Post non-visual content on social media: It refers to the sharing of experiences in the form of non-visual posts on social media and forums.

Substitutive perceived product/service value: It is characterised as the comprehensive evaluation by the customer of the outcomes associated with utilising a service or product, grounded in perceptions of what is received and what is given.

Functional perceived product/service value: It is characterised as the customer's comprehensive evaluation of the usefulness of a product, rooted in perceptions of what is received and what is given.

Reduced risk in online purchasing: It is defined as a diminishing perception of potential drawbacks in terms of performance, financial concerns, time constraints, safety, social aspects and psychological factors in online purchase.

Decision comfort: It is defined as the degree of psychological (and physiological) ease, contentment and well-being one feels in relation to a specific decision.

Decision confidence: It is defined as a cognition-based evaluation influenced by factors such as the balance of arguments for and against the chosen option, the amount of information available prior to the decision and between alternative conflicts.

References

Acquila-Natale, E., & Iglesias-Pradas, S. (2021). A matter of value? Predicting channel preference and multichannel behaviors in retail. *Technological Forecasting and Social Change, 162*, 120401.

Akarsu, T. N., Foroudi, P., & Melewar, T. (2020). What makes Airbnb likeable? Exploring the nexus between service attractiveness, country image, perceived authenticity and experience from a social exchange theory perspective within an emerging economy context. *International Journal of Hospitality Management, 91*, 102635.

Akarsu, T., Melewar, T., Mouroti, O., & Foroudi, P. (2018). *The impact of brand sensuality and brand experience on consumers' fashion product purchases: The moderating role of religiosity.* http://eprints.soton.ac.uk/id/eprint/434606

Akhtar, N., Kim, W. G., Ahmad, W., Akhtar, M. N., Siddiqi, U. I., & Riaz, M. (2019). Mechanisms of consumers' trust development in reviewers' supplementary reviews: A reviewer-reader similarity perspective. *Tourism Management Perspectives, 31*, 95–108.

Alba, J., Lynch, J., Weitz, B., Janiszewski, C., Lutz, R., Sawyer, A., & Wood, S. (1997). Interactive home shopping: Consumer, retailer, and manufacturer incentives to participate in electronic marketplaces. *Journal of Marketing, 61*(3), 38–53.

Allal-Chérif, O., Simón-Moya, V., & Ballester, A. C. C. (2021). Intelligent purchasing: How artificial intelligence can redefine the purchasing function. *Journal of Business Research, 124*, 69–76.

Alqayed, Y., Foroudi, P., Kooli, K., Foroudi, M. M., & Dennis, C. (2022). Enhancing value co-creation behaviour in digital peer-to-peer platforms: An integrated approach. *International Journal of Hospitality Management, 102*, 103140.

Alqayed, Y., Foroudi, P., Kooli, K., Foroudi, M., & Ferri, M. A. (2021). Exploring value co-creation concept: A bibliometric analysis of 20 years of research and theory. *Sustainable Branding: Ethical, Social, and Environmental Cases and Perspectives*, 291–309.

Anderson, J. C., & Gerbing, D. W. (1988). Structural equation modeling in practice: A review and recommended two-step approach. *Psychological Bulletin, 103*(3), 411.

Ariely, D. (1998). Combining experiences over time: The effects of duration, intensity changes and on-line measurements on retrospective pain evaluations. *Journal of Behavioral Decision Making, 11*(1), 19–45.

Ariely, D., & Zauberman, G. (2003). Differential partitioning of extended experiences. *Organizational Behavior and Human Decision Processes, 91*(2), 128–139.

ARK Investment Management LLC. (2020). Parcel drone delivery: Capitalizing on tech breakthroughs. https://ark-invest.com/articles/analyst-research/parcel-drone-delivery/

Arnould, E. J., & Price, L. L. (1993). River magic: Extraordinary experience and the extended service encounter. *Journal of Consumer Research, 20*(1), 24–45.

Atalay, A. S., & Meloy, M. G. (2011). Retail therapy: A strategic effort to improve mood. *Psychology and Marketing, 28*(6), 638–659.

Aw, E. C. X., Tan, G. W. H., Cham, T. H., Raman, R., & Ooi, K. B. (2022). Alexa, what's on my shopping list? Transforming customer experience with digital voice assistants. *Technological Forecasting and Social Change, 180*, 121711.

Babin, B. J., Darden, W. R., & Griffin, M. (1994). Work and/or fun: Measuring hedonic and utilitarian shopping value. *Journal of Consumer Research, 20*(4), 644–656. https://doi.org/10.1086/209376

Bag, S., Pretorius, J. H. C., Gupta, S., & Dwivedi, Y. K. (2021). Role of institutional pressures and resources in the adoption of big data analytics powered artificial intelligence, sustainable manufacturing practices and circular economy capabilities. *Technological Forecasting and Social Change, 163*, 120420.

Balakrishnan, J., & Dwivedi, Y. K. (2021). Conversational commerce: Entering the next stage of AIpowered digital assistants. *Annals of Operations Research*, 1–35.

Balakrishnan, J., & Foroudi, P. (2020). Does corporate reputation matter? Role of social media in consumer intention to purchase innovative food product. *Corporate Reputation Review, 23*, 181–200.

Bandura, A., & Walters, R. H. (1963). *Social learning and personality development.* Holt Rinehart and Winston.

Barry, J. M., Dion, P., & Johnson, W. (2008). A cross-cultural examination of relationship strength in B2B services. *Journal of Services Marketing, 22*(2), 114–135.

Barta, S., Gurrea, R., & Flavián, C. (2023). How augmented reality increases engagement through its impact on risk and the decision process. *Cyberpsychology, Behavior, and Social Networking, 26*(3), 177–187.

Barta Sergio, G. R., & Carlos, F. (2019). How augmented reality increases engagement through its impact on risk and the decision process. *Cyberpsychology, Behavior, and Social Networking*, 2–3.

Bhagat, R., Chauhan, V., & Bhagat, P. (2023). Investigating the impact of artificial intelligence on consumer's purchase intention in e-retailing. *Foresight, 25*(2), 249–263.

Bickart, B., & Schindler, R. M. (2001). Internet forums as influential sources of consumer information. *Journal of Interactive Marketing, 15*(3), 31–40.

Brakus, J. J., Schmitt, B. H., & Zarantonello, L. (2009). Brand experience: What is it? How is it measured? Does it affect loyalty? *Journal of Marketing, 73*(3), 52–68.

Brown, A. B., & Venkatesh, V. V. (2005). Qjarterty. *Management Information Systems Research Center, 29*(3), 399–426.

Centre for Economics and Business Research. (2021). *Retail week: The £21bn opportunity – How digital investment can transform the retail sector.* https://cebr. com/reports/retail-week-the-21bn-opportunity-how-digital-investment-can-transform-the-retail-sector/

Chattaraman, V., Kwon, W. S., Ross, K., Sung, J., Alikhademi, K., Richardson, B., & Gilbert, J. E. (2024). 'Smart' choice? Evaluating AI-based mobile decision bots for in-store decision-making. *Journal of Business Research, 183*, 114801.

Chatterjee, P. (2001). Online reviews: Do consumers use them? *Advances in Consumer Research, 28*(1), 129–133.

Chen, Y. L., Chen, J. M., & Tung, C. W. (2006). A data mining approach for retail knowledge discovery with consideration of the effect of shelf-space adjacency on sales. *Decision Support Systems, 42*(3), 1503–1520.

Chen, Y., & Xie, J. (2008). Online consumer review: Word-of-mouth as a new element of marketing communication mix. *Management Science, 54*(3), 477–491.

Cheng, L. C., & Sun, L. M. (2012). Exploring consumer adoption of new services by analyzing the behavior of 3G subscribers: An empirical case study. *Electronic Commerce Research and Applications, 11*(2), 89–100.

Chung, M., Ko, E., Joung, H., & Kim, S. J. (2020). Chatbot e-service and customer satisfaction regarding luxury brands. *Journal of Business Research, 117*, 587–595.

Churchill, G. A., Jr. (1979). A paradigm for developing better measures of marketing constructs. *Journal of Marketing Research, 16*(1), 64–73.

Cukier, K. (2021). Commentary: How AI shapes consumer experiences and expectations. *Journal of Marketing, 85*(1), 152–155.

Cuomo, M. T., Tortora, D., Foroudi, P., Giordano, A., Festa, G., & Metallo, G. (2021). Digital transformation and tourist experience co-design: Big social data for planning cultural tourism. *Technological Forecasting and Social Change, 162*, 120345.

Duan, Y., Edwards, J. S., & Dwivedi, Y. K. (2019). Artificial intelligence for decision making in the era of Big Data–evolution, challenges and research agenda. *International Journal of Information Management, 48*, 63–71.

Dwivedi, Y. K., Hughes, L., Ismagilova, E., Aarts, G., Coombs, C., Crick, T., Duan, Y., Dwivedi, R., Edwards, J., Eirug, A., Galanos, V., Ilavarasan, P. V., Janssen, M., Jones, P., Kar, A. K., Kizgin, H., Kronemann, B., Lal, B., Lucini, B., … & Williams, M. D. (2021). Artificial Intelligence (AI): Multidisciplinary perspectives on emerging challenges, opportunities, and agenda for research, practice and policy. *International Journal of Information Management, 57*, 101994.

Ellis, A. (1962). *Reason and emotion in psychotherapy.* Lyle Stuart.

Esfahani, M. S., & Reynolds, N. (2021). Impact of consumer innovativeness on really new product adoption. *Marketing Intelligence & Planning, 39*(4), 589–612.

Fakhreddin, F., & Foroudi, P. (2022). Instagram influencers: The role of opinion leadership in consumers' purchase behavior. *Journal of Promotion Management, 28*(6), 795–825.

Filieri, R. (2015). What makes online reviews helpful? A diagnosticity-adoption framework to explain informational and normative influences in e-WOM. *Journal of Business Research, 68*(6), 1261–1270.

Finn, A. (2012). Customer delight: Distinct construct or zone of nonlinear response to customer satisfaction? *Journal of Services Research, 15*(1), 99–110.

Fornell, C., & Larcker, D. F. (1981). Structural equation models with unobservable variables and measurement error: Algebra and statistics. https://doi.org/10.1177/002224378101800313

Foroudi, P. (2019). Influence of brand signature, brand awareness, brand attitude, brand reputation on hotel industry's brand performance. *International Journal of Hospitality Management, 76*, 271–285.

Foroudi, P. (2020). Corporate brand strategy: Drivers and outcomes of hotel industry's brand orientation. *International Journal of Hospitality Management, 88*, 102519.

Foroudi, P. (2023). Conceptualizing, measuring, and managing marketing assets: Developing the marketing assets, communication focus, and capability nexus. *Corporate Reputation Review, 26*(3), 203–222.

Foroudi, P., Cuomo, M. T., & Foroudi, M. M. (2020). Continuance interaction intention in retailing: Relations between customer values, satisfaction, loyalty, and identification. *Information Technology & People, 33*(4), 1303–1326.

Foroudi, P., & Dennis, C. (2023). *Researching and analysing business: Research methods in practice*. Routledge.

Foroudi, M. M., & Foroudi, P. (2021). *Corporate brand design: Developing and managing brand identity*. Routledge.

Foroudi, P., Gupta, S., Sivarajah, U., & Broderick, A. (2018). Investigating the effects of smart technology on customer dynamics and customer experience. *Computers in Human Behavior, 80*, 271–282.

Foroudi, P., Jin, Z., Gupta, S., Foroudi, M. M., & Kitchen, P. J. (2018). Perceptional components of brand equity: Configuring the symmetrical and asymmetrical paths to brand loyalty and brand purchase intention. *Journal of Business Research, 89*, 462–474.

Foroudi, P., & Marvi, R. (2019). Love is the bridge between you and everything: Relationships of identity, experience, and benevolence to travelers' loyalty and willingness to purchase. In *Tourism, hospitality and digital transformation* (pp. 47–72). Routledge.

Foroudi, P., Marvi, R., & Colmekcioglu, N. (2022). Antecedents and consequences of co-creation value with a resolution of complex P2P relationships. *International Journal of Contemporary Hospitality Management, 34*(12), 4355–4388.

Foroudi, P., Marvi, R., Cuomo, M. T., Bagozzi, R., Dennis, C., & Jannelli, R. (2023). Consumer perceptions of sustainable development goals: Conceptualization, measurement and contingent effects. *British Journal of Management, 34*(3), 1157–1183.

Foroudi, P., Marvi, R., & Kizgin, H. (2020). The others: The role of individual personality, cultural acculturation, and perceived value on towards firm's social media and acculturation orientation. *International Journal of Information Management, 52*, 102075.

Foroudi, P., Marvi, R., & Nazarian, A. (2019). Whispering experience: Configuring the symmetrical and asymmetrical paths to travelers' satisfaction and passion. In *Place branding: Connecting tourist experiences to places*. Routledge.

Foroudi, P., Melewar, T. C., & Gupta, S. (2014). Linking corporate logo, corporate image, and reputation: An examination of consumer perceptions in the financial setting. *Journal of Business Research, 67*(11), 2269–2281.

Foroudi, P., Yu, Q., Gupta, S., & Foroudi, M. M. (2019). Enhancing university brand image and reputation through customer value co-creation behaviour. *Technological Forecasting and Social Change, 138,* 218–227.

Gefen, D., Straub, D., & Boudreau, M. C. (2000). Structural equation modeling and regression: Guidelines for research practice. *Communications of the Association for Information Systems, 4*(1), 7.

Giese, J. L., & Cote, J. A. (2000). Defining consumer satisfaction. *Academy of Marketing Science Review, 1*(1), 1–22.

Goli, M., Sahu, A. K., Bag, S., & Dhamija, P. (2023). Users' acceptance of artificial intelligence-based chatbots: An empirical study. *International Journal of Technology and Human Interaction, 19*(1), 1–18.

Gupta, S., Foroudi, P., & Yen, D. (2018). Investigating relationship types for creating brand value for resellers. *Industrial Marketing Management, 72,* 37–47.

Ha, S. H., Bae, S. M., & Park, S. C. (2002). Customer's time-variant purchase behavior and corresponding marketing strategies: An online retailer's case. *Computers & Industrial Engineering, 43*(4), 801–820.

Haenlein, M., Kaplan, A., Tan, C. W., & Zhang, P. (2019). Artificial intelligence (AI) and management analytics. *Journal of Management Analytics, 6*(4), 341–343.

Hasan, M. R., Abdunurova, A., Wang, W., Zheng, J., & Shams, S. R. (2021). Using deep learning to investigate digital behavior in culinary tourism. *Journal of Place Management and Development, 14*(1), 43–65.

He, Z., Zhou, Y., Wang, J., Li, C., Wang, M., & Li, W. (2021). The impact of motivation, intention, and contextual factors on green purchasing behavior: New energy vehicles as an example. *Business Strategy and the Environment, 30*(2), 1249–1269.

Heller, J., Chylinski, M., de Ruyter, K., Mahr, D., & Keeling, D. I. (2019). Let me imagine that for you: Transforming the retail frontline through augmenting customer mental imagery ability. *Journal of Retailing, 95*(2), 94–114.

Holbrook, M. B. (2000). The millennial consumer in the texts of our times: Experience and entertainment. *Journal of Macromarketing, 20*(2), 178–192.

Hsieh, J. K., Kunz, W. H., & Wu, A. Y. (2023). Virtual gifting behavior on new social media: The perspectives of the community gift-giving model and face-negotiation theory. *Internet Research, 33*(4), 1597–1632.

Hsu, C. L., & Lin, J. C. C. (2021). Factors affecting customers' intention to voice shopping over smart speaker從智慧音箱品質、互補性與隱私風險探討影響智慧音箱使用者語音購物因素. *Service Industries Journal, 0*(0), 1–21. https://doi.org/10.1080/02642069.2021.2008913

Hu, N., Liu, L., & Zhang, J. J. (2008). Do online reviews affect product sales? The role of reviewers' characteristics and temporal effects. *Information Technology and Management, 9,* 201–214.

Huang, J. H., & Chen, Y. F. (2006). Herding in online product choice. *Psychology and Marketing, 23*(5), 413–428.

Huang, M. H., & Rust, R. (2018). Artificial intelligence in service. *Journal of Services Research, 21*(2), 155–172.

Huang, M. H., & Rust, R. T. (2021). A strategic framework for artificial intelligence in marketing. *Journal of the Academy of Marketing Science, 49*(1), 30–50. https://doi.org/10.1007/S11747-020-00749-9/TABLES/4

Hyde, K. F. (2000). Recognising deductive processes in qualitative research. *Qualitative Market Research: An International Journal, 3*(2), 82–90.

Jain, S., Basu, S., Dwivedi, Y. K., & Kaur, S. (2022). Interactive voice assistants – Does brand credibility assuage privacy risks. *Journal of Business Research,* 701–717. https://doi.org/10.1016/j.jbusres.2021.10.007

Jain, S., & Gandhi, A. V. (2021). Impact of artificial intelligence on impulse buying behaviour of Indian shoppers in fashion retail outlets. *International Journal of Innovation Science, 13*(2), 193–204.

Jang, Y. T. J., Liu, A. Y., & Ke, W. Y. (2022). *Exploring smart retailing: Anthropomorphism in voice shopping of smart speaker.* Information Technology and People. https://doi.org/10.1108/ITP-07-2021-0536

Jeon, Y. A. (2022). Let me transfer you to our AI-based manager: Impact of manager-level job titles assigned to AI-based agents on marketing outcomes. *Journal of Business Research, 145*(March), 892–904. https://doi.org/10.1016/j.jbusres.2022.03.028

Jessen, A., Hilken, T., Chylinski, M., Mahr, D., Heller, J., Keeling, D. I., & de Ruyter, K. (2020). The playground effect: How augmented reality drives creative customer engagement. *Journal of Business Research, 116,* 85–98.

Jin, N. P., Lee, S., & Lee, H. (2013). Examining the effects of perceived value and satisfaction on customer loyalty: A case of full-service restaurants in South Korea. *Journal of Hospitality Marketing & Management, 22*(3), 307–326. https://doi.org/10.1080/19368623.2013.744661

Kalsoom, U., Foroudi, P., Melewar, T., & Chapman, A. (2023). Marketing in the industry 4.0: The role of mobile technologies to enhance consumer brand experience, brand advocacy, and brand purchase intentions. In *Digital transformation and corporate branding* (pp. 241–258). Routledge.

Kar, B., Tripathy, A., & Pathak, M. D. (2022). What causes product returns in online purchases? A review and research agenda. *Prabandhan: Indian Journal of Management, 15*(4), 46–62.

Katakam, B. S., Bhukya, R., Bellamkonda, R. S., & Samala, N. (2021). Longitudinal analysis versus cross-sectional analysis in assessing the factors influencing shoppers' impulse purchase behavior – Do the store ambience and salesperson interactions really matter? *Journal of Retailing and Consumer Services, 61,* 102586.

Kautish, P., & Khare, A. (2022). Investigating the moderating role of AI-enabled services on flow and awe experience. *International Journal of Information Management, 66,* 102519.

Kautish, P., Purohit, S., Filieri, R., & Dwivedi, Y. K. (2023). Examining the role of consumer motivations to use voice assistants for fashion shopping: The mediating role of awe experience and eWOM. *Technological Forecasting and Social Change, 190,* 122407.

Kharfan, M., Chan, V. W. K., & Firdolas Efendigil, T. (2021). A data-driven forecasting approach for newly launched seasonal products by leveraging machine-learning approaches. *Annals of Operations Research, 303*(1–2), 159–174. https://doi.org/10.1007/s10479-020-03666-w

Kim, J. W., Lee, B. H., Shaw, M. J., Chang, H. L., & Nelson, M. (2001). Application of decision-tree induction techniques to personalized advertisements on internet storefronts. *International Journal of Electronic Commerce, 5*(3), 45–62. https://doi.org/10.1080/10864415.2001.11044215

Kim, S. Y., Kim, J. U., & Park, S. C. (2017). The effects of perceived value, website trust and hotel trust on online hotel booking intention. *Sustainability, 9*(12), 2262.

Kumar, V., Dixit, A., Javalgi, R. G., & Dass, M. (2016). Research framework, strategies, and applications of intelligent agent technologies (IATs) in marketing. *Journal of the Academy of Marketing Science, 44*, 24–45.

Lalicic, L., & Weismayer, C. (2021). Consumers' reasons and perceived value co-creation of using artificial intelligence-enabled travel service agents. *Journal of Business Research, 129*, 891–901.

Lefever, S., Dal, M., & Matthíasdóttir, Á. (2007). Online data collection in academic research: Advantages and limitations. *British Journal of Educational Technology, 38*(4), 574–582.

Lei, C., Hossain, M. S., & Wong, E. (2023). The impact of experience quality and perceived value on customer satisfaction with advanced technology services. *International Journal of Technology and Human Interaction, 19*(2), 58–77. https://doi.org/10.4018/IJTHI.2023040104

Lemon, K. N., & Verhoef, P. C. (2016). Understanding customer experience throughout the customer journey. *Journal of Marketing, 80*(6), 69–96. https://doi.org/10.1509/jm.15.0420

Leung, W. K., Chang, M. K., Cheung, M. L., & Shi, S. (2022). VR tourism experiences and tourist behavior intention in COVID-19: An experience economy and mood management perspective. *Information Technology and People, 36*(3), 1095–1125. https://doi.org/10.1108/ITP-06-2021-0423

Li, L., Ma, S., Han, X., Zheng, C., & Wang, D. (2020). Data-driven online service supply chain: A demand-side and supply-side perspective. *Journal of Enterprise Information Management, 34*(1), 365–381. https://doi.org/10.1108/JEIM11-2019-0352

Lin, Z., & Filieri, R. (2015). 'Airline passengers' continuance intention towards online check-in services: The role of personal innovativeness and subjective knowledge. *Transportation Research Part E: Logistics and Transportation Review, 81*, 158–168. https://doi.org/10.1016/j.tre.2015.07.001

Luo, X., Tong, S., Fang, Z., & Qu, Z. (2019). Frontiers: Machines vs. humans: The impact of artificial intelligence chatbot disclosure on customer purchases. *Marketing Science, 38*(6), 937–947.

Ma, R., & Wang, W. (2021). Smile or pity? Examine the impact of emoticon valence on customer satisfaction and purchase intention. *Journal of Business Research, 134*, 443–456.

MacCallum, R. C., & Austin, J. T. (2000). Applications of structural equation modeling in psychological research. *Annual Review of Psychology, 51*(1), 201–226.

Maeng, A., & Aggarwal, P. (2018). Facing dominance: Anthropomorphism and the effect of product face ratio on consumer preference. *Journal of Consumer Research, 44*(5), 1104–1122. https://doi.org/10.1093/jcr/ucx090

Majeed, M., Asare, C., Fatawu, A., & Abubakari, A. (2022). An analysis of the effects of customer satisfaction and engagement on social media on repurchase intention in the hospitality industry. *Cogent Business & Management, 9*(1), 2028331.

Marvi, R., Hollebeek, L. D., & Foroudi, P. (2022). Mapping customer engagement's intellectual: A multi-method bibliometric approach and future directions. In *The Emerald handbook of multi-stakeholder communication* (pp. 393–432). Emerald Publishing Limited.

Maslowska, E., Malthouse, E. C., & Collinger, T. (2016). The customer engagement ecosystem. *Journal of Marketing Management, 32*(5–6), 469–501.

Mehmannavazan, S., Foroudi, P., & Haghighinasab, M. (2023). Examining the impact of brand authenticity on purchase intention: A study of consumers' perception in the context of clothing industry in Iran. In *Digital transformation and corporate branding* (pp. 204–240). Routledge.

Mogaji, E., Soetan, T. O., & Kieu, T. A. (2021). The implications of artificial intelligence on the digital marketing of financial services to vulnerable customers. *Australasian Marketing Journal, 29*(3), 235–242.

Monroe, K. B. (1990). *Pricing: Making Profitable Decisions* (2nd ed.). McGraw-Hill.

Montgomery, A. L., Hosanagar, K., Krishnan, R., & Clay, K. B. (2004). Designing a better shopbot. *Management Science, 50*(2), 189–206. https://doi.org/10.1287/mnsc.1030.0151

Morotti, E., Stacchio, L., Donatiello, L., Roccetti, M., Tarabelli, J., & Marfia, G. (2022). Exploiting fashion x-commerce through the empowerment of voice in the fashion virtual reality arena: Integrating voice assistant and virtual reality technologies for fashion communication. *Virtual Reality, 26,* 1–14.

Mustak, M., Salminen, J., Plé, L., & Wirtz, J. (2021). Artificial intelligence in marketing: Topic modeling, scientometric analysis, and research agenda. *Journal of Business Research, 124,* 389–404.

Nankali, A., Seyyedamiri, N., Gholipour, T. H., Foroudi, P., Khajeheian, D., & Dekamini, F. (2022). Brand co-innovation in the sharing economy: A conceptual framework from insight to performance-based value co-creation and customer engagement. In *The Emerald handbook of multi-stakeholder communication* (pp. 541–562). Emerald Publishing Limited.

Nazarian, A., Atkinson, P., Foroudi, P., & Soares, A. (2021). Working together: Factors affecting the relationship between leadership and job satisfaction in Iranian HR departments. *Journal of General Management, 46*(3), 229–245.

Nazir, S., Khadim, S., Asadullah, M. A., & Syed, N. (2023). Exploring the influence of artificial intelligence technology on consumer repurchase intention: The mediation and moderation approach. *Technology in Society, 72,* 102190.

Nazir, S., Tayyab, A., Sajid, A., ur Rashid, H., & Javed, I. (2012). How online shopping is affecting consumers buying behavior in Pakistan? *International Journal of Computer Science Issues (IJCSI), 9*(3), 486.

Nica, E., Sabie, O. M., Mascu, S., & Luţan, A. G. (2022). Artificial intelligence decision-making in shopping patterns: Consumer values, cognition, and attitudes. *Economics, Management, and Financial Markets, 17*(1), 31–43.

Nicolaou, A. I., & McKnight, D. H. (2006). Perceived information quality in data exchanges: Effects on risk, trust, and intention to use. *Information Systems Research, 17*(4), 332–351.

Oliver, R. L., Rust, R. T., & Varki, S. (1997). Customer delight: Foundations, findings, and managerial insight. *Journal of Retailing, 73*(3), 311–336.

Omar, H., Klibi, W., Babai, M. Z., & Ducq, Y. (2023). Basket data-driven approach for omnichannel demand forecasting. *International Journal of Production Economics, 257,* 108748.

Ozdemir, S., Gupta, S., Foroudi, P., Wright, L. T., & Eng, T.-Y. (2020). Corporate branding and value creation for initiating and managing relationships in B2B markets. *Qualitative Market Research: An International Journal, 23*(4), 627–661.

Pansari, A., & Kumar, V. (2017). Customer engagement: The construct, antecedents, and consequences. *Journal of the Academy of Marketing Science, 45,* 294–311.

Papanagnou, C. I., & Matthews-Amune, O. (2018). Coping with demand volatility in retail pharmacies with the aid of big data exploration. *Computers & Operations Research, 98,* 343–354.

Park, I., Lee, J., Lee, D., Lee, C., & Chung, W. Y. (2022). Changes in consumption patterns during the COVID-19 pandemic: Analyzing the revenge spending motivations of different emotional groups. *Journal of Retailing and Consumer Services, 65,* 102874.

Patel, V., Kautish, P., & Patel, N. (2024). Impact of quality of AR apps on customer brand engagement, word-of-mouth and purchase intention: moderating role of perceived brand value. *International Journal of Electronic Marketing and Retailing, 15*(3), 330–349.

Perez-Vega, R., Kaartemo, V., Lages, C. R., Razavi, N. B., & Männistö, J. (2021). Reshaping the contexts of online customer engagement behavior via artificial intelligence: A conceptual framework. *Journal of Business Research, 129,* 902–910.

Peter, J. P. (1979). Reliability: A review of psychometric basics and recent marketing practices. *Journal of Marketing Research, 16*(1), 6–17.

Pillai, R., Sivathanu, B., & Dwivedi, Y. K. (2020). Shopping intention at AI-powered automated retail stores (AIPARS). *Journal of Retailing and Consumer Services, 57,* 102207.

Prentice, C., Dominique Lopes, S., & Wang, X. (2020). Emotional intelligence or artificial intelligence – An employee perspective. *Journal of Hospitality Marketing & Management, 29*(4), 377–403.

Ray, A., & Bala, P. K. (2021). User generated content for exploring factors affecting intention to use travel and food delivery services. *International Journal of Hospitality Management, 92,* 102730.

Retail Economics. (2023). *The impact of online retail.* https://www.retaileconomics.co.uk/report-online-retail/

Rick, S. I., Pereira, B., & Burson, K. A. (2014). The benefits of retail therapy: Making purchase decisions reduces residual sadness. *Journal of Consumer Psychology, 24*(3), 373–380.

Rita, P., Ramos, R., Borges-Tiago, M. T., & Rodrigues, D. (2022). Impact of the rating system on sentiment and tone of voice: A Booking.com and TripAdvisor comparison study. *International Journal of Hospitality Management, 104,* 103245.

Ritchie, J., Spencer, L., & O'Connor, W. (2003). Carrying out qualitative analysis. *Qualitative Research Practice: A Guide for Social Science Students and Researchers,* 219–262.

Rodgers, S. (2003). The effects of sponsor relevance on consumer reactions to internet sponsorships. *Journal of Advertising, 32*(4), 67–76.

Rodgers, W., & Nguyen, T. (2022). Advertising benefits from ethical artificial intelligence algorithmic purchase decision pathways. *Journal of Business Ethics, 178*(4), 1043–1061.

Rodgers, W., Yeung, F., Odindo, C., & Degbey, W. Y. (2021). Artificial intelligence-driven music biometrics influencing customers' retail buying behavior. *Journal of Business Research, 126,* 401–414.

Ruiz-Alba, J. L., Abou-Foul, M., Nazarian, A., & Foroudi, P. (2022). Digital platforms: Customer satisfaction, eWOM and the moderating role of perceived technological innovativeness. *Information Technology & People, 35*(7), 2470–2499.

Samudro, A., & Sumarwan, U. (2020). The influence of perceived value on customer satisfaction and behavioral intentions: The role of Islamic retailers in Indonesia. *Journal of Islamic Marketing, 11*(6), 1769–1782. https://doi.org/10.1108/JIMA-04-2020-0113

Scarpi, D., Pizzi, G., & Visentin, M. (2014). Shopping for fun or shopping to buy: Is it different online and offline? *Journal of Retailing and Consumer Services, 21*(3), 258–267.

Sharma, A., Dwivedi, R., Mariani, M. M., & Islam, T. (2022). Investigating the effect of advertising irritation on digital advertising effectiveness: A moderated mediation model. *Technological Forecasting and Social Change, 180,* 121731.

Sharma, A., Fadahunsi, A., Abbas, H., & Pathak, V. K. (2022). A multi-analytic approach to predict social media marketing influence on consumer purchase intention. *Journal of Indian Business Research, 14*(2), 125–149.

Shin, E., Chung, T., & Damhorst, M. L. (2021). Are negative and positive reviews regarding apparel fit influential? *Journal of Fashion Marketing and Management: International Journal, 25*(1), 63–79.

Shumanov, M., Cooper, H., & Ewing, M. (2022). Using AI predicted personality to enhance advertising effectiveness. *European Journal of Marketing, 56*(6), 1590–1609.

Solnet, D., Boztug, Y., & Dolnicar, S. (2016). An untapped gold mine? Exploring the potential of market basket analysis to grow hotel revenue. *International Journal of Hospitality Management, 56,* 119–125.

Soltani, M., Foroudi, P., & Nasab, M. H. (2023). Examining the impact of online customer engagement on non-financial performance considering the roles of brand attitude, customer co-creation, customer equity, and (e-) word-of-mouth. In *Digital transformation and corporate branding* (pp. 259–285). Routledge.

Speicher, M. (2018, March). Shopping in virtual reality. In *2018 IEEE conference on virtual reality and 3D user interfaces (VR)* (pp. 1–2). IEEE.

Statista. (2022). *Artificial Intelligence market size/revenue comparisons 2021.* Statista. https://www.statista.com/statistics/941835/artificial-intelligence-market-size-revenue-comparisons/. Accessed on April 27, 2022.

Steenkamp, J. B. E., & Baumgartner, H. (2000). On the use of structural equation models for marketing modeling. *International Journal of Research in Marketing, 17*(2–3), 195–202.

Sweeney, J. C., & Soutar, G. N. (2001). Consumer perceived value: The development of a multiple item scale. *Journal of Retailing, 77*(2), 203–220.

Tsai, C. Y., & Huang, S. H. (2015). A data mining approach to optimise shelf space allocation in consideration of customer purchase and moving behaviours. *International Journal of Production Research, 53*(3), 850–866.

Vandecasteele, B., & Geuens, M. (2010). Motivated consumer innovativeness: Concept, measurement, and validation. *International Journal of Research in Marketing, 27*(4), 308–318.

Venkatraman, M. P., & Price, L. L. (1990). Differentiating between cognitive and sensory innovativeness: Concepts, measurement, and implications. *Journal of Business Research, 20*(4), 293–315.

Verhoef, P. C., Lemon, K. N., Parasuraman, A., Roggeveen, A., Tsiros, M., & Schlesinger, L. A. (2009). Customer experience creation: Determinants, dynamics and management strategies. *Journal of Retailing*, *85*(1), 31–41.

Vitezić, V., & Perić, M. (2021). Artificial intelligence acceptance in services: Connecting with Generation Z. *Service Industries Journal*, *41*(13–14), 926–946.

Vlačić, B., Corbo, L., e Silva, S. C., & Dabić, M. (2021). The evolving role of artificial intelligence in marketing: A review and research agenda. *Journal of Business Research*, *128*, 187–203.

Wagner, T., & Rudolph, T. (2010). Towards a hierarchical theory of shopping motivation. *Journal of Retailing and Consumer Services*, *17*(5), 415–429.

Wang, J. J., Wang, L. Y., & Wang, M. M. (2018). Understanding the effects of eWOM social ties on purchase intentions: A moderated mediation investigation. *Electronic Commerce Research and Applications*, *28*, 54–62.

Weathers, D., Sharma, S., & Wood, S. L. (2007). Effects of online communication practices on consumer perceptions of performance uncertainty for search and experience goods. *Journal of Retailing*, *83*(4), 393–401.

Weber, F., & Schütte, R. (2019). A domain-oriented analysis of the impact of machine learning—The case of retailing. *Big Data and Cognitive Computing*, *3*(1), 11.

Wen Wan, E., Peng Chen, R., & Jin, L. (2017). Judging a book by its cover? The effect of anthropomorphism on product attribute processing and consumer preference. *Journal of Consumer Research*, *43*(6), 1008–1030.

Wu, L., Chen, K. W., & Chiu, M. L. (2016). Defining key drivers of online impulse purchasing: A perspective of both impulse shoppers and system users. *International Journal of Information Management*, *36*(3), 284–296.

Wu, K., & Cheng, T.-F. (2018). Assessing the effects of perceived value and satisfaction on loyalty: A study of Airbnb. *Journal of Quality Assurance in Hospitality & Tourism*, *19*(2), 190–210. https://doi.org/10.1080/1528008X.2017.1392352

Wu, R. S., & Chou, P. H. (2011). Customer segmentation of multiple category data in e-commerce using a soft-clustering approach. *Electronic Commerce Research and Applications*, *10*(3), 331–341.

Xia, F., Chatterjee, R., & Venkatesh, R. (2022). Leveraging social interaction among customers: Referral reward versus collective buying. *Journal of Interactive Marketing*, *57*(4), 583–600.

Xu, J., Zhang, H., Li, X., & Xue, H. (2022). Investigating the relationship between perceived value and customer satisfaction in the mobile payment service context. *Frontiers in Psychology*, *13*, 875. https://doi.org/10.3389/fpsyg.2022.887521

Yang, Z., Zhang, H., & Xie, E. (2017). Relative buyer-supplier relational strength and supplier's information sharing with the buyer. *Journal of Business Research*, *78*, 303–313.

Yin, J., & Qiu, X. (2021). AI technology and online purchase intention: Structural equation model based on perceived value. *Sustainability*, *13*(10), 5671.

Yuan, L., & Dennis, A. R. (2019). Acting like humans? Anthropomorphism and consumer's willingness to pay in electronic commerce. *Journal of Management Information Systems*, *36*(2), 450–477.

Zeithaml, V. A. (1988). Consumer perceptions of price, quality, and value: A means-end model and synthesis of evidence. *Journal of Marketing*, *52*(3), 2–22.

Zha, D., Foroudi, P., Jin, Z., & Melewar, T. (2022a). Making sense of sensory brand experience: Constructing an integrative framework for future research. *International Journal of Management Reviews, 24*(1), 130–167.

Zha, D., Foroudi, P., Melewar, T., & Jin, Z. (2022b). Assessing the psychological impact of the pandemic narrative in the media on hospitality consumption mood. In *The Emerald handbook of multi-stakeholder communication* (pp. 31–49). Emerald Publishing Limited.

Zha, D., Foroudi, P., Melewar, T., & Jin, Z. (2022c). Experiencing the sense of the brand: The mining, processing and application of brand data through sensory brand experiences. *Qualitative Market Research: An International Journal, 25*(2), 205–232.

Zha, D., Marvi, R., & Foroudi, P. (2023). Synthesizing the customer experience concept: A multimodularity approach. *Journal of Business Research, 167*, 114185.

Zha, D., Marvi, R., & Foroudi, P. (2024). Embracing the paradox of customer experiences in the hospitality and tourism industry. *International Journal of Management Reviews, 26*(2), 163–186.

Zha, D., Melewar, T., Foroudi, P., & Jin, Z. (2020). An assessment of brand experience knowledge literature: Using bibliometric data to identify future research direction. *International Journal of Management Reviews, 22*(3), 287–317.

Chapter 9

Encouraging Sustainable Behavior Among Hotel Employees

Shazia Luidens, Guido Berens and Ronny Reshef

Erasmus University, The Netherlands

Abstract

This chapter investigates the relationship between sustainable human resource (HR) practices and employee intentions to engage in sustainable behavior within an eco-friendly hotel. Specifically, we examine the influence of internal sustainability orientation, supervisory support, training, and rewards, as well as the mediating role of employees' knowledge of the resort's sustainability practices.

Keywords: Sustainable human resource (HR) practices; employee sustainable behavior; employee support; employee training; employee rewards; sustainability orientation; eco-friendly hotels

Introduction

Over the years, tourism has become one of the fastest-growing economic sectors worldwide (UNWTO, 2022). It is the primary source of income of many countries and has created numerous economic and employment opportunities. However, the tourism industry is also responsible for less desirable consequences since it causes considerable pressure on the environment. Tourism uses a significant number of natural resources and produces large amounts of waste (Scanlon, 2007). The environmental impacts of this rapidly growing industry cannot be neglected much longer, and as such, the concept of sustainable tourism has been created during discussions on how to develop tourism in an environmentally friendly manner (Hunter & Green, 1995).

In order to achieve sustainable tourism, stakeholders such as hotels need to act (Schmudde, 2019). Hotels have been facing increased pressure from society to become more sustainable in their business practices. The growth of environmental

Business Strategies and Ethical Challenges in the Digital Ecosystem, 197–224

Copyright © 2025 Shazia Luidens, Guido Berens and Ronny Reshef

Published under exclusive licence by Emerald Publishing Limited

doi:10.1108/978-1-80455-069-420241009

awareness among consumers and investors, as well as the number of regulations on environmental and social issues, intensifies the necessity to act. Therefore, hotels have incorporated sustainability practices and policies within their organization not only to address the issue of sustainability but also to gain a competitive advantage and diversify themselves from competitors (Jones et al., 2014).

After forming policies and practices to manage sustainability, organizations are faced with the challenge of motivating their employees to engage in sustainable behavior in the workplace de facto (Cantor et al., 2012). According to previous research, the support and behavior of employees are crucial for guaranteeing the long-term viability of sustainability practices (Del Brío et al., 2007).

Stimulating employees to become environmentally conscious and actively participate in sustainability-related activities is therefore gaining importance for organizations. Such consciousness can have a significant impact on the company's reputation and revenues (Cantor et al., 2012). Employees engaging in sustainable behavior can strengthen the competitive advantage and efficiency of sustainable practices within an organization, thereby improving the organization's overall economic and environmental performance (Daily & Huang, 2001; Zhang et al., 2020).

Employee behavior can be divided into two categories, namely in-role and extra-role behavior (Van Dyne & LePine, 1998). In-role behavior refers to the behavior that is expected or required from employees while performing their job, whereas extra-role behavior refers to the behavior of employees beyond their formal job requirements. In this chapter, the focus will be on the extra-role sustainable behavior of employees at Boarco Beach Resort (see the Case Study). The reason for this is that extra-role sustainable behavior has particularly been a challenge that the resort has been facing for the past years.

The importance of overcoming the challenge of engaging employees in sustainable behavior, especially in the tourism and hospitality industry, is high. This stems from the fact that tourism not only depends on natural resources but is also a labor-intensive industry with many employees (Rezapouraghdam et al., 2019). Apart from the formal work-related sustainability requirements, employees must understand and engage in the sustainability practices of the resort. This is vital in order to achieve long-term environmental and social goals and maintain the effectiveness of the existing practices that are in place (Daily & Huang, 2001).

Through sustainable human resource (HR) practices, which are policies in place to achieve desired environmental and social outcomes, organizations can encourage their employees to engage in sustainable behavior (Kramar, 2014). By understanding how these practices encourage employees to engage in sustainable behavior, the resort can move forward with its sustainability ambitions and enhance its reputation and revenues. Therefore, this chapter aims to answer the following research question:

> How do sustainable human resource practices encourage hotel employees to engage in sustainable behavior?

The primary goal of the research is to add to the understanding of employees' sustainable behavior by studying the case of Boarco Beach Resort. This can assist the tourism industry in achieving long-term sustainability goals and maintaining the effectiveness of the practices that are in place. The results of the research can be used by similar resorts in an effort to achieve sustainable behavior from their employees in the workplace.

Despite the expanse of academic literature on the significant contribution of sustainable human resource management (HRM) to the environmental performance of a company, there are only few studies in which the relationship between sustainable HR practices and employees' sustainable behavior is empirically tested (e.g., Paillé et al., 2014). This chapter aims to add to the research gap on the critical role of employees in an organization for achieving corporate sustainability and how to encourage them to engage in sustainable behavior (Jabbour & Santos, 2008).

Hotels and Sustainability

Over the years, hotels have coped with economic crises, societal issues, and environmental catastrophes. In the recent decades, sustainability has become an increasingly important issue within hotels since the pressure to become economically, socially, and environmentally responsible continues to grow (Bader, 2005). Additionally, both business and leisure travelers express a growing interest in sustainability when it comes to finding a place to stay (Henry, 2013). As travelers stay in hotels to experience the surrounding environment, hotels are responsible for preserving this environment if they wish to maintain their business in the long run. By incorporating sustainable business practices into their organization, hotels can therefore continue to depend on their surrounding environment for longevity and profitability (Bader, 2005).

The most common sustainable practices in hotels include reducing energy consumption, buying local and environmentally friendly products, lowering waste production, eliminating the use of disposable packaging, and recycling products and materials (Fien, 2002; Stalcup et al., 2014). While most of these practices are aimed at decreasing the environmental footprint, there are also other sustainable practices that are more socially oriented. Some examples can be donating money to local charities or campaigns and contributing used hotel furniture and appliances (Nicholls & Kang, 2012). Aside from the environmental and social benefits of sustainable practices, there could be financial benefits as well to adopting such practices by hotels. These include saving costs through long-term financial stability, increased attractiveness for investors, longevity and long-term profitability, and improved value of assets due to long-term business capability (Bader, 2005).

However, there are also barriers to implementing sustainable practices in a hotel. While there are both external and internal barriers, the latter have a more substantial influence on the implementation of sustainable practices (Becherer & Helms, 2014). Human resources, in contrast to financial ones, are harder to obtain and sustain in an organization (Hillary, 2004). Additionally, implementing sustainable practices in an organization causes substantial costs and at times even fails, for instance, due to a lack of sustainability knowledge and skills within the organization (Tzschentke et al., 2004). Therefore, focusing on the improvement of human resources is a reasonable precondition for implementing sustainability within organizations.

Encouraging Sustainable Behavior in the Work Environment

Employees play a crucial role in corporate sustainability as they can strengthen the competitive advantage and efficiency of these practices within an organization as a result of their behavior (Ahuja et al., 2019; Del Brío et al., 2007; Zhang et al., 2020). By engaging in sustainable behavior and showing willingness to adopt sustainable practices within their organization, employees can influence the innovation of a company, as well as its economic and environmental performance (Daily & Huang, 2001; Ruiz-Pérez et al., 2021). However, organizations are still confronted with the challenge of encouraging employees to engage in sustainable behavior. The main challenges related to incorporating sustainability within an organization stem from the vast amount of required changes in the organization, which often lead to internal opposition (Cantor et al., 2012).

The manner in which organizations show their appreciation for their employees and their contributions has a substantial influence on the behavior of employees (Eisenberger et al., 1986). For example, if an employee is recognized or awarded for a sustainability initiative they came up with, they are more likely to engage in such behavior. Often, how employees are treated in an organization has to do with the HR practices in place and the manner in which employees have engaged with their supervisors and other employees in the past (Aselage & Eisenberger, 2003). Therefore, sustainable behavior of employees can be encouraged through sustainable HRM.

The purpose of sustainable HRM is to achieve positive social and environmental outcomes through HR practices (Kramar, 2014). Incorporating sustainable HR practices in an organization could also improve the recruitment and retention of employees within an organization. This is crucial, especially in the hotel industry, where the employee turnover rate is high (Berns et al., 2009; Iverson & Deery, 1997). There is also an increased interest in working for green companies by job candidates, and companies find that employees' involvement in sustainability has a considerable impact on the company. Employee engagement in sustainable behavior can result in several actions, such as being involved in sustainability practices, thinking about improvements regarding sustainability in their own work routines, and coming up with suggestions to be more sustainable (Cantor et al., 2012). In the long term, employees' sustainable behavior can contribute to the sustainability goals of an organization and the effectiveness of sustainability practices (Daily & Huang, 2001).

Theoretical Framework

The theoretical framework that will be used during this research is adopted from a study by Pellegrini et al. (2018). In this study, the role of sustainable HR practices in influencing employee behavior for corporate sustainability was examined. The sustainable behavior of employees can be separated into two categories, namely in-role and extra-role behavior. Both types of behavior refer to the individual behavior of employees rather than large-scale sustainability strategies implemented by organizations (Ramus & Steger, 2000).

In-role behavior is related to the official requirements of the employee's job; it is required of employees to take sustainability into account when performing specific tasks related to their job. For example, a sustainability manager can be responsible for developing and carrying out sustainability projects and a salesperson selling sustainable products would be responsible for promoting such products to customers. On the other hand, extra-role behavior is related to the employees' actions beyond their formal job requirements, in which they intently take the initiative to engage in sustainable behavior in their workplace (Pellegrini et al., 2018). Such initiatives could include finding new ways of incorporating sustainability into the organization, making suggestions or reflecting on current sustainability practices of the organization, participating in sustainability initiatives and events organized by the organization, and promoting the sustainability image of the organization to others (Boiral & Paillé, 2012). During this research, the extra-role behavior of employees will be the focus because sustainable behavior is not an official job requirement of the hotel's employees.

Sustainable behavior among employees can be encouraged by supplying them with knowledge, skills, and motivation to act (Young et al., 2015). There are several ways in which a company can do this. In this research, four factors that can influence an employee's sustainability knowledge, and, in turn, their sustainable behavior will be studied. These four factors are internal sustainability orientation, supervisory support, training, and rewards.

Internal Sustainability Orientation

Employees' perceptions of a company's sustainability vision and practices can influence their behavior. To engage employees in sustainable behavior, a company needs to communicate the importance and subject matter of sustainability within their organization (Pellegrini et al., 2018). Research has proven that the employees' perception of sustainability policies within an organization affects their inclination to support environmental initiatives of the company (Ramus & Steger, 2000). Moreover, clear communication on sustainability policies, procedures, and practices within an organization has also been proven to encourage sustainable behavior among employees (Norton et al., 2014). The internal sustainability orientation of the company perceived by employees thus affects their understanding of the importance of sustainability, and, consequently, it influences their engagement in sustainable behavior. Therefore, the following hypothesis is formulated:

> *H1.* The internal sustainability orientation of the company perceived by employees positively influences employees' sustainable behavior.

Supervisory Support

Supervisory support can be defined as the employees' perception of the resources and feedback given by supervisors to understand and participate in sustainability initiatives and practices in the workplace environment (Susskind et al., 2003). Supervisors have a unique position in an organization, since they can influence both their employees and the top management. They interact with many employees daily and have the necessary resources and authority to make changes within an organization (Boiral et al., 2018). Therefore, supervisors are some of the most substantial agents of change regarding sustainability and are able to encourage sustainable behavior among others in the workplace (Cantor et al., 2012). Further, supervisory support can be pivotal. In the paper by Ramus and Steger (2000), their results showed that support from supervisors contributed to the initiatives of employees in improving the environmental performance of a company. Additionally, supervisory support has been linked to the successful implementation of sustainable practices in an organization (Daily & Huang, 2001). By providing support to employees, supervisors play an essential role in encouraging staff members to engage in sustainable behavior. Hence, the following hypothesis is formulated:

H2. Supervisory support positively influences employees' sustainable behavior.

Training

Training is an important way of developing employees and an investment in the human capital of the organization. Consecutively, it can increase the capacity and performance of the organization (Ahmad & Schroeder, 2003; Van Iddekinge et al., 2009). Sustainability training is aimed at increasing the environmental awareness of employees, improving their capability to make sustainability-related decisions, and carrying out sustainable actions in the workplace (Sammalisto & Brorson, 2008; Sarkis et al., 2010). Besides enhancing employees' knowledge and skills, sustainability training can also help them understand and commit to the values and practices of the organization.

Saeed et al. (2019) found that training is the most consistently successful practice in promoting sustainable behavior among employees. Training helps in shifting the mindset and attention of employees and positively influences the implementation of sustainable practices within an organization (Daily & Huang, 2001; Sarkis et al., 2010). Therefore, sustainability training is essential when it comes to implementing change in an organization and influencing employee behavior. Consequently, the following hypothesis is formulated:

H3. Sustainability training positively influences employees' sustainable behavior.

Rewards

Rewards are a way to motivate employees through benefits and can influence their behavior and commitment to an organization (Terera & Ngirande, 2014). A good rewards system gives employees the feeling that their organization values their contributions, independent decision-making, and professional behavior (Boyt et al., 2001). In terms of motivating sustainable behavior, the rewards given to employees should reflect the organization's values and commitment to sustainability (Daily & Huang, 2001). They can either be financial rewards, such as bonuses and allowances, or nonfinancial rewards, such as appreciation and recognition. Monetary rewards are one of the main factors in motivating employees, as it fulfills their basic needs. Additionally, financial rewards could also meet individuals' need for authority, status, and belonging within society (Yousaf et al., 2014). Rewards can thus have a substantial influence on the behavior of employees toward sustainability within an organization. Therefore, the following hypothesis is formulated:

H4. Rewards given for sustainable actions positively influence employees' sustainable behavior.

Sustainability Knowledge of the Resort

The way in which an organization communicates about its sustainability practices influences the knowledge of employees about these practices and the way this knowledge transfers between the employees (Harms, 2011). When the company has a strong internal sustainability orientation, employees see managers and supervisors as highly knowledgeable on sustainability practices and policies within an organization, which would enable knowledge transfer between employees. Through supervisory support, department managers of hotels can help employees understand and contribute to sustainability practices. This can significantly influence the commitment of staff members to the resort's sustainability practices and the successful implementation of these practices (Chan & Hawkins, 2010). In addition to internal sustainability orientation and supervisory support, training also plays an essential role in increasing the sustainability knowledge of employees (Sarkis et al., 2010). Another way to increase the sustainability knowledge of employees is through rewards, as they motivate employees to exchange knowledge among each other (Bartol & Srivastava, 2002).

When employees are highly knowledgeable about the sustainability practices of the organization, it can help them in the decision-making process on matters related to sustainability. Often, individuals avoid situations in which their knowledge is not sufficient in order to reduce the chances of making a mistake. Due to the high level of uncertainty in such situations, individuals may decide it is best not to engage in any behavior altogether (Chan et al., 2014). Indeed, Boswell et al. (2006) have shown that knowledge about the organization's strategy and the role of employees in implementing this strategy is vital to help employees contribute to it, especially when the employee behavior that is needed is extra-role behavior. Therefore, the following hypothesis is formulated:

> *H5*. Sustainability knowledge of the resort acts as a mediator between internal sustainability orientation, supervisory support, training, rewards, and the sustainable behavior of employees.

The theoretical framework of this research can be seen in Fig. 9.1, in which the knowledge of employees on the sustainability practices of the resort acts as a mediator between the four sustainable HR practices and employees' sustainable behavior. The relationships between the four practices, employees' sustainability knowledge, and sustainable behavior will be empirically tested in this research to determine which measures need to be taken by hotels to encourage their employees to engage in sustainable behavior within the workplace.

Research Methodology

This study was conducted in collaboration with Boarco Beach Resort, an eco-friendly hotel located in Aruba, during 2022. They are renowned for being one of the greenest hotels in the Caribbean. For many years, they have incorporated sustainability into their resort; however, it remains a challenge to do so in cooperation with their employees. Therefore, this research is focused on the sustainable behavior of their employees and how they engage with sustainability within their work environment.

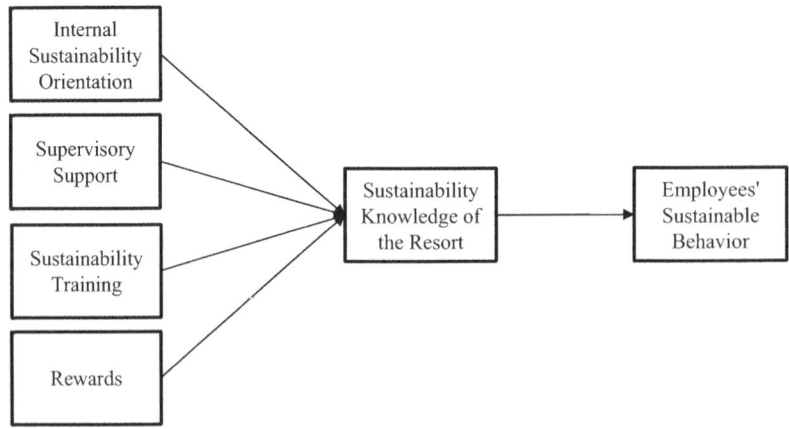

Fig. 9.1.   Theoretical Framework of the Research.

Research Design and Data Collection

The research was conducted using a survey where an online questionnaire was distributed among the target audience. The survey questions were based on academic literature and information from the resort's website and staff. It was pre-tested with the interim sustainability manager of the resort to see whether the questionnaire was clear and complete. She gave feedback on the terminology used in the questionnaire to make it more comprehensible for the employees and suggested including questions regarding employees' income and purchasing behavior of environmentally friendly products, among others. Although these questions were not relevant for the purpose of this research, they were included in the questionnaire to give the resort more insights into their employees' sustainable behavior.

After the feedback was incorporated into the online questionnaire, it was approved by the interim sustainability manager of the resort, thus giving it internal validity. A link to the online questionnaire was then sent to the supervisors and managers of each department via email to distribute among their employees. Initially, employees were given 10 days to fill out the survey. The number of responses was still low after 5 days; therefore, a reminder email was sent to the supervisors of each department to encourage more responses from their employees. The reminder email was not effective, and, consequently, it was decided to extend the deadline by four more days. The extension of the deadline was helpful, and eventually the data was collected over a period of two weeks. The final number of participants in the online questionnaire was 39 employees.

Participants

The research method used during the study was a census method, which means that all members of the population were studied. In accordance with the interim sustainability manager of the hotel, the three largest departments of the hotel were selected as the population for this research as they could bring about the most substantial change in employees' sustainable behavior. These departments were namely Housekeeping, Front Office, and Food & Beverage, with 114 employees in total, including management positions. The initial goal was to achieve at least a 50% response rate, as previous research indicates that the average response rate for surveys at the individual level is around 52% (Baruch & Holtom, 2008). It was expected for the number of responses to differ per department, as each one has a different number of employees as well as different degrees of access to a computer or mobile phone.

Questionnaire Design

Before designing the questionnaire in Qualtrics, a meeting was held with the supervisor and manager of each company department. The purpose of these meetings was to get an insight into the past, current, and future attempts of the resort to motivate its employees to engage in sustainable behavior. The information provided by the resort, together with measurement scales from academic literature, provided the basis for the online questionnaire. It was designed in a way to answer the research question as well as to provide Boarco Beach Resort with insightful information about their employees.

The questionnaire was written in English and opened with a short introduction regarding the purpose of the research. Participants were informed that their contribution was completely anonymous and confidential. After the participants consented to participate in the questionnaire, they were asked questions regarding their gender, age, level of education, job tenure, company department, and income level. For the questions on gender, age, and income level, there was an option for the participant to select "prefer not to say." As these questions could be sensitive for the participant, this option allows them to continue the questionnaire without having to disclose this information.

The questionnaire continued with a section on a Savings and Loans program offered for their employees (which is not relevant to test our hypotheses so will not be further discussed in this chapter). The next section of the questionnaire measured the dependent and independent variables of the research (Table A1) and will be explained in the following areas of this chapter.

Dependent Variables

The dependent variable in this research is employees' sustainable behavior. To measure the dependent variable, five statements were given to the participant in which they could indicate how often they engage in certain sustainable activities during their job. A five-point Likert scale ranging from "Always" to "Never" was used for these statements. An example of these statements is: "During my lunch break in the cafeteria, I only take as much food as I can eat." All the statements in the question were related to the extra-role sustainable behavior of employees.

Independent Variables

There are four independent variables influencing the dependent variable in the research's framework, namely "employees' sustainable behavior." These variables are the employees' internal sustainability orientation, supervisory support, sustainability training, and rewards.

In order to measure the independent variables, statements were given to the respondent in which they could indicate to which extent they agree or disagree with the statements. A Likert scale ranging from "strongly agree" to "strongly disagree" was used for these questions. The statements were based on academic literature in which they discussed different ways that employees can be encouraged or motivated to engage in environmental sustainability (Boyt et al., 2001; Eisenberger et al., 1986; Ramus, 2001; Susskind et al., 2003). The statements were adjusted to this research and in accordance with the interim sustainability manager of the resort.

Mediator

The employee's knowledge of the resort's sustainability practices acts as a mediator between the dependent variable and the independent variables. To measure employees' sustainability knowledge of the resort, eight true or false statements were given to the participant (Table A2). The statements are general sustainability practices of the resort and not specific to any department, giving the participants an equal chance of knowing the correct answer.

Control Variable

The control variable present in this research is the company department in which employees work in at the resort. The control variable "company department" could show differences in the sustainable behavior of employees among the departments, separately from the independent variables. The control variable was used to provide a more valid estimate of the relationships between the independent variables and sustainability knowledge and behavior of employees across the three different company departments of the resort (Housekeeping, Front Office, and Food & Beverage).

Data Analysis and Results

Sample

A total number of 39 employees responded to the online questionnaire, resulting in a 34% response rate. From the total responses, 22 respondents were male, 16 respondents were female, and one respondent preferred not to say their gender. Most respondents were below the age of 45 and had been working for Boarco Beach Resort for 0–5 years. The response rate per department was as follows: Housekeeping (22%), Front Office (74%), and Food & Beverage (25%).

Data Preparation

For the independent variables, the mean of the items for each concept was taken to show the average score per independent variable. For sustainability knowledge, the items were recorded into dummy variables with correct answers as "1" and incorrect answers as "0." The total number of correct responses per respondent was then added to create the new variable "total sustainability knowledge." As for the control variable "company department," again, the items were recorded into dummy variables. The department with the highest number of responses was used as the reference category, which was the Front Office.

Preliminary Analysis

Before performing the data analysis, we checked the reliability of our measures as well as the validity of the assumptions of regression analysis. In order to check for the internal consistency of each independent variable, Cronbach's alpha was estimated. The results can be seen in Table 9.1.

Table 9.1. Cronbach's Alpha for Each Independent Variable.

Independent Variable	Cronbach's Alpha	Level of Internal Consistency
Internal sustainability orientation	0.819	High
Supervisory support	0.910	High
Sustainability training	0.766	Acceptable
Rewards	0.698	Acceptable

The Cronbach's alpha of "sustainability training" and "rewards" would be substantially higher if one item from each construct was deleted. Since these items were problematic in comparison to the rest of the items in the question, they were removed. Cronbach's alpha for "sustainability training" was now 0.849, and for "rewards," it was 0.911. Therefore, the level of internal consistency went from acceptable to high for these two independent variables.

Checks of the assumptions of regression analysis showed no issues regarding linearity, multicollinearity, heteroskedasticity, or normality. There were a few outliers, which seem to be valid observations. For the model predicting sustainability knowledge, the results do not substantially change when removing the outliers, so it was decided to keep them in the dataset. However, for the model predicting sustainable behavior, the results do substantially change when removing the outliers. Specifically, none of the independent variables had a significant effect on sustainable behavior when the outliers were left in, whereas there were two significant effects when the outliers were removed. We therefore decided to remove the four outliers for that analysis.

Table 9.2 shows the means, standard deviations, and correlations of all constructs in our model. There do not seem to be any extremely high or low scores or correlations in our study.

Hypotheses Tests

To test *H1* through *H4*, we ran a multiple regression analysis predicting employees' sustainable behavior from the independent and control variables. The dependent variable in the analysis is "employees' sustainable behavior," which was measured on a 5-point Likert scale. The mean of these items was taken to show the average score per respondent for the dependent variable.

The regression model was statistically significant ($p = 0.043$) and had an R square value of 0.353, meaning that the predictor variables explain 35.3% of the variability of the dependent variable. As shown in Table 9.3, the only predictor variables that were statistically significant were "internal sustainability orientation" ($p = 0.035$) and "supervisory support" ($p = 0.049$). Both variables had a positive relationship with the dependent variable "employees' sustainable behavior." Thus, the results of

Table 9.2. Descriptives and Correlations.

	Mean	Std. Dev.	1.	2.	3.	4.	5.	6.	7.
1. Internal sustainability orientation	1.82	0.72							
2. Supervisory support	1.86	0.95	0.20						
3. Sustainability training	2.27	0.93	0.64	0.46					
4. Rewards	2.67	1.21	0.48	0.32	0.67				
5. Sustainability knowledge	6.36	1.14	−0.01	0.15	0.21	0.28			
6. Sustainable behavior	2.15	0.68	0.19	0.12	0.10	0.05	−0.20		
7. Housekeeping	0.21	0.41	0.49	−0.31	0.21	0.33	0.29	0.19	
8. Food & beverage	0.36	0.49	−0.21	0.00	−0.34	−0.31	−0.38	0.03	−0.38

Table 9.3. Coefficients of the Effects of Sustainable Human Resource Practices on Sustainable Behavior.

Model	Unstandardized B	Sig.
(Constant)	1.171	0.001
Internal sustainability orientation	0.433	0.035
Supervisory support	0.269	0.049
Sustainability training	−0.045	0.793
Rewards	−0.075	0.537
Housekeeping	0.173	0.582
Food & beverage	−0.042	0.843

the regression model suggest that the employees' sustainable behavior can be improved by increasing their internal sustainability orientation of the resort and by increasing the support given by supervisors.

To test *H5*, about the mediating role of sustainability knowledge, we ran two additional regression models. First, a multiple regression was run to predict employees' sustainability knowledge of the resort from internal sustainability orientation, supervisory support, sustainability training, and rewards. Additionally, the company departments were added as control variables in the regression model. This model was statistically significant ($p = 0.037$) with an R square value of 0.327, which means that the independent variables explain 32.7% of the variability of the dependent variable.

The coefficients in Table 9.4 show that the independent variable "internal sustainability orientation" ($p = 0.038$) and company department "housekeeping" ($p = 0.034$) are significantly related to our mediator (sustainability knowledge). The independent variable "internal sustainability orientation" has a negative

Table 9.4. Coefficients of the Effects of Sustainable Human Resource Practices on Sustainability Knowledge of the Resort.

Model	Unstandardized B	Sig.
(Constant)	6.359	<0.001
Internal sustainability orientation	−0.746	0.038
Supervisory support	0.348	0.132
Sustainability training	0.173	0.580
Rewards	0.090	0.644
Housekeeping	1.286	0.034
Food & beverage	−0.533	0.181

Table 9.5. Coefficients of the Effects of Sustainable Human Resource Practices and Sustainability Knowledge on Sustainable Behavior.

Model	Unstandardized B	Sig.
(Constant)	1.792	0.020
Internal sustainability orientation	0.351	0.113
Supervisory support	0.288	0.038
Sustainability training	−0.023	0.896
Rewards	−0.073	0.544
Sustainability knowledge	−0.091	0.348
Housekeeping	0.306	0.376
Food & beverage	−0.087	0.688

relationship with the mediator (−0.746), whereas the control variable "housekeeping" has a positive relationship with the mediator (+1.286). Thus, the results of the regression model suggest that the employees' sustainability knowledge of the resort can be improved by reducing their internal sustainability orientation. Additionally, there is a substantial difference among the company departments when it comes to employees' sustainability knowledge of the resort.

Second, to test the effect of sustainability knowledge on sustainable behavior (the second step in the mediating process), we ran a multiple regression model predicting sustainable behavior from sustainability knowledge, the independent variables, and the control variables. The ANOVA results showed that this regression model was not statistically significant ($p = 0.056$), meaning that the predictor variables do not significantly influence employees' sustainable behavior. Indeed, as can be seen in Table 9.5, the effect of sustainability knowledge on sustainable behavior is not significant. In fact, the only significant effect is that of "supervisory support." Therefore, the variable "sustainability knowledge of the resort" does not act as a mediator of the effects of sustainable HR practices.

Discussion

The behavior of employees plays a crucial role in strengthening sustainability within an organization (Zhang et al., 2020). However, it remains a challenge for organizations to engage their employees in sustainable behavior. Especially in the hotel industry, where organizations have a high employee turnover rate (Iverson & Deery, 1997), the support and commitment of employees is of vital importance. Therefore, research on this topic and how it can be implemented in practice is of the essence. Hence, this research aimed to answer the following question: "How do sustainable HR practices encourage hotel employees to engage in sustainable behavior?" The main findings of this research are discussed below.

The research model aims to explain the extra-role sustainable behavior of hotel employees and to analyze the relationship between employees' sustainable behavior and sustainable HR practices. Organizational policies and managerial procedures that include sustainability targets can possibly encourage employees to engage in sustainable behavior if they stimulate and motivate employees to commit to sustainability (Aguilera et al., 2007). Additionally, the research model tests the mediating role of employees' knowledge of sustainability practices of the resort.

As the results from this research show, the employees' internal sustainability orientation of the resort leads to an increase in their sustainable behavior. It is one of the four sustainable HR practices to influence employee behavior for sustainability, based on the research model by Pellegrini et al. (2018). The results from the data analysis show that the employee's perception of the internal sustainability orientation of the resort significantly influenced and increased their sustainable behavior and was in accordance with the results from the study by Pellegrini et al. (2018).

When a company clearly communicates the importance and subject matter of sustainability practices, the perception of employees changes and leads to an increase in their understanding of sustainability within the organization, therefore affecting their sustainable behavior. Additionally, the results from the data analysis also show that supervisory support significantly influenced and increased employees' sustainable behavior, which was also in accordance with the results from the study by Pellegrini et al. (2018). Within an organization, supervisors play a crucial role in motivating employees to engage in sustainable behavior. By providing employees with the necessary tools and feedback, they can understand, participate, and contribute to the sustainability practices of their organization.

On the other hand, sustainability training and rewards did not influence the sustainable behavior of employees. The results from the data analysis show that the effects of these practices were not statistically significant and are consistent with the findings of Pellegrini et al. (2018). While previous studies have shown that training and rewards have an effect on sustainable behavior (Ramus & Killmer, 2007), the results from this research suggest otherwise. A possible explanation for this discrepancy could be in the specific characteristics of the case. The data obtained from the questionnaire showed that sustainability training is not offered on a regular basis at the resort and that the participants would like more training to be provided to them. As for rewarding and recognizing employees for their sustainability initiatives and contributions to the environment in their daily job, the participants indicated they were not recognized or rewarded enough. However, the participants also suggested that if there were a monthly sustainability nomination in place, they would be more motivated to engage with sustainability at the resort. These findings might be the reason why the effects of training and rewards are not significant in this research, as respondents might not (yet) have a strong opinion on the resort's training and rewards. While training and rewards are often perceived by organizations to be some of the most effective ways of stimulating behavior, organizations should "not rely on rewards and training as universal and cost-effective solutions for shaping employees' sustainable behavior" (Pellegrini et al., 2018, p. 1229). Extra-role sustainable behavior requires extra time and attention from employees aside from their job requirements. Therefore, employees are often motivated to engage in such behavior by individual and organizational values rather than rewards (Chatman, 1989).

Lastly, the mediating role of "sustainability knowledge of the resort" between the four practices and employees' sustainable behavior was investigated. The results showed that employees' sustainability knowledge of the resort could be improved by reducing their internal sustainability orientation of the resort. Additionally, there is a substantial difference among the company departments in terms of employees' sustainability knowledge of the resort. However, because there was no significant effect of "sustainability knowledge of the resort" on employees' sustainable behavior, it could not be confirmed that "sustainability knowledge of the resort" acted as a mediator in the research model. Although previous research has shown that knowledge can be a significant predictor of behavior, the same cannot be concluded from the findings of this research.

The main research question, "How do sustainable HR practices encourage the hotel employees of Boarco Beach Resort to engage in sustainable behavior?" was answered by concluding that internal sustainability orientation and supervisory support encourage hotel employees to engage in sustainable behavior. The results from this study are in line with previous research that proves that employees are more inclined to engage in sustainable behavior when there is clear communication on sustainability within the organization and sufficient managerial support (Norton et al., 2014; Pellegrini et al., 2018; Ramus & Steger, 2000). Improving the way in which employees perceive their organization's commitment to sustainability can lead to employees incorporating sustainability values within themselves and their organization (Raineri & Paillé, 2016). A small example of this is when the participants were asked about the resort's Savings & Loans program in the online questionnaire. At first, 1/3 of the respondents did not know about the program. After informing the participants about it, about half of them would make use of the program to reduce their carbon footprint. When giving the respondents a clear example of how they could use the program, more than half (62%) of the respondents were willing to reduce their carbon footprint (and thus, engage in sustainable behavior).

Furthermore, the outcomes of this research confirm that supervisory support is crucial for encouraging employees to engage in sustainable behavior in the workplace. Supervisors play an active role in shifting toward sustainability by influencing how employees perceive the subject matter and importance of sustainability within an organization. Additionally, by having direct and regular communication with employees, supervisors provide the required tools and feedback that make it easier for employees to incorporate sustainable behavior into their daily work life. Therefore, top management in an organization should make sure that sustainable practices and policies are well understood by supervisors. When they are provided with clear instructions and resources, supervisors can become successful change agents and can transform sustainability practices and policies into individual actions (Cantor et al., 2012; Pellegrini et al., 2018).

Managerial Implications

The primary purpose of this study was to give recommendations to Boarco Beach Resort on how they could encourage their employees to engage in sustainable behavior. As the results show, the sustainable HR practices that significantly and positively influence their employees' sustainable behavior are internal sustainability orientation and supervisory support. Supervisors play a crucial role in influencing the relationship between these practices and employees' sustainable behavior.

Most employees at the resort are aware of the importance of sustainability. However, when there is too much or confusing sustainability information, they indicated that the resort could help them more with organizing and making sense of this information. Additionally, employees indicated that they need more guidance with incorporating sustainability in the workplace. Supervisors should thus openly communicate and engage in conversations around the topic of sustainability. There is also a need to make sure that supervisors understand and are committed to the sustainability practices and policies within the resort in order to help employees incorporate these into their daily work life. For example, supervisors can give employees the responsibility of fulfilling small tasks related to sustainability or allow them to participate in the decision-making process around sustainability practices that involve them, thereby stimulating them to come up with new sustainability ideas. Without guidance and support from supervisors, employees will be less encouraged to participate in sustainable practices at the resort. The support of supervisors and clear communication about sustainability practices and policies, including concrete actions that employees can take during their daily job, can help encourage sustainable behavior in the workplace and ultimately guarantee the long-term success of sustainability practices of the resort.

Theoretical Implications

The research's results add insights into the sustainable behavior of employees in the tourism industry, as previous studies have typically focused on employees' sustainable behavior in other sectors (such as the fashion industry). Additionally, this study contributed to the gap in academic literature by empirically testing the influence of sustainable HR practices on employees' sustainable behavior. This study also adds to the understanding of the topic of employees' sustainable behavior and allows for researchers to further discuss and explore the managerial aspects of employees' sustainable behavior. In addition to its empirical findings, this study serves as a practical example for other hotels in the tourism industry that are facing the same challenge with their employees.

According to the results of this study, training and rewards do not have an influence on the sustainable behavior of employees. This provides the possibility for future academics to further investigate the nature of these practices and perhaps other factors that might motivate employees to engage in sustainable behavior, such as job satisfaction or environmental values.

Limitations of the Research

The main limitation of this research was the small number of respondents, possibly due to the fact that the supervisors of two company departments became ill during the data collection period. The response rate was 34%, meaning that a higher percentage of nonresponse means a higher risk of nonresponse bias. For example, employees that do not engage in sustainable behavior or do not find the topic of sustainability interesting or important would be less likely to participate in this research. Therefore, it is difficult to make concrete conclusions for the entire population when the response rate is not so high.

Even though the sample of respondents was representative of the company departments, a higher number of respondents would have increased the validity of the study. Additionally, the exclusion of the other company departments could have led to there being no statistical differences between the three company departments in their employees' sustainable behavior. Thus, all departments of the resort could be included next time as this could give more diversified answers and perhaps lead to a difference in the sustainable behavior of the resort's employees.

Another limitation of this research was that it had to be conducted from a distance. Thus, data had to be collected through an online questionnaire which was distributed by the managers and supervisors of each company department. Given the fact that the questionnaire was about the sustainable behavior of employees working for a sustainable company and that it was distributed to them by their supervisors, employees could have felt pressured to give answers that were expected from them.

Suggestions for Further Research

Although there were several limitations to this research, it builds a foundation for the resort to encourage their employees in sustainable behavior and provides considerable room for further research to expand upon. The finding that training and rewards do not have a significant influence on employees' sustainable behavior in this situation gives future researchers the opportunity to explore the effectiveness of alternative sustainable HR practices. Additionally, future research could address the limitations of this study by using different data collection tools, such as interviews or experiments, to gain better insights into how sustainable HR practices affect employees' sustainable behavior. Conducting the research in-person and in private with employees, thus not on behalf of management, would also reduce the pressure on employees to give expected answers, thereby making the results as reliable as possible. As for the limitation on the number of respondents, all departments of the resort could be included next time, and perhaps an incentive could be given to the employees to participate in the research.

Conclusion

This chapter investigated the relationship between sustainable HR practices and the inclination of employees to engage in sustainable behavior in order to support sustainability within an organization. Based on previous literature, the research model was created that connects four sustainable HR practices to the sustainable behavior of employees, namely internal sustainability orientation, supervisory support, training, and rewards. Additionally, the mediating role of employees' knowledge of sustainability practices of the resort was examined in relation to the four practices and employees' sustainable behavior. The research was conducted in collaboration with Boarco Beach Resort, an eco-friendly hotel located on an island. Like many other companies, they are facing the challenge of encouraging their employees to engage in sustainable behavior. During this research, the extra-role behavior of employees was looked at, meaning the behavior that employees engage in that does not relate to their job requirements.

The results of this research show that when the resort clearly communicates about the importance of their sustainability practices to their employees by helping them understand and participate in these activities in addition to supervisory support, employees are more likely to be encouraged to engage in sustainable behavior. Although we expected sustainability training and rewards to have an influence on the sustainable behavior of employees, the results showed that both these practices did not have statistically significant effects. The results of the current study provide the resort – and other hotels – with data-driven insights on how to encourage their employees in sustainable behavior to achieve their long-term sustainability goals and maintain the effectiveness of their sustainability practices.

Case Study

Boarco Beach Resort is a Caribbean Carbon Neutral resort. On the island where it is located, tourism is a multimillion-dollar industry responsible for almost 60% of the island's economy and around 80% of the total jobs on the island.

Ever since the resort was founded, it has focused on incorporating sustainability into its business practices by investing in environmental technologies and systems, as well as environmentally safe products. For example, the resort uses solar panels to heat water, water reducers to limit water flow, and reuses water from sinks and showers to irrigate the gardens. In addition to the sustainability of its own practices, it supports a wide range of sustainability efforts in the local community, such as a donkey sanctuary, a beach cleanup, and the introduction of a law banning plastic bags. The resort has received numerous environmental awards and certifications for its sustainability efforts. On its website, the company prominently displays its sustainability efforts as well as a central section labeled "What we are not." In the latter, they explain to guests why they do not offer things like all-inclusive service (namely, to stimulate guests to visit local restaurants), steaming-hot whirlpools, or plastic water bottles.

Despite its long history in sustainable practices, the resort is currently facing the same challenge as other companies after implementing policies and practices to manage sustainability: the sustainable behavior of their employees. A lot (if not most) of its many sustainability initiatives require the cooperation of its employees. For example, initiatives like the reduction of energy and water consumption, the reuse of leftover breakfast bread for croutons and bread pudding, a recycling contest in which resort guests act as judges for crafts created by employees, and employees helping guests to adopt stray dogs, all require the active involvement of employees. The resort has an active Green Team, in which each department is represented. However, this might not always be sufficient to make sustainability "top of mind" for employees in their busy day-to-day work.

Case Study Questions

(1) How can the resort managers increase their support toward employees when it comes to sustainability initiatives?
(2) How can Boarco Beach Resort communicate their sustainability efforts to their employees?
(3) Which other factors could possibly encourage employees of the resort to engage in sustainable behavior and why?

Key Terms and Definitions

Extra-role sustainable behavior: Employees' actions beyond their formal job requirements, in which they take the initiative to engage in sustainable behavior in the workplace.
Internal sustainability orientation: The way in which employees perceive a company's sustainability vision and practices.
Rewards: Stimuli provided to employees to reinforce desired behavior.
Supervisory support: The resources and feedback given by supervisors to understand and participate in sustainability initiatives and practices in the workplace environment.
Sustainability knowledge of the resort: Employees awareness and understanding of the resort's sustainability practices.
Sustainability training: Education aimed at increasing the environmental awareness of employees, improving their capability to make sustainability-related decisions, and carrying out sustainable actions in the workplace.
Sustainable HR practices: Policies in place to achieve desired environmental and social outcomes.

References

Aguilera, R. V., Rupp, D. E., Williams, C. A., & Ganapathi, J. (2007). Putting the S back in corporate social responsibility: A multilevel theory of social change in organizations. *Academy of Management Review, 32*(3), 836–863.

Ahmad, S., & Schroeder, R. G. (2003). The impact of human resource management practices on operational performance: Recognizing country and industry differences. *Journal of Operations Management*, (21), 19–43.

Ahuja, J., Panda, T. K., Luthra, S., Kumar, A., Choudhary, S., & Garza-Reyes, J. A. (2019). Do human critical success factors matter in adoption of sustainable manufacturing practices? An influential mapping analysis of multi-company perspective. *Journal of Cleaner Production*, *239*, 117981.

Aselage, J., & Eisenberger, R. (2003). Perceived organizational support and psychological contracts: A theoretical integration. *Journal of Organizational Behavior: The International Journal of Industrial, Occupational and Organizational Psychology and Behavior*, *24*(5), 491–509.

Bader, E. E. (2005). Sustainable hotel business practices. *Journal of Retail and Leisure Property*, *5*(1), 70–77.

Bartol, K. M., & Srivastava, A. (2002). Encouraging knowledge sharing: The role of organizational reward systems. *Journal of Leadership & Organizational Studies*, *9*(1), 64–76.

Baruch, Y., & Holtom, B. C. (2008). Survey response rate levels and trends in organizational research. *Human Relations*, *61*(8), 1139–1160.

Becherer, R. C., & Helms, M. M. (2014). Green goals in organizations: Do small businesses engage in environmentally friendly strategies? *Journal of Small Business Strategy*, *24*(1), 1–18.

Berns, M., Townend, A., Zayna, K., Balagopal, B., Reeves, M., Hopkins, M., & Kruschwitz, N. (2009). The business of sustainability. Findings and insights from the first annual business of sustainability survey and the global thought leaders research project. *MIT Sloan Management Review*, *51*(1), 20–26.

Boarco Beach Resort. (2022). https://www.bucuti.com/resort/eco-friendly

Boiral, O., & Paillé, P. (2012). Organizational citizenship behaviour for the environment: Measurement and validation. *Journal of Business Ethics*, *109*(4), 431–445.

Boiral, O., Raineri, N., & Talbot, D. (2018). Managers' citizenship behaviors for the environment: A developmental perspective. *Journal of Business Ethics*, *149*, 395–409.

Boswell, W. R., Bingham, J. B., & Colvin, A. J. (2006). Aligning employees through "line of sight". *Business Horizons*, *49*(6), 499–509.

Boyt, T. E., Lusch, R. F., & Naylor, G. (2001). The role of professionalism in determining job satisfaction in professional services: A study of marketing researchers. *Journal of Service Research*, *3*(4), 321–330.

Cantor, D. E., Morrow, P. C., & Montabon, F. (2012). Engagement in environmental behaviors among supply chain management employees: An organizational support theoretical perspective. *Journal of Supply Chain Management*, *48*(3), 33–51.

Chan, E. S., & Hawkins, R. (2010). Attitude towards EMSs in an international hotel: An exploratory case study. *International Journal of Hospitality Management*, *29*(4), 641–651.

Chan, E. S. W., Hon, A. H. Y., Chan, W., & Okumus, F. (2014). What drives employees' intentions to implement green practices in hotels? The role of knowledge, awareness, concern and ecological behavior. *International Journal of Hospitality Management*, *40*, 20–28.

Chatman, J. A. (1989). Improving interactional organizational research: A model of person-organization fit. *Academy of Management Review*, *14*(3), 333–349.

Daily, B. F., & Huang, S. C. (2001). Achieving sustainability through attention to human resource factors in environmental management. *International Journal of Operations & Production Management, 21*(12), 1539–1552.

Del Brío, J. Á., Fernandez, E., & Junquera, B. (2007). Management and employee involvement in achieving an environmental action-based competitive advantage: An empirical study. *International Journal of Human Resource Management, 18*(4), 491–522.

Eisenberger, R., Huntington, R., Hutchison, S., & Sowa, D. (1986). Perceived organizational support. *Journal of Applied Psychology, 71*(3), 500–507.

Fien, J. (2002). Advancing sustainability in higher education: Issues and opportunities for research. *Higher Education Policy, 15*(2), 143–152.

Harms, D. (2011). Environmental sustainability and supply chain management—A framework of cross-functional integration and knowledge transfer. *Journal of Environmental Sustainability, 1*(1), 9.

Henry, L. (2013). *The greening of America-including hotels, will going green push me further into the black! Trends in the hotel industry, USA Edition 2013* (pp. 14–17). PKF Consulting.

Hillary, R. (2004). Environmental management systems and the smaller enterprise. *Journal of Cleaner Production, 12*(6), 561–569.

Hunter, C., & Green, H. (1995). *Tourism and the environment: A sustainable relationship?* Routledge.

Iverson, R. D., & Deery, M. (1997). Turnover culture in the hospitality industry. *Human Resource Management Journal, 7*(4), 71–82.

Jabbour, C. J. C., & Santos, F. C. A. (2008). The central role of human resource management in the search for sustainable organizations. *International Journal of Human Resource Management, 19*(12), 2133–2154.

Jones, P., Hillier, D., & Comfort, D. (2014). Sustainability in the global hotel industry. *International Journal of Contemporary Hospitality Management, 26*(1), 5–17.

Kramar, R. (2014). Beyond strategic human resource management: Is sustainable human resource management the next approach? *International Journal of Human Resource Management, 25*(8), 1069–1089.

Nicholls, S., & Kang, S. (2012). Going green: The adoption of environmental initiatives in Michigan's lodging sector. *Journal of Sustainable Tourism, 20*(7), 953–974.

Norton, T. A., Zacher, H., & Ashkanasy, N. M. (2014). Organisational sustainability policies and employee green behaviour: The mediating role of work climate perceptions. *Journal of Environmental Psychology, 38*, 49–54. https://doi.org/10.1016/j.jenvp.2013.12.008

Paillé, P., Chen, Y., Boiral, O., & Jin, J. (2014). The impact of human resource management on environmental performance: An employee-level study. *Journal of Business Ethics, 121*(3), 451–466.

Pellegrini, C., Rizzi, F., & Frey, M. (2018). The role of sustainable human resource practices in influencing employee behavior for corporate sustainability. *Business Strategy and the Environment, 27*(8), 1221–1232.

Raineri, N., & Paillé, P. (2016). Linking corporate policy and supervisory support with environmental citizenship behaviors: The role of employee environmental beliefs and commitment. *Journal of Business Ethics, 137*(1), 129–148.

Ramus, C. A. (2001). Organizational support for employees: Encouraging creative ideas for environmental sustainability. *California Management Review, 43*(3), 85–105.

Ramus, C. A., & Killmer, A. B. (2007). Corporate greening through prosocial extra-role behaviours–a conceptual framework for employee motivation. *Business Strategy and the Environment, 16*(8), 554–570.

Ramus, C. A., & Steger, U. (2000). The roles of supervisory support behaviors and environmental policy in employee 'ecoinitiatives' at leading-edge European companies. *Academy of Management Journal, 43*(4), 605–626.

Rezapouraghdam, H., Alipour, H., & Arasli, H. (2019). Workplace spirituality and organization sustainability: A theoretical perspective on hospitality employees' sustainable behavior. *Environment, Development and Sustainability, 21*(4), 1583–1601.

Ruiz-Pérez, F., Lleo, A., & Ormazabal, M. (2021). Employee sustainable behaviors and their relationship with corporate sustainability: A Delphi study. *Journal of Cleaner Production, 329,* 129742.

Saeed, B. B., Afsar, B., Hafeez, S., Khan, I., Tahir, M., & Afridi, M. A. (2019). Promoting employee's proenvironmental behavior through green human resource management practices. *Corporate Social Responsibility and Environmental Management, 26*(2), 424–438.

Sammalisto, K., & Brorson, T. (2008). Training and communication in the implementation of environmental management systems (ISO 14001): A case study at the University of Gävle, Sweden. *Journal of Cleaner Production, 16*(3), 299–309.

Sarkis, J., Gonzalez-Torre, P., & Adenso-Diaz, B. (2010). Stakeholder pressure and the adoption of environmental practices: The mediating effect of training. *Journal of Operations Management, 28*(2), 163–176.

Scanlon, N. L. (2007). An analysis and assessment of environmental operating practices in hotel and resort properties. *International Journal of Hospitality Management, 26*(3), 711–723.

Schmudde, U. (2019). *Sustainable city development by tourism over cross-sectoral industries: A case study in Central Sweden* (Vol. 238, pp. 527–541). WIT Transactions on Ecology and the Environment. https://doi.org/10.2495/SC190461

Stalcup, L. D., Deale, C. S., & Todd, S. Y. (2014). Human resources practices for environmental sustainability in lodging operations. *Journal of Human Resources in Hospitality & Tourism, 13*(4), 389–404.

Susskind, A. M., Kacmar, K. M., & Borchgrevink, C. P. (2003). Customer service providers' attitudes relating to customer service and customer satisfaction in the customer-server exchange. *Journal of Applied Psychology, 88*(1), 179–187.

Terera, S. R., & Ngirande, H. (2014). The impact of rewards on job satisfaction and employee retention. *Mediterranean Journal of Social Sciences, 5*(1), 481–487.

Tzschentke, N., Kirk, D., & Lynch, P. A. (2004). Reasons for going green in serviced accommodation establishments. *International Journal of Contemporary Hospitality Management, 16*(2), 116–124.

United Nations World Tourism Organization (UNWTO). (2022). Tourism – An economic and social phenomenon: Why tourism? https://www.unwto.org/why-tourism

Van Dyne, L., & LePine, J. A. (1998). Helping and voice extra-role behaviors: Evidence of construct and predictive validity. *Academy of Management Journal, 41*(1), 108–119.

Van Iddekinge, C. H., Ferris, G. R., Perrewe, P. L., Perryman, A. A., Blass, F. R., & Heetderks, T. D. (2009). Effects of selection and training on unit-level performance over time: A latent growth modeling approach. *Journal of Applied Psychology, 94*(4), 829–843.

Young, W., Davis, M., McNeill, I. M., Malhotra, B., Russell, S., Unsworth, K., & Clegg, C. W. (2015). Changing behaviour: Successful environmental programmes in the workplace. *Business Strategy and the Environment, 24*(8), 689–703.

Yousaf, S., Latif, M., Aslam, S., & Saddiqui, A. (2014). Impact of financial and non-financial rewards on employee motivation. *Middle-East Journal of Scientific Research, 21*(10), 1776–1786.

Zhang, L., Wu, J., Chen, H., & Nguyen, B. (2020). Does one bad apple ruin a firm's green brand image? Examining frontline service employees' environmentally irresponsible behaviors. *European Journal of Marketing, 54*(10), 2501–2521.

Appendices

Table A1. Research Variables With Their Corresponding Items and Measurement Scales.

Variable	Items	Measurement Scale
Internal sustainability orientation	(1) Boarco makes an effort to let every employee understand the importance of sustainability.	Five-point Likert scale (Strongly agree to Strongly disagree)
	(2) Boarco notifies their employees about sustainability changes in the resort.	
	(3) Boarco uses information systems (such as email, bulletin boards, etc.) to share information about sustainability with their employees.	
	(4) Boarco gives complete and accurate information regarding sustainability topics.	

(Continued)

Table A1. *(Continued)*

Variable	Items	Measurement Scale
	(5) Boarco helps organize and make sense of information when there is too much or confusing sustainability information.	
Supervisory support	(1) My supervisor encourages me to come up with new sustainability ideas.	Five-point Likert scale (Strongly agree to Strongly disagree)
	(2) I can easily discuss concerns around sustainability with my supervisor.	
	(3) My supervisor is open to receiving feedback or suggestions on the sustainability matters of the resort.	
Sustainability training	(1) Boarco commits resources and time for employees to attend sustainability training.	Five-point Likert scale (Strongly agree to Strongly disagree)
	(2) Sustainability training is offered on a regular basis.	
	(3) Boarco encourages participation in any activity in which an employee would like to learn and develop their sustainability skills, such as a workshop or webinar.	
	(4) Boarco makes sure that employees have the required tools to do their job in a sustainable way.	
	(5) I would want more sustainability training to be offered to employees.	
Rewards	(1) Boarco gives recognition to employees who do something good for the environment in their daily job.	Five-point Likert scale (Strongly agree to Strongly disagree)

Table A1. *(Continued)*

Variable	Items	Measurement Scale
	(2) Boarco rewards or recognizes its employees' sustainability initiatives.	
	(3) A monthly sustainability nomination would motivate me to engage (more) with sustainability at the resort.	
Sustainability knowledge	(1) Boarco is a certified Carbon Neutral resort.	True/False
	(2) Energy-saving technology is used in the rooms and Elements restaurant.	
	(3) The guests' bed linens and towels are changed every day.	
	(4) Aluminum, glass, and cardboard are recycled at Boarco.	
	(5) Boarco uses the most eco-friendly products available.	
	(6) Ingredients for food are sourced almost 100% locally.	
	(7) All plants on the resort's property are native to Aruba.	
	(8) Food and textile waste are thrown away.	
Employees' sustainable behavior	(1) During my lunch break in the cafeteria, I only take as much food as I can eat.	Five-point Likert scale (Always to Never)
	(2) I participate in the monthly beach clean-ups.	
	(3) During my daily job, I think about how I can work in the most sustainable way possible.	

(Continued)

Table A1. *(Continued)*

Variable	Items	Measurement Scale
	(4) I use a reusable water canteen at work.	
	(5) I often think of ways to be (more) sustainable in my organization.	

Table A2. True or False Statements From the Online Questionnaire.

Statement	True or False	Positive or Negative
• Boarco is a certified Carbon Neutral resort	True	Positive
• Energy-saving technology is used in the rooms and elements restaurant	True	Positive
• The guests' bed linens and towels are changed every day	False	Negative
• Aluminum, glass, and cardboard are recycled at Boarco	True	Positive
• Boarco uses the most eco-friendly products available	True	Positive
• Ingredients for food are sourced almost 100% locally	False	Positive
• All plants on the resort's property are native to Aruba	True	Positive
• Food and textile waste are thrown away	False	Negative

Part III

Business Strategies for Technological Adoption

This part speaks to the "Technological Adoption" aspect of your title. It focuses on how businesses can strategically adopt emerging technologies.

Chapter 10

Smart Retailing Adoption and Digital Business Strategy in the Time of the Crisis

Edem Kofi Boni and S. Asieh H. Tabaghdehi

Brunel University London, UK

Abstract

The retail industry has experienced significant transformations driven by digitalization and the challenges posed by the COVID-19 pandemic. This chapter aims to explore the impact of digitalization on retail business models and understand consumer purchasing habits during emergencies. This chapter will examine the influence of scarcity and competitive arousal on consumer choices, the effects of stock-outs on brand and store preferences, price sensitivity, waiting times and the shift towards online shopping. Additionally, it will address concerns about social exclusion in digital channels and the potential for bridging the gap between offline and online shopping experiences.

Keywords: Smart retaining; digital transformation customer purchasing behaviour; digital ethics; privacy; trust; crisis

Introduction: Overview of the COVID-19 Pandemic and Its Impact on Retailers

The continuous progression of digitalization and the rapid advancement of smart technologies have had a profound impact on the retail industry, driving significant innovation. This transformation has been further accelerated by the unprecedented challenges posed by the COVID-19 crisis. Notably, there has been a substantial surge in global online shopping volumes from February 2020 to April 2021, resulting in a remarkable 35% increase in the market capitalization of the retail sector (Bradley et al., 2021). As a result, the retail industry has witnessed a notable rise in innovative business models aimed at meeting the ever-increasing

Business Strategies and Ethical Challenges in the Digital Ecosystem, 227–244
Copyright © 2025 Edem Kofi Boni and S. Asieh H. Tabaghdehi
Published under exclusive licence by Emerald Publishing Limited
doi:10.1108/978-1-80455-069-420241010

and dynamic expectations of consumers (Aslam, 2023; Kullak et al., 2023; Mostaghel et al., 2022; Swani et al., 2023). This surge in innovation encompasses various aspects, including the adoption of technology, integration of supply chains, management of logistics and the implementation of digital marketing strategies (Crespo et al., 2023; de Lucas Ancillo & Gavrila Gavrila, 2023; Gavrila Gavrila & de Lucas Ancillo, 2021). Due to some retailers' early adoption of cutting-edge digital business models during the pandemic, there was a clear disparity between industry leaders and laggards in terms of market value growth (Bradley et al., 2021). These forward-thinking retailers, who proactively embraced innovative digital strategies and technologies, positioned themselves at the forefront of the industry's evolution. By leveraging digitalization to optimize their operations, enhance consumer experiences and transform their business models, they gained a competitive edge. Their early adoption of digitalization proved instrumental in navigating the unprecedented challenges brought about by the pandemic. As consumer behaviours rapidly shifted towards online channels, these digitally savvy retailers were well-prepared to meet changing demands and capitalize on the growing digital market. The result was a significant increase in market value, indicating recognition from investors of the resilience and future potential of these digitally enabled retailers. Their ability to harness the power of advanced digital technologies, such as data analytics, artificial intelligence (AI) and personalized marketing, enabled them to deliver tailored experiences, attract and retain consumers and drive revenue growth.

In contrast, retailers that were slower to embrace digital transformation encountered greater difficulties during the pandemic. Their traditional business models struggled to adapt to the rapidly changing landscape, making it challenging for them to compete effectively, particularly against digitally native disruptors. Consequently, the gap between these laggards and the industry leaders who had embraced digitalization widened significantly. This divergence in market value growth serves as a compelling reminder of the critical importance of retailers embracing digital transformation. It underscores the need for ongoing innovation, investment in digital capabilities and proactive adaptation to evolving consumer expectations. The experiences of retailers who had already embraced advanced digital business models highlight the strategic imperative for the industry to prioritize digitalization to thrive and succeed in the dynamic and increasingly digital-driven retail landscape. The effects and benefits derived from digitalization in the retail business model are evident for several reasons. Firstly, retailers typically rely on third-party suppliers for their products, making a streamlined supply chain management system vital for their competitiveness. Secondly, retailers serve as the final link in the supply chain and have direct engagement with end consumers (Dahlke et al., 2021; Ganotakis et al., 2023). By leveraging digitalization to enhance consumer interactions, retailers can drive higher sales and overall performance. Lastly, the retail industry is one of the largest sectors in many economies, characterized by its substantial workforce and value creation (Foroudi et al., 2018; Jain et al., 2022; Pantano, 2014). Retailers play a crucial role as intermediaries in the supply chain, making digitalization-driven innovation highly relevant (Dahlke et al., 2021; Ganotakis et al., 2023; Mostaghel et al., 2022).

Consequently, it becomes imperative to deepen our understanding of how digitalization enables business model innovation in the retail industry, both in practical and theoretical terms. Through a comprehensive study of the relationship between digitalization and business model transformation, valuable insights can be gained to guide retailers in adapting to the rapidly evolving landscape and maximizing the benefits of digitalization. Digitalization, defined as the utilization of digital technologies to transform business models and create new sources of revenue and value within industrial ecosystems (Parida et al., 2019), has a profound impact on the retail industry. It goes beyond the mere introduction of new technologies and focuses on understanding the implementation and use of digitalization. In the empirical context of retail, digitalization significantly affects various aspects of business models, including value creation, value delivery and value capture. One example of digitalization's impact on value creation is the use of AI in analyzing social media content. Retailers can gain more precise insights into consumer behaviour, leading to improved marketing decision-making in a shorter time frame (Alabed et al., 2022; Fredström et al., 2022; Nazir et al., 2023). Similarly, the utilization of chatbots and robot-generated responses enables prompt and accurate consumer inquiries, enhancing the value delivery process (Aw et al., 2022; Hoyer et al., 2020). Virtual reality (VR) is also utilized to augment the consumer experience, further enhancing value delivery (Battisti et al., 2022; Holzmann & Gregori, 2023; Mostaghel et al., 2022). In terms of value capture, there is a growing experimentation with cryptocurrency, blockchain and big data analytics, which are expected to have a lasting impact on retail revenue models (Mostaghel et al., 2022).

The digitalization-driven innovation of retail business models has attracted considerable interest from marketing and innovation management scholars. However, existing research in this area is limited in scope and lacks a comprehensive perspective. Previous studies have focused on specific aspects of digitalization-driven retail business model innovation, leaving a gap in understanding the transformative role of digitalization in retail business models. The current trajectory of the retail industry remains uncertain for both researchers and practitioners, as the emergence of advanced technologies presents both opportunities and challenges (Meyer et al., 2023; Paul & Rosenbaum, 2020). The contemporary global landscape is undergoing profound transformations that significantly influence consumer perceptions and behaviours in the retail sector, leaving a lasting impact beyond the emergency. These changes compel consumers to reconsider their established habits and preferences, leading to noteworthy shifts. Primarily, consumers may switch from their usual retailers to other competitors due to factors such as spatial proximity and product assortment availability during the emergency. The crisis-induced disruptions prompt individuals to reassess their loyalty to familiar retailers, driving them to explore alternatives that better cater to their immediate needs and circumstances. Secondly, the assistance provided by certain retailers during the emergency can foster a sense of attachment and gratitude among consumers, potentially resulting in continued patronage even after the crisis subsides. Consumers are likely to develop loyalty and trust towards retailers that demonstrated support and responsiveness during challenging times. Conversely, retailers perceived as unwilling or unable to accommodate consumers' needs, such as providing delivery slots for loyal patrons, may experience a decrease in consumer attachment. Furthermore, the pandemic-induced changes in shopping habits have led consumers to discover and embrace new services and conveniences previously overlooked. Notably, older consumers, who were initially hesitant to engage in online purchases, have now embraced the safety and benefits.

Consumers' Purchasing Behaviour During Emergencies

Recent literature has emphasized the influential role of perceived scarcity in shaping consumer choices (Hamilton et al., 2019; Serravalle et al., 2023). The global lockdown imposed due to the COVID-19 outbreak in early 2020 triggered substantial shifts in behaviour and habits for both consumers and retailers (Serravalle et al., 2023). This unprecedented event led to a significant increase in online activities, including shopping, entertainment and communication (Ishrat et al., 2023; Santiago et al., 2022), resulting in information overload characterized by an abundance of available information for consumers. Within this context, the perception of content relevance in the purchase decision process can be influenced (Jiang & Stylos, 2021; Serravalle et al., 2023). While previous research has demonstrated that scarcity enhances the perceived value of unavailable goods (Verhallen & Robben, 1994; Yuen et al., 2022), it has also been observed that the scarcity of products, as opposed to resources, can have contrasting effects. On one hand, scarcity can augment the value attributed to scarce products (Cialdini, 1993, 2021); on the other hand, it can diminish the significance of the purchase context (Shah et al., 2015). During the global lockdown, consumers exhibited unprecedented stockpiling behaviours, deviating from their customary shopping patterns. Essential items such as hand sanitizers, surgical masks and toilet tissue quickly became scarce, followed by seemingly unrelated products like yeast, pasta and detergents (Pantano et al., 2020). The scarcity of these products resulted in an increase in negative behaviours, such as anxiety, among consumers, leading to disruptions in their rational purchasing decisions (Serravalle et al., 2023).

Two significant phenomena that emerged during the initial waves of the COVID-19 pandemic contributed to this situation: the scarcity effect and competitive arousal. The scarcity effect, originally explored in commodity theory (Brock, 1968), posits that the value of a commodity is heightened when it is scarce or unavailable (Brock, 1968). As a result, consumers tend to desire scarce products more than others because they associate owning these items with feelings of personal distinctiveness or uniqueness (Brock, 1968; Lynn, 1991; Serravalle et al., 2023). This desire for scarce products engenders a sense of anxiety and competition among consumers, referred to as "competitive arousal" in the literature (Allport, 1924; Serravalle et al., 2023). Competitive arousal encompasses the competitive nature of a purchase situation and the belief that one must compete with other buyers to achieve a specific goal within a particular buying context (Nichols, 2012; Park & Li, 2023; Song et al., 2021). In non-emergency periods, stock-outs in groceries are infrequent occurrences. However, the repeated exposure to stock-outs during emergencies can elicit unexpected responses from consumers, and these responses may persist beyond the emergency period. Previous studies have shown that when consumers encounter a temporary product shortage, they typically adapt by either choosing an alternative brand or shopping at a different store. This behaviour is a common response to such situations, as demonstrated in previous study (Hoang & Breugelmans, 2022; Ngoh & Groening, 2022; Pizzi & Scarpi, 2013). Nonetheless, the recurrent unavailability of specific brands (due to stock-outs) and stores (due to lockdown measures) could bring about a more profound transformation in consumer preferences, ultimately impacting the distribution of product choices even after the stores return to their normal operating conditions.

The panic-driven stockpiling also influenced consumers' price sensitivity, leading to many individuals accepting significant price increases for certain product categories. Additionally, government-imposed regulations, including limitations on gatherings and enforcement of social distancing measures, resulted in long queues forming outside stores, with consumers sometimes enduring hours of waiting. Previous research has demonstrated a negative relationship between waiting time and consumer satisfaction (Anić et al., 2010; Papagiannidis et al., 2022). However, the long-term impact of extended waiting times during emergencies on consumer satisfaction remains uncertain. The limited access to physical store premises, coupled with heightened health concerns, triggered a surge in demand for alternative distribution channels. The COVID-19 emergency has accelerated the growth of online shopping, also known as smart retailing, which had previously seen gradual progress over the past decade. This surge in online shopping can be attributed to various factors, including the safety concerns associated with physical stores during the pandemic. Online platforms offer convenience and accessibility, appealing not only to tech-savvy individuals but also to older and less technologically adept consumers who may have been hesitant to engage in online shopping before. However, alongside the benefits of online shopping, concerns regarding social exclusion arise from the accelerated shift to digital channels. While online shopping partially alleviates the negative effects of social isolation by providing individuals with the ability to procure necessary goods without leaving their homes, it is important to recognize the potential implications for consumer well-being. Social exclusion refers to the feeling of being disconnected from society or excluded from social interactions, and it can have detrimental effects on mental health and overall life satisfaction.

In a comparative perspective, traditional offline shopping (brick and mortar) has traditionally offered a social aspect that online shopping may lack. Physical stores often serve as social spaces where individuals can engage in face-to-face interactions with store employees and other consumers, fostering social connection, personal recommendations and a sense of community. Offline shopping experiences allow consumers to browse and compare products physically, engaging their senses in a way that online shopping cannot replicate. Moreover, offline shopping offers immediate gratification through the ability to touch, try on or examine products before making a purchase decision. This tactile experience is absent in the online shopping process, where consumers rely on product descriptions, images and reviews to inform their choices. The absence of physical interaction with products can lead to uncertainty and dissatisfaction if the purchased items do not meet consumers' expectations. However, online shopping platforms have been working to bridge the gap between virtual and physical shopping experiences. Some platforms have implemented features such as augmented reality (AR) and VR technologies, which allow consumers to visualize products in their physical environment or virtually try on items. These advancements aim to enhance the online shopping experience and address some of the limitations associated with social exclusion and a lack of sensory engagement. Furthermore, retailers and governments have implemented various measures to comply with public regulations, leading to an increased adoption and acceptance of smart technologies in the retail sector. These technologies include chatbots, face recognition systems, voice assistance and GPS tracking. Although the use and disclosure of personal data typically raise privacy concerns among consumers, the perceived benefits of employing more invasive technology during emergencies may enhance consumers' willingness to disclose personal information. This, in turn, enables effective tracking of their shopping activities, which contributes to the containment efforts of the virus. However, it remains uncertain whether these adaptations will persist beyond the emergency period and if privacy concerns will continue to diminish. In conclusion, the COVID-19 pandemic has triggered significant shifts in consumer behaviour and preferences. Factors such as product scarcity, price sensitivity, extended waiting times, reliance on online shopping and acceptance of biometric surveillance have influenced consumer responses during this crisis. Understanding the long-term effects of these changes is crucial for retailers and policymakers as they address the post-pandemic landscape. Further research is needed to investigate the lasting impact on consumer decision-making and the potential adaptations that may emerge in the aftermath of this extraordinary period.

Recommendations

The COVID-19 pandemic has served as a catalyst for the digital transformation of the retail industry. To meet the evolving expectations of consumers, retailers have been compelled to adopt innovative business models. This academic discussion aims to present solutions and recommendations that can assist retailers in effectively addressing the challenges and controversies arising from the pandemic, while also leveraging digitalization to drive business model innovation.

One crucial recommendation for retailers is to proactively embrace digital transformation by adopting innovative digital strategies and technologies that optimize operations, enhance consumer experiences and transform business models. The adoption of digital technologies enables retailers to leverage data analytics, AI and personalized marketing to tailor experiences, attract and retain consumers and drive revenue growth. Early adopters who embraced digitalization gained a competitive edge during the pandemic, underscoring the strategic importance of digital transformation.

Streamlining the supply chain is another key aspect for retailers to remain competitive. Digitalization enables improved supply chain visibility, collaboration and efficiency, thereby enhancing the overall performance of retailers and their ability to meet dynamic consumer demands. Retailers should streamline their supply chains through digitalization by leveraging technologies such as blockchain and data analytics to optimize inventory management, demand forecasting and logistics. Retailers should harness the power of data analytics and AI to gain insights into consumer behaviour, improve marketing decision-making and deliver personalized consumer experiences. The utilization of data analytics and AI allows retailers to analyze social media content and other data sources, providing precise insights into consumer behaviour. This information enables retailers to better understand their target audience, tailor offerings and optimize marketing strategies.

Retailers should invest in technologies that enhance value delivery to consumers, such as chatbots, VR and other immersive experiences. By leveraging digitalization, retailers can provide prompt and accurate consumer service through chatbots and create immersive shopping experiences using VR technology. These innovations improve convenience, efficiency and consumer satisfaction, leading to increased loyalty and revenue growth. Digitalization provides opportunities for retailers to explore new revenue streams. By experimenting with emerging technologies, retailers can leverage blockchain for secure transactions, utilize big data analytics to drive insights and potentially adopt cryptocurrency for seamless and efficient transactions. Retailers should experiment with emerging technologies such as cryptocurrency, blockchain and big data analytics to develop innovative revenue models.

The pandemic-induced changes in consumer behaviour necessitate retailers to prioritize consumer loyalty. By demonstrating responsiveness to consumer needs, providing convenient services like home deliveries and cashless payments, retailers can build trust and secure long-term consumer loyalty. Retailers should focus on building consumer loyalty by providing exceptional support during challenging times and offering convenient services. Given the rapidly evolving landscape, retailers should invest in research to understand the transformative impact of digitalization on retail business models. This knowledge will guide decision-making, enabling retailers to handle the rapid changes of the retail landscape effectively. Retailers should adopt a research-oriented approach, staying informed about emerging trends, technologies and consumer dynamics.

Retailers should prioritize the development and enhancement of their e-commerce infrastructure to meet the demands of online shopping during crises. This includes ensuring robust website performance, minimizing downtime and accurately tracking inventory levels. By investing in scalable infrastructure, retailers can handle increased online traffic and provide a seamless shopping experience for consumers. Delivery and fulfilment processes are critical during crises, especially when there is a surge in online orders. Retailers should leverage technology to optimize their logistics operations, including the use of automation, route optimization algorithms and last-mile delivery solutions. By streamlining delivery processes, retailers can ensure timely and efficient order fulfilment, minimizing delays and improving consumer satisfaction.

In-store technology that minimizes physical contact and prioritizes safety should be adopted. Retailers should invest in contactless payment solutions, self-checkout systems and advanced store technologies to reduce touchpoints and provide a safe shopping environment. This includes leveraging computer vision, sensor fusion and deep learning algorithms to enable frictionless shopping experiences and minimize physical interactions. Retailers should harness the power of data analytics to understand changing consumer behaviour and personalize their offerings. By analyzing consumer data, retailers can identify trends, preferences and purchase patterns, allowing them to tailor their marketing strategies and product recommendations. This personalization enhances the consumer experience, increases consumer loyalty, and drives sales during challenging times.

Effective communication with consumers is crucial during crises. Retailers should leverage technologies such as SMS notifications, email updates, and mobile apps to provide timely and transparent information about order status, delivery updates, and any changes to store operations. This helps build trust, keeps consumers informed, and ensures they feel valued and supported. Retailers should study and learn from successful case studies, such as a Supermarket and Online Retailer, to understand how technology can be effectively adopted during crises. By analyzing the strategies and solutions implemented by these industry leaders, retailers can gain valuable insights and adapt them to their specific business contexts. It is important to identify best practices and tailor them to suit their own operations and consumer base.

Hence, crises require retailers to continuously innovate and adapt to changing circumstances. Retailers should stay updated on the latest technological advancements and trends, such as emerging digital platforms, automation solutions, and delivery options. By embracing innovation and remaining flexible, retailers can proactively respond to challenges, meet consumer expectations and ensure long-term business continuity. By embracing digital transformation, enhancing supply chain management, leveraging data analytics and AI, improving value delivery, experimenting with new revenue models, building consumer loyalty, conducting research and staying informed, retailers can address the challenges presented by the COVID-19 pandemic and leverage digitalization for business model innovation. These solutions and recommendations enable retailers to adapt to evolving consumer expectations, drive growth and thrive in the increasingly digital-driven retail landscape.

Future Research Directions

Future research should focus on investigating the adoption and impact of smart retailing technologies during times of crisis. This includes studying the implementation of technologies such as IoT, AI, big data analytics and robotics in retail settings and evaluating their effectiveness in improving operational efficiency, consumer experience and overall business performance. Research can explore the challenges and barriers to adopting smart retailing technologies, as well as the organizational and managerial factors that influence successful implementation. In the face of crises, retailers need to develop resilient and adaptable digital business strategies. Future research can examine the characteristics and components of effective digital business strategies that enable retailers to manage through challenging times. This includes investigating the role of agility, flexibility and innovation in digital business models, as well as exploring strategies for managing risks and uncertainties. Research can also focus on understanding how digital business strategies can contribute to the long-term sustainability and competitiveness of retail organizations.

The future of smart retailing lies in delivering personalized and immersive consumer experiences. Research should explore the ways in which smart retailing technologies can be leveraged to enhance consumer engagement and create memorable experiences. This includes investigating the use of AR, VR, personalized recommendations and interactive touchpoints to create unique and tailored experiences for consumers. Future research can also examine the impact of consumer engagement and experience on consumer satisfaction, loyalty and purchase behaviour. As smart retailing technologies become more prevalent, it is essential to examine the ethical and social implications they may have. Future research should delve into topics such as data privacy, security and transparency in the collection and use of consumer data. Additionally, research can explore the impact of smart retailing on employment and workforce dynamics, as well as the potential socio-economic consequences of automation and robotics in retail settings. Understanding these ethical and social implications is crucial for developing responsible and sustainable smart retailing practices.

The role of AI and machine learning in optimizing inventory management, demand forecasting and supply chain coordination in smart retailing. The impact of smart retailing technologies on sustainability and environmental performance, including the reduction of waste, energy consumption and carbon emissions in retail operations. The influence of social media and online platforms on consumer engagement and brand-building strategies in the context of smart retailing. The integration of offline and online consumer experiences in smart retailing, including strategies for creating seamless omni-channel experiences and leveraging consumer data across different touchpoints. By addressing these future research directions and exploring the suggested issues, researchers can contribute to the understanding and advancement of smart retailing adoption and digital business strategy during times of crisis. The viability and effectiveness of different paradigms, models and implementation programs can be evaluated, leading to the development of best practices and insights for retailers to thrive in the evolving digital landscape.

Conclusion

This chapter focuses on consumers' purchasing habits during emergencies, particularly during the COVID-19 pandemic. It discusses the impact of perceived scarcity, competitive arousal and panic-driven stockpiling on consumer behaviour. It also explores the shifts in price sensitivity, extended waiting times and the surge in online shopping during the pandemic. This chapter examines the benefits and concerns associated with online shopping, including social exclusion and the absence of sensory engagement in virtual shopping experiences. It highlights the adoption of smart technologies by retailers and governments, such as chatbots, face recognition systems, GPS tracking and the potential trade-offs between privacy concerns and public health measures. In conclusion, the COVID-19 pandemic has had profound effects on consumer behaviour and preferences. The scarcity of essential products and the competitive arousal among consumers resulted in disruptions in rational purchasing decisions. Consumers exhibited panic-driven stockpiling and accepted significant price increases for certain product categories. The pandemic also accelerated the growth of online shopping, providing convenience and accessibility while raising concerns about social exclusion. Offline shopping offers social interaction, sensory engagement and immediate gratification, but online platforms are bridging the gap through technologies like AR. Retailers and governments have implemented various technological solutions to comply with regulations and contain the virus, raising questions about privacy and the long-term sustainability of these adaptations.

This chapter also presents case studies of a Supermarket and Online Retailer, highlighting their effective technological adoption during the pandemic. The Supermarket expanded its click and collect service, implemented mobile apps, self-checkout systems and inventory management solutions. The Online Retailer leveraged warehouse automation, machine learning algorithms, contactless delivery and advanced logistics to manage the surge in online orders. The case study questions provided facilitate a deeper analysis of these retailers' approaches, technological solutions and the lessons other retailers can learn from their successes and shortcomings. Overall, this chapter emphasizes the importance of understanding the long-term effects of the pandemic on consumer decision-making and the need for further research to explore the lasting impact and potential adaptations in the post-pandemic era.

Case Study

Retailers Demonstrating Effective Technological Adoption For Business Continuity During Crisis

The COVID-19 pandemic presented unprecedented challenges to retailers worldwide, including those based in the United Kingdom. In response, retailers like the Supermarket, Online Retailer and competing stores showcased remarkable resilience and adaptability through the strategic use of technology to ensure business continuity. These case studies shed light on how these UK-based retailers effectively employed technology-driven solutions such as click and collect services, digital innovations and supply chain optimization to address pandemic challenges and meet evolving consumer needs.

Case Study SUPERMARKET

During the COVID-19 pandemic, the Supermarket, the United Kingdom's leading supermarket chain, effectively adopted technology to address the surge in online orders and demand for contactless shopping options (Hodgson, 2021). In addition to expanding their click and collect service, the Supermarket implemented innovative digital solutions to enhance their operations and improve the overall shopping experience. For instance, they introduced a user-friendly mobile application that allowed consumers to browse products, create shopping lists and place orders from the comfort of their homes. The app provided real-time updates on product availability and allowed consumers to schedule their preferred collection times for click and collect orders. This seamless mobile shopping experience catered to the growing demand for online grocery shopping, providing a convenient and safe shopping solution during the pandemic. To streamline in-store shopping, the Supermarket introduced self-checkout systems, enabling consumers to independently scan and pay for their items, reducing queues and minimizing physical contact. This system not only expedited payments but also allowed the Supermarket to allocate more staff to other areas of the store, ensuring efficient operations and improved consumer satisfaction. Furthermore, the Supermarket utilized technology to enhance inventory management, ensuring product availability through advanced data analytics and AI. By accurately forecasting consumer demand and optimizing stock levels, the Supermarket effectively prevented stock-outs and met the increased demand for groceries during the pandemic. Apart from click and collect, the Supermarket introduced a home delivery service to cater to consumers preferring doorstep deliveries. By expanding their delivery capabilities and implementing contactless options, the Supermarket provided consumers with a safe and convenient way to receive their orders. Improved consumer communication channels, including SMS notifications and email updates, kept shoppers informed and engaged. Transparent and timely communication contributed to consumer satisfaction and trust during uncertain times. The Supermarket's proactive technological adoption made it a leader in the retail industry, setting an example for UK-based retailers on using technology effectively for business continuity in challenging times.

Case Study ONLINE RETAILER

As a global e-commerce giant, the Online Retailer faced a significant surge in online shopping during the pandemic. To address this and ensure timely deliveries, the Online Retailer relied on its advanced technological infrastructure and logistics capabilities. They implemented warehouse automation, utilizing robots and AI-powered systems to optimize order picking and fulfilment processes.

Machine learning algorithms were deployed to forecast consumer demand and provide personalized product recommendations, enhancing the shopping experience. The Online Retailer also offered contactless delivery, allowing consumers to receive orders without physical contact. The Online Retailer's extensive use of warehouse automation streamlined order processing, reducing time and increasing fulfilment accuracy. Machine learning algorithms predicted high-demand products, optimized inventory management and provided personalized product recommendations based on consumer behaviour. The Online Retailer's contactless delivery service assured consumer safety during the pandemic. They optimized delivery routes, reduced transit times and provided accurate delivery estimates through advanced route optimization algorithms and real-time tracking systems. The Online Retailer's commitment to consumer service was reflected in AI-powered chatbots, providing 24/7 customer support and issue resolution. In summary, the Online Retailer's technological adoption during the pandemic allowed them to handle surging online shopping demands while ensuring timely deliveries. By embracing warehouse automation, machine learning, contactless delivery services, advanced logistics solutions and AI-powered consumer support, the Online Retailer maintained high consumer satisfaction levels. Through these technological innovations, the Online Retailer set a benchmark for UK-based retailers, demonstrating how technology can ensure business continuity and consumer satisfaction during crises.

The COVID-19 pandemic heightened the need for retailers to embrace and utilize technology in response to changing consumer demands and challenges. In this analysis, we compare two prominent retailers, the Supermarket and the Online Retailer, regarding their technological shortcomings during the pandemic. By examining their technological responses, we can gain insights into the different approaches taken by these industry leaders and evaluate the effectiveness of their strategies.

E-Commerce Infrastructure and Scalability: One notable technological shortcoming observed during the COVID-19 pandemic was the limited e-commerce infrastructure and scalability of retailers. The Supermarket, as a traditional brick-and-mortar retailer, faced challenges in quickly expanding its online operations to keep up with the surge in demand. The company experienced website crashes, slow loading times and inventory inaccuracies, which led to frustrated consumers unable to complete their purchases. On the other hand, the Online Retailer, with its established and robust e-commerce infrastructure, demonstrated greater preparedness in terms of technology. The company effectively managed the increased online traffic, ensured a seamless user experience and successfully processed a significant number of orders. The Online Retailer's scalable and reliable technological infrastructure enabled it to meet consumers' expectations and maintain its position as a leading e-commerce platform.

Delivery and Fulfilment Optimization: Efficient delivery and fulfilment operations became paramount during the pandemic as more consumers turned to online shopping. Supermarket encountered difficulties in optimizing its delivery processes to meet the surge in online orders. The company struggled to ensure deliveries were made on time and faced challenges in adapting its logistics systems to handle the increased volume. Conversely, the Online Retailer leveraged its advanced logistics capabilities and innovative technologies to optimize its delivery operations. The company introduced robotics and automation into its warehouses for enhanced efficiency and faster order processing. Furthermore, the Online Retailer's investment in last-mile delivery solutions like drone delivery and the Online Retailer Lockers offered consumers contactless options that were both convenient and safe.

Contactless Payments and In-Store Technology: The COVID-19 pandemic necessitated retailers adopting contactless payment methods as well as implementing advanced in-store technologies that minimized physical contact and prioritized the safety of both consumers and employees. Supermarket encountered difficulties when it came to quickly implementing contactless payment solutions in its stores. As a result, consumers faced longer lines and had to touch more surfaces during the checkout process. On the other hand, the Online Retailer's technologically advanced stores like the Online Retailer Go offered frictionless shopping experiences through the use of computer vision, sensor fusion and deep learning algorithms. These stores allowed consumers to shop without physically checking out, which reduced touchpoints and improved overall safety.

Analysis

In terms of data analytics and personalization, retailers needed to effectively utilize these tools to understand changing consumer behaviour and tailor their offerings accordingly. The Supermarket struggled to leverage consumer data for providing personalized recommendations and targeted promotions during the pandemic. The company found it difficult to adapt its marketing strategies to meet the evolving needs and preferences of consumers. In contrast, the Online Retailer excelled in data analytics capabilities by offering personalized recommendations and targeted marketing campaigns. By understanding changing buying patterns through consumer data, the Online Retailer was able to adjust its product offerings and provide tailored shopping experiences. The focus on personalization contributed to consumer satisfaction and loyalty during the pandemic.

Table 10.1 summarizes the technological transformation and adoption of the Supermarket and the Online Retailer during the COVID-19 pandemic, highlighting their disparities in e-commerce infrastructure, delivery optimization, contactless payments and data analytics. The Supermarket faced challenges in adapting to the surge in online demand and implementing advanced technologies, whereas the Online Retailer demonstrated greater readiness and effectiveness in leveraging its existing infrastructure and innovative solutions. In conclusion, when comparing the Supermarket's response with that of the Online Retailer's technological strategies during the COVID-19 pandemic, it becomes evident that there were significant shortcomings in various areas for the Supermarket. These included challenges in e-commerce infrastructure scalability, delivery optimization, contactless payments and data analytics. On the other hand, the Online Retailer demonstrated greater technological readiness and effectiveness in these

Table 10.1. Comparison Review of Technological Transformation and Adoption in Supermarket and Online Retailer.

Technological Shortcomings	Supermarket	Online Retailer
E-commerce infrastructure	Limited online operations and scalability	Established and robust e-commerce infrastructure
	Website crashes, slow loading times, inventory	Effectively managed increased online traffic,
	Inaccuracies	Seamless user experience and order processing
Delivery and fulfilment Optimization	Difficulties in optimizing delivery processes and	Leveraged advanced logistics capabilities and
	Adapting logistics systems to handle increased volume	Innovative technologies for efficient operations
		And faster order processing
Contactless payments and In-store technology	Challenges in implementing contactless payment	Technologically advanced stores (e.g., online retailer
	Solutions, resulting in longer lines and increased	Go) provided frictionless shopping experiences
	Physical contact during checkout	Through computer vision and sensor fusion
Data analytics and personalization	Struggled to leverage consumer data for personalized	Excelled in data analytics capabilities, offering
	Recommendations and targeted promotions	Personalized recommendations and targeted
		Marketing campaigns

areas by leveraging its robust e-commerce infrastructure, optimizing delivery operations, implementing contactless payment solutions and utilizing data analytics for personalization. These contrasting outcomes offer valuable insights for other retailers looking to enhance their technological capabilities in responding to future crises. It is crucial for retailers to invest in scalable e-commerce infrastructure, optimize delivery and fulfilment operations, adopt contactless payment options and leverage data analytics for personalization. By addressing these shortcomings and learning from successful strategies, retailers can better serve their consumers, ensure business continuity and successfully address future emergencies.

Case Study Questions

(1) How did retailers, specifically the Supermarket and the Online Retailer, leverage technology to enhance their click and collect services during the COVID-19 pandemic, adapting to changing consumer needs?
(2) What technological solutions did the Supermarket and the Online Retailer employ to manage the surge in online orders and ensure timely deliveries during the pandemic?
(3) In a comparative analysis of the Supermarket and the Online Retailer, what technological shortcomings were identified, particularly in terms of e-commerce infrastructure, delivery optimization, contactless payments and data analytics? What lessons can other retailers learn from both these shortcomings and successful strategies?

Key Terms and Definitions

Transparent and timely communication: Transparent and timely communication refers to the practice of openly sharing relevant information with stakeholders in a clear, honest and timely manner.

e-commerce infrastructure scalability: E-commerce infrastructure scalability refers to the ability of an e-commerce platform to efficiently and effectively adapt and expand its technological resources and capabilities in response to changes in demand, traffic volume and business growth.

Leverage data analytics: Leveraging data analytics involves harnessing the power of data to gain insights, make informed decisions and drive strategic actions within an organization.

References

Alabed, A., Javornik, A., & Gregory-Smith, D. (2022). AI anthropomorphism and its effect on users' self-congruence and self–AI integration: A theoretical framework and research agenda. *Technological Forecasting and Social Change, 182.* https://doi.org/10.1016/j.techfore.2022.121786

Allport, F. H. (1924). *Social psychology*. Houghton.

Anić, I. D., Radas, S., & Miller, J. C. (2010). 'Antecedents of consumers' time perceptions in a hypermarket retailer. *The Service Industries Journal, 31*(5), 809–828. https://doi.org/10.1080/02642060903067530

Aslam, U. (2023). Understanding the usability of retail fashion brand chatbots: Evidence from customer expectations and experiences. *Journal of Retailing and Consumer Services, 74.* https://doi.org/10.1016/j.jretconser.2023.103377

Aw, E. C. X., Tan, G. W. H., Cham, T. H., Raman, R., & Ooi, K. B. (2022). Alexa, what's on my shopping list? Transforming customer experience with digital voice assistants. *Technological Forecasting and Social Change, 180.* https://doi.org/10.1016/j.techfore.2022.121711

Battisti, S., Agarwal, N., & Brem, A. (2022). Creating new tech entrepreneurs with digital platforms: Meta-organizations for shared value in data-driven retail ecosystems. *Technological Forecasting and Social Change, 175.* https://doi.org/10.1016/j.techfore.2021.121392

Bradley, C., Kohli, S., Kuijpers, D., & Smith, T. R. (2021). How retailers can improve their performance in the post-COVID world. *McKinsey.* https://www.mckinsey.com/industries/retail/our-insights/why-retail-outperformers-are-pulling-ahead#/. Accessed on July 3, 2023.

Brock, T. C. (1968). Implications of commodity theory for value change. In *Psychological foundations of attitudes* (pp. 243–275). Elsevier. https://doi.org/10.1016/B978-1-4832-3071-9.50016-7

Cialdini, R. B. (1993). *Influence: The psychology of persuasion.* William Morrow and Company.

Cialdini, R. B. (2021). *Influence, new and expanded: The psychology of persuasion.* HarperCollins. https://books.google.co.uk/books?id=4uf8DwAAQBAJ

Crespo, N. F., Crespo, C. F., Silva, G. M., & Nicola, M. B. (2023). Innovation in times of crisis: The relevance of digitalization and early internationalization strategies. *Technological Forecasting and Social Change, 188.* https://doi.org/10.1016/j.techfore.2022.122283

Dahlke, J., Bogner, K., Becker, M., Schlaile, M. P., Pyka, A., & Ebersberger, B. (2021). Crisis-driven innovation and fundamental human needs: A typological framework of rapid-response COVID-19 innovations. *Technological Forecasting and Social Change, 169.* https://doi.org/10.1016/j.techfore.2021.120799

de Lucas Ancillo, A., & Gavrila Gavrila, S. (2023). The impact of research and development on entrepreneurship, innovation, digitization and digital transformation. *Journal of Business Research, 157.* https://doi.org/10.1016/j.jbusres.2022.113566

Foroudi, P., Gupta, S., Sivarajah, U., & Broderick, A. (2018). Investigating the effects of smart technology on customer dynamics and customer experience. *Computers in Human Behavior, 80,* 271–282. https://doi.org/10.1016/j.chb.2017.11.014

Fredström, A., Parida, V., Wincent, J., Sjodin, D., & Oghazi, P. (2022). What is the market value of artificial intelligence and machine learning? The role of innovativeness and collaboration for performance. *Technological Forecasting and Social Change, 180.* https://doi.org/10.1016/j.techfore.2022.121716

Ganotakis, P., Angelidou, S., Saridakis, C., Piperopoulos, P., & Dindial, M. (2023). Innovation, digital technologies, and sales growth during exogenous shocks. *Technological Forecasting and Social Change, 193.* https://doi.org/10.1016/j.techfore.2023.122656

Gavrila Gavrila, S., & de Lucas Ancillo, A. (2021). Spanish SMEs' digitalization enablers: E-Receipt applications to the offline retail market. *Technological Forecasting and Social Change, 162.* https://doi.org/10.1016/j.techfore.2020.120381

Hamilton, R., Thompson, D., Bone, S., Chaplin, L. N., Griskevicius, V., Goldsmith, K., Hill, R., John, D. R., Mittal, C., O'Guinn, T., Piff, P., Roux, C., Shah, A., & Zhu, M. (2019). The effects of scarcity on consumer decision journeys. *Journal of the Academy of Marketing Science,* 532–550. https://doi.org/10.1007/s11747-018-0604-7

Hoang, D., & Breugelmans, E. (2022). "Sorry, the product you ordered is out of stock": Effects of substitution policy in online grocery retailing. *Journal of Retailing.* https://doi.org/10.1016/j.jretai.2022.06.006

Hodgson, J. (2021). Tesco eyes more delivery slots for online customers after big digital sales growth during pandemic. *Evening Standard.* https://www.standard.co. uk/business/leisure-retail/Tesco-sales-over-ps53-billion-pandemic-year-online-growth-b929562.html. Accessed on July 5, 2023.

Holzmann, P., & Gregori, P. (2023). The promise of digital technologies for sustainable entrepreneurship: A systematic literature review and research agenda. *International Journal of Information Management.* https://doi.org/10.1016/j. ijinfomgt.2022.102593

Hoyer, W. D., Kroschke, M., Schmitt, B., Kraume, K., & Shankar, V. (2020). Transforming the customer experience through new technologies. *Journal of Interactive Marketing, 51,* 57–71. https://doi.org/10.1016/j.intmar.2020.04.001

Ishrat, I., Hasan, M., Farooq, A., & Khan, F. M. (2023). Modelling of consumer challenges and marketing strategies during crisis. *Qualitative Market Research: An International Journal.* https://doi.org/10.1108/qmr-12-2021-0149

Jain, G., Kamble, S. S., Ndubisi, N. O., Shrivastava, A., Belhadi, A., & Venkatesh, M. (2022). Antecedents of Blockchain-Enabled E-commerce Platforms (BEEP) adoption by customers—A study of second-hand small and medium apparel retailers. *Journal of Business Research, 149,* 576–588. https://doi.org/10.1016/j. jbusres.2022.05.041

Jiang, Y., & Stylos, N. (2021). Triggers of consumers' enhanced digital engagement and the role of digital technologies in transforming the retail ecosystem during COVID-19 pandemic. *Technological Forecasting and Social Change, 172.* https://doi.org/10.1016/j.techfore.2021.121029

Kullak, F. S., Baier, D., & Woratschek, H. (2023). How do customers meet their needs in in-store and online fashion shopping? A comparative study based on the jobs-to-be-done theory. *Journal of Retailing and Consumer Services, 71.* https://doi.org/10. 1016/j.jretconser.2022.103221

Lynn, M. (1991). Scarcity effects on value: A quantitative review of the commodity theory literature. *Psychology and Marketing, 8*(1), 43–57. https://doi.org/10.1002/ mar.4220080105

Meyer, P., Roth, A., & Gutknecht, K. (2023). Service robots in organisational frontlines—A retail managers' perspective. *Journal of Retailing and Consumer Services, 70.* https://doi.org/10.1016/j.jretconser.2022.103173

Mostaghel, R., Oghazi, P., Parida, V., & Sohrabpour, V. (2022). Digitalization driven retail business model innovation: Evaluation of past and avenues for future research trends. *Journal of Business Research, 146,* 134–145. https://doi.org/10. 1016/j.jbusres.2022.03.072

Nazir, S., Khadim, S., Ali Asadullah, M., & Syed, N. (2023). Exploring the influence of artificial intelligence technology on consumer repurchase intention: The mediation and moderation approach. *Technology in Society, 72.* https://doi.org/10.1016/ j.techsoc.2022.102190

Ngoh, C. lyn, & Groening, C. (2022). The effect of COVID-19 on consumers' channel shopping behaviors: A segmentation study. *Journal of Retailing and Consumer Services, 68.* https://doi.org/10.1016/j.jretconser.2022.103065

Nichols, B. S. (2012). The development, validation, and implications of a measure of consumer competitive arousal (CCAr). *Journal of Economic Psychology, 33*(1), 192–205. https://doi.org/10.1016/j.joep.2011.10.002

Pantano, E. (2014). Innovation management in retailing: From consumer perspective to corporate strategy. *Journal of Retailing and Consumer Services*, 825–826. https://doi.org/10.1016/j.jretconser.2014.02.017

Pantano, E., Pizzi, G., Scarpi, D., & Dennis, C. (2020). Competing during a pandemic? Retailers' ups and downs during the COVID-19 outbreak. *Journal of Business Research, 116*, 209–213. https://doi.org/10.1016/j.jbusres.2020.05.036

Papagiannidis, S., Almanos, E., Bourlakis, M., & Dennis, C. (2022). The pandemic consumer response: A stockpiling perspective and shopping channel preferences. *British Journal of Management*. https://doi.org/10.1111/1467-8551.12616

Parida, V., Sjödin, D., & Reim, W. (2019). Reviewing literature on digitalization, business model innovation, and sustainable industry: Past achievements and future promises. *Sustainability*. MDPI. https://doi.org/10.3390/su11020391

Park, J., & Li, W. (2023). "I got it FIRST": Antecedents of competitive consumption of a new product. *Journal of Retailing and Consumer Services, 73*. https://doi.org/10.1016/j.jretconser.2023.103367

Paul, J., & Rosenbaum, M. (2020). Retailing and consumer services at a tipping point: New conceptual frameworks and theoretical models. *Journal of Retailing and Consumer Services, 54*. https://doi.org/10.1016/j.jretconser.2019.101977

Pizzi, G., & Scarpi, D. (2013). When out-of-stock products DO backfire: Managing disclosure time and justification wording. *Journal of Retailing, 89*(3), 352–359. https://doi.org/10.1016/j.jretai.2012.12.003

Santiago, J., Borges-Tiago, M. T., & Tiago, F. (2022). Is firm-generated content a lost cause? *Journal of Business Research, 139*, 945–953. https://doi.org/10.1016/j.jbusres.2021.10.022

Serravalle, F., Mahabubul Alam, G., & Giacosa, E. (2023). "We are out of toilet paper": Testing the mediating effect of product scarcity on consumers' competitive arousal in family firms. *Journal of Business Research, 164*. https://doi.org/10.1016/j.jbusres.2023.114012

Shah, A. K., Shafir, E., & Mullainathan, S. (2015). Scarcity frames value. *Psychological Science, 26*(4), 402–412. https://doi.org/10.1177/0956797614563958

Song, M., Choi, S., & Moon, J. (2021). Limited time or limited quantity? The impact of other consumer existence and perceived competition on the scarcity messaging—Purchase intention relation. *Journal of Hospitality and Tourism Management, 47*, 167–175. https://doi.org/10.1016/j.jhtm.2021.03.012

Swani, K., Milne, G. R., & Brown, B. P. (2023). The benefits of meeting buyer privacy expectations across information, time, and space dimensions. In *Industrial marketing management* (pp. 14–26). Elsevier Inc. https://doi.org/10.1016/j.indmarman.2023.04.013

Verhallen, T. M. M., & Robben, H. S. J. (1994). Scarcity and preference: An experiment on unavailability and product evaluation. *Journal of Economic Psychology, 15*(2), 315–331.

Yuen, K. F., Tan, L. S., Wong, Y. D., & Wang, X. (2022). Social determinants of panic buying behaviour amidst COVID-19 pandemic: The role of perceived scarcity and anticipated regret. *Journal of Retailing and Consumer Services, 66*. https://doi.org/10.1016/j.jretconser.2022.102948

Chapter 11

Predicting Mobile Commerce Adoption: The SEM-MLP Approach

Zeinab Zamani[a], Ameneh Khadivar[a], Hamid Padash[b], Javad Shekarkhah[c] and Morteza Akbari[b]

[a]Alzahra University, Iran
[b]University of Tehran, Iran
[c]Allameh Tabataba'i University, Iran

Abstract

This chapter recognizes and ranks the factors that impact the adoption of mobile commerce (MC) by users. The results showed that compatibility, perceived usefulness (PU), perceived risk (PR), mobility, and perceived cost (PC) have a significant effect on the adoption of MC by users. The results of multilayer perceptron (MLP) showed that mobility, among other model variables, had the greatest impact on the adoption of MC, and PC had the lowest effect on the adoption of MC. The comparison of the MLP model with linear regression illustrates that the predictive power of MLP outperforms the linear regression model in predicting MC adoption.

Keywords: Mobile commerce; technology adoption; artificial neural network; structural equation modeling; multilayer perceptron

Introduction

Rapid improvements in mobile technology have prompted a greater adoption of mobile devices and an increase in their use in different aspects of our life. Mobile penetration, or the number of mobile subscribers per 100 people, is 96.4% globally (International Telecommunication Union, 2021); however, it is significantly greater (125.8%) in industrialized countries. Smartphones and tablets are employed as communication devices that provide wireless internet access in addition to voice communication. In developing countries, smartphones have the highest ranking in

Business Strategies and Ethical Challenges in the Digital Ecosystem, 245–265
Published under exclusive licence by Emerald Publishing Limited
doi:10.1108/978-1-80455-069-420241011

internet connectivity. Commercial activity, i.e., purchasing and vending of services and products, via wireless networks and using mobile devices is known as mobile commerce (m-commerce or MC), and it is one of the fastest-growing industries. Duffey (1997, as cited in Madan & Yadav, 2019, p. 131) introduces the concept of MC. He believes that MC is providing electronic commerce capabilities to the final users (or customers) using wireless technology. MC shares core business ideas, such as making commercial dealings over an electronic device. Moreover, MC is considered as a step forward (Coursaris & Hassanein, 2002). The term m-commerce refers to conducting trade utilizing wireless electronic systems, and it allows commercial transactions over wireless systems. It combines the benefits of traditional e-commerce (EC) with the added benefit of mobility. It entails using mobile systems, such as tablets, smartphones, and personal digital assistants (PDAs), capable of transacting.

MC is a subcategory of EC that provides the possibility of transactions through the internet without any time or place restrictions. It introduces entirely new possibilities, such as location-based services. The ability of MC as a business model has been unlocked in recent years because of advancements in internet technology (i.e., 5G) as well as the increasing demand for mobile communication devices. Today's mobile phone is more than simply a means of communication; it's a complicated device that provides data transfer and wireless internet access. Its use has expanded far beyond simply connecting individuals to a variety of additional services such as internet surfing, entertainment, and online shopping, which is leading to the growing popularity of MC.

A review of technology literature indicates that technology has gone through three periods so far. The first course, which began in 1972, was the personal computer course. The second course, which began in 1990 and lasted until 2000, was the internet era. The third course, which began in 2000 and continues to this day, is the period of technology and mobile internet, which has led to the formation of MC (Mahatanankoon et al., 2005). Moreover, it is predicted that by 2030, a revolution and huge changes in the field of technology will take place. For example, by 2022, one million trillion sensors will be linked to the internet. It is predicted that 10% of reading eyeglasses will be linked to the internet by 2023, and the first cell phone that can be implanted in the human body will be commercially available by 2023 (Marguerite, 2021). Because of the growing use of mobile phones and changing consumer tastes, marketers have created a variety of mobile-based applications that allow customers to do transactions using their mobile devices. The tendency today is to move away from wired networks and toward wireless networks. According to several analysts, the rate of expansion of MC differs by country. This suggests that certain fundamental elements influence MC adoption. In comparison to many other countries with similar socioeconomic and demographic features, the research illustrates that MC in developing economies had a reasonable success rate. This disparity can be explained by the fact that mobile phones are more frequently used in developing countries, whereas financial services (e.g., trading, insurance, and banking) are still in their infancy.

Iran is a developing country with a high potential for MC services as the internet penetration rate in Iran is reported at 70% (The Official Portal of Measuring Information Society of Iran, 2022). Adoption, on the other hand, is still low, indicating that there are barriers to MC acceptance among West Asian customers.

The MC market in Iran is still in its initial stages, and in such a context, the main issue is consumers' willingness to adopt new technologies (Faqih, 2016; Wu & Wang, 2005). With a better comprehension of the elements that impact users' decisions to conduct transactions on mobile devices, MC potential is likely to grow. Consistent with the latest data published by the West Asian Ministry of Communications and Information Technology, the number of mobile broadband subscribers in Iran reached 41 million and 57 thousand by the end of June 2017. This shows that the penetration rate of mobile phone subscribers in Iran has increased by 104% compared to 2013. Mobile phones are a prerequisite for MC, and based on statistics, 25% of wireless users with their mobile devices will be somehow involved in MC (Mahatanankoon et al., 2005). All this indicates the opportunity for the growth of MC in Iran. Subsequently, many businesses strive to take advantage of this opportunity, and they have turned to the use of MC. Does the question arise what factors affect the acceptance of MC by customers? And which of these factors is more important in the prediction of their behavioral intention? Consequently, the current study is conducted to seek to answer these questions. The results of this study will help businesses and commercial organizations to decide on how to participate in MC by providing information on the factors affecting customer MC adoption.

M-Commerce

The term m-commerce was originally used in 1997, and since then, numerous scholars have defined it in a variety of ways. Tiwari and Buse (2007), for example, defined MC as any monetary transaction undertaken to utilize mobile devices via a mobile telecommunication network. Turban et al. (2002) proposed a broader definition of MC in such a way that MC, also known as m-business, refers to using mobile devices and wireless networks to conduct e-commerce. In sum, it encompasses any operations relating to potential business transactions carried out via a wireless network using a handheld mobile system (Tarasewich et al., 2002). Vittet-Philippe and Navarro (2000 as cited in Islam et al., 2011, p. 81) have a different perspective on MC and see it as the advancement of EC, and they define MC as "an EC for users on the move."

MC encompasses a novel variety of services, business methods, and technological innovations that distinguish it from regular EC. The exchange of information, commodities, services, and money transactions electronically is referred to as EC (Turban et al., 2002). MC, in addition to the benefits of traditional EC, also provides mobility and loanability. In comparison with desktop computers, mobile devices, like cell phones, have limitations for instance smaller screen displays and low bandwidth. On the other hand, these restrictions resulted in the development of various mobile applications that allow access to the internet anywhere and anytime (Sadeh, 2003).

Theoretical Framework of the Study

The models available in the literature for technology adoption are divided into two general categories. The first category includes the models that examine the adoption of technology from the perspective of users, and the second category constitutes the models that investigate technology adoption by organizations. As an example, Brynjolfsson and McElheran (2016) propose a model that examines the speed of data-driven decision-making in American companies between 2010 and 2015, and in another study, Brynjolfsson et al. (2021) provide a model for accepting predictive analytics in the organization. Davis (1989) developed a technology acceptance model (TAM) that is one of the most common and reliable models for forecasting user acceptance; David's proposed model has introduced perceived ease of use (PEOU) and perceived usefulness (PU) as the determinants of user behavior in accepting technology, but it often seems as insufficient. Therefore, several studies have proposed extending TAM with other components to predict customer behavior better (Wei et al., 2009; Wu & Wang, 2005). Accordingly, social influence (Chong et al., 2012; Tan et al., 2014), perceived risk (PR) (Dai & Palvi, 2009; Tan et al., 2014), perceived cost (PC) (Chong et al., 2012; Dai & Palvi, 2009; Tan et al., 2014), trust (Akbari, Keshavarz, et al., 2020; Akbari, Rezvani, et al., 2020, 2021), enjoyment (Dai & Palvi, 2009), variety of services (Chong et al., 2012), subjective norm (Akbari, Keshavarz, et al., 2020; Akbari, Moradi, et al., 2021; Dai & Palvi, 2009), compatibility (Akbari, Keshavarz, et al., 2020; Dai & Palvi, 2009), mobility (Dai & Palvi, 2009), and variety of services (Dai & Palvi, 2009) are examples of factors that previous researchers have added to the TAM model based on the nature of technology was studied.

Perceived Usefulness

PU is consistently proven to have a major impact on new technology uptake. PU is the extent to which an individual believes that involvement in online trans-actions through MC boosts their productivity. Research has proven the impor-tance of PU in adopting technology in different dimensions, for example, mobile payment (Shin, 2009), internet banking (Chong et al., 2010), mobile internet (Kim et al., 2007), 5G technology (Akbari, Rezvani, et al., 2021), and mobile services (Zarmpou et al., 2012). Some researchers have investigated and demonstrated the effect of demographic variables, such as gender (e.g., Liébana-Cabanillas et al., 2014; Wei et al., 2009) on PU. Since the significant effect of PU on user intention to adopt MC is validated in the body of literature (Chong, 2013; Dai & Palvi, 2009), this variable is considered one of the variables of TAM in the current study. Hence, it could conceivably be hypothesized that:

H1. PU significantly increases customer intention to use (ITU) m-commerce (MC).

Perceived Ease of Use

PEOU is the extent to which an individual believes that engaging in online transactions through MC is facile and does not necessitate many endeavors. This variable is considered a key component in technology adoption models. PEOU widely applied as an influencing variable among studies that have focused on internet-related topics, such as e-services (Featherman et al., 2010), mobile payment (Liébana-Cabanillas et al., 2014; Schierz et al., 2010; Shin, 2009), ride-hailing (Akbari, Seyyedamiri, et al., 2020), ridesharing (Akbari, Moradi et al., 2021) and internet banking (Cheng et al., 2006; Kim et al., 2007). Chong (2013), for example, provides evidence that PEOU was an influential variable in MC adoption. Bhatti (1970) showed that this factor is an antecedent of behavioral intention to use (ITU) MC among both Malaysian and Chinese users. In a cross-cultural study of Chinese and American users, Dai and Palvi (2009) discovered that PEOU affects m-commerce acceptance among Chinese consumers, but not among Americans. Thus, it is anticipated that PEOU increases the users' ITU m-commerce. Hence, it could conceivably be hypothesized that:

H2. PEOU significantly increases customer ITU m-commerce (MC).

Perceived Risk

PR is financial, psychological, or/and service risks consumers may face while doing online trades (Wu & Wang, 2005). Because sensitive individual data are frequently saved on users' mobile phones, the security and privacy issues associated with MC trades can be substantial (Chong, 2013). MC is doing financial transactions through mobile devices, which many consider dangerous. This element has been identified as important in understanding the rate of adoption of mobile technology by several studies (Chong et al., 2012; Madan & Yadav, 2016; Natarajan et al., 2017; Thakur & Srivastava, 2013). Users expect the platform they use to be secure and not endanger their personal and banking data. Hence, PR will be negatively related to their ITU a platform. Subsequently, it could conceivably be hypothesized that:

H3. PR significantly decreases customer ITU m-commerce.

Perceived Cost

PC is generally described as costs of using MC such as equipment costs and access costs. Consistent with behavioral decision theory, users make a cost–benefit analysis for both PU and PEOU. Users encounter non-negligible costs when moving between brands in diverse marketplaces (Chen & Hitt, 2002; Plouffe et al., 2001). There are certain additional costs associated with switching from wired EC to MC. According to Constantinides (2002), three significant components that make MC more costly than wired EC are equipment expenses, access charges, and trade fees. Furthermore, internet consumers have been enraged by aggravating encounters such as poor quality, sluggishness, or missing connections. Consumers, however, must foot the bill for all of these annoyances. M-commerce providers should create cost-cutting solutions that persuade current and prospective users to access portals at any time and from anywhere. Without a doubt, it is expected that the investments would conclude a long-term income stream from loyal customers, more than compensating for the cost. Otherwise, m-commerce would struggle to survive since users can get the same information or outcomes from other sources (Rock, 2000). Higher PCs lower the tendency of the customer to use a platform. Hence, it could conceivably be hypothesized that:

H4. PC significantly decreases customer ITU m-commerce.

Compatibility

Compatibility is reliably linked to technology adoption (Agarwal & Prasad, 1998). The extent to which the innovation is seen to be matchable with the potential users' existing values, prior experiences, and needs is referred to as compatibility (Akbari, Keshavarz, et al., 2020; Sonnenwald et al., 2001). In other words, compatibility is described as the extent to which engaging in online trading through MC is compatible with the beliefs, values, past experiences, and current requirements of potential users. Adoption will be more favorable if there is a high level of compatibility. Hence, it could conceivably be hypothesized that:

H5. Compatibility significantly increases customer ITU m-commerce.

Mobility

The most important feature of mobile technology is mobility, which is a considerable benefit over traditional systems (Kim et al., 2010). Movable capability means that MC can be used anyplace, at any time, or even when traveling. Whereas both mobility and usefulness are advantages of technology, the fundamental distinction is that usefulness encompasses all of technology's advantages, while mobility encompasses just mobile technology's advantages (Mallat et al., 2009). Mobility has a strong favorable impact on users' attitudes regarding mobile payment systems, their desire to use them, and their perceived utility (Schierz et al., 2010). Hence, it could conceivably be hypothesized that:

H6. Mobility has a positive significant impact on customer ITU m-commerce.

Variety of Services

Even though m-commerce has a wide range of applications, the variety of services provided by electronic commerce websites is still higher (Chong et al., 2012). MC services include entertainment, communication, transaction, and information services (Sadeh, 2003). As a result, the diversity of MC services provided affects

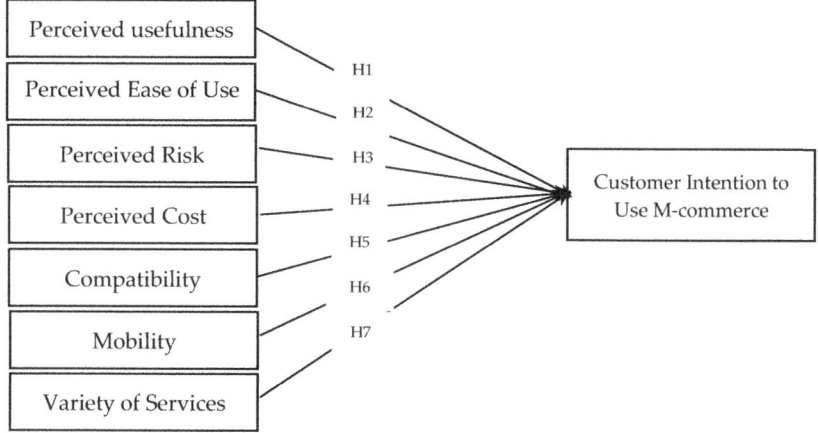

Fig. 11.1.   Conceptual Model of Research.

MC adoption intention (Chong, 2013). Hence, it could conceivably be hypothesized that:

H7. A variety of services significantly increases customer ITU m-commerce.

The conceptual model developed by the present study is shown in Fig. 11.1. Among the innovations of the present conceptual model can be: (1) simultaneous study of the direct impact of seven factors PU, PEOU, PR, PC, compatibility, mobility, and variety of services on the ITU MC, (2) the use of a multi-analytical approach including structural equations modeling, artificial neural networks, and regression to test the model and to test its predictive power.

Methods

The current study is applied research, and its results help companies to expand their MC usage. In addition, consistent with the nature of the data and the data collection method, this is descriptive survey research. It is also a cross-sectional study because it examines data related to a certain period (i.e., the data collection took place in July 2021). West Asian users of mobile phones that can connect to the internet and are members of various apps and social media networks make up the statistical population of the current study. By sampling approach, the questionnaire was created online and made available on social media networks. Finally, 290 participants finished the survey after 20 days. The items for the questionnaire were derived from the literature, and the questionnaire's validity was validated by several professors and EC professionals. According to Liébana-Cabanillas et al. (2017), a seven-point Likert scale (i.e., 1 indicates strongly disagree and 7 means strongly agree) was also used to measure the questions. Confirmatory factor analysis and structural equation modeling (SEM) using SmartPLS 3.0 were utilized to evaluate hypotheses and to examine the model fit. The accuracy of the model prediction was then measured using neural network analysis and regression to determine the importance of each of the confirmed factors in the preanalysis of neural networks. In addition, the predictive power of the model is determined by comparing the results of regression analysis and neural network analysis. The neural network analysis and regression were carried out using SPSS 22.0.

Results

Demographic analysis of the participants in this study states that 46.2% of the participants were male and 53.8% were female. It was also found that 6% of participants were between 24 and 28 years old, 59.1% were between 25 and 34 years old, 30.2% were between 35 and 44 years old, and 4.6% were more than 45 years old. The majority of the participants have higher education levels. In this way, 6 of the participants were in high school, 25 were a diploma, 86 were a bachelor's degree, 110 had a master's degree, and 63 had a PhD degree or were doctoral students.

Since the proposed model of the present research is original, the first, factor analysis was performed on this model. For factor analysis, the measurement model must be tested. In structural equations, the relationship between observable variables (i.e., questionnaire questions) and latent variables (i.e., main variables) is called the measurement model. Fig. 11.2 is the output of SmartPLS software that provides the loading factors and the path coefficients. The numbers between the visible variables and the invisible variables are called loading factors. To test factor analysis, all loading factors must be both above 0.4 and be significant at least at a 95% confidence interval. Fig. 11.2 shows that all these loading factors are above 0.4, and the significance of all of them was confirmed using the t-test indicating a good explanation of the model; therefore, the measurement models are used for the latent variables, without any modification.

Moreover, to test the validity and reliability of the questionnaire, four criteria of Cronbach's alpha, average variance extracted (AVE), composite reliability, and divergent validity were employed. The results of Cronbach's alpha test and composite reliability show that the value of these two factors for all model variables is greater than the threshold of 0.7, which confirms the reliability of the data collection tool in this research. The results of the assessment of the measurement model disclose that the measurement tool employed in this research has a high convergence validity because the value of AVE for all variables is above 0.5, which indicates that each of the hidden variables can express more than half of the variance of their observable variables (see Table 11.1).

Divergent validity or discriminant validity is also examined to make sure that the observable variables are only related to the corresponding latent variables not to the other latent variables. Fornell–Larker criterion by comparing the second root of the AVE tests the divergent validity. As can be observed in Table 11.2, for all variables, the second root of the AVE (elements of the main diameter of the table) is greater than its correlation coefficient with other variables. In this way, the divergent validity of the model is confirmed.

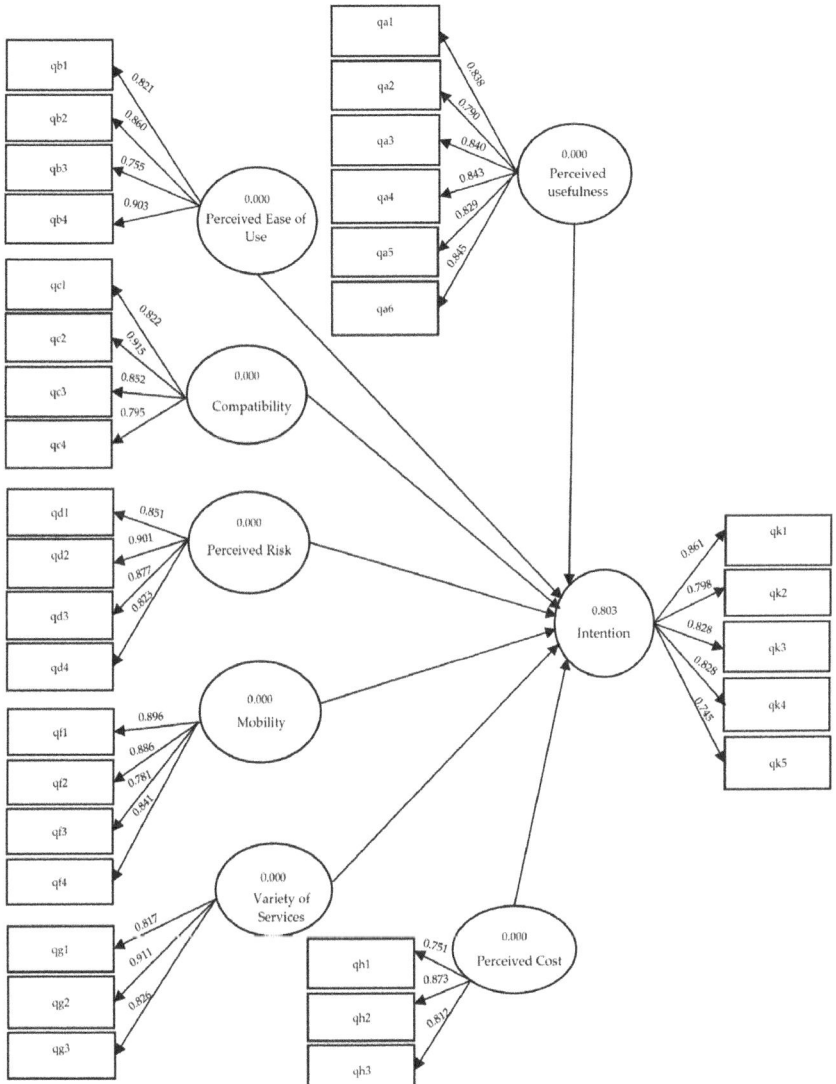

Fig. 11.2.   Loading Factors of the Questionnaire Variables.

Hypotheses Test

Table 11.3 shows hypothesis testing results. According to Table 11.3, the path coefficients of hypotheses *H1*, *H3*, *H4*, *H5*, and *H6* are significant at least at the 95% confidence level. Therefore, these hypotheses are considered confirmed. Since the path coefficients associated with *H2* and *H7* are not significant

Table 11.1. Model Reliability and Validity Test Results.

Variables	AVE	α	CR
Perceived usefulness	0.691	0.910	0.931
Perceived ease of use	0.700	0.856	0.903
Perceived risk	0.745	0.886	0.921
Perceived costs	0.661	0.745	0.854
Compatibility	0.718	0.868	0.910
Mobility	0.729	0.876	0.915
Variety of services	0.727	0.810	0.888

(i.e., their corresponding t-value is less than 1.96), these two hypotheses are rejected. In other words, not enough evidence is found to confirm the impact of PEOU and a variety of services on customer ITU m-commerce. The confirmation of other hypotheses implies that PU, compatibility, and mobility have a positive significant impact (due to the positive coefficient of the path coefficient) on customer ITU m-commerce. It is also proved that PR and PC have a negative significant impact (due to the positive coefficient of the path coefficient) on customer ITU m-commerce.

The last row of Table 11.3 shows that R^2 associated with the variable of customer intention is 80.3%, which illustrates that these variables together can explain 80.3% of the changes in the customer's m-commerce. This value is higher than the threshold of 0.67, which indicates the considerable power of the model. Another indicator in examining the explanatory power of the model is the predictive relevance (Q^2) criterion, which determines the predictive power of the model. The value of Q^2 for the model is 52.5%, which is higher than the threshold of 0.35 and indicates the high predictive power of the model. Finally, the goodness of fit (GoF) metric is used to check the appropriateness of the overall model fit. To calculate GoF, the commonality index and the coefficient of determination (R^2) are used (see Eq. 11.1). The commonality index is calculated as the mean of the squared correlations linking each observable variable to the corresponding hidden variable across all blocks. The output of SmartPLS 3.0 showed that the communality index for this model is 0.705; consequently, the GoF of 0.752 was obtained using Eq. (11.1), which indicates a strong overall fit of the model.

$$\text{GOF} = \sqrt{\text{Communality} \times R^2} = \sqrt{0.705 \times 0.803} = 0.752 \qquad (11.1)$$

Neural Network Analysis

In this study, the common method of the back-propagation method, namely the multilayer perceptron (MLP) network, has been used. MLP benefits from a

Table 11.2. Divergent Validity Result Test.

Convergent Validity	Perceived Cost	Mobility	Compatibility	Customer Intention	Perceived Ease of Use	Perceived Risk	Perceived Usefulness	Variety of Services
Perceived cost	0.661	—	—	—	—	—	—	—
Mobility	0.206	0.729	—	—	—	—	—	—
Compatibility	0.233	0.526	0.718	—	—	—	—	—
Customer intention	0.311	0.590	0.680	0.678	—	—	—	—
Perceived ease of use	0.236	0.497	0.593	0.522	0.700	—	—	—
Perceived risk	0.181	0.383	0.490	0.545	0.437	0.745	—	—
Perceived usefulness	0/265	0.500	0.712	0.648	0.571	0.413	0.691	—
Variety of services	0.170	0.460	0.515	0.416	0.428	0.403	0.496	0.727

Table 11.3. Structural Model Coefficients and Model Fit Metrics.

Hypotheses	Path Coefficient	*t*-value	Result
Perceived usefulness → Customer intention	0.205	1.99	Confirmed
Perceived ease of use → Customer intention	−0.036	0.44	Not confirmed
Perceived risk → Customer intention	−0.035	2.86	Confirmed
Perceived cost → Customer intention	−0.123	2.25	Confirmed
Compatibility→ Customer intention	0.246	2.39	Confirmed
Mobility→ Customer intention	0.22	3.04	Confirmed
Variety of Services→ Customer intention	0.094	1.27	Not confirmed
R^2	0.803		
Q^2	0.525		

two-stage supervised learning step. In the first step, the input data are entered into the network, and the features are added to the next layer. At this stage, the weights are fixed, and at the end, the network output is calculated. In the second step, the network weights are adjusted according to the error-correction learning, the error signal is propagated to the previous layers, and the weights are corrected accordingly. In designing a neural network model, the number of layers, the number of hidden neurons, learning algorithms, activator function, learning rate, number of repetitions, data normalization, learning, and testing set size must be specified. The complete neural network structure of this research is in three layers, including an input layer, a hidden layer, and an output layer.

The count of independent variables determines the count of the neurons in the input layer. Identifying the number of middle layers (hidden) neurons is not an easy task and is mostly done through trial and error and the rule of thumb to improve overall network performance. In general, as the count of hidden-layer neurons increases, the network's ability to detect the complexities of the patterns in the training phase increases, but this may reduce the possibility of network generalization (Raut et al., 2018). Therefore, a balance must be struck between the two to improve overall network performance.

Despite the importance of the number of hidden layer neurons, there is no one-size-fits-all rule for choosing the optimal number. Different factors affect the number of hidden neurons such as sample size, training algorithm, neural network architecture, and the count of latent layers (Zhu et al., 2020). In addition, neurons in the output layers are the same as dependent variables.

In this study, neural networks were modeled using SPSS 22.0 in which the count of input layer neurons according to the results obtained from the modeling

Table 11.4. Weights Related to the Middle Layer of the MLP Model.

Input Neurons	Neuron 1	Neuron 2	Neuron 3
Perceived usefulness	−0.446	0.317	−1.532
Compatibility	−0.097	−0.246	−0.552
Perceived risk	0.265	−0.776	−0.999
Mobility	0.028	−0.317	−0.727
Perceived cost	0.302	−0.248	1.000
Output neurons (customer intention to use m-commerce)	−1.159	−0.910	−0.157

of structural equations in the previous stage is equal to five independent variables (i.e., PU, PR, PC, compatibility, and mobility) related to five confirmed hypotheses of the study. While the output layer contains a dependent variable called the customer ITU m-commerce. Hence, the count of neurons in the hidden layer is considered three. The sigmoid function is employed as the activation function for latent and output layer neurons. To increase the performance of the training phase, e.g., shortening the training time, all the variables were normalized to 0 and 1. The data were divided into two categories: training data and testing data. The share of training data was 70% of the data, and the share of testing data was 30% of the data. The neural network model with the weights of the middle layers is shown in Table 11.4.

Sensitive Analysis

The sensitivity analysis measures the importance of each predictor in forming the neural network. In other words, it shows the importance of each of the independent variables in determining the independent values. Normalization of this importance is achieved by dividing the values of importance by their largest value and is expressed as a percentage. The results of the sensitivity analysis according to Table 11.5 show that mobility is the most important variable in predicting customer ITU m-commerce, followed by PU, compatibility, PR, and PC, respectively.

Table 11.5. The Importance of Each Independent Variable in Predicting the Dependent Variable.

Variable	Normalized Importance	Variable	Normalized Importance
Mobility	0.100	PR	0.76
Perceived usefulness	0.998	PC	0.54
Compatibility	0.78		

Regression Analysis Versus the Neural Network Algorithm

The output of regression analysis disclosed that PU, compatibility, PR, mobility, and PC have a significant impact on customer ITU m-commerce (see Table 11.6). It is also found that these five variables can explain 80% of the changes in the dependent factor (i.e., Adjusted R^2 = 0.8). The research regression model is given in Eq. (11.2).

$$\text{Consumer Intention} = \beta_0 + \beta_1 \text{ Use fulness} + \beta_2 \text{ Risk} + \beta_3 \text{ Cost} \\ + \beta_4 \text{ Compatibility} + \beta_5 \text{ Mobility} \tag{11.2}$$

Durbin–Watson statistic value is close to 2, indicating a lack of autocorrelation among the variables. The value of F of the model was 107.763 which is significant at a 5% error level and shows that the model is generally significant, and as a minimum, one of the variables has a significant linear relevance with the dependent variable. According to Table 11.6, the PC has a negative significant impact (due to the negative coefficient of -0.104) and a significant relationship (t-statistic equal to -2.841) (at the level of 5% error) on the customer ITU m-commerce. However, other variables have a positive significant relevance with customer intentions.

In comparing the predictive power of artificial neural network algorithms with other methods, most previous studies indicate the superiority of artificial neural networks over common prediction techniques such as ordinary least squares regression, logit regression, and separator analysis. The Root Mean Square Error (RMSE) and the Mean Absolute Percentage Error (MAPE) are employed to compare the neural network and regression performance, and its results are shown in Table 11.7.

A comparison of the predictive power of the MLP model and regression using two accuracy metrics of MSRE and MAPE discloses that the prediction error rate

Table 11.6. Summary of Regression Model Test Results.

Model	Coefficient	Standard Error	*t*-value	Sig.
B0	1.335	0.359	3.722	0.000
Perceived usefulness	0.214	0.076	3.722	0.006
Compatibility	0.275	0.073	3.749	0.000
Perceived risk	0.190	0.050	3.807	0.000
Mobility	0.179	0.054	3.342	0.001
Perceived cost	−0.104	0.037	−2.841	0.005
Model Power		*Model Assumptions*		
Durbin Watson	1.99	R	0.90	
ANOVA (*F*)	107.763	R^2	0.81	
F Sig.	0.000	Adjusted R^2	0.80	

Table 11.7. Comparison of the Predictive Power of the Models.

Models	RMSE	MAPE
MLP	0. 431	0. 071
Linear regression	0. 446	0. 0717

of the MLP model was slightly lower than regression in both metrics, in this study. This finding indicates that MLP outperforms regression in the prediction of customer ITU m-commerce.

Conclusion

The current study ranked the variables affecting the customer ITU m-commerce. Firstly, it was found that PU, compatibility, PR, mobility, and PC have a significant impact on customer ITU m-commerce, which is in line with the results of Liébana-Cabanillas et al. (2017), Zarmpou et al. (2012), Wei et al. (2009), and Wu and Wang (2005). However, the results of the structural analysis revealed that PEOU and a variety of services have no significant effect on customer ITU m-commerce. The lack of relevance between PEOU and the behavioral intention of using MC is consistent with the results of Liébana-Cabanillas et al. (2017), Wu and Wang (2005), and Zarmpou et al. (2012). However, respondents indicated that they tend to accept MC because of the usefulness and desirability of MC, such as spending less time and not because of its ease of use. The lack of impact of diversity of mobile services and applications on ITU m-commerce is not according to the results of research by Chong et al. (2012), who also claim that the diversity of services significantly affects the behavioral intention of users to use MC. This difference in results may be due to cultural differences and technological contexts in the two countries. As the results of the study of Akbari, Rezvani, et al. (2021) showed, adoption technology differs between developed and developing countries.

A comparison of accuracy metrics of the linear regression model and MLP model showed that the outputs of this Artificial Neural Network (ANN) model have a lower error in predicting customer behavior. This finding is following the findings of Madan and Yadav (2019) and Liébana-Cabanillas et al. (2017). Therefore, this model is proposed to predict the intentions of customers to use MC. The output of this model ranked the variables affecting customer behavior as follows: mobility, PU, compatibility, PR, and PC, respectively. In other words, the possibility of using MC in any place and time, i.e., the mobility feature, was recognized as the most important feature affecting customer ITU m-commerce, in this study. In the research of Liébana-Cabanillas et al. (2017), compatibility was identified as the most important factor, followed by participation, trust, and usefulness. The difference in the results is due to the cultural context and the type of application, i.e., mobile banking.

Managerial Implications

The contributions of the current research help m-commerce to understand better their user behavior. In addition, it is found that mobility PU has the most important effect on users' decision in using m-commerce; therefore, it is recommended to the mobile service providers to consider these factors in both developing services as well as marketing activities.

According to findings mobile devices due to their small size, lightweight and portability have a high effect on the acceptance of MC by customers. Organizations should keep in mind that MC is still somewhat new in Iran, so given the high volume of mobile phone users in Iran, it is a good opportunity for them to come up with plans and strategies to transition to m-commerce and facilitate trades using mobile applications. On the other hand, when entering a mobile business, they should keep in mind that those programs can be remarkably different from other trading methods in terms of time savings or effectiveness and follow-up of transactions. They should try to gain customers' trust in m-commerce in effective ways and emphasize the mobility and usefulness of using m-commerce in their advertisements.

Limitations and Future Research

One of the most important limitations of this study is that this is cross-sectional research in which the study was done at a point in time. It is suggested that future research be conducted at time intervals that allow for the observation of changes in customer perceptions. This is especially true when m-commerce platforms have been analyzed. Second, the research was limited to a single country's area. As a result, conducting a cross-cultural study to examine the tastes of different cultures might be beneficial. Third, a comparison of the settings of various demographic groups would be better, particularly when using age as a criterion for separating survey respondents.

Case Study

As the results of the study showed, PU, compatibility, mobility, PR, and PC have a significant effect on the adoption of MC by customers. Here, one case of the banking industry that uses MC is presented. Please read the case and answer its questions.

Colour Banking Company is an West Asian digital bank, where all banking services are carried out with a mobile application and are completely online. The Colour Banking Company mobile bank (e.g., mobile application) provides services such as opening a bank account in less than 7 minutes, online identification, free issuance of a bank card, free delivery of a card to a person's address in less than 10 working days, 24/7 customer support service, smart money transfer, discounts and refunds when shopping, automatic bill payment. The Colour Banking Company application can be installed by downloading the application from the Colour Banking Company website and launching it by entering the mobile phone number that is in the person's name, registering your friend's identification code, and entering the national number. After completing the identification process in Colour Banking Company, the individual's account will be verified and activated within 2 hours at most. Then you can order the card from inside the application and deliver it to the address you want. In Colour Banking Company, the account opening is completely free and without fees, and there is no need to maintain a minimum balance in the bank account. The Colour Banking Company application has various features, including the possibility of entering the application using the fingerprint defined in the mobile phone, the possibility of entering the application using the face scan defined in the mobile phone, and the possibility of receiving the login password in case of forgetting the password or receiving the initial password, and also online chat inside the program.

Case Study Questions

(1) To what extent do people need the use of MC compared to electronic and traditional commerce in the banking industry?
(2) What indicators have been followed by Colour Banking Company regarding the acceptance of MC?
(3) What other measures can be taken to improve the adoption of MC to Colour Banking Company?

Key Terms and Definitions

Customer intention: The intention is the customer's desire to use m-commerce. Review of the previous study indicates that intention is a reasonable predictor of technology use.
Mobile commerce: M-commerce refers to the use of mobile, wireless systems to communicate and make transactions.
Technology adoption: The decision by a person to obtain and use a novel innovation or invention.

References

Agarwal, R., & Prasad, J. (1998). A conceptual and operational definition of personal innovativeness in the domain of information technology. *Information Systems Research*, 9(2), 204–215. https://doi.org/10.1287/isre.9.2.204

Akbari, M., Keshavarz, M., Rezvani, A., Bakhtiar, A., & Shahriari, E. (2020). Drivers of 5 G technology acceptance: A Bayesian approach. *European Journal of International Management*, 1(January). https://doi.org/10.1504/EJIM.2022.10048391

Akbari, M., Moradi, A., Seyyedamiri, N., Zúñiga, M. Á., Rahmani, Z., & Padash, H. (2021). Consumers' intentions to use ridesharing services in Iran. *Research in Transportation Business & Management*, 41(December), 100616. https://doi.org/10.1016/j.rtbm.2020.100616

Akbari, M., Rezvani, A., Shahriari, E., Zúñiga, M. A., & Pouladian, H. (2020). Acceptance of 5 G technology: Mediation role of trust and concentration. *Journal of Engineering and Technology Management, 57*(July–September), 101585. https://doi.org/10.1016/j.jengtecman.2020.101585

Akbari, M., Rezvani, A., Zúñiga, M. A., & Shahriari, E. (2021). How the theory of planned behaviour and flow theory contribute to the acceptance of 5G technology? *European Journal of International Management.* https://doi.org/10.1504/EJIM.2021.10037606

Akbari, M., Seyyedamiri, N., Zúñiga, M. Á., Padash, H., & Shakiba, H. (2020). Evidence for acceptance of ride-hailing services in Iran. *Transportation Research Record, 2674*(11), 289–303. https://doi.org/10.1177/0361198120942224

Bhatti, T. (1970). Exploring factors influencing the adoption of mobile commerce. *Journal of Internet Banking and Commerce, 12*(3), 1–13. Corpus ID: 18246885.

Brynjolfsson, E., Jin, W., & McElheran, K. (2021). The power of prediction: Predictive analytics, workplace complements, and business performance. *Business Economics, 56*(4), 217–239. http://dx.doi.org/10.2139/ssrn.3849716

Brynjolfsson, E., & McElheran, K. (2016). The rapid adoption of data-driven decision-making. *The American Economic Review, 106*(5), 133–139. https://doi.org/10.1257/aer.p20161016

Chen, P. Y., & Hitt, L. M. (2002). Measuring switching costs and the determinants of customer retention in Internet-enabled businesses: A study of the online brokerage industry. *Information Systems Research, 13*(3), 255–274. https://doi.org/10.1287/isre.13.3.255.78

Cheng, T. E., Lam, D. Y., & Yeung, A. C. (2006). Adoption of internet banking: An empirical study in Hong Kong. *Decision Support Systems, 42*(3), 1558–1572. https://doi.org/10.1016/j.dss.2006.01.002

Chong, A. Y. L. (2013). A two-staged SEM-neural network approach for understanding and predicting the determinants of m-commerce adoption. *Expert Systems with Applications, 40*(4), 1240–1247. https://doi.org/10.1016/j.eswa.2012.08.067

Chong, A. Y. L., Chan, F. T., & Ooi, K. B. (2012). Predicting consumer decisions to adopt mobile commerce: Cross country empirical examination between China and Malaysia. *Decision Support Systems, 53*(1), 34–43. https://doi.org/10.1016/j.dss.2011.12.001

Chong, A. Y. L., Ooi, K. B., Lin, B., & Tan, B. I. (2010). Online banking adoption: An empirical analysis. *International Journal of Bank Marketing, 28*(4), 267–287. https://doi.org/10.1108/02652321011054963

Constantinides, E. (2002). The 4S web-marketing mix model. *Electronic Commerce Research and Applications, 1*(1), 57–76. https://doi.org/10.1016/S1567-4223(02)00006-6

Coursaris, C., & Hassanein, K. (2002). Understanding m-commerce: A consumer-centric model. *The Quarterly Journal of Electronic Commerce, 3,* 247–272.

Dai, H., & Palvi, P. C. (2009). Mobile commerce adoption in China and the United States: A cross-cultural study. *ACM SIGMIS – Data Base: The Database for Advances in Information Systems, 40*(4), 43–61. https://doi.org/10.1145/1644953.1644958

Davis, F. D. (1989). Perceived usefulness, perceived ease of use, and user acceptance of information technology. *MIS Quarterly, 13*(3), 319–340. https://doi.org/10.2307/249008

Faqih, K. M. (2016). An empirical analysis of factors predicting the behavioral intention to adopt Internet shopping technology among non-shoppers in a developing country context: Does gender matter? *Journal of Retailing and Consumer Services, 30*(May), 140–164. https://doi.org/10.1016/j.jretconser.2016.01.016

Featherman, M. S., Miyazaki, A. D., & Sprott, D. E. (2010). Reducing online privacy risk to facilitate e-service adoption: The influence of perceived ease of use and corporate credibility. *Journal of Services Marketing, 24*(3), 219–229. https://doi.org/10.1108/08876041011040622

International Telecommunication Union. (2021). *Measuring the information society report*. International Telecommunication Union. https://www.itu.int/en/ITU-D/Statistics/Pages/publications/misr2018.aspx. Accessed on January 11, 2021.

Islam, M. A., Khan, M. A., Ramayah, T., & Hossain, M. M. (2011). The adoption of mobile commerce service among employed mobile phone users in Bangladesh: Self-efficacy as a moderator. *International Business Research, 4*(2), 80–89. https://doi.org/10.5539/ibr.v4n2p80

Kim, H. W., Chan, H. C., & Gupta, S. (2007). Value-based adoption of mobile internet: An empirical investigation. *Decision Support Systems, 43*(1), 111–126. https://doi.org/10.1016/j.dss.2005.05.009

Kim, C., Mirusmonov, M., & Lee, I. (2010). An empirical examination of factors influencing the intention to use mobile payment. *Computers in Human Behavior, 26*(3), 310–322. https://doi.org/10.1016/j.chb.2009.10.013

Liébana-Cabanillas, F., Marinković, V., & Kalinić, Z. (2017). A SEM-neural network approach for predicting antecedents of m-commerce acceptance. *International Journal of Information Management, 37*(2), 14–24. https://doi.org/10.1016/j.ijinfomgt.2016.10.008

Liébana-Cabanillas, F., Sánchez-Fernández, J., & Muñoz-Leiva, F. (2014). The moderating effect of experience in the adoption of mobile payment tools in Virtual Social Networks: The m-Payment Acceptance Model in Virtual Social Networks (MPAM-VSN). *International Journal of Information Management, 34*(2), 151–166. https://doi.org/10.1016/j.ijinfomgt.2013.12.006

Madan, K., & Yadav, R. (2016). Behavioural intention to adopt mobile wallet: A developing country perspective. *Journal of Indian Business Research, 8*(3), 227–244. https://doi.org/10.1108/JIBR-10-2015-0112

Madan, K., & Yadav, R. (2019). A two-stage SEM-neural network analysis to predict drivers of m-commerce in India. *International Journal of Electronic Marketing and Retailing, 10*(2), 130–149. http://dx.doi.org/10.1504/IJEMR.2019.10018834

Mahatanankoon, P., Wen, H. J., & Lim, B. (2005). Consumer-based m-commerce: Exploring consumer perception of mobile applications. *Computer Standards & Interfaces, 27*(4), 347–357. https://doi.org/10.1016/j.csi.2004.10.003

Mallat, N., Rossi, M., Tuunainen, V. K., & Öörni, A. (2009). The impact of use context on mobile services acceptance: The case of mobile ticketing. *Information & Management, 46*(3), 190–195. https://doi.org/10.1016/j.im.2008.11.008

Marguerite, R. (2021). The mobile phone of the future will be implanted in your head (2016). https://www.cnet.com/tech/services-and-software/the-mobile-phone-of-the-future-will-be-implanted-in-your-head/. Accessed on January 16, 2021.

Natarajan, T., Balasubramanian, S. A., & Kasilingam, D. L. (2017). Understanding the intention to use mobile shopping applications and its influence on price sensitivity. *Journal of Retailing and Consumer Services, 37*(July), 8–22. https://doi. org/10.1016/j.jretconser.2017.02.010

Plouffe, C. R., Hulland, J. S., & Vandenbosch, M. (2001). Richness versus parsimony in modeling technology adoption decisions—Understanding merchant adoption of a smart card-based payment system. *Information Systems Research, 12*(2), 208–222. http://dx.doi.org/10.1287/isre.12.2.208.9697

Raut, R. D., Priyadarshinee, P., Gardas, B. B., & Jha, M. K. (2018). Analyzing the factors influencing cloud computing adoption using three stage hybrid SEM-ANN-ISM (SEANIS) approach. *Technological Forecasting and Social Change, 134,* 98–123. https://doi.org/10.1016/j.techfore.2018.05.020

Rock, J. (2000). Mobile commerce: The next big thing or just plain hype. *The Weekly Corporate Growth Report, 1121*(18), 11093–11104.

Sadeh, N. (2003). *M-commerce: Technologies, services, and business models.* John Wiley & Sons.

Schierz, P. G., Schilke, O., & Wirtz, B. W. (2010). Understanding consumer acceptance of mobile payment services: An empirical analysis. *Electronic Commerce Research and Applications, 9*(3), 209–216. https://doi.org/10.1016/j.elerap. 2009.07.005

Shin, D. H. (2009). Towards an understanding of the consumer acceptance of mobile wallet. *Computers in Human Behavior, 25*(6), 1343–1354. https://doi.org/10.1016/j. chb.2009.06.001

Sonnenwald, D. H., Maglaughlin, K. L., & Whitton, M. C. (2001). Using innovation diffusion theory to guide collaboration technology evaluation: Work in progress. In *Proceedings tenth IEEE international workshop on enabling technologies: Infrastructure for collaborative enterprises. WET ICE 2001* (pp. 114–119). IEEE. http:// dx.doi.org/10.1109/ENABL.2001.953399

Tan, G. W. H., Ooi, K. B., Leong, L. Y., & Lin, B. (2014). Predicting the drivers of behavioral intention to use mobile learning: A hybrid SEM-Neural Networks approach. *Computers in Human Behavior, 36*(July), 198–213. https://doi.org/10. 1016/j.chb.2014.03.052

Tarasewich, P., Nickerson, R. C., & Warkentin, M. (2002). Issues in mobile e-commerce. *Communications of the Association for Information Systems, 8*(January), 41–64. http://dx.doi.org/10.17705/1CAIS.00803

Thakur, R., & Srivastava, M. (2013). Customer usage intention of mobile commerce in India: An empirical study. *Journal of Indian Business Research, 5*(1), 52–72. https://doi.org/10.1108/17554191311303385

The Official Portal of Measuring Information Society of Iran. (2022). *The Information and Communication Technology Development Index 2017.* The Official Portal of Measuring Information Society of Iran. https://mis.ito.gov.ir/ictindex/view international/19. Accessed on January 6, 2022.

Tiwari, R., & Buse, S. (2007). *The mobile commerce prospects: A strategic analysis of opportunities in the banking sector* (p. 233). Hamburg University Press. https://doi. org/10.15460/HUP.16

Turban, E., King, D., Lee, J., & Viehland, D. (2002). Electronic commerce: A managerial perspective 2002. *Prentice Hall, 13*(975285), 4.

Wei, T. T., Marthandan, G., Chong, A. Y. L., Ooi, K. B., & Arumugam, S. (2009). What drives Malaysian m-commerce adoption? An empirical analysis. *Industrial Management & Data Systems*, *109*(3), 370–388. https://doi.org/10.1108/02635570910939399

Wu, J. H., & Wang, S. C. (2005). What drives mobile commerce?: An empirical evaluation of the revised technology acceptance model. *Information & Management*, *42*(5), 719–729. https://doi.org/10.1016/j.im.2004.07.001

Zarmpou, T., Saprikis, V., Markos, A., & Vlachopoulou, M. (2012). Modeling users' acceptance of mobile services. *Electronic Commerce Research*, *12*(2), 225–248. https://doi.org/10.1007/s10660-012-9092-x

Zhu, T., Guo, Y., Wang, C., & Ni, C. (2020). Inter-hour forecast of solar radiation based on the structural equation model and ensemble model. *Energies*, *13*(17), 4534. https://doi.org/10.3390/en13174534

Chapter 12

A Literature Review of the Sharing Economy Adoption: Insights on Influencing Factors

Maryam Khodayari[a], Morteza Akbari[a] and Pantea Foroudi[b]

[a]University of Tehran, Iran
[b]Brunel University London, UK

Abstract

The factors involved in and obstacles to sharing economy adoption have been studied with several methods, and several models have occurred to clarify the underlying procedure of sharing economy (SE) adoption, which provide contradictory and scattered findings. This chapter seeks to offer a scientific outline of the academic structure of the SE adoption domain.

Keywords: Sharing economy; collaborative consumption; collaborative economy; technology acceptance; technology adoption

Introduction[1]

With the development of information technology and sharing systems facilitated by the internet, a new paradigm called the sharing economy (SE) (Akarsu et al., 2020; Akbari et al., 2022b; Belk, 2014; Chatterjee et al., 2022) has been created to respond to concerns such as the climate crisis, environmental issues, and the depletion of natural resources. SE uses advanced technologies (Cuomo et al., 2021; Foroudi et al., 2017, 2018, 2019, 2020) to integrate and collect dispersed resources and share usage rights on the internet platform to meet consumer needs (Foroudi et al., 2020, 2022; Hafeez et al., 2018, 2019; Zhu et al., 2017). With the emergence of innovative and emerging technologies, the way of doing business

---

[1]Figure color descriptions are present in this chapter, and the digital version contains color figures.

Business Strategies and Ethical Challenges in the Digital Ecosystem, 267–304
Copyright © 2025 Maryam Khodayari, Morteza Akbari and Pantea Foroudi
Published under exclusive licence by Emerald Publishing Limited
doi:10.1108/978-1-80455-069-420241012

has changed, which has forced many entrepreneurs to innovate, and these innovations disrupt traditional businesses (Imani et al., 2020; Rajabi et al., 2022; Richter et al., 2017). As a disruptive innovation, SE creates opportunities and challenges for entrepreneurs (Chuah et al., 2021; Ruiz-Alba et al., 2022). SE also creates opportunities for unemployed people, increasing social interactions, improving reciprocity, and enabling them to access resources that they might not otherwise have (Dillahunt & Malone, 2015; Kathan et al., 2016). Therefore, SE can improve social problems such as overconsumption, contamination, and scarcity (Hamari et al., 2016; Laukkanen & Tura, 2020). Adding ecological, societal, and financial value to the value proposition provided by businesses helps create a more sustainable civilization (Cocquyt et al., 2020). By sharing assets and resources, companies can be more flexible and respond faster to market changes (Grondys, 2019). Realizing the benefits it provides to individuals and society, a large number of SE-based businesses have been established around the world, which represents an emerging trend (Ahsan, 2020).

In addition to the opportunities created, SE is associated with many challenges and risks. Risks include theft and damage of personal assets (Lutz et al., 2018), uncertainty and fear of opportunism caused by users' inability to evaluate products or services (Chen et al., 2014; Yang et al., 2019), cyberattacks on online operating systems that lead to personal information violations (Lutz et al., 2018), surveillance and ambiguous rules and regulations, trust in online platforms and particularly trust in strangers, which are critical issues and the main barriers to SE (Chen et al., 2014; So et al., 2018; Tussyadiah & Pesonen, 2018). In the era of the Fourth Industrial Revolution, SE is mentioned as a smart solution to manage resources (Grondys, 2019); however, to date, it has not been widely adopted (Hira, 2017; Kathan et al., 2016). Therefore, companies are missing out on the opportunities the Fourth Industrial Revolution offers. On the other hand, some argue that the performance of businesses based on SE differs from region to region (Ajwani-Ramchandani et al., 2021).

The review of previous articles on the aspects affecting SE adoption shows opposing findings. For instance, Bąk et al. (2022) found that among the most important motivations, sustainability is more important. As an example, the use of Uber services is meaningfully affected by details linked to two pillars of sustainability – *social* and *economic*. Examining shared services in India, Kaushal and Prashar (2022) found that perceived intimacy as intrinsic motivation and economic benefits as extrinsic motivation are the strongest determinants of Indian users' attitudes and intention to continuously use the SE. Amaro et al. (2019) also found that Millennials' intent to book on Airbnb is influenced by subjective norms, willingness to stay, unique variety, attitude, and economic benefits. Risk and purchase channels do not affect booking intention. So et al. (2018) showed that neither social interaction nor risk had an important effect on consumer behavior toward Airbnb, while price value, home amenities, and distrust could only indirectly influence consumer behavior through attitude to influence their behavioral intention. However, risk, benefits, platform trust, and platform quality are key determinants of users' intention to contribute to Uber (Lee et al., 2018).

From the overview of previous studies, we found that the reasons for users' SE adoption vary (Bawack & Kamdjoug, 2018) in different geographical locations around the world and among different countries due to the existence of diverse business models, conflict between different stakeholders, and different and complex policies and regulations (Hossain, 2020; Muñoz & Cohen, 2017). For the above reasons, to achieve the benefits and reduce the limitations of the SE, it is essential to recognize the critical factors involved in and barriers to the successful adoption of the SE.

Although recent studies (Teubner, 2022; Tran et al., 2019) have been conducted, given the up-to-date analysis in the current study, the objectives of this article are: (1) to study the knowledgeable structure of SE adoption literature done co-citation analysis (CCA) and to identify key knowledgeable traditions and (2) to recognize potential study directions for upcoming investigation. To achieve the specified goals, citation and co-citation analyses were performed as follows. In the first phase, to survey the present status of papers in SE adoption, the distribution of papers in countries, the top articles, and the most authoritative journals were examined through citation analysis. Next, CCA was performed to survey an extensive range of thematic sections.

This article reviewed 305 articles on July 17, 2022, in the period 1975–2022. To overwhelm the contradictions and fill the study gaps, the current research is looking for the structure and nature of SE adoption. Results find that the main subjects in this field contain different methods of exchange, motivation, barriers to participation, theories used in SE adoption, and sustainability. The findings also suggest that insufficient study has been done on the impact of a series of factors at the *micro* level (including the individual level: Electronic word of mouth (eWOM), self-disclosure, self-efficacy, word of mouth (WOM), and the firm level: Brand awareness and brand image) and at the *macro* level (political factor: Policy and regulations, social factor: Culture and perceived legitimacy, environmental factor: Perceived physical risks, technology factor: Information accurateness and availability). In addition, according to the review of previous studies, researchers have often investigated the factors of success and influence on SE adoption, so our suggestion for future research is to consider limitations and obstacles including institutional and market challenges at the macro level as well.

Method

Review Questions

Based on the topics stated in the overview, which are (a) the importance of the subject, (b) rapid changes in businesses, (c) changing the paradigm toward sustainable consumption, (d) neglecting some significant features of SE adoption in prior studies, and (e) the need for an inclusive review of the issue, three key research questions were raised. (i) What are the success and effective issues for the adoption of SE? (ii) What are the barriers to and challenges of SE adoption? (iii) What factors should be considered by researchers in this field in future research?

Database

Bibliometric analysis (BA) is a broad and detailed method for investigating and evaluating a large amount of scientific data. This method is intended to understand the interrelationships between journal citations and to summarize the up-to-date status of a current or developing research topic (Donthu et al., 2021). BA includes several methods such as citation analysis (CA), keyword co-occurrence, CCA, or co-authoring analysis (Dias, 2019). BA has been employed in prior studies to survey diverse areas like blockchain technology (Kuzior & Sira, 2022), sharing economy (Akbari et al., 2022b), supply chain innovation (Malacina & Teplov, 2022), the evolution of eWOM (Akbari et al., 2022a), and social innovation (Foroudi et al., 2020).

The Clarivate Analytics-WoS database was used to obtain the data used in this study. Although there are several internationally recognized databases, the Web of Science (WoS) database has the uppermost standards for research (Merigó et al., 2015). The WoS database is more prevalent in many papers that employ the bibliographic technique to investigate their particular subjects (Akbari, Khodayari, et al., 2020; Chae, 2022; Malacina & Teplov, 2022).

Procedure and Data

To recover the records of this chapter, the search in the core collection section of the WoS database, which is hereinafter referred to as WoS for short, was extracted on July 17, 2022, from 1975 to 2022. The search formula is as follows: "share* economy*" OR "collaborative* consumption*" OR "collaborative* economy*" AND "acceptance*" OR "adoption*." The publishing field is a "Topic." Searching for these keywords in the topic section, we retrieved 369 records. Then, by applying the filter of "Articles," the number of these records fell to 313 records. The remaining documents comprised proceeding papers (45), early access (16), review articles (15), and book chapters (2). In the third step, by filtering English, 305 articles were extracted. Other articles were in other languages, including Spanish (2 articles), Portuguese (5), and Russian (1).

The Analytical Methods and Software

Basic bibliometric studies analyze the citations in a given area. CA measures the similarity among documents, journals, countries, or institutes over the occurrence where two items are independently cited by single or further items (Xu et al., 2021). With the basic presumption that if two papers are co-cited by a third publication, then they may be conceptually connected, CCA is being used more often to map networks of concepts in scientific domains (Kleinberg, 2003). This likelihood rises with the number of co-citations, enabling us to establish a solid connection between the papers (Kashani et al., 2022).

CA

Diverse facets of a research area can be examined, depending on the unit of analysis chosen. After searching and choosing keywords, the stages of bibliographic study need the vastness of the study to be determined to run a comprehensive search (Zupic & Čater, 2015). In this study, we primarily performed a CA. CA enables academics to comprehend the level of activity in a given field and the appropriate journals, reveal the researchers' study performance, and identify research directions for the future (Chabowski et al., 2018; Ferreira et al., 2016). The most common CA units include papers, authors, sources, institutes, cited references, and countries. This analysis is based on the statement that the scholars cite documents that they consider important (Chabowski et al., 2018).

CCA

This study applied CCA to find subdomains of SE adoption research. After collecting the articles from WoS, the data were transferred to the VOSviewer software to implement the full structure used for CCA. Using this software, a co-citation network of cited references was drawn for further analysis. Regarding all the analysis stages and the software used in each stage, the method is briefed in Fig. 12.1.

Outcomes

Publication Trends

In this study, 305 articles with 6,025 citations related to SE adoption have been reviewed. As shown in Fig. 12.2, the number of studies has increased continuously every year, which indicates the growth of researchers' interest in this field.

The Most Productive Countries

Through CA, Table 12.1 shows countries by number of citations, in order from most cited to least, in the area of SE adoption. The three most cited countries in this field are the United States with 62 articles and 1842 citations, People's Republic of China with 68 articles and 1,347 citations, and England with 37 articles and 1,015 citations. Fig 12. 3, taken from Datawrapper, shows a map of countries by the number of citations from minimum to maximum citations in SE adoption. Countries highlighted in pink have the least citations, countries highlighted in green have the most citations, and countries highlighted in gray have no data.

The Most Cited Journals

Through CA, Table 12.2 and Fig. 12.4 display the most cited journals in SE adoption as follows: *Journal of Cleaner Production, Electronic Commerce*

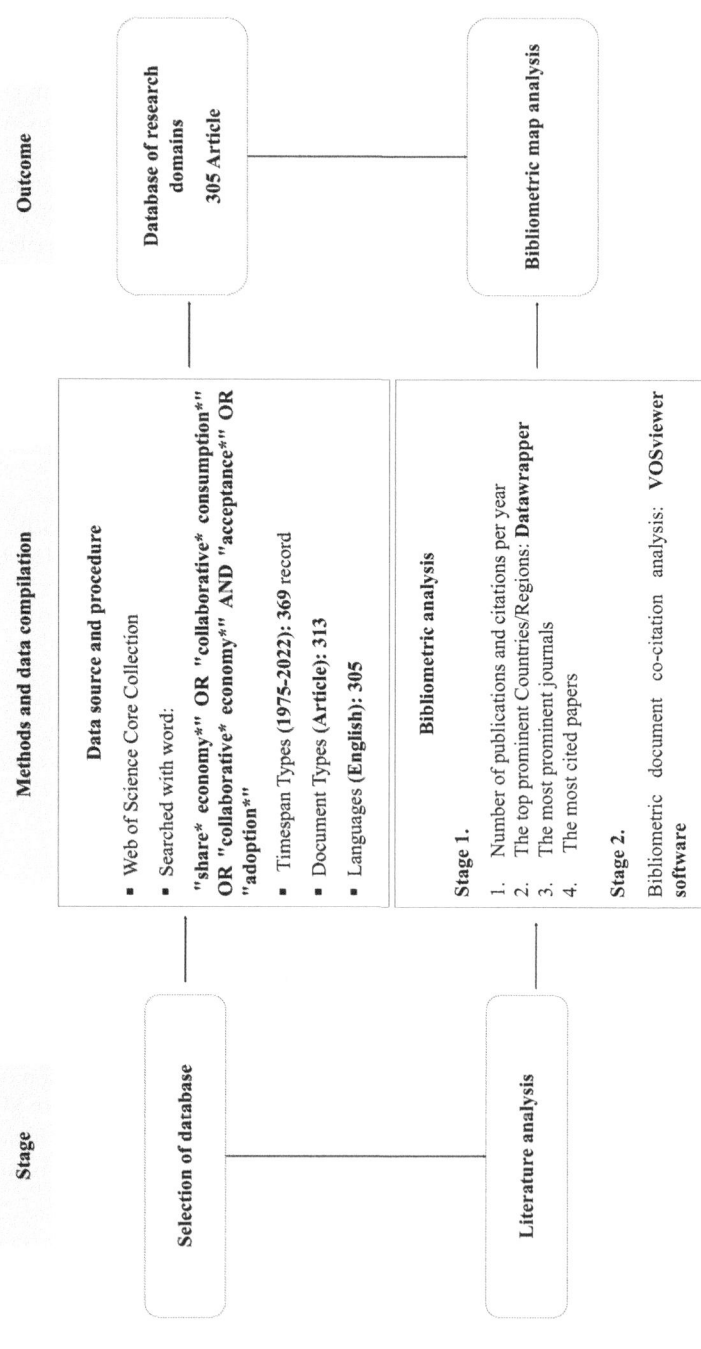

Fig. 12.1.   Methodological Approach. *Source:* Authors' Presentation.

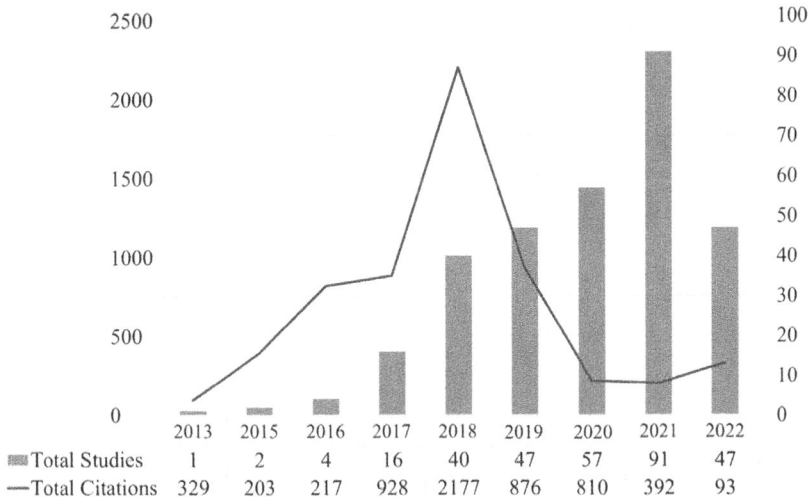

	2013	2015	2016	2017	2018	2019	2020	2021	2022
▬ Total Studies	1	2	4	16	40	47	57	91	47
—Total Citations	329	203	217	928	2177	876	810	392	93

Fig. 12.2. Number of Articles and Citations of Each Article per Year.

Table 12.1. The Most Productive Countries Based on the Rate of Citation.

Country	Documents	Citations	Country	Documents	Citations
USA	62	1842	South Korea	14	189
People's Republic of China	68	1,347	Australia	19	168
England	37	1,015	Italy	10	163
Germany	25	533	Denmark	5	149
Canada	12	482	Switzerland	6	115
India	20	331	Portugal	6	93
Spain	13	284	Brazil	11	69
Singapore	6	252	Malaysia	7	51
Netherlands	10	238	Iran	6	25
France	15	228	Turkey	5	11
Taiwan	18	193			

Number of citations from the
lowest to the highest citation

11   1842

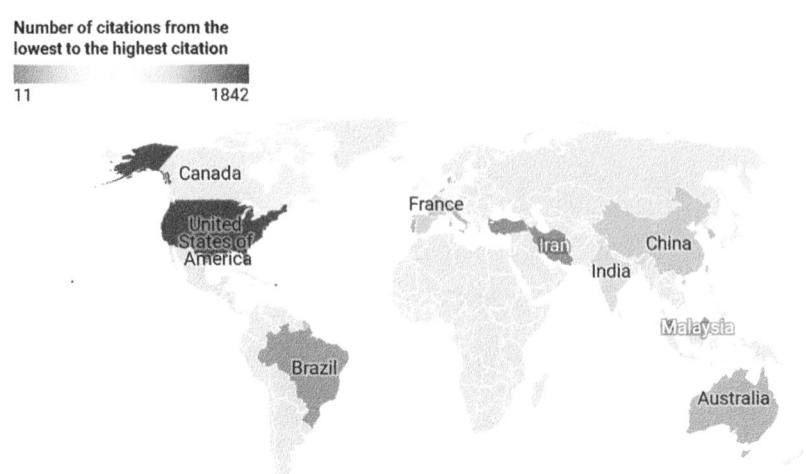

Fig. 12.3.   Map of Countries Based on the Number of Citations.
Source: Created with www.datawrapper.de

Research and Applications, and *International Journal of Contemporary Hospitality Management*. From 2013 to 2022, 15 articles on SE adoption were available in the *Journal of Cleaner Production*, which has the most citations with 751 citations; five articles in *Electronic Commerce Research and Applications* (401 citations); and

Table 12.2. Most Cited Journals in SE Adoption.

Source	Documents	Citations
Journal of Cleaner Production	15	751
Electronic Commerce Research and Applications	5	401
International Journal of Contemporary Hospitality Management	5	222
Journal of Consumer Marketing	5	221
Technological Forecasting and Social Change	9	195
International Journal of Hospitality Management	7	188
Sustainability	24	159
Transportation Research Part F-Traffic Psychology and Behavior	6	158
Journal of Retailing and Consumer Services	6	140
Journal of Business Research	8	77
Information Technology & People	6	28

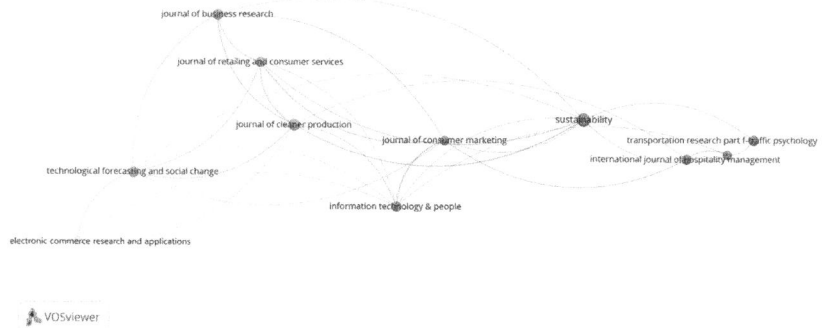

Fig. 12.4.   Mapping of the Most Cited Journals in SE Adoption.

five articles in the *International Journal of Contemporary Hospitality Management* (222 citations). Table 2 shows the most published citations in the scope of the SE adoption along with the frequency of their citations.

The Most Cited Articles

Recognition of highly cited publications serves as a significant measure to comprehend author rank and provides a basis for additional research. Looking for the highly cited documents on SE adoption (see Fig. 12.3), Hamari's (2013) study has attracted the most attention. In this article, he introduces the social and cognitive impact and determination of users' goals as a strong predictor of the acceptance and use of gamification programs. The next most cited article, by Guttentag et al. (2018), examines the motivations of tourists to use Airbnb. The third most popular paper is by So et al. (2018), which states that the fee rate, fun, and aids of a home meaningfully impact users' attitude toward Airbnb. Table 12.3 shows an overview of the most cited articles with at least 100 citations in SE adoption.

CCA

CCA was performed with the cited references to well recognize the theoretical necessities of 305 articles. An original sample of 16,672 cited references was concentrated in documents with at least 25 citations, subsequent in 28 articles related to SE adoption (see Table 12.4). Fig. 12.5 displays the bibliometric network based on CCA, which contains four clusters.

Cluster A: Methods of Exchange

This cluster includes 10 articles about new methods of exchange. The new methods of exchange discussed in the articles of this cluster are sharing (Belk, 2007, 2010), access-based consumption (Bardhi et al., 2012), commercial sharing

Table 12.3. Most Cited Articles in SE Adoption.

Authors	Motivations	Theories	Methodology	Effective Factors	Constraints	Citations
Hamari (2013)	Gamification mechanisms alone do not automatically lead to important growth in usage in the studied useful service.	• Social influence • Social proof theory • Theory of planned behavior • Flow theory	A multivariate test (MANOVA)	• Social comparison • Goal setting	—	329
Guttentag et al. (2018)	Tourists' motivations for using Airbnb.	Innovation adoption	An exploratory factor analysis	• Interaction • Home Benefits • Novelty • SE ethos • Local authenticity	—	306
So et al. (2018)	Fee rate, fun, and aids of a home meaningfully impact the attitude toward Airbnb.	The theory of planned behavior	Mixed-methods approach: Qualitative method: semi-structured focus group interviews. Quantitative method: Survey	• Price Value • Authenticity • Novelty • Enjoyment • Social interactions • Home Benefits	• Perceived risk • Distrust • Insecurity	209

Piscicelli et al. (2014)	Examining how users' values affect the acceptance and diffusion of collaborative consumption.	Social psychological models of behaviors and social practice theory	Mixed-methods approach: Qualitative method: a case study. Quantitative method: Survey	• Security • Conformity • Tradition • Benevolence • Universalism • Self-direction • Stimulation • Hedonism • Achievement • Power	—	182
Edbring et al. (2016)	The consumer's attitude toward consumption models is very different depending on the product group.	—	Mixed-methods approach: Qualitative method: semi-structured interviews. Quantitative method: Survey	Motivations for secondhand consumption: • Attitudes economic reasons • Environmental reasons • Desire to be unique • Other: quality, inaccessibility, unique design, and fun Motivations for access-based consumption: • Attitudes • Flexibility • Financial reasons	Obstacles to secondhand use: Concern for health, pests The desire for new goods Obstacles to access-based consumption: Want to own Concern for health Newness with the idea Financial barriers worry Ecological barriers Obstacles to sharing and	176

(*Continued*)

Table 12.3. (*Continued*)

Authors	Motivations	Theories	Methodology	Effective Factors	Constraints	Citations
				• Temporary nature of use • Environmental reasons Motivations for sharing and collaborative consumption: • Practical for rarely used products • Reasons for stability	collaborative consumption: Want to own Concern for health Fear of producing inaccessibility Absence of trust in others Unreasonable and complicated	
Kumar et al. (2018)	SE amenities are mainly accepted by generation y, while other groups are still in the initial phases of acceptance.	Social exchange, self-determination, and reciprocal altruism	Interview	• Attributes of generations	–	159
Hwang and Griffiths (2017)	The explicit dimensions of value perceptions have diverse effects on the attitude and empathy of customers to shared consumption services.	Theory of reasoned action	Structural equation modeling	• Utilitarian value • Hedonic value • Symbolic value • Empathy • Attitude	–	132

Author (year)	Finding	Theory	Method		Factors	No.
Zhu et al. (2017)	Self-efficacy is an essential aspect that has an impact on consumer perception. Useful value, emotive value, and community value are important backgrounds of the overall value of ride-sharing apps.	Social cognitive theory. Perceived value theory.	Partial least squares path modeling (pls-pm)		• Self-efficacy • Functional value • Emotive value • Community value • Knowledge cost • Hazard cost • Value • Attitude	123
Parente et al. (2018)	The SE phenomenon has led to the adoption of platform businesses around the world, which in turn creates an excellent chance for upcoming study.	International business theories	Literature review	-	• Competitors • Regulations	121
Lee et al. (2018)	Risks, benefits, faith in the platform, and platform qualities were important predictors of users' intent to contribute to Uber.	Theory of reasoned action	The structural equation modeling technique	—	• Perceived platform qualities • Trust in the platform • Perceived risks • Perceived benefits	114
Min et al. (2019)	Comparative benefit, compatibility, complication,	Technology acceptance model (TAM)	The structural equation	—	• Relative advantage • Compatibility	108

(Continued)

Table 12.3. (*Continued*)

Authors	Motivations	Theories	Methodology	Effective Factors	Constraints	Citations
	observability, and community impact have an important effect on usefulness and ease of use.	Diffusion of innovation theory (DIT)	modeling technique	• Complication • Observability • Community influence • Usefulness • Ease of use • Attitudes		
Prieto et al. (2017)	Demographic variables play an important role in individual choice behavior regarding car-sharing services.	—	Survey	Demographic variables	—	106
Barnes and Mattsson (2017)	Consumer intentions are primarily driven by economic, environmental, and social aids mediated by utility and enjoyment, in turn by a sense of belonging to a shared public.	Theory of reasoned action (TRA)	Partial least squares path modeling	• Economic benefits • Environmental benefits • Social benefits • Enjoyment and sense of belonging • Social influence • Trust and structural assurance	—	104

Table 12.4. Co-Citation Network of Cited References in SE Adoption.

Cluster	Label	Citations	Theme	Details
A	Albinsson and Yasanthi Perera (2012)	28	Methods of exchange	• Sharing • Access-based consumption
	Bardhi et al. (2012)	70		• Commercial sharing systems
	Barnes and Mattsson (2016)	26		• Pseudo-sharing • Collaborative consumption
	Belk (2007)	27		
	Belk (2010)	34		
	Belk (2014)	105		
	Benoit et al. (2017)	33		
	Botsman and Rogers (2010)	63		
	Hamari et al. (2016)	128		
	Lamberton and Rose (2012)	50		
B	Bucher et al. (2016)	25	Participation motivation and barriers	*Motivations:* • Amenities
	Cheng (2016)	31		• Cost saving
	Ert et al. (2016)	34		• Desirability
	Guttentag (2015)	34		• Economic benefits (value)
	Möhlmann (2015)	76		• Enjoyment • Familiarity
	Tussyadiah (2015)	30		• Monetary • Moral
	Tussyadiah (2016)	33		• Satisfaction • Service quality
	Zervas et al. (2017)	43		• Socio-hedonic • Sustainability and economic benefits • Trust • Usefulness

(Continued)

Table 12.4. *(Continued)*

Cluster	Label	Citations	Theme	Details
				Barriers: • Lack of economic benefits • Lack of efficiency in the field of technology • Lack of trust
C	Ajzen (1991)	67	Theories used in the SE adoption	The theory of reasoned action (TRA)
	Davis et al. (1989)	35		The theory of planned behavior (TPB)
	Davis (1989)	67		The technology acceptance model (TAM)
	Lee et al. (2018)	27		The model of personal computer utilization (MPCU)
	Venkatesh and Davis (2000)	35		The motivational model (MM)
	Venkatesh et al. (2003)	53		Decomposed Theory of Planned Behavior (DTPB)
	Venkatesh (2012)	31		Combined TAM and TPB (C-TAM-TPB)
				The social cognitive theory (SCT)
				Innovation diffusion theory (IDT)
				A unified theory of acceptance and use of technology (UTAUT)
D	Böcker and Meelen (2017)	32	Sustainability	• Economic
	Cohen and Kietzmann (2014)	27		• Environmental • Social effects
	Martin (2016)	34		

systems (Lamberton & Rose, 2012), pseudo-sharing (Belk, 2014), and collaborative consumption (CC) (Belk, 2014; Benoit et al., 2017; Botsman & Rogers, 2010).

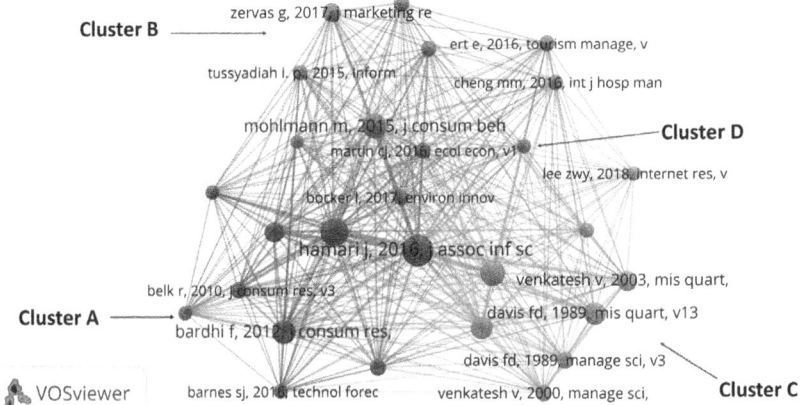

Fig. 12.5.   Co-Citation Grid of Cited References in SE Adoption.

Belk (2007) defined sharing as the act and process of distributing our property to others for their use, as well as receiving the property of others for our use. Then in 2010, the study introduced sharing in family or circle of friends. Access-based consumption is also defined as a deal that may be mediated by a market in which no transmission of rights takes place (Bardhi et al., 2012). Commercial sharing systems are marketer-managed platforms that give clients the chance to enjoy the benefits of products without taking ownership. It is considered competition between consumers for a limited supply of a common product (Lamberton & Rose, 2012). Pseudo-sharing is a commercial connection masquerading as public sharing; but it is not sharing (Belk, 2014). Collaborative consumption is a three-way exchange between a platform, a service provider, and a customer where there is no transfer of ownership but the use of a low-use asset for an agreed (short) time, through market mechanisms (Benoit et al., 2017). Finally, Eckhardt et al. (2019) defined the SE as a technologically enabled socioeconomic system that has five main features (impermanent access, the transmission of economic rate, platform intermediation, extensive client character, and crowd-sourced supply).

Collaborative consumption and SE are two of the most current innovative forms of consumption in the context of Web 2.0 (Belk, 2014). These two concepts are relatively new, have various names, and are often used interchangeably, and the differences between them are often ignored (Belk, 2014). The difference between these two methods of exchange has not been considered in the existing studies in this cluster (Barnes & Mattsson, 2016; Belk, 2010) which examine the reasons for consumers' willingness to participate in CC (Benoit et al., 2017; Hamari et al., 2016).

Cluster B: Participation Motivation and Barriers

Eight articles in this cluster examine the range of different motivations and barriers to sharing. During the design of a model based on the theory of planned behavior, Bucher et al. (2016) introduced three motives as factors affecting the attitude and intention to share; these are *moral, socio-hedonic*, and *monetary*. Also, they identified three predictors of sharing motives which are materialism, sociability, and volunteerism. Tussyadiah (2015) investigated the motivations of and obstacles to using Airbnb services in the hotel industry and named two motivations of social aspects of sustainability and economic benefits and three obstacles which are lack of trust, lack of efficiency in the field of technology, and lack of economic benefits. In 2016, to better understand the behavioral characteristics of users in the SE, he examined the factors that affect their satisfaction and intention to use Airbnb services again. User satisfaction is influenced by factors such as enjoyment, economic benefits (value), and amenities (Tussyadiah, 2016). In another study of this cluster, Ert et al. (2016) focused their attention on the appearance of sellers' photos on Airbnb platforms. The presence of these photos can have a significant impact on users' decisions because users infer the reliability of the host from these photos, and their choice is influenced by this inference.

Möhlmann (2015) obtained results by examining two samples, one of the car-sharing users and the other of the home-sharing users. In the first study, he found that the variables of cost saving, familiarity, service quality (Akbari, Seyyed Amiri, et al., 2020), trust, and desirability have a positive effect on user satisfaction (Akbari, Moradi, et al., 2020). Also, the variables belonging to society and desirability have a positive effect on the probability of re-choosing the previous service. In the second study, he found that the four variables of cost savings, familiarity, trust, and usefulness positively affect satisfaction. In addition, familiarity and usefulness have a positive and significant effect on the probability of choosing the sharing option again. In this study, satisfaction has a positive effect on the likelihood of choosing the sharing option again.

Cluster C: Theories Used in the SE Adoption

The articles in this cluster focus on introducing technology acceptance models and theories related to SE adoption. Table 12.5 describes the theories in detail.

Cluster D: Sustainability

The three articles in this cluster examine the relative importance of (1) economic, (2) social, and (3) environmental incentives for participation in SE. SE is (1) a financial opportunity, (2) an additional sustainable form of consumption, and (3) a path toward a decentralized, fair, and sustainable economy (Martin, 2016). In addition to economic consequences, SE has positive environmental and social effects (Böcker & Meelen, 2017; Botsman & Rogers, 2010). Various researchers have proposed different motivations for participation in the SE. Bardhi et al. (2012) and Bellotti et al. (2015) stated that there are economic motivations for the car-sharing platform,

Table 12.5. Theories Used in the SE Adoption.

Source	Theory	Description
Fishbein and Ajzen (1977)	TRA	With the first theory of technology acceptance, attitude affects behavior and is a one-dimensional or multidimensional aspect. This theory is designed to explain almost every human behavior. This theory is moderated by the two main constructs of attitude toward behavior and mental norm.
Ajzen (1991)	TPB	TPB is an extension of TRA that has been expanded by adding behavioral control. This theory is moderated by three main constructs. Attitude toward behavior and mental norm and behavioral control as a new construct.
Taylor and Todd (1995)	DTPB	This model examines dimensions such as belief, attitude, mental norms, and perceived behavioral control by separating them into specific belief dimensions in more detail. This theory shows that behavioral intention is a direct determinant of behavior.
Davis (1989); Venkatesh and Davis (2000)	TAM	In this model, two technology acceptance criteria replace the TRA's attitude toward behavior: usefulness and perceived ease of use.
Venkatesh and Davis (2000)	TAM2	TAM2 was expanded from TAM to explain perceived usefulness and ease of use from the perspective of social influence and cognitive instrumental processes. Social influence processes refer to subjective, voluntary, and image norm cases. Cognitive instrumental processes refer to job relevance, output quality, demonstrability of results, and perceived ease.

(Continued)

Table 12.5. *(Continued)*

Source	Theory	Description
Mathieson (1991)	C-TAM-TPB	This model was developed by combining the TPB (social psychology domain) model with TAM (information technology domain) to achieve better use of TPB in technology acceptance. This model combines TPB predictors with the usefulness of TAM to provide a hybrid model.
Thompson et al. (1991)	MPCU	This theory states that PC use may be influenced by people's feelings toward PC use, social norms, expected consequences, habits, and facilitating circumstances. Behavior is directly influenced by social aspects, consequences, influence, and facilitating circumstances.
Rogers (2003)	IDT	This theory focuses on individual differences in novelty. Four main factors determine behavior: innovation, communication channels, time, and social systems. Rogers stated five features of innovation that affect people's behavior and express the degree of adoption of innovation. These include comparative advantage, compatibility, complication, testability, and observability.
Davis et al. (1992)	MM	Two main factors of motivation; extrinsic and intrinsic motivation. Extrinsic motivation to use technology was expressed as the usefulness of technology use, and intrinsic motivation to use technology was expressed as enjoyment of technology use.

Table 12.5. *(Continued)*

Source	Theory	Description
Bandura (1986)	SCT	The main feature of this theory is its social influence and its influence on external and internal social reinforcement. This theory also values people's previous experiences. These experiences influence reinforcements and expectations, regardless of whether a person engages in a particular behavior or not, and reveal the reasons why a person engages in that behavior.
Venkatesh (2012); Venkatesh et al. (2003)	UTAUT	This theory integrates key elements from eight models previously used in the field of information technology. Each of the previous models tries to predict and explain user behavior using different independent variables. A single model was developed based on the conceptual and empirical similarities between these eight models.

Zipcar. On the other hand, other researchers argued that environmental motivations underlie participation in the SE (Botsman & Rogers, 2010; Gansky, 2010). For example, people participate in accommodation sharing because they want to interact with their local host (Tussyadiah, 2015). In another study, Cohen and Kietzmann (2014) introduced a sustainable business model in three mobility sectors using agency theory and communication between government and providers. SE business models are full of paradoxes, and there is a fundamental need to generate a model that aligns the power of agents (SE providers) and managers (governments).

Discussion

Based on CA and CCA, the motivations for SE adoption have been discussed much more than the barriers and challenges facing SE adoption. SE businesses in any field often face a variety of challenges such as market and institutional challenges (Roberts, 2020). Upon arrival, these businesses must quickly build an ecosystem of users and service providers and engage with local regulators, administrators, and community groups to gain acceptance. The key to their survival and success is the ability to adapt their digital platform and business model to consistently take advantage of opportunities and address concerns as they arise. On the other hand, a series of factors influencing the adoption of SE has received less attention from researchers and requires more research (see Fig. 12.6). In the following, each of these factors is discussed at the *micro* level (including the individual level: eWOM, self-disclosure, self-efficacy, WOM, and the firm level: Brand awareness and brand image) and at the *macro* level (political factor: Policy and regulations, social factor: Culture and perceived legitimacy, environmental factor: Perceived physical risks, technology factor: Information accurateness and availability).

Macro level:

Policy and Regulations – Since SE does not meet regulatory standards, the government should support the benefits and innovation of initiatives in the startup stages (Reddick et al., 2020). For example, client security and privacy are emergent as regulatory conflicts (Berke, 2016; Katz, 2015), so the examination of this aspect of SE and regulatory problems (Katz, 2015) are relatively new issues. Strict regulation is not necessary since SE has a self-regulatory characteristic that reduces risk, and strict regulation can hinder startup innovation. Academics are

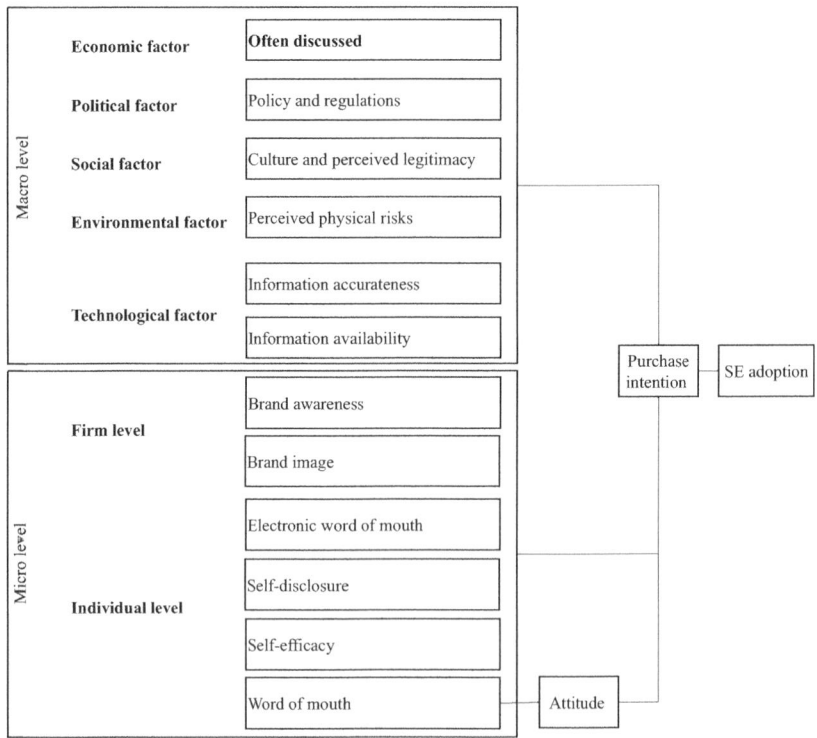

Fig. 12.6.   Study Gap.

still unable to offer a strong regulatory outline. Since SE is a new phenomenon, are conventional regulatory frameworks appropriate as the first step to overwhelming SE challenges, or does it require an entirely different set of guidelines and rules? This research field needs deeper scientific study.

Culture and Perceived Legitimacy – Limited studies are investigating the influence of culture on SE adoption. Culture includes human behaviors and social norms, knowledge, beliefs, arts, laws, customs, abilities, and habits of people in these groups (Chen & Lin, 2020; Tylor, 1871). Many researchers consider social norms to be a very effective factor in user attitudes (Akbari, Moradi, et al., 2020; Bae et al., 2017; Fishbein & Ajzen, 1977), and user attitudes also affect user's intention to use and accept technology (Boateng et al., 2019). When SE is approved by others, people will develop a positive attitude toward it. The influence of social norms on attitude is particularly evident in SE because its platforms are community-based (Kong et al., 2020; Mao & Lyu, 2017). As a new form of the organization operating in a new market category, SE may not fit with existing cultural designs. SE platforms may raise regulatory and normative issues that differ from those traditionally observed. Normative issues arise when SE platforms do not seem to adhere to the norms and values of the social environment. In other words, to operate, grow, and survive requires understanding and acceptance among the target market actors (Aldrich & Fiol, 1994; Humphreys & Latour, 2013). Such support is granted in the form of legitimacy, which is defined as the public perception of organizational actions as desirable or appropriate in a social system (Ackermann et al., 2022; Suchman, 1995).

Perceived Physical Risks – Perceived physical risks are considered equivalent to customers' perception that a product may harm their body if they consume it (Mitchell & Boustani, 1992). Individual and physical worries about personal security can play a main part in consumer decision-making (Novelli et al., 2018). As an example, the physical risks of being infected with COVID-19 may decrease users' requests for goods and services since they want to evade exposure to physical risks. Perceived risk exacerbates anxiety and hurts behavioral intention (Matiza, 2020). Previous research (Bae & Chang, 2021; Floyd et al., 2004; Stefani et al., 2008) has confirmed the implications of perceived risk for users' consumption decisions.

Information Accurateness and Availability – Accurate delivery of information is aimed at eliminating knowledge imbalances and conveying correct content to stakeholders (Pertheban et al., 2020). Customers tend to evaluate the information published by other users to plan their use of SE products/services. On the other hand, other stakeholders also need reliable statistics (Jung et al., 2021). To plan guidelines, legislators and experts also need access to statistical information, analysis, and survey reports (Hong et al., 2019). Therefore, communication technologies and SE platforms should provide more details about shared products and services (Mandić & Praničević, 2019). Mobile phones encourage such a sharing lifestyle by supporting a wide range of applications that can be accessed anytime, anywhere. These are new methods of information delivery that have a great impact on users' intention to use and purchase by making content more available (Herrero et al., 2018).

Micro level:

Brand Awareness – Brand awareness depends on whether a brand name comes to mind when consumers think of a particular product category. Brand awareness has a positive and significant effect on purchase decisions, and the more customers know about a brand, the more effective it is in their purchase decision (Novansa & Ali, 2017) because when users are aware of a specific brand, the chance of choosing that brand among similar products is higher (Ilyas et al., 2020). A well-known brand can win the competition with other brands and become a choice to further increase purchase intention (Rahmi et al., 2022)

Brand Image – Brand image is the customer's current perception of a particular brand (Foroudi, 2023; Foroudi et al., 2019, 2020; Kotler & Keller, 2021). Brand image can be defined as a set of unique associations in the minds of customers (Pradana et al., 2021). Brand image is the key driver of brand equity which refers to users' understanding and feelings about a brand and influences consumer behavior (Foroudi & Foroudi, 2021; Solihin, 2021). A good or positive image of the brand should have an effect of added value on users. If a brand has a bad image, consumers are not interested in buying; conversely, a positive brand image lasts for a long time, and users are more inclined to buy it (Wydyanto & Ilhamalimy, 2021). Based on the findings of Savitri et al. (2022), brand image has an impact on users' purchase intention.

Word of Mouth – WOM as a form of social business is one of the most effective sources of information transfer by consumers (Akarsu et al., 2022; Akbari et al., 2022a; Colmekcioglu et al., 2022; Foroudi et al., 2021; Keiningham et al., 2018; Soltani et al., 2023). By creating awareness, changing or confirming the opinions of users, creating interest in buying products, and influencing the behavior of consumers as they purchase (Pitt et al., 2018; Risselada et al., 2014), WOM affects the acceleration of new purchases and the acceptance (Kumar et al., 2016) and encouragement of repeat purchases (Iyengar et al., 2015).

Electronic Word of Mouth – eWOM is an important source of information about products/services. eWOM is the process of dynamic and continuous change among consumers about a product/service that is available to many people and institutions through the internet (Ismagilova et al., 2020). Customers have access to more product/service reviews from multiple sources than ever before. Web 2.0 advancements allow users to share experiences, opinions, and feedback about products and services with other consumers, and eWOM is becoming increasingly popular among consumers. Worldwide, these reviews are read by users before making a purchase decision (Senecal & Nantel, 2004). eWOM is the most trusted source of information, and consumers rely on eWOM for their purchases after recommendations from friends (Nielsen, 2013). Research has shown that users' online reviews have a great influence on their purchase decisions (Filieri & McLeay, 2014; Senecal & Nantel, 2004).

Self-disclosure – Self-disclosure, which has often been neglected in research, acts as a basis for building trust and reducing risk in the SE. Self-disclosure by service providers not only builds consumer trust but also reduces their risk perception. When consumers and service providers are objectively similar, consumers do not pay much attention to the information disclosed by service providers, but when there is no objective similarity, consumers pay more attention to the personal information shared by service providers (Teubner, 2022; Tran et al., 2022).

Self-efficacy – Considering social learning theory, self-efficacy refers to a person's belief in their ability to perform a specific task (Bandura, 1986; Madawala et al., 2023; Tsarenko & Strizhakova, 2013). When people have low self-efficacy, they cannot manage situations effectively. Users may clearly understand the perceived value of SE but do not intend to use it due to their lack of confidence in using it. On the other hand, consumers with high self-efficacy will be confident in their ability and will put in significant effort to complete the purchase (Yi & Gong, 2008). Consumers with high perceived control experience high self-efficacy and are likely to have strong purchase intentions (Li et al., 2018). Self-efficacy as a predictor of adoption intention has been investigated by other researchers (Tams et al., 2018; Zhu et al., 2022).

Conclusion

In this article, bibliometric analysis, we examined the studies conducted between 1975 and 2022 in the field of SE adoption, using the WoS database. Quantitative statistics were extracted from the bibliography, and descriptive analysis was undertaken. The main information about the data includes the number of articles and the number of citations each had each year, the most productive countries, prominent journals, and most highly cited articles in this field. The three most important countries are the United States, People's Republic of China, and England. Prominent journals include the *Journal of Cleaner Production, Electronic Commerce Research and Applications*, and the *International Journal of Contemporary Hospitality Management*. Three highly cited articles in this field were written by the authors Hamari (2013), Guttentag et al. (2018), and Kam et al. (2018). Also, CCA was mapped with the help of VOSviewer software. Using CCA, four clusters were introduced: (A) Methods of exchange (sharing, access-based consumption, commercial sharing systems, pseudo-sharing, and collaborative consumption), (B) Participation motivation and barriers (Motivations: amenities, cost saving, desirability, economic benefits (value), enjoyment, familiarity, monetary, moral, satisfaction, service quality, socio-hedonic, sustainability and economic benefits, trust, and usefulness, Barriers: lack of economic benefits, lack of efficiency in the field of technology, and lack of trust), (C) Theories used in the SE adoption (TRA, TPB, DTPB, TAM, TAM2, C-TAM-TPB, MPCU, IDT, MM, SCT, and UTAUT), and (D) Sustainability (economic environmental and social effects).

We also found that there has not been enough study on the impact of a series of factors at the micro level (including the individual level: eWOM, self-disclosure, self-efficacy, WOM, and the firm level: Brand awareness and brand image) and at the macro level (political factor: Policy and regulations, social factor: Culture and perceived legitimacy, environmental factor: Perceived physical risks, technology factor: Information accurateness and availability). In addition, according to the review of previous studies, researchers have often investigated the factors of success and influence on SE adoption, so our suggestion for future research is to consider limitations and obstacles including institutional and market challenges at the macro level as well.

Limitations and Future Research Directions

One of the limitations of this research is the use of the WoS as a database. It is recommended that other data sources are used in future work, such as Scopus or Google Scholar, although WoS is one of the most reliable databases. It is also suggested that future studies be adjusted and reviewed based on a different number of citations. In addition, in this research, only documents in English have been reviewed. Other languages will be useful for future studies.

Case Study

In the past few years, the public perception of shared goods and/or services has changed fundamentally. For example, house sharing has become widely popular. Increasing sharing of property or personal assets provides an opportunity to earn money and minimize costs. One of the reasons for the formation of Airbnb is the insufficient number of hotel rooms (Gunter et al., 2020). Airbnb became a pioneer in housing sharing and has uniquely changed travel accommodations. It provides unique access to the home, experience, and being part of a local community around the world and offers innovative solutions for consumers by providing an online platform to access their community. Launched in 2008, the company has disrupted the hotel industry and is seen as a threat to the traditional business model as it offers lower priced accommodations and addresses the shortage of hotel rooms in high demand. However, traditional companies have retaliated and asked government agencies to protect them by setting regulations (Guttentag, 2017). What makes Airbnb unique is the collaboration between the local community by creating a platform to connect with people around the world and offering their underutilized rooms for a fee.

For about nine years, the concept of "home away from home" has become a success story at Airbnb and is present in more than 191 countries around the world (Ackerman, 2021). Airbnb is a trusted social marketplace for people to list, discover, and book unique accommodations around the world. The initial idea was to rent out their rooms like a bedroom where guests can sleep on their air mattresses during peak periods when there is a shortage of hotel rooms in cities due to a large number of tourists and conventions. They soon realized the potential need of this market.

Unlike traditional hotels, Airbnb leverages its room capacity by scaling hosts that can provide space and match it to travelers (Reinhold & Dolnicar, 2021). This allows Airbnb to save on the cost of maintaining physical assets. Also, Airbnb facilitates and provides an online platform that enables users and guests to register, create a personal profile, and match needs based on the participant's needs. One of the main reasons for Airbnb's exponential growth over the years is Millennials' trust in innovations and strangers. Participants consider familiarity, utility (financial benefits), and hedonic value as their motivations for participating in sharing community. However, studies cannot ignore the fact that fee or price and applied reasons are the main reasons why travelers participate in public sharing. Trust plays an important role in the SE. Now, the challenge for SE businesses is to maintain the level of customer trust to guarantee sustainable development.

Case Study Questions

(1) By what mechanisms can SE-based providers/companies gain the trust of users to use and adopt SE?
(2) What is the role of the government in the SE adoption by society and businesses?
(3) What is the competitive advantage of managers due to the use of SE?

Key Terms and Definitions

Sharing Economy: A technologically enabled socioeconomic system that has five main features (permanent access, economic rate transfer, platform intermediation, extensive customer personality, and crowd-sourced supply).

Collaborative Consumption: A set of source circulation systems in which clients temporarily or permanently "acquire" and "provide" valued properties or facilities through direct communication with other clients or an intermediary.

Collaborative Economy: This is a market where clients count on each other instead of large firms to accomplish their requirements and requests.

Technology Acceptance: This is an attitude to technology, and it is influenced by numerous aspects. A user who has got a new technology has not yet adopted it – there are other phases beyond simple buying, and this is where acceptance plays a vital role. If a user purchases a product and then rejects it, full adoption is unlikely to occur.

Technology Adoption: This is a process – it starts with the user's awareness of the technology and ends with the user's acceptance of the technology and its full use. Someone who embraces technology is likely to replace it when it breaks, find innovative uses for it, and cannot imagine life without it.

References

Ackerman, K. (2021, December 10). Case study: Airbnb – Future Sensor – Medium. *The Medium.* https://medium.com/future-sensor/case-study-airbnb-7f4e2a66184c

Ackermann, C. L., Matson-Barkat, S., & Truong, Y. (2022). A legitimacy perspective on sharing economy consumption in the accommodation sector. *Current Issues in Tourism, 25*(12), 1947–1967. https://doi.org/10.1080/13683500.2021.1935789

Ahsan, M. (2020). Entrepreneurship and ethics in the sharing economy: A critical perspective. *Journal of Business Ethics*, *161*(1), 19–33. https://doi.org/10.1007/s10551-018-3975-2

Ajwani-Ramchandani, R., Figueira, S., de Oliveira, R. T., Jha, S., Ramchandani, A., & Schuricht, L. (2021). Towards a circular economy for packaging waste by using new technologies: The case of large multinationals in emerging economies. *Journal of Cleaner Production*, *281*(January), 125139. https://doi.org/10.1016/j.jclepro.2020.125139

Ajzen, I. (1991). The theory of planned behavior. *Organizational Behavior and Human Decision Processes*, *50*(2), 179–211. https://doi.org/10.4135/9781446249215.n22

Akarsu, T. N., Foroudi, P., & Melewar, T. (2020). What makes Airbnb likeable? Exploring the nexus between service attractiveness, country image, perceived authenticity and experience from a social exchange theory perspective within an emerging economy context. *International Journal of Hospitality Management*, *91*, 102635.

Akarsu, T. N., Marvi, R., & Foroudi, P. (2022). Forty-nine years of sensory research literature: A review on its development, foundation and future research directions. *European Journal of International Management*. https://doi.org/10.1504/EJIM.2022.10051055

Akbari, M., Amiri, N. S., Zúñiga, M. Á., Padash, H., & Shakiba, H. (2020). Evidence for acceptance of ride-hailing Services in Iran. *Transportation Research Record*, *2674*(11), 289–303. https://doi.org/10.1177/0361198120942224

Akbari, M., Foroudi, P., Fashami, R. Z., Mahavarpour, N., & Khodayari, M. (2022a). Let us talk about something: The evolution of e-WOM from the past to the future. *Journal of Business Research*, *149*(September), 663–689. https://doi.org/10.1016/j.jbusres.2022.05.061

Akbari, M., Foroudi, P., Khodayari, M., Zaman Fashami, R., Shahabaldini Parizi, Z., & Shahriari, E. (2022b). Sharing Your Assets: A Holistic Review of Sharing Economy. *Journal of Business Research*, *140*(February), 604–625. https://doi.org/10.1016/j.jbusres.2021.11.027

Akbari, Khodayari, M., Danesh, M., Davari, A., & Padash, H. M. (2020). A bibliometric study of sustainable technology research. *Cogent Business and Management*, *7*(1), 1–25. https://doi.org/10.1080/23311975.2020.1751906

Akbari, M., Moradi, A., SeyyedAmiri, N., Zúñiga, M. Á., Rahmani, Z., & Padash, H. (2020). Consumers' intentions to use ridesharing services in Iran. *Research in Transportation Business & Management*, (December). https://doi.org/10.1016/j.rtbm.2020.100616

Albinsson, P. A., & Yasanthi Perera, B. (2012). Alternative marketplaces in the 21st century: Building community through sharing events. *Journal of Consumer Behaviour*, *11*(4), 303–315. https://doi.org/10.1002/cb.1389

Aldrich, H. E., & Fiol, C. M. (1994). Fools rush in? The institutional context of industry creation. *Academy of Management Review*, *19*(4), 645–670. https://doi.org/10.5465/amr.1994.9412190214

Amaro, S., Andreu, L., & Huang, S. (2019). Millenials' intentions to book on Airbnb. *Current Issues in Tourism*, *22*(18), 2284–2298. https://doi.org/10.1080/13683500.2018.1448368

Bae, S. Y., & Chang, P.-J. (2021). The effect of coronavirus disease-19 (COVID-19) risk perception on behavioural intention towards 'untact' tourism in South Korea during the first wave of the pandemic (March 2020). *Current Issues in Tourism*, *24*(7), 1017–1035. https://doi.org/10.1080/13683500.2020.1798895

Bae, S. J., Lee, H., Suh, E.-K., & Suh, K.-S. (2017). Shared experience in pretrip and experience sharing in posttrip: A survey of Airbnb users. *Information & Management*, *54*(6), 714–727. https://doi.org/10.1016/j.im.2016.12.008

Bąk, A., Nawrocka, E., & Jaremen, D. E. (2022). "Sustainability" as a motive for choosing shared-mobility services: The case of polish consumers of Uber Services. *Sustainability*, *14*(10), 6352. https://doi.org/10.3390/su14106352

Bandura, A. (1986). *Social foundations of thought and action* (pp. 23–28). https://doi.org/10.4135/9781446221129.n6

Bardhi, F., Eckhardt, G. M., Bardhi, F., & Eckhardt, G. M. (2012). Access-based consumption: The case of car sharing. *Journal of Consumer Research*, *39*(4), 881–898. https://doi.org/10.1086/666376

Barnes, S. J., & Mattsson, J. (2016). Understanding current and future issues in collaborative consumption: A four-stage Delphi study. *Technological Forecasting and Social Change*, *104*(March), 200–211. https://doi.org/10.1016/j.techfore.2016.01.006

Barnes, S. J., & Mattsson, J. (2017). Technological forecasting & social change understanding collaborative consumption: Test of a theoretical model. *Technological Forecasting and Social Change*. https://doi.org/10.1016/j.techfore.2017.02.029

Bawack, R. E., & Kamdjoug, J. R. K. (2018). Adequacy of UTAUT in clinician adoption of health information systems in developing countries: The case of Cameroon. *International Journal of Medical Informatics*, *109*(August), 15–22. https://doi.org/10.1016/j.tourman.2018.01.009

Belk, R. (2007). Why not share rather than own? *The Annals of the American Academy of Political and Social Science*, *611*(1), 126–140.

Belk, R. (2010). Sharing. *Journal of Consumer Research*, *36*(5), 715–734. https://doi.org/10.1086/612649

Belk, R. (2014). You are what you can access: Sharing and collaborative consumption online. *Journal of Business Research*, *67*(8), 1595–1600. https://doi.org/10.1016/j.jbusres.2013.10.001

Bellotti, V., Ambard, A., Turner, D., Gossmann, C., Demkova, K., & Carroll, J. M. (2015). A muddle of models of motivation for using peer-to-peer economy systems. In *Proceedings of the 33rd Annual ACM Conference on Human Factors in Computing Systems* (pp. 1085–1094). ACM.

Benoit, S., Baker, T. L., Bolton, R. N., Gruber, T., & Kandampully, J. S. (2017). A triadic framework for collaborative consumption (CC): Motives, activities and resources & capabilities of actors. *Journal of Business Research*, *79*(November), 219–227. https://doi.org/10.1016/j.jbusres.2017.05.004

Berke, D. (2016). Products liability in the sharing economy. *Yale Journal on Regulation*, *33*(2), 603.

Boateng, H., Kosiba, J. P. B., & Okoe, A. F. (2019). Determinants of consumers' participation in the sharing economy: A social exchange perspective within an emerging economy context. *International Journal of Contemporary Hospitality Management*, *31*(2), 718–733. https://doi.org/10.1108/IJCHM-11-2017-0731

Böcker, L., & Meelen, A. A. H. (2017). Sharing for people, planet or profit? Analysing motivations for intended sharing economy participation. *Innovation Studies Utrecht (ISU) Working Paper Series*, *23*(02), 28–39. https://doi.org/10.1016/J.EIST.2016.09.004

Botsman, R., & Rogers, R. (2010). *What's mine is yours: The rise of collaborative consumption.* https://archive.org/details/whatsmineisyours0000bots/page/n9/mode/2up

Bucher, E., Fieseler, C., & Lutz, C. (2016). What's mine is yours (for a nominal fee) – Exploring the spectrum of utilitarian to altruistic motives for Internet-mediated sharing. *Computers in Human Behavior, 62*(September), 316–326. https://doi.org/10.1016/j.chb.2016.04.002

Chabowski, B., Kekec, P., Morgan, N. A., Hult, G. T. M., Walkowiak, T., & Runnalls, B. (2018). An assessment of the exporting literature: Using theory and data to identify future research directions. *Journal of International Marketing, 26*(1), 118–143. https://doi.org/10.1509/jim.16.0129

Chae, B. K. (2022). Mapping the evolution of digital business research: A bibliometric review. *Sustainability, 14*(12), 6990. https://doi.org/10.3390/su14126990

Chatterjee, S., Chaudhuri, R., Vrontis, D., & Foroudi, P. (2022). Dark side of sharing economy: Examining the unethical practices and its impact on coopetition and firm performance. *Journal of Business-To-Business Marketing, 29*(1), 69–85.

Chen, D., Lai, F., & Lin, Z. (2014). A trust model for online peer-to-peer lending: A lender's perspective. *Information Technology and Management, 15*(4), 239–254. https://doi.org/10.1007/s10799-014-0187-z

Chen, S., & Lin, N. (2020). Culture, productivity and competitiveness: Disentangling the concepts. *Cross Cultural & Strategic Management, 28*(1), 52–75. https://doi.org/10.1108/CCSM-02-2020-0030

Cheng, M. (2016). Sharing economy: A review and agenda for future research. *International Journal of Hospitality Management, 57*(August), 60–70. https://doi.org/10.1016/j.ijhm.2016.06.003

Chuah, S. H.-W., Tseng, M.-L., Wu, K.-J., & Cheng, C.-F. (2021). Factors influencing the adoption of sharing economy in B2B context in China: Findings from PLS-SEM and fsQCA. *Resources, Conservation and Recycling, 175*(December), 105892. https://doi.org/10.1016/j.resconrec.2021.105892

Cocquyt, A., Crucke, S., & Slabbinck, H. (2020). Organizational characteristics explaining participation in sustainable business models in the sharing economy: Evidence from the fashion industry using conjoint analysis. *Business Strategy and the Environment, 29*(6), 2603–2613. https://doi.org/10.1002/bse.2523

Cohen, B., & Kietzmann, J. (2014). Ride on! Mobility business models for the sharing economy. *Organization & Environment, 27*(3), 279–296. https://doi.org/10.1177/1086026614546199

Colmekcioglu, N., Marvi, R., Foroudi, P., & Okumus, F. (2022). Generation, susceptibility, and response regarding negativity: An in-depth analysis on negative online reviews. *Journal of Business Research, 153*, 235–250.

Cuomo, M. T., Tortora, D., Foroudi, P., Giordano, A., Festa, G., & Metallo, G. (2021). Digital transformation and tourist experience co-design: Big social data for planning cultural tourism. *Technological Forecasting and Social Change, 162*, 120345.

Davis, F. D. (1989). Perceived usefulness, perceived ease of use, and user acceptance of information technology. *MIS Quarterly, 13*(2), 319–340. https://doi.org/10.2307/249008

Davis, F. D., Bagozzi, R. P., & Warshaw, P. R. (1989). User Acceptance of computer technology: A comparison of two theoretical models. *Management Science, 35*(8), 982–1003. https://www.jstor.org/stable/2632151

Davis, F. D., Bagozzi, R. P., & Warshaw, P. R. (1992). Extrinsic and intrinsic motivation to use computers in the workplace. *Journal of Applied Social Psychology*, *22*(14), 1111–1132. https://doi.org/10.1111/j.1559-1816.1992.tb00945.x

Dias, G. P. (2019). Fifteen years of e-government research in Ibero-America: A bibliometric analysis. *Government Information Quarterly*, *36*(3), 400–411. https://doi.org/10.1016/j.giq.2019.05.008

Dillahunt, T. R., & Malone, A. R. (2015). The promise of the sharing economy among disadvantaged communities. In *Proceedings of the 33rd Annual ACM Conference on Human Factors in Computing Systems* (pp. 2285–2294). https://doi.org/10.1145/2702123.2702189

Donthu, N., Kumar, S., Mukherjee, D., Pandey, N., & Lim, W. M. (2021). How to conduct a bibliometric analysis: An overview and guidelines. *Journal of Business Research*, *133*(September), 285–296. https://doi.org/10.1016/j.jbusres.2021.04.070

Eckhardt, G. M., Houston, M. B., Jiang, B., Lamberton, C., Rindfleisch, A., & Zervas, G. (2019). Marketing in the sharing economy. *Journal of Marketing*, *83*(5), 5–27. https://doi.org/10.1177/0022242919861929

Edbring, E. G., Lehner, M., & Mont, O. (2016). Exploring consumer attitudes to alternative models of consumption: Motivations and barriers. *Journal of Cleaner Production*, *123*(June), 5–15. https://doi.org/10.1016/j.jclepro.2015.10.107

Ert, E., Fleischer, A., & Magen, N. (2016). Trust and reputation in the sharing economy: The role of personal photos in Airbnb. *Tourism Management*, *55*(August), 62–73. https://doi.org/10.1016/j.tourman.2016.01.013

Ferreira, J. J. M., Fernandes, C. I., & Ratten, V. (2016). A co-citation bibliometric analysis of strategic management research. *Scientometrics*, *109*(1), 1–32. https://doi.org/10.1007/s11192-016-2008-0

Filieri, R., & McLeay, F. (2014). E-WOM and accommodation: An analysis of the factors that influence travelers' adoption of information from online reviews. *Journal of Travel Research*, *53*(1), 44–57. https://doi.org/10.1177%2F0047287513481274

Fishbein, M., & Ajzen, I. (1977). Belief, attitude, intention, and behavior: An introduction to theory and research. *Philosophy and Rhetoric*, *10*(2), 411–450.

Floyd, M. F., Gibson, H., Pennington-Gray, L., & Thapa, B. (2004). The effect of risk perceptions on intentions to travel in the aftermath of September 11, 2001. *Journal of Travel & Tourism Marketing*, *15*(2–3), 19–38. https://doi.org/10.1300/J073v15n02_02

Foroudi, P. (2023). Conceptualizing, measuring, and managing marketing assets: Developing the marketing assets, communication focus, and capability nexus. *Corporate Reputation Review*, *26*(3), 203–222.

Foroudi, P., Akarsu, T. N., Marvi, R., & Balakrishnan, J. (2020). Intellectual evolution of social innovation: A bibliometric analysis and avenues for future research trends. *Industrial Marketing Management*, *93*(February), 446–465. https://doi.org/10.1016/j.indmarman.2020.03.026

Foroudi, P., Cuomo, M. T., & Foroudi, M. M. (2020). Continuance interaction intention in retailing: Relations between customer values, satisfaction, loyalty, and identification. *Information Technology & People*, *33*(4), 1303–1326.

Foroudi, M. M., & Foroudi, P. (2021). *Corporate brand design: Developing and managing brand identity*. Routledge.

Foroudi, P., Gupta, S., Nazarian, A., & Duda, M. (2017). Digital technology and marketing management capability: Achieving growth in SMEs. *Qualitative Market Research: An International Journal, 20*(2), 230–246.

Foroudi, P., Gupta, S., Sivarajah, U., & Broderick, A. (2018). Investigating the effects of smart technology on customer dynamics and customer experience. *Computers in Human Behavior, 80*, 271–282.

Foroudi, P., Marvi, R., & Imani, S. (2020). The impact of internal marketing on knowledge sharing capability. *European Journal of International Management.* https://doi.org/10.1504/EJIM.2022.10056741

Foroudi, P., Palazzo, M., & Sabina, K. (2022). When Love Takes over: Boosting love towards Airbnb brand. *Corporate Reputation Review*, 1–15.

Foroudi, P., Palazzo, M., & Sultana, A. (2021). Linking brand attitude to word-of-mouth and revisit intentions in the restaurant sector. *British Food Journal, 123*(13), 221–240.

Foroudi, P., Yu, Q., Gupta, S., & Foroudi, M. M. (2019). Enhancing university brand image and reputation through customer value co-creation behaviour. *Technological Forecasting and Social Change, 138*, 218–227.

Gansky, L. (2010). *The mesh: Why the future of business is sharing.* Penguin.

Grondys, K. (2019). Implementation of the sharing economy in the B2B Sector. *Sustainability, 11*(14), 3976. https://doi.org/10.3390/su11143976

Gunter, U., Önder, I., & Zekan, B. (2020). Modeling Airbnb demand to New York City while employing spatial panel data at the listing level. *Tourism Management, 77*, 104000. https://doi.org/10.1016/j.tourman.2019.104000

Guttentag, D. (2015). Airbnb: Disruptive innovation and the rise of an informal tourism accommodation sector. *Current Issues in Tourism, 18*(12), 1192–1217. https://doi.org/10.1080/13683500.2013.827159

Guttentag, D. (2017). Regulating innovation in the collaborative economy: An examination of Airbnb's early legal issues. In *Tourism on the verge* (pp. 97–128). https://doi.org/10.1007/978-3-319-51799-5_7

Guttentag, Smith, S., Potwarka, L., & Havitz, M. (2018). Why tourists choose Airbnb: A motivation-based segmentation study. *Journal of Travel Research, 57*(3), 342–359. https://doi.org/10.1177/0047287517696980

Hafeez, K., Alghatas, F. M., Foroudi, P., Nguyen, B., & Gupta, S. (2019). Knowledge sharing by entrepreneurs in a virtual community of practice (VCoP). *Information Technology & People, 32*(2), 405–429.

Hafeez, K., Foroudi, P., Nguyen, B., Gupta, S., & Alghatas, F. (2018). How do entrepreneurs learn and engage in an online community-of-practice? A case study approach. *Behaviour & Information Technology, 37*(7), 714–735.

Hamari, J. (2013). Electronic Commerce Research and Applications Transforming homo economicus into homo ludens: A field experiment on gamification in a utilitarian peer-to-peer trading service. *Electronic Commerce Research and Applications, 12*(4), 236–245. https://doi.org/10.1016/j.elerap.2013.01.004

Hamari, J., Sjöklint, M., & Ukkonen, A. (2016). The sharing economy: Why people participate in collaborative consumption. *Journal of the Association for Information Science and Technology, 67*(9), 2047–2059.

Herrero, A., San Martín, H., & Collado, J. (2018). Market orientation and SNS adoption for marketing purposes in hospitality microenterprises. *Journal of*

Hospitality and Tourism Management, 34, 30–40. https://doi.org/10.1016/j.jhtm. 2017.11.005

Hira, A. (2017). Profile of the sharing economy in the developing world: Examples of companies trying to change the world. *Journal of Developing Societies, 33*(2), 244–271. https://doi.org/10.1177/0169796x17710074

Hong, J. H., Kim, B. C., & Park, K. S. (2019). Optimal risk management for the sharing economy with stranger danger and service quality. *European Journal of Operational Research, 279*(3), 1024–1035. https://doi.org/10.1016/j.ejor.2019.06.020

Hossain, M. (2020). Sharing economy: A comprehensive literature review. *International Journal of Hospitality Management, 87*(July 2018). https://doi.org/10. 1016/j.ijhm.2020.102470

Humphreys, A., & Latour, K. A. (2013). Framing the game: Assessing the impact of cultural representations on consumer perceptions of legitimacy. *Journal of Consumer Research, 40*(4), 773–795. https://doi.org/10.1086/672358

Hwang, J., & Griffiths, M. A. (2017). Share more, drive less: Millennials value perception and behavioral intent in using. https://doi.org/10.1108/JCM-10-2015-1560

Ilyas, G. B., Rahmi, S., Tamsah, H., Munir, A. R., & Putra, A. H. P. K. (2020). Reflective model of brand awareness on repurchase intention and customer satisfaction. *The Journal of Asian Finance, Economics and Business, 7*(9), 427–438. https://doi.org/10.13106/jafeb.2020.vol7.no9.427

Imani, S., Foroudi, P., & Marvi, R. (2020). Praise of intra-organizational social capital and knowledge sharing behaviors in MNCs. *European Journal of International Management.*

Ismagilova, E., Dwivedi, Y. K., & Slade, E. (2020). Perceived helpfulness of eWOM: Emotions, fairness and rationality. *Journal of Retailing and Consumer Services, 53,* 101748. https://doi.org/10.1016/j.jretconser.2019.02.002

Iyengar, R., Van den Bulte, C., & Lee, J. Y. (2015). Social contagion in new product trial and repeat. *Marketing Science, 34*(3), 408–429. https://doi.org/10.1287/mksc. 2014.0888

Jung, J., Park, E., Moon, J., & Lee, W. S. (2021). Exploration of sharing accommodation platform Airbnb using an extended technology acceptance model. *Sustainability, 13*(3), 1185. https://doi.org/10.3390/su13031185

Kam, K., So, F., Oh, H., & Min, S. (2018). Motivations and constraints of Airbnb consumers : Findings from a mixed-methods approach. *Tourism Management, 67,* 224–236. https://doi.org/10.1016/j.tourman.2018.01.009

Kashani, E. S., Radosevic, S., Kiamehr, M., & Gholizadeh, H. (2022). The intellectual evolution of the technological catch-up literature: Bibliometric analysis. *Research Policy, 51*(7), 104538. https://doi.org/10.1016/j.respol.2022.104538

Kathan, W., Matzler, K., & Veider, V. (2016). The sharing economy: Your business model's friend or foe? *Business Horizons, 59*(6), 663–672. https://doi.org/10.1016/j. bushor.2016.06.006

Katz, V. (2015). Regulating the sharing economy. *Berkeley Technology Law Journal, 30*(4), 1067–1126. https://doi.org/10.15779/Z38HG45

Kaushal, L. A., & Prashar, A. (2022). Determinants of service consumer's attitudes and behavioral intentions towards sharing economy for sustainable consumption: An emerging market perspective. *Journal of Global Information Technology Management, 25*(2), 137–158. https://doi.org/10.1080/1097198X.2022.2062993

Keiningham, T. L., Rust, R. T., Lariviere, B., Aksoy, L., & Williams, L. (2018). A roadmap for driving customer word-of-mouth. *Journal of Service Management*, *29*(1), 2–38. https://doi.org/10.1108/JOSM-03-2017-0077

Kleinberg, J. (2003). Bursty and hierarchical structure in streams. *Data Mining and Knowledge Discovery*, *7*(4), 373–397. https://doi.org/10.1023/A:1024940629314

Kong, Y., Wang, Y., Hajli, S., & Featherman, M. (2020). In sharing economy we trust: Examining the effect of social and technical enablers on millennials' trust in sharing commerce. *Computers in Human Behavior*, *108*(July), 105993. https://doi.org/10.1016/j.chb.2019.04.017

Kotler, P., & Keller, K. (2021). *Marketing Management* (15th global edition). Pearson Education Limited. http://dspace.vnbrims.org:13000/xmlui/handle/123456789/5050

Kumar, A., Bezawada, R., Rishika, R., Janakiraman, R., & Kannan, P. K. (2016). From social to sale: The effects of firm-generated content in social media on customer behavior. *Journal of Marketing*, *80*(1), 7–25. https://doi.org/10.1509/jm.14.0249

Kumar, V., Lahiri, A., & Dogan, O. B. (2018). A strategic framework for a profitable business model in the sharing economy. *Industrial Marketing Management*, *69*, 147–160. https://doi.org/10.1016/j.indmarman.2017.08.021

Kuzior, A., & Sira, M. (2022). A bibliometric analysis of blockchain technology research using VOSviewer. *Sustainability*, *14*(13), 8206. https://doi.org/10.3390/su14138206

Lamberton, C. P., & Rose, R. L. (2012). When is ours better than mine? A framework for understanding and altering participation in commercial sharing systems. *Journal of Marketing*, *76*(4), 109–125. https://doi.org/10.1509/jm.10.0368

Laukkanen, M., & Tura, N. (2020). The potential of sharing economy business models for sustainable value creation. *Journal of Cleaner Production*, *253*(20), 120004. https://doi.org/10.1016/j.jclepro.2020.120004

Lee, Z. W. Y., Chan, T. K. H., Balaji, M. S., Chong, A. Y., & Lee, Z. W. Y. (2018). Why people participate in the sharing economy: An empirical investigation of Uber. *Internet Research*, *28*(3), 829–850. https://doi.org/10.1108/IntR-01-2017-0037

Li, Y., Xu, Z., & Xu, F. (2018). Perceived control and purchase intention in online shopping: The mediating role of self-efficacy. *Social Behavior and Personality*, *46*(1), 99–105. https://doi.org/10.2224/sbp.6377

Lutz, C., Hoffmann, C. P., Bucher, E., & Fieseler, C. (2018). The role of privacy concerns in the sharing economy. *Information, Communication & Society*, *21*(10), 1472–1492. https://doi.org/10.1080/1369118X.2017.1339726

Madawala, K., Foroudi, P., & Palazzo, M. (2023). Exploring the role played by entrepreneurial self-efficacy among women entrepreneurs in tourism sector. *Journal of Retailing and Consumer Services*, *74*, 103395.

Malacina, I., & Teplov, R. (2022). Supply chain innovation research: A bibliometric network analysis and literature review. *International Journal of Production Economics*, *251*(September), 108540. https://doi.org/10.1016/j.ijpe.2022.108540

Mandić, A., & Praničević, D. G. (2019). Progress on the role of ICTs in establishing destination appeal: Implications for smart tourism destination development. *Journal of Hospitality and Tourism Technology*, *10*(4), 791–813. https://doi.org/10.1108/JHTT-06-2018-0047

Mao, Z., & Lyu, J. (2017). Why travelers use Airbnb again? An integrative approach to understanding travelers' repurchase intention. *International Journal of*

Contemporary Hospitality Management, *29*(9), 2464–2482. https://doi.org/10.1108/IJCHM-08-2016-0439

Martin, C. J. (2016). The sharing economy: A pathway to sustainability or a nightmarish form of neoliberal capitalism? *Ecological Economics*, *121*(January), 149–159. https://doi.org/10.1016/j.ecolecon.2015.11.027

Mathieson, K. (1991). Predicting user intentions: Comparing the technology acceptance model with the theory of planned behavior. *Information Systems Research*, *2*(3), 173–191. https://doi.org/10.1287/isre.2.3.173

Matiza, T. (2020). Post-COVID-19 crisis travel behaviour: Towards mitigating the effects of perceived risk. *Journal of Tourism Futures*, *8*(1), 99–108. https://doi.org/10.1108/JTF-04-2020-0063

Merigó, J. M., Mas-Tur, A., Roig-Tierno, N., & Ribeiro-Soriano, D. (2015). A bibliometric overview of the Journal of Business Research between 1973 and 2014. *Journal of Business Research*, *68*(12), 2645–2653. https://doi.org/10.1016/j.jbusres.2015.04.006

Min, S., Kam, K., So, F., & Jeong, M. (2019). Consumer adoption of the Uber mobile application: Insights from diffusion of innovation theory and technology acceptance model. *Journal of Travel & Tourism Marketing*, *36*(7), 770–783. https://doi.org/10.1080/10548408.2018.1507866

Mitchell, V. W., & Boustani, P. (1992). Consumer risk perceptions in the breakfast cereal market. *British Food Journal*, *94*(4), 17–26. https://doi.org/10.1108/00070709210011534

Möhlmann, M. (2015). Collaborative consumption: Determinants of satisfaction and the likelihood of using a sharing economy option again. *Journal of Consumer Behaviour*, *14*(3), 193–207. https://doi.org/10.1002/cb.1512

Muñoz, P., & Cohen, B. (2017). Mapping out the sharing economy: A configurational approach to sharing business modeling. *Technological Forecasting and Social Change*, *125*, 21–37. https://doi.org/10.1016/j.techfore.2017.03.035

Nielsen, J. (2013). The reviews are in: Yelp users are four-star consumers. https://www.nielsen.com/us/en/insights/article/2013/the-reviews-are-in–yelp-users-are-four-star-consumers.html

Novansa, H., & Ali, H. (2017). Purchase decision model: Analysis of brand image, brand awareness and price (Case study SMECO Indonesia SME products). *Saudi Journal of Humanities and Social Sciences*, *2*(8), 621–632. https://doi.org/10.21276/sjhss

Novelli, M., Burgess, L. G., Jones, A., & Ritchie, B. W. (2018). 'No Ebola... still doomed'–The Ebola-induced tourism crisis. *Annals of Tourism Research*, *70*(May), 76–87. https://doi.org/10.1016/j.annals.2018.03.006

Parente, R. C., Geleilate, J. G., & Rong, K. (2018). The sharing economy globalization phenomenon: A research agenda. *Journal of International Management*, *24*(1), 52–64. https://doi.org/10.1016/j.intman.2017.10.001

Pertheban, S., Narayana Samy, G., & Shanmugam, B. (2020). A systematic literature review: Information accuracy practices in tourism. *Journal of Quality Assurance in Hospitality & Tourism*, *21*(1), 1–30. https://doi.org/10.1080/1528008X.2018.1563016

Piscicelli, L., Cooper, T., & Fisher, T. (2014). The role of values in collaborative consumption: Insights from a product-service system for lending and borrowing in the UK. *Journal of Cleaner Production*, 1–9. https://doi.org/10.1016/j.jclepro.2014.07.032

Pitt, C., Eriksson, T., Plangger, K., & Dabirian, A. (2018). Accommodation market labels and customers reviews: An abstract. *Academy of Marketing Science World Marketing Congress*, 539–540. https://doi.org/10.1007/978-3-030-02568-7_146

Pradana, A. F. P., Hasan, S., Putra, A. H. P. K., & Kalla, R. (2021). Moderating of SERVQUAL on E-WOM, Product Quality, and Brand Image on and E-commerce Purchase Intention. *Golden Ratio of Mapping Idea and Literature Format*, 2(1), 36–51. https://doi.org/10.52970/grmilf.v2i1.135

Prieto, M., Baltas, G., & Stan, V. (2017). Car sharing adoption intention in urban areas: What are the key sociodemographic drivers. *Transportation Research Part A*, *101*, 218–227. https://doi.org/10.1016/j.tra.2017.05.012

Rahmi, S., Ilyas, G. B., Tamsah, H., & Munir, A. R. (2022). Perceived risk and its role in the influence of brand awareness on purchase intention: Study of Shopee users. *Jurnal Siasat Bisnis*, *26*(1), 97–109. https://doi.org/10.20885/jsb.vol26.iss1.art7

Rajabi, A. A., Mirmehdi, S. M., Foroudi, P., & Azimi, E. (2022). Use of social media functionality for improving information sharing, problem-solving, and co-production in a B2B context. *Iranian Journal of Information Processing and Management*, *38*(Special Issue), 105–145.

Reddick, C. G., Zheng, Y., & Liu, T. (2020). Roles of government in regulating the sharing economy: A case study of bike sharing in China. *Information Polity*, *25*(2), 219–235. https://doi.org/10.3233/IP-190207

Reinhold, S., & Dolnicar, S. (2021). *The evolution of Airbnb's business model* (pp. 17–78). https://doi.org/10.6084/m9.figshare.14195957

Richter, C., Kraus, S., Brem, A., Durst, S., & Giselbrecht, C. (2017). Digital entrepreneurship: Innovative business models for the sharing economy. *Creativity and Innovation Management*, *26*(3), 300–310. https://doi.org/10.1111/caim.12227

Risselada, H., Verhoef, P. C., & Bijmolt, T. H. A. (2014). Dynamic effects of social influence and direct marketing on the adoption of high-technology products. *Journal of Marketing*, *78*(2), 52–68. https://doi.org/10.1509/jm.11.0592

Roberts, A. (2020). Liminal movement by digital platform-based sharing economy ventures: The case of Uber technologies. *Strategic Management Journal*, *43*(3), 447–475. https://doi.org/10.1002/smj.3148

Rogers, E. M. (2003). *Diffusion of innovations* (p. 551). Free Press.

Ruiz-Alba, J. L., Abou-Foul, M., Nazarian, A., & Foroudi, P. (2022). Digital platforms: Customer satisfaction, eWOM and the moderating role of perceived technological innovativeness. *Information Technology & People*, *35*(7), 2470–2499.

Savitri, C., Hurriyati, R., Wibowo, L., & Hendrayati, H. (2022). The role of social media marketing and brand image on smartphone purchase intention. *International Journal of Data and Network Science*, *6*(1), 185–192. https://doi.org/10.5267/j.ijdns.2021.12.016

Senecal, S., & Nantel, J. (2004). The influence of online product recommendations on consumers' online choices. *Journal of Retailing*, *80*(2), 159–169. https://doi.org/10.1016/j.jretai.2004.04.001

So, K. K. F., Oh, H., & Min, S. (2018). Motivations and constraints of Airbnb consumers: Findings from a mixed-methods approach. *Tourism Management*, *67*(August), 224–236. https://doi.org/10.1016/j.tourman.2018.01.009

Solihin, D. (2021). The influence of brand image and atmosphere store on purchase decision for Samsung brand smartphone with buying intervention as intervening variables (study on Samsung experience store Krawaci customers). *International Journal of Social Science and Business, 5*(2). https://doi.org/10.23887/ijssb.v5i2.30847

Soltani, M., Foroudi, P., & Nasab, M. H. (2023). Examining the impact of online customer engagement on non-financial performance considering the roles of brand attitude, customer co-creation, customer equity, and (e-) word-of-mouth. In *Digital transformation and corporate branding* (pp. 259–285). Routledge.

Stefani, G., Cavicchi, A., Romano, D., & Lobb, A. E. (2008). Determinants of intention to purchase chicken in Italy: The role of consumer risk perception and trust in different information sources. *Agribusiness: An International Journal, 24*(4), 523–537. https://doi.org/10.1002/agr.20177

Suchman, M. C. (1995). Managing legitimacy: Strategic and institutional approaches. *Academy of Management Review, 20*(3), 571–610. https://doi.org/10.5465/amr. 1995.9508080331

Tams, S., Legoux, R., & Léger, P.-M. (2018). Smartphone withdrawal creates stress: A moderated mediation model of nomophobia, social threat, and phone withdrawal context. *Computers in Human Behavior, 81*, 1–9. https://doi.org/10.1016/j.chb.2017.11. 026

Taylor, S., & Todd, P. A. (1995). Understanding information technology usage: A test of competing models. *Information Systems Research, 6*(2), 144–176.

Teubner, T. (2022). More than words can say: A randomized field experiment on the effects of consumer self-disclosure in the sharing economy. *Electronic Commerce Research and Applications, 54*(July–August), 101175. https://doi.org/10.1016/j. elerap.2022.101175

Thompson, R. L., Higgins, C. A., & Howell, J. M. (1991). Personal computing: Toward a conceptual model of utilization. *MIS Quarterly, 15*(1), 125–143. https:// doi.org/10.2307/249443

Tran, B. X., Latkin, C. A., Vu, G. T., Nguyen, H. L. T., Nghiem, S., Tan, M.-X., Lim, Z.-K., Ho, C. S. H., & Ho, R. C. M. (2019). The current research landscape of the application of artificial intelligence in managing cerebrovascular and heart diseases: A bibliometric and content analysis. *International Journal of Environmental Research and Public Health, 16*(15). https://doi.org/10.3390/ijerph16152699

Tran, T. T. H., Robinson, K., & Paparoidamis, N. G. (2022). Sharing with perfect strangers: The effects of self-disclosure on consumers' trust, risk perception, and behavioral intention in the sharing economy. *Journal of Business Research, 144*(May), 1–16. https://doi.org/10.1016/j.jbusres.2022.01.081

Tsarenko, Y., & Strizhakova, Y. (2013). Coping with service failures: The role of emotional intelligence, self-efficacy and intention to complain. *European Journal of Marketing*. https://doi.org/10.1108/03090561311285466

Tussyadiah, I. P. (2015). An exploratory study on drivers and deterrents of collaborative consumption in travel 1. *Information and Communication Technologies in Tourism, 27*(December), 817–830.

Tussyadiah, I. P. (2016). Factors of satisfaction and intention to use peer-to-peer accommodation. *International Journal of Hospitality Management, 55*(May), 70–80. https://doi.org/10.1016/j.ijhm.2016.03.005

Tussyadiah, I. P., & Pesonen, J. (2018). Drivers and barriers of peer-to-peer accommodation stay–an exploratory study with American and Finnish travellers. *Current Issues in Tourism, 21*(6), 703–720. https://doi.org/10.1080/13683500.2016.1141180

Tylor, E. B. (1871). *Primitive culture: Researches into the development of mythology, philosophy, religion, art and custom* (Vol. 2). J. Murray.

Venkatesh, V. (2012). Consumer acceptance and use of information technology: Extending the unified theory. *MIS Quarterly, 36*(1), 157–178. https://doi.org/10.2307/41410412

Venkatesh, V., & Davis, F. D. (2000). A theoretical extension of the technology acceptance model: Four longitudinal field studies. *Management Science, 46*(2), 185–204. https://doi.org/10.1287/mnsc.46.2.186.11926

Venkatesh, V., Morris, M. G., Davis, G. B., & Davis, F. D. (2003). User acceptance of information technology: Toward a unified view. *MIS Quarterly, 27*(3), 425–478. https://doi.org/10.2307/30036540

Wydyanto, W., & Ilhamalimy, R. R. (2021). Determination of Trust and purchase decisions: Analysis of brand image and price (marketing management literature review). *Dinasti International Journal of Management Science, 2*(3), 506–516. https://doi.org/10.31933/DIJMS.V2I3.745

Xu, Z., Ge, Z., Wang, X., & Skare, M. (2021). Technological Forecasting & Social Change Bibliometric analysis of technology adoption literature published from 1997 to 2020. *Technological Forecasting and Social Change, 170*(May), 120896. https://doi.org/10.1016/j.techfore.2021.120896

Yang, S.-B., Lee, K., Lee, H., & Koo, C. (2019). In Airbnb we trust: Understanding consumers' trust-attachment building mechanisms in the sharing economy. *International Journal of Hospitality Management, 83*(October), 198–209. https://doi.org/10.1016/j.ijhm.2018.10.016

Yi, Y., & Gong, T. (2008). The electronic service quality model: The moderating effect of customer self-efficacy. *Psychology and Marketing, 25*(7), 587–601. https://doi.org/10.1002/mar.20226

Zervas, G., Proserpio, D., & Byers, J. W. (2017). The rise of the sharing economy: Estimating the impact of Airbnb on the hotel industry. *Journal of Marketing Research, 54*(5), 687–705. https://doi.org/10.1509/jmr.15.0204

Zhu, G., So, K. K. F., & Hudson, S. (2017). Inside the sharing economy: Understanding consumer motivations behind the adoption of mobile applications. *International Journal of Contemporary Hospitality Management, 29*(9), 2218–2239. https://doi.org/10.1108/IJCHM-09-2016-0496

Zhu, G., Zheng, J., & Chen, Y. (2022). Acceptance of free-floating car sharing: A decomposed self-efficacy-based value adoption model. *Transportation Letters, 14*(5), 524–534. https://doi.org/10.1080/19427867.2021.1903132

Zupic, I., & Čater, T. (2015). Bibliometric methods in management and organization. *Organizational Research Methods, 18*(3), 429–472. https://doi.org/10.1177/1094428114562629

Part IV
Ethical and Strategic Challenges in the Digital Age

This part addresses the "Ethical Challenges in Digital Business Ecosystem," covering topics related to ethics, trust, and strategic adaptations, particularly in challenging times.

Chapter 13

The Web Watches and Remembers Everything: The Ethical Implications of Digital Footprints in SMEs Performance

S. Asieh H. Tabaghdehi, Ozlem Ayaz, Ainurul Rosli, Prena Tambay and Waheed Mughal

Brunel University London, UK

Abstract

As a result of COVID-19 outbreak, the rapid digital transformation has drastically changed the way we work as individuals as well as the organisations. Our constant engagement online has become a natural phenomenon. Whenever we go online, we leave a trail of digital data behind us either actively or passively. For a common customer, employee or even an employer, issues regarding data protection and data security are challenging. For instance, who owns the Digital Footprint Data? Do the employees have the skills to protect customers' data online? How are small and medium enterprises (SMEs) handling the ethical issues around digital footprints? These are some primary questions SMEs are currently facing in the transition of digital transformation. These questions have profound ethical implications for SMEs' digital footprints during the COVID-19 outbreak and beyond, which have been explored further in this study.

Keywords: Digital footprint; digital data; digital ethics; privacy; trust; transparency; Small Medium Enterprise (SME)

Introduction

The COVID-19 pandemic reshaped the outlines of our daily lives in ways we could never have imagined. The familiar landscape of busy offices, in-person meetings and the tangible exchange of paperwork was replaced by a new normal.

Business Strategies and Ethical Challenges in the Digital Ecosystem, 307–318
doi:10.1108/978-1-80455-069-420241013

In this transformed reality, our reliance on technology took centre stage. Working from home, learning the art of managing overflowing inboxes and engaging in virtual meetings via platforms like Zoom became the order of the day. For many, this was a novel experience. Remarkably, over half of Europe's remote workers who embarked on this journey during the pandemic had never experienced the remote work landscape before. Today, we spend much of our time online, generating enormous amounts of personal data (Chamorro-Premuzic & Nahai, 2017). COVID-19 has resulted in even more data, as more of us work from home, shop online and choose online entertainment.

Simultaneously, over half of Small and Medium-sized Enterprises (SMEs) found themselves more anxious about digitalisation than any other challenge. In the digital age, a single data breach can echo with costly consequences, affecting both a company's reputation and its financial health. As the world pivoted towards remote work, a transformation that continues to exert its influence, the digital footprints of organisations and individuals alike expanded. The greater the footprint, the greater the risks. The term 'digital footprint' surfaced in conversations, carrying connotations of both mystery and peril. But what exactly is a digital footprint? In its essence, a digital footprint is the indelible trail of data that each of us leaves behind whenever we go online. Have you ever experienced one of those moments when you mistakenly hit 'reply all' on an email containing a snarky remark? If so, you've inadvertently magnified your digital footprint, expanding it through a simple oversight.

This study aims to unravel the complicated concept of digital footprints. We want to shed light on what the digital footprint signifies, the implications it carries and the responsible ways in which we can address this ever-evolving digital landscape. As we investigate the digital footprint challenges and opportunities, we will uncover their significance not just for individuals but also for SMEs and organisations at large. SMEs play a significant role in the national economy by providing various goods and services, creating job opportunities, developing regional economies and communities, encouraging competition in the market and offering innovation. SMEs account for 48% of the UK private sector employment, 33% of annual UK private sector turnover and 99% of all private sector businesses (Shehata et al., 2017).

Active and Passive Digital Footprint

The concept of digital footprints can be categorised into two main types: passive and active. Passive digital footprints encompass the data that individuals inadvertently leave behind without being fully aware that it might be utilised by other parties (Wook et al., 2019). These passive digital footprints can comprise a wide range of information, including cookies, location data, browsing history and more. They are generated as a natural consequence of our online activities, often without our explicit consent.

On the other hand, active digital footprints are created when users intentionally and consciously share information about themselves online (Wook et al., 2019). This sharing can take place through various means, such as social media posts, personal blog entries or interactions on websites and applications. However, irrespective of whether a digital footprint is passive or active, it is important to recognise that all digital footprints are traceable. Our experts strongly believe that individuals who contribute to passive digital footprints should have the opportunity to review and, if they choose, restrict the usage of these data. This approach emphasises the importance of user consent and control over their digital presence, even for information they may not have been aware they were sharing in the first place. This perspective aligns with the principles of privacy and data protection in the digital age.

Navigating Digital Footprints in the Wake of COVID-19: Ethical Implications for SMEs and Their Control Over Data

In today's digital age, the way we communicate and share information has evolved dramatically. Whether it's through email, Zoom, WhatsApp or various other sharing platforms, our reliance on digital channels for communication has become the norm. While these platforms have undoubtedly enhanced our ability to connect and collaborate, they have also introduced a new set of challenges, particularly concerning data security and trust. The convenience of digital communication often comes at the cost of uncertainty. As we send messages, documents or information, we can never be entirely certain that our data is guaranteed to remain safe and secure. This is a concern that has become increasingly apparent, as instances of data breaches and fraudulent activities have risen.

One significant issue is the unauthorised copying and manipulation of emails. In some cases, malicious individuals may copy an email and alter its contents to suit their own purposes. This deceptive practice involves using the original sender's name, creating an illusion that the communication is legitimate. As a result, recipients may find it challenging to distinguish between authentic and altered messages, leading to a breach of trust and potential harm. In this landscape of digital uncertainty, it becomes paramount for individuals, businesses and organisations to take proactive measures to safeguard their data and communication channels. This includes implementing robust cybersecurity measures, ensuring data encryption and educating users about potential risks and best practices for maintaining the integrity of their digital interactions.

As we continue to rely on digital platforms for communication and information sharing, the need for vigilance and a commitment to data security has never been greater, particularly in SMEs. It is imperative that we address these challenges collectively to protect our digital identities and maintain trust in the digital domain. Even before the COVID-19 pandemic outbreak, SMEs were not well equipped to handle such a rush to digital adoption which blur the boundaries between organisational and personal information (Guha et al., 2018). The more personal information is included in any equation, the more it interferes with the privacy of the individuals concerned. Striving to break through in the digital world, many SMEs are taking minimal and vague steps, especially after the COVID-19 outbreak. Thus, these questions emerge: to whom does this digital footprint belong and who, ultimately, has control over it. These are the critical questions for organisations to consider how SMEs can better understand their digital footprints and their ethical implications both at organisational and individual levels. Specifically, cybersecurity risks pose serious threats to mature information societies which depend on digital technologies to function and flourish (Floridi, 2016), which was highly observed after the COVID-19 outbreak.

Furthermore, the increasing reliance on digital technologies and growing focus on online data collection have raised privacy concerns among internet users (Flyverbom et al., 2019). According to Martin (2020), 'privacy violations are valued akin to security violations in creating distrust in firms and in consumer (un)willingness to engage with firms. They further indicated that consumers' privacy expectations are to be met by the organisations.

Existing literature suggests that concerns over trust and risk are major hindrances to the wide adoption of business to customer (B2C) e-commerce in banking (Yousafzai et al., 2003). Ambiguity over rules, roles and regulations causes negative consequences, while a transparency-based sharing framework produces positive results (Köbis et al., 2021). Perceived security and perceived privacy hugely influence the customers' trust. However, 'a clear understanding of the meaning and significance of transparency has yet to emerge in the stakeholder literature' (Schnackenberg & Tomlinson, 2016). Furthermore, there is a major need for increasing transparency without jeopardising the potential of trust-based commercial sharing (Köbis et al., 2021).

Navigating the Digital Ethics Landscape: Transparency, Accountability and Privacy

Technology is driving our economy, politics and everyday life – but that also brings risks. Transparency, accountability and explainability are crucial for building trust in digital technology. Open surveillance and concerns over privacy are major challenges (Flyverbom et al., 2019). Nonetheless, a distinction exists between personal data and open data, and privacy considerations may vary between the two categories. Personal data can be directly linked to an individual and is legally protected. Open data encompasses elements like gender, email addresses, postal codes, dates of birth and social media contacts, and it can be exchanged without the subject's consent. The resulting confusion and ambiguity regarding personal and open data have significant implications for digital ethics, necessitating a comprehensive understanding of the issue by both customers and employees. However, the literature highlights that no online data is personal or private anymore. For example, Chamorro-Premuzic and Nahai (2017) argue that the concept of 'personal', which once meant 'private', no longer exists, because our data is widely available in the public domain. However, securing personal data can restrict our ability to enjoy free and personalised services online. Therefore, informed consent is crucial in deciding what to share online.

In current digital settings, news media and less popular online spaces empower individuals to actively express public dissent. This trend of enabling individuals, including employees, to voice public dissent is known as employee anonymous online dissent (EAOD). The phenomenon of EAOD, where disgruntled employees use online channels to 'blow the whistle' on their employers, raises issues of accountability and ethics because such employees have access to the anonymised data anyway (Ravazzani & Mazzei, 2018). Transparency and trust are equally important for customers, employees and employers. Transparency wins stakeholders' trust in organisations (Schnackenberg & Tomlinson, 2016). However, advanced artificial intelligence (AI) has made informed consent a dead commodity because businesses increasingly rely on algorithms that are data-trained sets of decision rules (Kim & Routledge, 2022). This implies that the firms use data to benefit their businesses regardless of consent.

Data and Methods

An In-Depth Exploration of the Ethical Implications of Digital Footprints on SMEs

In the exploration of understanding the complex ethical landscape surrounding digital footprints and their impact on the performance of SMEs, this study employed netnography within the dynamic and professional platform of LinkedIn and Tweeter to understand people's lived online experience from many perspectives. This section explains the framework, data collection and analytical approach utilised in our investigation, which facilitated a profound understanding of this multifaceted phenomenon. Our research methodology primarily hinged on netnography, a qualitative research approach initially championed by Kozinets (1998) and further refined by Belz and Baumbach (2010). This approach serves as a digital ethnographic tool that allowed us to venture into the online setting of LinkedIn, a prolific professional networking platform. The objective was to engage in immersive data collection within this digital ecosystem and unravel the ethical nuances of digital footprints.

Leveraging LinkedIn: An Audience of Over 11,000 Views and 200 Comments

LinkedIn, renowned for its stature as a global hub of professionals, became our virtual field site for this netnographic exploration. Within this dynamic platform, we embarked on a journey of interaction, engaging with a diverse and extensive audience that exceeded 11,000 views, sparking vibrant discussions with over 200 comments. This expansive engagement formed the bedrock of our data collection, allowing us to collect invaluable insights into the ethical sides of digital footprints as perceived by a broad spectrum of LinkedIn users. We purposefully sought out and interacted with communities of academics, researchers and businesses, each offering their unique perspectives on the diverse dimensions of digital footprints. The consolidation of these diverse viewpoints contributed to a comprehensive understanding of the ethical implications inherent to digital footprints. The COVID-19 pandemic, a transformative event that reshaped the digital landscape, served as a crucial reference point. Our netnography concentrated on collecting data post-pandemic, investigating into the lived experiences of individuals and organisations as they address the digital terrain during and after the global health crisis. This temporal specificity added depth and relevance to our analysis, ensuring that the ethical implications were captured in the most current and pertinent light. Hence, the data and methods employed in this study reflect a dedicated effort to comprehensively explore the ethical dimensions of digital footprints on SMEs' performance. Through netnography on the LinkedIn platform, we tapped into the collective wisdom of diverse online communities, focusing on post-pandemic experiences, and, thus, our findings are imbued with rich contextual portrayals of the evolving ethical landscape of digital footprints in the modern digital era.

Data Analysis

The Significance of Digital Footprint in SMEs

Digital footprint covers all aspects of activities performed online and it has commercial value (Dwork & Mulligan, 2013). So, organisations have access to the digital footprints generated from customers which can be and used as base for various commercial objectives (Abril et al., 2012). However, this access has raised many issues in relation to and digital ethics such as data privacy, data security, surveillance and web tracing. Although SMEs have limited resources to become resilient to data projection, they are equally responsible to implement the effective policies for data handling and processing like any of the big organisations. For SMEs, financial constraints, a knowledge-technology gap, digitally skilled labour and lack of policies and procedures on handling digital data are the major challenges. The first emphasis of our research is that the technology is rapidly changing, knowledge among the public remains idle; and how can educational institutions provide adequate training and education to bridge the knowledge-technology gap are the primary questions for policymakers.

As quoted by one of our participants the digital footprint is 'In short, clickstream data'. It was also mentioned by another participant that 'Although it's any data in the system that is connected with me, I tend to think of it as something negative that may come back and bite me'. Hence, the importance of having policies regarding data privacy, surveillance, General Data Protection Regulation (GDPR) and cyber security is vital for SMEs in creating value for their respective businesses. Hence, for responsible practice, it is equally important for employees, employers and customers to draw boundaries between professional and personal activities on digital platforms. But again, as a second emphasis of this research, if organisations use personal activities of the employees as a surveillance tool to punish them at the workplace, it leaves a big question: how can personal and professional life be separated on social media? This has been highlighted by one of the participants that 'Back then we didn't think to use it as an asset for building up your reputation. These days, I use social media very differently, I always think about which content to post, how it's interesting or adds value to my followers, etc.'. She then continued that 'From the business perspective, I think it is absolutely crucial'.

Ethical Dimensions of Digital Footprints

The ethical consequences of digital footprint are not limited to the business, they equally impact social behaviour (image, identity) and the role of community is vital in using them positively. As the third emphasis, for responsible digital footprint management, there is a dire need to create new roles/responsibilities to manage data within the SMEs. This will promote transparency and accountability in processing the digital data. It has been debated by one of our respondents that 'policy can and must work on safety online, actually the United Kingdom is trying to work in this direction, unfortunately making some actions unlawful or adding fines is not enough. What we need is a culture of truth (check that what you see online is really what it seems) and a culture of accountability and responsibility (do your part in keeping the online world true). An interesting exercise may be asking non-tech savvy people what they prefer between easy authentication and security that their credentials can't be stolen. You'll be surprised how many will choose the first. There is not enough understanding of the risks associated with our web-surfing'.

Promoting Transparency and Accountability

Lack of capability in controlling data shared with key partners has also ethical consequences in terms of transparency and accountability. Hence, the final emphasis of this study is that data privacy leads to some clarity on regulatory focus. So, a collaborative ethical approach is needed to address the issues related to digital data ownership, handling and processing without compromising on privacy and security. As quoted by one of our participants 'I try not to mix my personal profiles of social media with my working profiles so that I can get privacy. I recently went through some social media profiles to change sharing settings of very old personal posts. Also, when I do not use a digital account I close it'. Furthermore, another participant indicated his concern as '1st thing that comes to my mind – Data Privacy. Footprints allow other people not just knowing where you've been but also where you're heading (yes, the power of AI and data analytics). This is where awareness on data privacy/security plays an important role'. Another participant debated that 'Although I am conscious of privacy on social media by not posting sensitive information. My personal data is still being collected all the time, the online subscriptions/newsletters, the forms I had to fill in with info like DoB, email, telephone, etc., which passively created a digital footprint. I do wonder how businesses manage this data'.

Data Privacy and Regulatory Focus

The further ethical implication of the misuse of the digital footprint data has been explored by other participants saying that 'Data security is one of the hot topics in our digital world, which all parties should reconsider and work further in order to protect people's privacy'. The way people work, opinions, preferences and interests have to be private. As a similar practice, the United States experienced how Digital footprint is important, during the 2016 Presidential election (Cambridge Analytica Case), how Election Propaganda was custom made and manipulated. This may have affected not only the United States but the entire World. While we may be concerned about protecting our privacy and personal data online, we generally do little about it. For example, research suggests that consumers care less about their privacy while using their social media accounts (Chamorro-Premuzic & Nahai, 2017).

Other respondents emphasised that concerns regarding privacy, the utilisation of personal data and transparency often lack clarity. Organisations are deficient in providing employees with the necessary training to clarify the implications of their online activities. Both customers and employees should be empowered with the choice to either delete their data or specify its usage and sharing preferences. They highlighted that every organisation should establish a strong protocol for protecting the digital data they gather while also devising a responsible approach for managing and governing these data. These measures are crucial in preventing data breaches and ensuring compliance with regulatory requirements.

Hence, digital footprint shouldn't create any discrimination. Like in all other fields 'Ethic' perspective should be discussed/highlighted more and more. The issue is global – but the solution starts at the local level. And that's why SMEs need education, training, support, resources and a regulatory framework to help them manage digital data in a more efficient and ethical way.

Conclusion

Digitalisation is an inevitable phenomenon of the modern age. We as individuals, businesses and organisations are connected to digital life one way or the other. Digital life has its own risks and implications. The open surveillance, trust, accountability, transparency, cyber security and a growing concern about issues of privacy are some of the most important challenges of this digital age (Flyverbom et al., 2019). This study sheds light on a significant revelation: a pervasive and concerning limitation in the understanding of digital footprints and their far-reaching implications among individuals. This finding underscores the critical importance of addressing this knowledge gap, as it has significant implications for personal privacy, data security and the ethical use of digital platforms. Within the digital landscape, a complex web of data trails is involved with every online interaction and transaction. Yet, our study highlights that many individuals possess only a brief grasp of digital footprints, often underestimating their breadth and depth. It is evident from our research that the implications of digital footprints extend far beyond the surface-level interactions most individuals are aware of. Beyond the simple understanding of basic online activities like posting, liking or sharing, a deeper comprehension of the layers of data collection, tracking mechanisms and data sharing is essential.

This limited understanding is a cause for concern, as it directly affects individuals' ability to protect their data privacy. A failure to recognise the full scope of one's digital footprint may unintentionally expose personal information to unintended parties. This, in turn, can lead to privacy breaches and potentially harmful consequences. Moreover, an inadequate understanding of digital footprints also leaves individuals vulnerable to security. Malicious actors and cyber threats can exploit these vulnerabilities, leading to unauthorised access, data breaches and identity theft. Such security breaches can have severe real-world consequences for individuals. The ethical dimension of digital footprints remains largely unexplored for those with limited understanding. Questions surrounding the responsible use of data, transparency in data collection and the consequences of data misuse often elude individuals who are unaware of the broader implications of their digital presence.

In light of these findings, there arises a clear call for enhanced digital literacy initiatives. Empowering individuals with the knowledge to address the digital landscape effectively, protect their data and make informed ethical choices is imperative. Digital literacy programs, educational institutions and awareness campaigns should aim to bridge this knowledge gap and equip individuals to be responsible digital citizens. This study uncovers a critical deficiency in individual understanding concerning digital footprints and their profound implications. This knowledge gap underscores the need for proactive efforts to enhance digital literacy and raise awareness about the essentials of digital footprints, data privacy and ethical considerations in the digital age.

Managerial Implication

In light of the rapid technological changes brought about by the COVID-19 pandemic, businesses have faced numerous challenges in adapting to this evolving landscape. Factors such as budget constraints and the need for continuous digital literacy have delayed the management process. This underscores the importance of providing additional support to SMEs in terms of data protection, data security and ethical digital practices. Among the various aspects of digital footprint, privacy emerges as a supreme concern. Privacy violations can be as detrimental as security breaches, leading to a loss of trust between firms and their customers. To mitigate these concerns, it is imperative for businesses to establish and communicate reasonable expectations of privacy for their consumers (Martin, 2020).

Furthermore, transparency plays a pivotal role in building and maintaining trust with stakeholders. The results of this study align with recent research that indicates consumers are often reluctant to safeguard their data or abandon social media platforms, even in the absence of complete trust in data security

(Chamorro-Premuzic & Nahai, 2017). Therefore, SMEs should prioritise transparency as a means of enhancing trust and credibility in their operations.

Theoretical Implication

The central theoretical implication revolves around the ethical utilisation and governance of digital footprints. Current discussions surrounding digital footprints often lack in-depth consideration of the precise locations where our data is being harnessed and stored, as well as the specific platforms involved. This theoretical gap underscores the need to explore the details of data management and analysis within digital environments. Furthermore, the theoretical framework highlights the scarcity of attention devoted to matters of fairness and inclusion on digital platforms. Understanding how various user groups are represented and how data-related decisions affect inclusivity is paramount within this context. Moreover, the issue of data ownership is another theoretical concern. The framework emphasises the need for more comprehensive reflection on who possesses and manages our data, alongside the ethical implications and potential ramifications arising from data analysis and utilisation. This highlights the necessity of advancing research and theoretical frameworks in digital footprint studies to explore further about the ethical data management, inclusivity and the implications of data ownership. It provides a foundation for future theoretical developments in the domain of digital footprint ethics.

Case Study

Navigating Digital Ethics in SMEs: The Impact of Digital Footprint

TechTech Solutions is an SME providing digital services, and its efforts to balance innovation with ethical considerations. TechTech Solutions recognised the significance of leveraging digital data to enhance its services. However, the company was confronted with ethical dilemmas related to user privacy, the transparency of data practices and establishing trust among its clientele.

TechTech Solutions initiated data collection to refine its offerings. However, heightened privacy concerns emerged as customers questioned the extent and purpose of data collection, emphasising the need for transparent data usage policies. Recognising the pivotal role of trust, TechTech Solutions revamped its approach. Transparent communication about data practices, the implementation of robust security measures and adherence to data protection regulations aimed to build trust among users. They embraced digital ethics by re-evaluating its data use policies. It implemented mechanisms for obtaining explicit user consent, anonymising sensitive data and ensuring that data-driven decisions align with ethical standards.

As an SME, TechTech Solutions faced challenges such as limited resources and expertise in navigating the complexities of digital ethics. Collaboration with industry forums, participation in ethical discussions and leveraging external through their progressive experience in the market, they experienced a positive shift in user perception. Transparent communication about data practices resulted in increased user trust. The company's commitment to digital ethics not only enhanced its reputation but also attracted ethically conscious customers. They realised that as a key survival strategy they must strike between utilising digital data for innovation and upholding digital ethics to ensure user privacy, trust and transparency. They focus more on how SMEs can proactively address ethical challenges, foster customer trust and thrive in the evolving digital landscape.

Case Study Questions

(1) How did TechTech Solutions address the challenge of leveraging digital data for innovation while simultaneously upholding ethical practices?
(2) What specific measures did they implement to address privacy concerns and establish transparent data usage policies?
(3) In revamping their approach, TechTech Solutions emphasised transparent communication about data practices to build trust among users. How did this commitment to transparency impact user perception and trust?
(4) As an SME, TechTech Solutions faced challenges related to limited resources and expertise in relation to digital ethics. How did they overcome these challenges, and what strategies did they employ to address the complexities of digital ethics?
(5) In what ways did collaboration with industry forums and participation in ethical discussions contribute to their ethical decision-making processes?

Key Terms and Definitions

Digital Footprint Data: Digital footprint data refers to the information generated by an individual's online activities and interactions across various digital platforms and devices.

Privacy Concerns: Privacy concerns refer to apprehensions and anxieties regarding the protection of personal information and the control individuals have over their own data in various contexts, particularly in digital environments.

Digital Trust: Digital trust refers to the confidence and reliability individuals, organisations and societies place in digital technologies, platforms and services to safeguard their interests, protect their privacy and deliver on promises.

Transparency: Transparency refers to the practice of openly providing information, insights and processes in a clear, honest and accessible manner.

Digital Ethics: Digital ethics refers to the moral principles, values and guidelines that govern the ethical use of digital technologies, data and platforms in society.

References

Abril, P. S., Levin, A., & Del Riego, A. (2012). Blurred boundaries: Social media privacy and the twenty-first-century employee. *American Business Law Journal*, *49*(1), 63–124.

Belz, F. M., & Baumbach, W. (2010). Netnography as a method of lead user identification. *Creativity and Innovation Management, 19*(3), 304–313.

Chamorro-Premuzic, T., & Nahai, N. (2017). Why we're so hypocritical about online privacy. *Harvard Business Review.* https://ipc.kingscollege.edu.np/wp-content/uploads/2022/03/H03N00-PDF-ENG.pdf

Dwork, C., & Mulligan, D. K. (2013). It's not privacy, and it's not fair. *Stanford Law Review, 66*, 35.

Floridi, L. (2016). Mature information societies—A matter of expectations. *Philosophy & Technology, 29*, 1–4.

Flyverbom, M., Deibert, R., & Matten, D. (2019). The governance of digital technology, big data, and the internet: New roles and responsibilities for business. *Business & Society, 58*(1), 3–19.

Guha, S., Harrigan, P., & Soutar, G. (2018). Linking social media to customer relationship management (CRM): A qualitative study on SMEs. *Journal of Small Business and Entrepreneurship, 30*(3), 193–214.

Kim, T. W., & Routledge, B. R. (2022). Why a right to an explanation of algorithmic decision-making should exist: A trust-based approach. *Business Ethics Quarterly, 32*(1), 75–102.

Köbis, N., Soraperra, I., & Shalvi, S. (2021). The consequences of participating in the sharing economy: A transparency-based sharing framework. *Journal of Management, 47*(1), 317–343.

Kozinets, R. V. (1998). On netnography: Initial reflections on consumer research investigations of cyberculture. *ACR North American Advances.* https://citeseerx.ist.psu.edu/document?repid=rep1&type=pdf&doi=2b29b0f040660c8032136ac243638b0d0b8630ac

Martin, K. (2020). Breaking the privacy paradox: The value of privacy and associated duty of firms. *Business Ethics Quarterly, 30*(1), 65–96.

Ravazzani, S., & Mazzei, A. (2018). Employee anonymous online dissent: Dynamics and ethical challenges for employees, targeted organisations, online outlets, and audiences. *Business Ethics Quarterly, 28*(2), 175–201.

Schnackenberg, A. K., & Tomlinson, E. C. (2016). Organizational transparency: A new perspective on managing trust in organization-stakeholder relationships. *Journal of Management, 42*(7), 1784–1810.

Shehata, N., Salhin, A., & El-Helaly, M. (2017). Board diversity and firm performance: Evidence from the UK SMEs. *Applied Economics, 49*(48), 4817–4832.

Wook, T. S. M., Mohamed, H. A. Z. U. R. A., Noor, S. F. M., Muda, Z. U. R. I. N. A., & Zairon, I. Y. (2019). Awareness of digital footprint management in the new media amongst youth. *Jurnal Komunikasi: Malaysian Journal of Communication, 35*(3), 407–421.

Yousafzai, S. Y., Pallister, J. G., & Foxall, G. R. (2003). A proposed model of e-trust for electronic banking. *Technovation, 23*(11), 847–860.

Chapter 14

The Political Challenge of AI in Modern Society: From National AI Strategy to the Algorithmic Elections

Lefteris Kretsos, S. Asieh H. Tabaghdehi and Ashley Braganza

Brunel University London, UK

Abstract

The transformative impact of artificial intelligence (AI) and technological advancements has captured the attention of various stakeholders, from researchers to policymakers and the general public. Despite the promise of AI's benefits, concerns persist regarding its ethical, privacy, security, and societal implications. Public trust in AI remains low, with fears surrounding its future use and governance growing among scholars and the public. These anxieties are fueled by media narratives raising scenarios such as the "AI revolution" or "AI apocalypse." Moreover, the prospect of technology-driven unemployment adds to this climate of anxiety. Meanwhile, AI's increasing geopolitical influence has shifted its focus from innovation to dominance, with national governments viewing it as a tool for competitive repositioning. However, AI also poses threats to democracy, as it facilitates the spread of misinformation and undermines electoral integrity. In this chapter, we explore further the challenges AI presents to modern society and democracy, focusing on political practices and electoral risks. Our analysis focuses on the political and social dimensions of AI, arguing that its impacts are shaped by specific political decisions rather than abstract technological dynamics. We emphasize the need to acknowledge and address the political implications of AI to foster a more informed discourse surrounding its deployment and regulation.

Keywords: Artificial Intelligence (AI); misinformation; fake news; election campaign; national AI strategy; public policy

Business Strategies and Ethical Challenges in the Digital Ecosystem, 319–331

Copyright © 2025 Lefteris Kretsos, S. Asieh H. Tabaghdehi and Ashley Braganza

Published under exclusive licence by Emerald Publishing Limited

doi:10.1108/978-1-80455-069-420241014

Introduction

The transformative impact of artificial intelligence (AI) and technological advancements has garnered significant attention from various stakeholders, including researchers, policymakers, businesses, and the general public. As AI technologies continue to advance, their implications extend to issues such as ethics, privacy, security, information transparency, economic disruption, and societal well-being (Buhmann & Fieseler, 2023; Helbing, 2019; Sheikh, 2020; Stephanidis et al., 2019). However, despite these developments, public trust in AI remains low. For instance, for the majority of Americans, concerns outweigh feelings of excitement about the benefits of AI in daily life (Ikkatai et al., 2023).

Similarly, scholars have highlighted a growing sense of fear and anxiety regarding the wide-ranging consequences of AI's future use and governance (He et al., 2019; Li & Huang, 2020; Nadarzynski et al., 2019; Zhan et al., 2023). These fears encompass broader perspectives of AI, often framed under media narratives and neologisms such as "AI revolution" or "AI apocalypse." Such terms are also used to describe potential impacts on specific areas, including automated driving systems (Boudette et al., 2022), privacy issues (Shin et al., 2022), and human rights violations due to advanced technologies in surveillance and policing (Rahwan et al., 2019; Zuboff, 2019).

A prominent source of anxiety and fear concerning AI revolves around the prospect of rising technology-driven unemployment. Alarming statistics from a survey by Goldman Sachs authored by Joseph Briggs and Devesh Kodnani in March 2023, for example, concluded that 300 million full-time jobs are at serious risk due to AI. In this climate of anxiety, it becomes crucial for modern organizations, academic institutions, and regulators to facilitate understanding of AI and its potential for the greater good.

However, the current state of affairs indicates a different reality, as AI has become a stream of technological supremacy and increased geopolitical influence rather than a tool for establishing healthy innovation ecosystems (Bradford, 2023; Mazzucato, 2018). Digital domination and influence in the modern geopolitical landscape play a significant role in the adoption and deployment of AI, with national governments viewing AI as a tool for national rebranding and competitive repositioning in the global division of work and production output (Foffano et al., 2020).

Simultaneously, AI poses serious threats to the foundations of democracy by making it easier for political actors to disseminate misinformation and manipulate public opinion, potentially affecting the integrity of national elections. AI-powered tools have the capacity to facilitate the spread of misinformation, challenging citizens' trust in the electoral system and potentially leading to reduced voter turnout, and a decline in democratic participation in the future.

In this chapter, we undertake a critical review of the challenges posed by AI to modern society and democracy, focusing on two illustrative examples of political practice and ritual. Both examples selected for analysis underscore the pronounced political implications inherent in the ongoing discourse surrounding AI deployment. The first example scrutinizes the National AI Strategy action plans, with a particular emphasis on the case of the United Kingdom. The second example delves into the emerging risks to democratic elections posed by AI-powered tools and examines the measures governments are implementing to address these risks and threats.

Our analysis offers a distinctive perspective on the contemporary discourse surrounding the AI imperative. In contrast to mainstream media narratives that often portray AI and its impact as technocentric and driven by abstract techno-logical dynamics, we contend that the influence of AI is fundamentally political and social, rather than merely industrial or technological. The advancements in AI yield outcomes that are closely tied to specific political decisions. Without these decisions in place, the consequences of AI and digitalization would manifest differently.

Grounded in this theoretical framework, we argue that both national action plans for AI strategy and policies aimed at safeguarding electoral integrity are essentially political decisions reflecting political priorities. The analysis presented in this chapter leads to the conclusion that the prevalent media focus tends to overlook this political dimension, contributing to the depoliticization of the modern AI discourse by presenting it as a technocratic, monolithic phenomenon.

National AI Strategies: A Global Undemocratic Race to Supremacy

The widespread implementation of AI has evolved into a national mission and objective, hailed as a pathway for human societies to attain unparalleled levels of knowledge, productivity, economic growth, prosperity, and societal advancement (Verschraegen et al., 2017). These political aspirations and visions are mirrored in national AI strategy plans, policy documents, government initiatives, and high-profile, albeit often exclusive, AI-related events, as well as the formation of dedicated committees and working groups comprising AI experts (Bareis & Katzenbach, 2022; Dutton, 2018).

AI is recognized as a linchpin in the ongoing digital and green transitions, prompting countries to periodically review and synchronize their policies across sectors such as agriculture, healthcare, finance, and gaming. National AI Strategy reports serve as governance tools, shaping policies for technology adoption and envisioning a technologically advanced future (The UK Leads Europe and Ranks Third Globally in Artificial Intelligence, 2021). They also represent strategic positioning and "rebranding" initiatives, outlining future measures and policy initiatives while allocating resources to AI research, application, and digital infrastructure investment (Jasanoff & Kim, 2009).

However, National AI Strategy reports often adopt a market-centric approach or reflect distinct political traditions and cultural values (Robinson, 2020). For example, in the United Kingdom, the national AI strategy prioritizes investment in AI to lead in advanced AI systems globally (Office for Artificial Intelligence. National AI Strategy, 2021). Yet, public engagement strategies to enhance trust in AI are not prioritized, and the strategy lacks mechanisms for citizen and insti-tutional participation in establishing more ethical AI systems. Consultative and social dialogue bodies for AI, with specific mandates and targets, are conspicuously absent from the strategy document. Additionally, there is no commitment to a long-term, well-funded partnership with educational institutions, media outlets, including popular platforms like BBC and YouTube, or other content platforms to raise awareness about AI issues and broader digitalization agendas.

The engagement activities outlined in the UK's national AI strategy report primarily target AI research and industry communities, specific projects like the NHS Lab, or consultations at high-ranking levels. If AI is considered more than a utility, posing a powerful force shaping people's lives, there's an evident need to include broader society in the development and debate around AI. However, the UK's National AI Strategy has certain deficits. The report fails to address the chronic underfunding of public institutions and the regional disparities in income and growth allocation, which have worsened since Brexit. Additionally, the United Kingdom's main competitors have significantly increased public spending on AI investments, often prioritizing key areas like healthcare services.

These aspects highlight that creating enthusiasm with a forward-looking vision and conveying messages for more focused AI deployment policies aren't sufficient to meet objectives. Successful delivery necessitates a capable and receptive organization, focus on the moral purpose of actions, and metrics study for success indicators (Barber, 2015).

Conversely, the European Union has introduced new governance instruments and funding streams, offering substantial financial support for AI investments and research projects with a €20 billion investment target in AI across the European Union (Brattberg et al., 2020). Notably, the Digital Europe Programme, with a budget of €7.9 billion for AI (2021–2027), aims to build strategic digital capacities and deploy digital technologies widely. The Recovery and Resilience Facility, contributing 20% of €670 billion for digital and AI projects until 2026, supports member states' recovery investments and reforms.

Additional resources for funding AI investments include funds from the European Investment Bank, European Central Bank, and national governments. In the United Kingdom, AI investments rely more on private initiatives, with a focus on London-centric projects. This poses a challenge for regional growth, considering 65% of the United Kingdom's AI companies are headquartered in London, and the remaining 35% concentrate mainly on high-income urban areas like Edinburgh, Oxford, Cambridge, and Manchester (businesswire, 2021). However, evidence on investment distribution in AI activity is more concerning. According to Beauhurst's 2022 report, equity funding distribution in the United Kingdom has worsened, with the South of England, especially London, claiming the majority (72%) of investments (Gov.UK, 2022). Such evidence contradicts the goal of making the United Kingdom the world leader in advanced AI systems, emphasizing the need for more synergies and dispersion of investment across the country.

The regional dimension's importance in innovation and dynamic capabilities is significant for a competitive economy (Boschma & Frenken, 2011). Scholars highlight factors such as infrastructural facilities, policy support, and historical background shaping a region's potential and opportunities (Labory & Bianchi, 2021).

Neglecting regional insights in national policies can lead to growing regional disparities, expanded inequalities, and human capital loss. To address this, implementing more friendly taxation for AI investments and establishing AI hubs outside London, including the Greater London region, is crucial. Public policies should emphasize regional needs.

Nevertheless, capturing the benefits of an AI-enabled economy requires innovation spread across regions and sectors, especially those addressing urgent challenges (Artificial Intelligence Sector Study, 2022). Although the UK prioritizes AI investments, healthcare and social care sectors still depend significantly on precarious work, as well as on migrant and unskilled labor (Forde et al., 2023). The National UK Strategy falls short in challenging this issue, lacking specific targets, milestones, and priorities for widespread AI adoption following an inclusive industrial strategy.

The UK government's commitment to becoming an AI leader faces challenges due to an optimistic outlook that does not adequately prepare the economy and society for imminent threats. A sector and region-led approach in AI regulation is lacking, and the pro-innovation approach to regulate AI, as outlined in the white paper by the Department for Science, Innovation, and Technology (March, 2023), suggests a delayed implementation of regulations. Despite some strengths, such as measurable action points and deadlines, and a focus on crucial areas like digital skills and data accessibility, the United Kingdom's strength in AI research does not guarantee a safe and sustainable future deployment of AI on a mass scale. Trust remains a paramount issue that cannot be neglected in the AI deployment landscape.

The recent developments in the UK government's National AI Strategy are more promising in addressing regulatory concerns. The new white paper (March, 2023) by the UK Department for Science, Innovation, and Technology (DSIT) focuses on creating a pro-innovation regulatory framework that promotes public trust in AI. It introduces a regulatory sandbox to bring regulators and innovators together, facilitating a better understanding of how regulations impact emerging AI technologies. Despite the UK government's decision not to propose new legislation, unlike the European Union and other countries, the DSIT white paper aims to empower regulators through guidelines, enabling statutory action when deemed necessary.

Notably, the emphasis on increasing public trust in AI is a significant aspect of the new strategy, acknowledging the need to address AI risks and safeguard fundamental values to drive AI adoption. The UK government also recognizes the importance of working closely with international partners and national governments to support more ethical approaches to AI.

However, both the 2021 National AI Strategy and the 2023 DSIT white paper continue the tradition of soft kind of regulation to support AI development and adoption. Ethical AI adoption is not actively promoted through the implementation of relevant projects in central government functions, reflecting the government's concerns about over-regulation and organizational flexibility.

In summary, addressing AI regulatory issues requires collaborative efforts and partnerships not only between government and industry but also across various organizations and institutions, including universities, trade unions, and social businesses. The challenges posed by AI demand regulations at both national and international levels, ensuring the maintenance of ethical standards universally. Regulators and politicians must recognize the transformative impact of AI on all aspects of economic and social life, including the functioning of democratic institutions.

While AI technologies offer unprecedented opportunities for efficiency, transparency, and innovation, they also bring unique challenges that can potentially impact the democratic principles underlying societies. The intersection of AI and democracy has sparked debates on fairness, accountability, privacy, and the overall influence of automation on decision-making processes (Helberger et al., 2020; Katyal, 2019). In the following discussion, we delve into the critical role of AI in shaping the democratic landscape, particularly its impact on the integrity of democratic elections.

AI, Fake News, and Elections

Fake news has been a persistent issue throughout history, with philosophers like Hannah Arendt highlighting the erosion of truth by continual lying from political leaders and institutions over time. In the modern context, fake news is defined as false, deceptive, or incorrect material resembling news media content. Citizens face challenges in forming informed opinions amid the vast information from traditional and social media. Egelhofer and Lecheler (2019) identified three pillars of fake news: low facticity, journalistic format, and intention to deceive.

Fake news extends beyond politics, influencing decisions in healthcare, as seen in pandemic-related conspiracy theories (Ahmad et al., 2022). Events like the Brexit referendum and Trump's 2016 victory intensified concerns about orchestrated propaganda, fake news, and the role of social media platforms in disrupting democracy (Bakir & McStay, 2018; Ball, 2017; Bennett & Livingston, 2018; Levinson, 2017). Scholars criticize the hegemony of big tech companies, highlighting issues of algorithmic curation and data-driven behavioral manipulation (Galloway, 2018; Leslie, 2023).

Explanations for fake news range from political and media power dynamics to issues of bias in media influencing democratic dialogue (Aoki, 2020; Bucy & Newhagen, 2019). Media's influence on political life, public discourse, and consent has been studied, emphasizing strong ties between media and the state (Bourdieu, 1991; Carey, 1989; Castells, 2009; Chomsky, 1998). The media is seen as a tool for reinforcing systems of domination and constructing reality (Adorno, 2001; Miliband, 1969). Current concerns include the fear of bots, misinformation, and hacking in the context of rising authoritarianism and populism, affecting political engagement and polarization (Graves & Wells, 2019; Mazzoleni & Voerman, 2017). While some studies suggest AI's positive role in driving voter participation (Muppasani et al., 2023), the growing use of digital marketing techniques by political parties raises ethical concerns, including disinformation campaigns and cybersecurity risks (Duffy et al., 2020).

The application of AI software tools poses a significant threat to electoral democracies, particularly when fraudulent AI-generated content is used in campaign ads, jeopardizing the integrity of democratic elections. Despite efforts by Natural Language Processing (NLP)-driven expert systems and detection mechanisms, media integrity has not reached a level where the global population feels secure from disinformation. Surveys from organizations like the Pew Research Centre, Oxford Reuters, and Eurobarometer indicate persistently low trust in media and political organizations.

The consequences of disinformation and a society lacking factual truths are severe risks to democracy and its various processes, especially elections (Lazer et al., 2018). In a post-truth society, subjective and sentimental approaches often prevail over logical argumentation, allowing fake news to overshadow well-researched journalism (Krause et al., 2019). AI technologies exacerbate the challenge of low trust in democratic institutions, introducing unprecedented levels of disinformation and fake news through webs of deceit. Deepfakes, microtargeting, harder-to-detect bots, and generative AI contribute to the creation of online information bubbles, potentially leading to political chaos in upcoming elections.

The urgency of addressing the risks posed by AI to democracy becomes crucial as several countries, including the United Kingdom, the United States, India, Indonesia, Mexico, and Taiwan, are scheduled to hold elections in 2024, collectively involving almost 4 billion people (World Economic Forum, 2024). Regulators and policy actors must prioritize safeguarding the integrity of these elections by implementing a plan that addresses not only human actors but also algorithmic and machine learning tools. This aligns with the principles outlined in articles 10 and 11 of the European Court of Human Rights, emphasizing freedom of expression, freedom of assembly and association, and the right to free and fair elections.

The comprehensive policy menu should involve all key stakeholders in the political environment and election process, including governments, media outlets, and the digital political consultancy industry. Additionally, there is a need for robust voter education, with a focus on more aggressive AI literacy interventions. Despite current research predominantly adopting a technical perspective, delving into specific technological problems and solutions within the computer science domain, a broader and more interdisciplinary approach is necessary to effectively combat AI-driven misinformation.

Scholarship should redirect its focus to a significant yet overlooked aspect of AI's impact on elections, particularly the capacity of AI tools to fabricate consensus during electoral processes. Elections serve as an opportune environment for political propaganda and manipulation, and AI technologies, especially generative AI, have the potential to shape consensus or dissent through persuasive means. At the current stage, a crucial question arises: "How does the proliferation of malicious narratives occur?"

To address this question, it is essential to recognize that past instances of voter manipulation, such as the Cambridge Analytica scandal and interference in the 2016 American elections, involved three fundamental components: (i) Malicious Actors (including hackers, bots, and malign accounts), (ii) Generated content (encompassing memes, long-form narratives, fake journalists, fabricated accounts, top search results dominance for keywords, and machine-generated dominance in public debates), and (iii) a dissemination process (encompassing pathways of dissemination, mechanisms of virality, and peer-to-peer transmission that facilitate the spread of fake news).

AI tools and technologies have a profound impact on all three aspects of voter manipulation. Firstly, AI lowers the cost of producing harmful and manipulative content, as seen in the case of deepfakes and synthetic media. These forms of content, often sensational and emotional (e.g., revenge porn, shocking videos, audio deepfakes, fake hot mic videos, and generated text), can be created by AI in various formats, including text, audio, or video, or a combination of them. What is particularly concerning is the novel way in which synthetic media makes it more likely for such content to be widely disseminated and go viral.

Secondly, AI influences the distribution of manipulative content by introducing more sophisticated automated accounts, enhancing the ability to evade platform detection algorithms, utilizing algorithmic recommendations, and improving curation and targeting.

Thirdly, AI chatbots, especially those employing Generative Adversarial Networks (GANs), have the potential to significantly amplify trustworthy images. Such malicious applications are more challenging to detect.

In summary, AI technologies present a significant threat to the effective functioning of political institutions and have the potential to erode voters' trust in elections, a fundamental aspect of the democratic process. These technologies can exert persuasive and mobilizing influences on voters, contributing to increased polarization in public discourse, reduced tolerance for opposing viewpoints, and the promotion of negative political messaging that targets vulnerable social groups. In essence, AI can have a detrimental impact on social solidarity and democratic engagement.

The implications of AI on national elections prompt critical reflections on the resilience of democracy in the digital age. While AI introduces innovative and efficient possibilities in the electoral process, it also brings forth risks related to misinformation and trust issues. Recognizing these challenges and formulating strategies to address them is crucial for preserving the integrity of democratic elections and fostering informed, free, and fair decision-making by citizens.

The deployment of AI technologies necessitates comprehensive regulatory interventions to establish a robust institutional framework. This framework should facilitate and expedite the evolution of media in the digital AI era, ensuring the appropriateness, quality, independence, and competitiveness of news products. However, it's important to note that the phenomenon of fake news in politics is not a new development. Above and beyond any technically advanced solution, the most effective remedy for combating fake news lies in the enhancement of critical thinking (Van Deursen & Van Dijk, 2009). Cultivating such thinking is essential for nurturing a more knowledgeable citizenry.

AI expert systems play a pivotal role in rebuilding trust in media and political institutions by supporting the aspiration that information presented to the public is impartial and authentic. Equally important is the prospect of instilling critical reading skills among citizens. For those ensnared in the post-truth dynamics of the digital realm, it becomes imperative to offer pathways that ensure the delivery of factual and investigative journalism content. To uphold a free and democratic society, citizens must leverage AI tools that empower them to critically assess and evaluate information.

Conclusion

AI has become a paramount focus in global policymaking, driven by the pursuit of innovation and growth. Unfortunately, there's a lack of emphasis on fostering public discussion and educating citizens, even at the primary school level, about how AI adoption aligns with democratic values. The crucial factor for the success of AI strategies is rebuilding public trust in both AI and democracy. However, these policy developments must be analyzed within their social contexts and power structures. In this analysis, we explore AI's risks to electoral integrity and formal national AI strategies. National AI Strategy reports serve as policy blueprints, setting missions, targets, and deadlines. Countries engage in a global AI race, recognizing that AI adoption will shape their future economic and geopolitical standing. However, transplanting national AI policies as a universal recipe for success overlooks the need for contextual considerations. Issues like improving the lives of elderly citizens or addressing precarious employment require a nuanced understanding of political, cultural, and path-dependent factors.

Examining the UK National AI Strategy reveals a celebration of technological progress linked with flexibility and a limited state role, distinct from Germany and Nordic countries (National AI Strategy, 2021). This emphasis on flexibility has long been considered a source of national advantage in the United Kingdom. The government's approach to Big Tech and data, exemplified by more flexible General Data Protection Regulation (GDPR) rules and warnings instead of fines, reflects this stance. However, this model is marked by high regional inequality, a continuation of the United Kingdom's historical economic pattern. In the context of AI's challenges to democratic institutions, especially in national elections, where citizens express their political will, AI disrupts traditional processes. AI-powered tools, while offering advantages, also introduce vulnerabilities. They facilitate the spread of misinformation, undermining the integrity of elections and eroding trust in democratic institutions. Trust is fundamental for a functioning democracy, and when citizens doubt the authenticity of elections, democracy itself is at risk. To address these challenges, a comprehensive National AI Strategy is essential. This strategy should include educational initiatives to enhance digital literacy, empower citizens to critically evaluate information, and strengthen laws and regulations to counter AI-driven disinformation. Creating an ecosystem for understanding AI's impact on organizations and society is crucial for navigating the transformative era ahead.

Case Study: A Case Study on National Strategies and Electoral Integrity

In recent years, the proliferation of AI technologies has sparked widespread debate and scrutiny regarding its implications for society and democracy. AI's transformative potential has led many nations to develop national strategies to harness its benefits and mitigate the relevant risks. These strategies often outline priorities, investments, and policies related to AI development. Additionally, concerns have arisen regarding AI's influence on electoral processes, including the spread of misinformation and threats to electoral integrity. For instance, in the United Kingdom (UK), the government launched its National AI Strategy in response to the growing importance of AI in various sectors. The strategy aims to position the United Kingdom as a global leader in AI innovation while ensuring responsible and ethical AI deployment. However, the development and implementation of the strategy reflect political priorities and trade-offs. For example, funding allocation and regulatory frameworks may be influenced by political considerations, shaping the trajectory of AI development in the country.

Particularly since the last few years, the emergence of AI-powered tools has raised concerns about their potential impact on electoral processes and democratic norms. The spread of misinformation, manipulate public opinion, and undermine trust in the electoral system such as the riots at the US capitol in January 2021. Governments worldwide are struggling with the challenge of safeguarding electoral integrity in the face of AI-driven threats. Measures such as increased transparency, regulation of political advertising, and cybersecurity enhancements are being considered and implemented to mitigate these risks.

Case Study Questions

(1) How do national AI strategies reflect the political priorities and trade-offs of a country?
(2) What are some specific challenges faced in safeguarding electoral integrity in the age of AI, and how can political will and action address these challenges?
(3) In what ways can policymakers, stakeholders, and civil society collaborate to ensure informed dialogue and decision-making regarding the ethical, social, and political implications of AI deployment and governance?

Key Terms and Definitions

Fake news: Fake news refers to deliberately fabricated or misleading information presented as legitimate news or factual reporting.
Misinformation: Misinformation refers to false or inaccurate information that is spread unintentionally or without malicious intent.
Electoral integrity: Electoral integrity refers to the adherence to democratic principles, fairness, and transparency in electoral processes, ensuring that elections are free, fair, and credible.

References

Adorno, T. (2001). *The culture industry: Selected essays on mass culture*. Routledge.
Ahmad, T., Aliaga Lazarte, E. A., & Mirjalili, S. (2022). A Systematic literature review on fake news in the COVID-19 Pandemic: Can AI propose a solution? *Applied Sciences, 12*(24), 12727.

Aoki, N. (2020). An experimental study of public trust in AI chatbots in the public sector. *Government Information Quarterly*, *37*(4), 101490.

Artificial Intelligence Sector Study. (2022). https://assets.publishing.service.gov.uk/media/641d71e732a8e0000cfa9389/artifical_intelligence_sector_study.pdf

Bakir, V., & McStay, A. (2018). Fake news and the economy of emotions. *Digital Journalism*, *6*(2), 154–175.

Ball, J. (2017). *Post-truth: How bullshit conquered the world*. Biteback Publishing.

Barber, M. (2015). *How to run a government: So that citizens benefit and taxpayers don't go crazy*. Penguin.

Bareis, J., & Katzenbach, C. (2022). Talking AI into being: The narratives and imaginaries of national AI strategies and their performative politics. *Science, Technology & Human Values*, *47*(5), 855–881.

Bennett, W. L., & Livingston, S. (2018). The disinformation order: Disruptive communication and the decline of democratic institutions. *European Journal of Communication*, *33*(2), 122–139.

Boschma, R., & Frenken, K. (2011). The emerging empirics of evolutionary economic geography. *Journal of Economic Geography*, *11*(2), 295–307.

Boudette, N. E., Metz, C., & Ewing, J. (2022). Tesla autopilot and other driver-assist systems linked to hundreds of crashes. *The New York Times*. https://www.nytimes.com/2022/06/15/business/self-driving-car-nhtsa-crash-data.html

Bourdieu, P. (1991). *Language and symbolic power*. Polity Press.

Bradford, A. (2023). *Digital empires: The global battle to regulate technology*. Oxford University Press.

Brattberg, E., Rugova, V., & Csernatoni, R. (2020). *Europe and AI: Leading, lagging behind, or carving its own way?* (Vol. 9). Carnegie Endowment for International Peace.

Briggs, J., & Kodnani, D. (2023). The potentially large effects of artificial intelligence on economic growth. *Global Economics Analyst*. Goldman Sachs.

Bucy, E. P., & Newhagen, J. E. (2019). Fake news finds an audience. *Journalism and Truth in an Age of Social Media*, 201–222.

Buhmann, A., & Fieseler, C. (2023). Deep learning meets deep democracy: Deliberative governance and responsible innovation in artificial intelligence. *Business Ethics Quarterly*, *33*(1), 146–179.

Carey, J. (1989). *Communication as culture*. Unwin Hyman.

Castells, M. (2009). *Communication power*. Oxford University Press.

Chomsky. (1998). *The common good*. Odonian Press.

Department for Science, Innovation, and Technology. (2023, March 29). *A pro-innovation approach to AI regulation*. https://www.gov.uk/government/publications/ai-regulation-a-pro-innovation-approach/white-paper;Department for Science

Duffy, S., Bruce, K., & Moroko, L. (2020). Customer orientation: Its surprising origins, tumultuous development and place in the future of marketing thought and practice. *Australasian Marketing Journal*, *28*(4), 181–188.

Dutton, T. (2018). An overview of national AI strategies. *Politics + AI*, 28.

Egelhofer, J. L., & Lecheler, S. (2019). Fake news as a two-dimensional phenomenon: A framework and research agenda. *Annals of the International Communication Association*, *43*(2), 97–116.

Foffano, F., Scantamburlo, T., Cortés, A., & Bissolo, C. (2020). *European Strategy on AI: Are we truly fostering social good?* arXiv preprint arXiv:2011.12863.

Forde, C., Alberti, G., Dolezalova, M., Bessa, I., Cutter, J., Ciupijus, Z., Morganti, E., & Graham, G. (2023). Migration in post-Brexit UK: Examining employer strategies and assessing their consequences for workers. In paper presented at the *Industrial Relations Conference in Europe*. https://www.dur.ac.uk/business/media/durham-university-business-school/about-us/departments/management-and-marketing/IREC2023-18-20-09-23.pdf

Galloway, S. (2018). *The Four: The Hidden DNA of Amazon, Apple, Facebook, and Google*. Random House Large Print.

Graves, L., & Wells, C. (2019). From information availability to factual account-ability. *Journalism and Truth in an Age of Social Media*, 39–57.

He, J., Baxter, S. L., Xu, J., Xu, J., Zhou, X., & Zhang, K. (2019). The practical implementation of artificial intelligence technologies in medicine. *Nature Medicine*, *25*(1), 30–36.

Helberger, N., Araujo, T., & de Vreese, C. H. (2020). Who is the fairest of them all? Public attitudes and expectations regarding automated decision-making. *Computer Law & Security Report*, *39*, 105456.

Helbing, D. (2019). *Societal, economic, ethical and legal challenges of the digital revolution: From big data to deep learning, artificial intelligence, and manipulative technologies* (pp. 47–72). Springer International Publishing.

Ikkatai, Y., Hartwig, T., Takanashi, N., & Yokoyama, H. M. (2023). Segmentation of ethics, legal, and social issues (ELSI) related to AI in Japan, the United States, and Germany. *AI and Ethics*, *3*(3), 827–843.

Jasanoff, S., & Kim, S. H. (2009). Containing the atom: Sociotechnical imaginaries and nuclear power in the United States and South Korea. *Minerva*, *47*, 119–146.

Katyal, S. K. (2019). Private accountability in the age of artificial intelligence. *UCLA Law Review*, *66*, 54.

Krause, N. M., Wirz, C. D., Scheufele, D. A., & Xenos, M. A. (2019). Fake news: A new obsession with an old phenomenon? In J. Katz & K. K. Mays (Eds.), *Journalism and truth in an age of social media* (pp. 58–78). Oxford University Press.

Labory, S., & Bianchi, P. (2021). Regional industrial policy in times of big disruption: Building dynamic capabilities in regions. *Regional Studies*, *55*(10–11), 1829–1838.

Lazer, D. M. J., Baum, M. A., Benkler, Y., Berinsky, A. J., Greenhill, K. M., Menczer, F., Metzger, M. J., Nyhan, B., Pennycook, G., Rothschild, D., Schudson, M., Sloman, S. A., Sunstein, C. R., Thorson, E. A., Watts, D. J., & Zittrain, J. L. (2018). The science of fake news. *Science*, *359*(6380), 1094–1096.

Leslie, D. (2023). The ethics of computational social science. In *Handbook of computational social science for policy* (pp. 57–104). Springer International Publishing.

Levinson, P. (2017). *Fake news in real context*. Connected Editions. Incorporated.

Li, J., & Huang, J. S. (2020). Dimensions of artificial intelligence anxiety based on the integrated fear acquisition theory. *Technology in Society*, *63*, 101410.

Mazzoleni, O., & Voerman, G. (2017). Memberless parties: Beyond the business-firm party model? *Party Politics*, *23*(6), 783–792.

Mazzucato, M. (2018). *The value of everything: Making and taking in the global economy*. Hachette.

Miliband, R. (1969). *The state in capitalist society*. Camelot Press.

Muppasani, B., Pallagani, V., Lakkaraju, K., Lei, S., Srivastava, B., Robertson, B., Hickerson, A., & Narayanan, V. (2023). On safe and useable chatbots for promoting voter participation. *AI Magazine*, *44*(3), 240–247. https://doi.org/10.1002/aaai.12109

Nadarzynski, T., Miles, O., Cowie, A., & Ridge, D. (2019). Acceptability of artificial intelligence (AI)-led chatbot services in healthcare: A mixed-methods study. *Digital health*, *5*, https://doi.org/10.1177/2055207619871808

National AI Strategy. (2021). https://assets.publishing.service.gov.uk/media/614db4d1e90e077a2cbdf3c4/National_AI_Strategy_-_PDF_version.pdf

Office for Artificial Intelligence. National AI Strategy. (2021). https://assets.publishing.service.gov.uk/government/uploads/system/uploads/attachment_data/file/1020402/National_AI_Strategy_-_PDF_version.pdf

Rahwan, I., Cebrian, M., Obradovich, N., Bongard, J., Bonnefon, J. -F., Breazeal, C., Crandall, J. W., Christakis, N. A., Couzin, I. D., Jackson, M. O., Jennings, N. R., Kamar, E., Kloumann, I. M., Larochelle, H., Lazer, D., McElreath, R., Mislove, A., Parkes, D. C., Pentland, A. S., Wellman, M. (2019). Machine behaviour. *Nature*, *568*(7753), 477–486. https://doi.org/10.1038/s41586-019-1138-y

Robinson, S. C. (2020). Trust, transparency, and openness: How inclusion of cultural values shapes Nordic national public policy strategies for artificial intelligence (AI). *Technology in Society*, *63*, 101421.

Sheikh, S. (Ed.). (2020). *Understanding the role of artificial intelligence and its future social impact*. IGI Global.

Shin, D., Kee, K. F., & Shin, E. Y. (2022). Algorithm awareness: Why user awareness is critical for personal privacy in the adoption of algorithmic platforms? *International Journal of Information Management*, *65*, 102494.

Stephanidis, C., Salvendy, G., Antona, M., Chen, J. Y. C., Dong, J., Duffy, V. G., Fang, X., Fidopiastis, C., Fragomeni, G., Fu, L. P., Guo, Y., Harris, D., Ioannou, A., Jeong, K. A., Konomi, S., Krömker, H., Kurosu, M., Lewis, J. R., Marcus, A., …, Zhou, J. (2019). Seven HCI grand challenges. *International Journal of Human-Computer Interaction*, *35*(14), 1229–1269. https://doi.org/10.1080/10447318.2019.1619259

The UK Leads Europe and Ranks Third Globally in Artificial Intelligence. (2021). https://www.businesswire.com/news/home/20211215005874/en/The-UK-Leads-Europe-and-Ranks-Third-Globally-in-Artificial-Intelligence

Van Deursen, A. J., & Van Dijk, J. A. (2009). Improving digital skills for the use of online public information and services. *Government Information Quarterly*, *26*(2), 333–340.

Verschraegen, G., Vandermoere, F., Braeckmans, L., & Segaert, B. (Eds.). (2017). *Imagined futures in science, technology and society* (1st ed.). Routledge. https://doi.org/10.4324/9781315440842

World Economic Forum. (2024). *The big election year: How to protect democracy in the era of AI*. https://www.weforum.org/agenda/2024/01/ai-democracy-election-year-2024-disinformation-misinformation/

Zhan, E. S., Molina, M. D., Rheu, M., & Peng, W. (2023). What is there to fear? Understanding multi-dimensional fear of AI from a technological affordance perspective. *International Journal of Human-Computer Interaction*, 1–18.

Zuboff, S. (2019). *Age of surveillance capitalism: The fight for a human future at the new frontier of power*. Public Affairs.

Chapter 15

How do Social Trust and Self-Efficacy Drive Collaborative Consumption? A Case of TaskRabbit[1]

Ming-yao Jen, Dorothy Yen and Kevin Lu

Brunel University London, UK

Abstract

This research investigates the role of trust and social capital in shaping consumer behaviour in collaborative consumption (CC) platforms. By integrating system quality, social referral and shared goals, this study aims to develop a comprehensive framework that explains how these factors influence social trust, self-efficacy and ultimately drive consumers' intention to adopt CC.

Keywords: Collaborative consumption (CC); social trust; self-efficacy; labour market; purchase intention

Key Points

- This study aims to explore the extent to which social trust influences individuals' intention to adopt collaborative consumption and the role of self-efficacy in facilitating the interactions.
- Drawing on social capital literature and social cognitive theory, a framework is developed to identify the antecedents of social trust and self-efficacy in collaborative consumption purchase intention.
- The analysis reveals that social trust, self-efficacy, shared goals, system quality and social referrals significantly impact purchase intention, emphasising the

[1]This chapter has been developed using parts of the thesis, Ming-yao (2021) Investigating factors affecting purchase intention in collaborative consumption: the antecedents of social trust and self-efficacy. Brunel University, London.

Business Strategies and Ethical Challenges in the Digital Ecosystem, 333–356
doi:10.1108/978-1-80455-069-420241015

importance of these factors in understanding and promoting collaborative consumption adoption.

Introduction

Collaborative consumption (CC) has become a prevalent form of exchange between individuals, as evidenced by a rapid 60% growth in 2017 (Ozcan et al., 2017). With 23% of the UK population actively using such services (Ozcan et al., 2017), CC is expected to be worth over £140 billion by 2025 (PwC, 2015). Moreover, CC has posed competitive threats to traditional incumbents (Eckhardt et al., 2019), ranging from transportation (e.g. Uber), lodging (e.g. Airbnb), financial services (e.g. Funding Circle), food services (e.g. Deliveroo) and the labour market (e.g. TaskRabbit). CC can be defined as 'a scalable socio-economic system that employs technology-enabled platforms to provide consumers with temporary access to tangible and intangible resources that may be crowdsourced' (Eckhardt et al., 2019, p. 7). CC can be traced throughout human history (Felson & Spaeth, 1978) as offering people ways to meet or for community members to help each other (Akbar & Hoffmann, 2022; Bardhi & Eckhardt, 2012). By providing social value, the development of CC helps to foster a sense of community, as it increases interpersonal interactions (Belk, 2007; Lee et al., 2021; Tóth et al., 2022). CC also helps reduce resource waste by encouraging consumers to exchange and reuse any unwanted or underutilised assets (Benoit et al., 2017), thus responding to calls for sustainable living through resource sharing and efficiency (Leismann et al., 2013). These benefits have attracted significant attention from various research communities, including information systems, marketing, economics and psychology, in discussing why and how the sellers and the platform owners could develop alternative business strategies that would help them increase their popularity (Celata et al., 2017; Lamberton & Rose, 2012; Tripp et al., 2022).

However, the existence of CC is often situated within the grey regulatory area, where the sellers or service providers in CC are random individuals rather than professionals (Sundararajan, 2016; Venkateswaran et al., 2021). For example, the gardener on TaskRabbit may be someone who is proficient in his/her own garden rather than a professionally trained gardener. Hence, CC transactions involve co-presence. Growing concern over the balance between trust and risk in the intention of using CC has emerged (Ert et al., 2016; Ter Huurne et al., 2017; Yao et al., 2022; Zhai et al., 2021). Trust in CC has been viewed as being embedded within its digital reputation system (Hamari & Koivisto, 2015; Tóth et al., 2022) and the users' digital profiles (Ert et al., 2016). Nevertheless, the extant literature on CC has not fully addressed the issues of lack of trust among the platform users, and nor have the studies attempted to understand the antecedents that drive trust. Since the factors that influence individuals' intention to adopt CC include perceived social value (Nadeem et al., 2020; Zhang et al., 2018) and a sense of community (Celata et al., 2017; Eckhardt et al., 2019), this study aims to explore to what extent trust affects people's intention to adopt CC.

Furthering the vital role of social trust, another relevant factor is self-efficacy, which helps individuals to form the belief that they are capable of completing the required tasks (Bandura, 2001). In the context of ridesharing, self-efficacy has been identified as a fundamental factor that drives the users' perceptions of value and their purchase intention (Zhu et al., 2017). This is because CC can only be facilitated when consumers trust that they are capable of navigating the CC platform and of completing the required tasks, such as proceeding with and subsequently evaluating the exchanges.

To explore how trust affects CC adoption, we draw on social capital literature (Nahapiet & Ghoshal, 1998) and social cognitive theory (Bandura, 1986) to develop a framework to identify the antecedents of social trust and self-efficacy in individuals' purchase intention on a CC platform. We tackle these unaddressed yet important factors in this chapter by addressing CC as a virtual community (Belk, 2007). While most of the studies on CC focus on ridesharing or lodging services (Eckhardt et al., 2019), our study focuses on the exchange in the labour market. Compared to lodgings (e.g. Airbnb) and transportation services (e.g. Uber), the labour market has platforms for the exchange of individuals' skills and time. In the example of TaskRabbit, the platform connects buyers to service providers and facilitates the exchange of everyday tasks, such as cleaning, moving heavy goods, delivering items and handyman work. Focusing on the United Kingdom and the relatively new market that TaskRabbit established in 2018, we conducted an online quantitative survey, with data collected from 373 TaskRabbit users. By empirically testing how social trust and self-efficacy drive CC purchase intention, this study sheds new light on the understanding of CC.

Main Focus of the Chapter

CC has been acknowledged as a type of exchange between peers and is described as being 'as old as humankind' by Belk (2014). CC is defined as an 'activity whereby a platform provider links a consumer that aims to temporarily utilise assets with a peer service provider, who grants access to these assets and with this delivers the core service' (Benoit et al., 2017, p. 220). As such, CC-related firms operate through the presence of a triadic framework, thereby making it essential that both consumers and sellers (or service providers) stay connected with the platform to transact with each other. CC's triadic model differs from the traditional business model in the following four dimensions: (1) crowd-based networks, (2) reduced transaction costs, (3) leveraging the use of information and communications technology (ICT) and (4) blurring the lines between professionalism and personalised service (Sundararajan, 2016).

Firstly, the crowd-based networks imply that each entity recognises the benefits generated from using the CC platforms. For example, customers receive a reduced price for services and goods that they want, while sellers (or service providers) obtain the monetary value from staying on the platform and delivering services by sharing their belongings or skills. Secondly, CC platforms that provide diversity in products and services are also likely to reduce transaction costs, such as the costs of contract negotiation. Thirdly, CC firms effectively use ICT to connect individuals together (Benoit et al., 2017). For instance, using matchmaking technology, Uber connects drivers and customers by providing them with the function of utilising drivers' own vehicles to serve customers who need a taxi service. Finally, the services and goods in CC are often supplied by individuals rather than professionals, which is often reflected as 'personalised service' (Sundararajan, 2016). Unlike in traditional rental services, where insurance companies can support damage to the rental goods, sharing in CC encompasses an obligation of care and responsibility from both sides of the service (Belk, 2007). For example, Uber drivers use their vehicles as taxis; thus, they run the risk that accidents may damage the vehicle.

Increasing CC purchase intention enhances high-impact capital that creates new opportunities for individuals, from resources and skills to time and economic value (Sundararajan, 2016). Möhlmann (2015) explored the determinants of using CC by observing the perceived benefits from participating on CC platforms, including cost-saving, community belonging and environmental impact. The increased number of individuals purchasing via CC also helps society to establish social capital by encouraging togetherness as a community (Belk, 2014; Chiu et al., 2006; Sundararajan, 2016; Tóth et al., 2022) and the broader set of individuals using CC can lead to a positive impact on the environment (Venkateswaran et al., 2021). For instance, fewer cars or goods are required, leading to resource sharing and efficiency (Leismann et al., 2013).

However, as the shared goods and services are booked via the internet, consumers are often unable to evaluate and inspect them beforehand. Hence, the fundamental element of CC involves interacting with strangers without the element of past behaviour and future interactions (Celata et al., 2017); thus, participating in CC means that both the customers and the sellers need to accept and embrace the inherent risk. This is heightened by the lack of rules or regulations in CC (Hartl et al., 2016; Venkateswaran et al., 2021); often, platform owners are not liable for the shared assets, the customers or the sellers (Sundararajan, 2016). Nevertheless, the existing literature tends to focus on promoting the benefits of CC and exploring how these benefits drive purchase intention of CC, but there is little discussion of the tension between trust and risk (Butschek et al., 2022; Ert et al., 2016; Ter Huurne et al., 2017). Since the triadic nature of CC is open and fully voluntary, hence, the users are typically strangers; this tension highlights the extent to which a particular CC firm would encounter trust-related challenges while encouraging purchase intention (Milanova & Maas, 2017; Venkateswaran et al., 2021; Yao et al., 2022).

To address this tension between risk and trust, we have developed eight hypotheses derived from the social capital perspective. Our research framework, which postulates that individuals' perception of social trust and self-efficacy can help address the trust–risk balance, thus increasing individuals' intention to purchase via CC. Moreover, the framework comprises four latent variables (individuals' perception of network stability, system quality, social referral and shared goals) to model individuals' antecedents of social trust and self-efficacy.

Social Trust

Social trust refers to the expectation that arises within a network of regular, trustworthy and cooperative interactions (Barber, 1983; Fukuyama, 1996; Nahapiet & Ghoshal, 1998). Social trust differs from generalised and particularised trust, as it is categorised as the trust in a community (Fukuyama, 1996), for example trust in society and trust in strangers. In this research context, social trust refers to a CC platform user's trust in others on the CC platform (Cha & Lee, 2022), believing that as a collective entity, they are trustworthy and reliable and are not engaging in opportunistic behaviour. Social trust serves as the foundation of collective behaviours that create productive cooperation and sustain peaceful and stable social relations (Newton, 2001).

Within the CC literature, trust has been referred to as one's social capital (Cha & Lee, 2022; Sundararajan, 2016; Tóth et al., 2022), trust in people (Belk, 2007) and trusting belief in a community (Ter Huurne et al., 2017; Tschang, 2021). However, most of the extended work is generally normative and does not explore trust in a collective entity. For example, Ert et al. (2016) found that when using Airbnb, hosts with profile photos are perceived as more trustworthy and so can charge higher prices than hosts without profile photos. In the context of car sharing, Bardhi and Eckhardt (2012) also discussed how customers like to remain anonymous to eliminate any possible negative effects in the future, while Hartl and Hofmann (2021) found that a badge system (e.g., identity check and certification) can be used as trust cues to increase individual driver's trust rating. Nevertheless, all of these studies tend to focus on how to increase trust in individual CC users, rather than increasing individual users' social trust in CC. Also, most studies in the domain have aimed to investigate the impact of two particular CC areas: peer-to-peer accommodation (Abdar & Yen, 2020; Ert et al., 2016) and peer-to-peer transportation (Bardhi & Eckhardt, 2012; Möhlmann, 2015). The extant literature has not discussed how social trust works in the peer-to-peer labour market.

Celata et al. (2017) posited three concepts of generalised reciprocity mechanisms in CC: sharing activities, resources and trust. Considering the triad of CC comprised of community-based initiatives, when users experience higher social trust towards other users in the same community and believe that together they can provide and sustain the exchange model as promised by the CC platform, they are more likely to engage in CC initiatives. Therefore, we postulate that individuals with higher social trust towards others on the CC platform are more likely to purchase via CC in the future:

> *H1.* A user's social trust towards others on a CC platform will increase the user's intention to purchase.

Self-Efficacy

Self-efficacy is defined as an individual's judgements of his/her own capabilities to perform a behaviour (Bandura, 1986), which indicates the degree of trust that one places on one's ability. Research focusing on sharing behaviour in virtual communities has established that perceived self-efficacy shapes individuals' belief in organising and executing actions (Hsu & Chiu, 2004), reflecting on the individual's trust in their own capability in participating on a CC platform and performing the required tasks effectively. Individuals with high self-efficacy are more likely to exercise sharing than those individuals with low self-efficacy (Tamjidyamcholo et al., 2013). In the context of ridesharing applications, Eckhardt et al. (2019) found that self-efficacy is regarded as an individual's capability in understanding the use of CC platforms and how CC could benefit them in their daily life, such as cost-saving.

Since one's self-efficacy in a particular technology serves as an anchor for the development of technology adoption (Compeau et al., 1999), we argue that when individuals perceive themselves as having the capability of understanding and performing the required tasks on a CC platform, these individuals are more likely to purchase via CC. Moreover, Yi and Hwang (2003) found that individuals' acceptance of new computer technology is affected by their perceived self-efficacy, and the higher an individual's score on self-efficacy, the higher their intention to use the new computer technology. Taken together, we, hypothesis as follows:

> *H2*. A user's (CC platform) self-efficacy will increase the user's intention to purchase.

Network Stability

Network stability is related to how frequently change of membership occurs in a network (Inkpen & Tsang, 2005). Networks regarded as highly stable, would not have a lot of users dropping out in one go and keep a steady growth in the number of registered members. In contrast, an unstable network may prevent the development of an eco-balanced CC triad. Sundararajan (2016) suggested that the connection among the members is the key facet that enables the exchange to occur, which consequently facilitates the trust among network members, leading to a more eco-balanced triadic model. In other words, as CC relies on the convergence of services and goods that are provided by individuals, a lack of service providers or a lack of consumers would be intolerable for the triadic model. For example, if low service availability is perceived, it is likely to reduce individuals' trust in the platform's ability to deliver the proclaimed promise or values.

Moreover, network stability contributes to individuals' evaluation of the overall value of using CC (Eckhardt et al., 2019). Gawer and Cusumano (2014) found that the network effect serves as the foundation of trust, especially for newcomers: the larger the size of a network, the higher the resulting number of users using the platform and the more positive the users' trust toward the platform. Inkpen and Tsang (2005) found that networks having a stable pool of members lead to long-lasting cooperative behaviour within organisations. While CC represents an organic and alternative format of human organisation, we argue that network stability plays an important role in serving an individual's social trust. Therefore, we propose the following hypothesis:

H3. A CC platform's network stability will increase a user's social trust towards the CC platform.

System Quality

Social capital theory emphasises the importance of well-structured networks and the resources embedded within them. System quality refers to the extent to which connectivity in a network is well structured and configured by the platform owners (Zhou, 2012). System quality has been viewed as a crucial factor in the development of a successful platform (Lei, 2021), as it facilitates and enhances the perception of overall connectivity among the members (Williams, 2006). Compared to traditional online business platforms, the premise of CC platforms is that they should increase the access speed, navigation and ease-of-use for both buyers and sellers, and simultaneously process the matching system to connect the users who are available online. Research has shown that CC platforms with poor system quality are likely to experience very limited growth (Zhang et al., 2018). From the social networking perspective, when individuals feel excluded from networks they desire to join, their perception of social trust is likely to decrease (Coleman, 1988; Fukuyama, 1996; Williams, 2006). For example, If a CC platform's system quality is lacking, leading to difficulties in accessing resources or services, users may perceive the platform as poorly structured and become less trusting of its capabilities if consumers cannot reach the sellers on the platform, they may perceive that the platform is poorly structured and that it is difficult to access the resources or services from the network. We, therefore, propose the following hypothesis:

H4. A CC platform's system quality will increase the user's social trust towards the CC platform.

Social Referral

Social referral refers to channels that keep the flow of information within the network or outside of the network, and it derives from social ties (Nahapiet & Ghoshal, 1998). Consumers frequently share information or knowledge actively with others in their network (Inkpen & Tsang, 2005). These pieces of information are often considered valuable because they help to reduce the search time and are often relevant to the members' topics of interest, especially if they are shared by family or friends (Nahapiet & Ghoshal, 1998). Moreover, Van Den Bulte et al. (2018) found that individuals' relationships with a firm will be strengthened when their acquaintance, family member or friend is also one of the firm's customers because such a social connection increases an individual's social trust and social value in and their bond with the firm (Huang et al., 2022). Therefore, we argue that social referral helps reduce the risk associated with signing up to and participating in a new CC platform with the problems of anonymity and grey regulations. As such, social referral may help improve a user's social trust towards a CC network. Following the same argument, we therefore propose:

H5. Social referral will increase a user's social trust towards the CC platform.

Furthermore, individuals' perception of self-efficacy is sporadic – an individual's decision depends on their physical and social environment (Tamjidyamcholo et al., 2013). This means that the perception of self-efficacy is shaped by individuals' social environment over time (Bandura, 1997). Being socially recognised by close others as having the capacity to engage with and achieve the tasks required for participating on a CC platform increases one's perceived self-efficacy regarding that CC platform. Using this rationale, we argue that when individuals are referred to participate on a CC platform by their friend or family member, they are more likely to regard themselves as having the capability to join in and become part of the community. This is because the invites from acquaintances and friends signal the desired social approval and recognition to consumers, which contribute to the evaluation of ones' own self-efficacy in navigating the same network (Arnould & Rose, 2016). Therefore, we propose:

H6. Social referral will increase a user's self-efficacy towards the CC platform.

Shared Goals

Shared goals refer to the 'collective goals and aspirations of the members of a cooperative network' (Tsai & Ghoshal, 1998, p. 157). It has been recognised as a set of practices that motivate cooperative behaviours (Inkpen & Tsang, 2005). When network members have the same vision regarding how they should work together, shared goals can promote the efficiency of communication and mutual understanding among the members, thus encouraging the sharing of ideas and resources within the network (Chow & Chan, 2008; Nahapiet & Ghoshal, 1998; Tsai & Ghoshal, 1998).

Studies have shown that having common goals signifies that network members have shared values in the cooperative process. For instance, Inkpen and Tsang (2005) found that shared goals among the employees reflect the firm's intellectual capital, which leads to better strategic alliances within the organisation. Zhang (2020) also revealed that having shared goals is an inclusive force in building and maintaining the collaborative behaviour in the networks. For instance, with the aim of facilitating a fair exchange, Airbnb requires all its users to respect each other's house rules, and if the customers damage the rented property, the service fee may not be returned and the profile may also receive a bad review. This explains why Tussyadiah (2016) found that both sellers and customers perceive a stronger sense of community and social benefits after using CC for accommodation sharing. Acknowledging the common goals (e.g. sharing fairly) may increase members' social trust towards the CC platform at the collective level. We therefore propose:

H7. Shared goals will increase a user's social trust in the CC platform.

Moreover, sharing common goals among the users means that the individuals are more likely to understand the tasks required and improve one's self-efficacy so that he or she can better achieve the common goal (Bandura, 1997). Individuals that score highly on shared goals tend to have a better understanding of the potential values resulting from collaborating with their peers. Theoretically, this will promote self-efficacy and will help maintain long-term relationships (Ventura et al., 2015). For example, when a CC platform user agrees with the platform's common goals (e.g. sharing fairly), this person is more likely to improve their self-efficacy so that he or she can participate on the CC platform to share fairly. Thus, we postulate:

H8. Shared goals will increase the user's self-efficacy towards the CC platform.

Analysis and Findings

Data analysis in this study was based on a PLS-SEM software called SmartPLS 3.0 to contemporaneously assess the measurement instrument and the conceptual model. This approach is considered appropriate as it can deliver valid results for studies that contain relatively complex models with small sample sizes (Chin, 1998). In addition, PLS-SEM has been identified as an effective tool for management-related studies that have a predictive research scope (Chin, 1998; Hair et al., 2021; Ringle et al., 2012).

Measurement Model

Following the steps of PLS-SEM recommended by Hair et al. (2021), the first step in PLS is to examine the convergent validity of the constructs by assessing the average variance extracted (AVE). The values of AVE should be larger than the generally recognised 0.5 for all constructs (Fornell & Larcker, 1981). Furthermore, following Werts et al. (1973), internal consistency should be assessed by using the composite reliability (CR) when the research model involves theoretical constructs. Acceptable values of CR should exceed 0.7 (Fornell & Larcker, 1981). All the AVE and CR values met the recommended threshold, indicating the absence of measurement error. To evaluate discriminant validity, two traditional assessments were evaluated: the first criterion, the cross-loadings criterion, was concerned with the indicator level, in which the loadings of the measures should be higher than their loadings on all other latent variables (Hair et al., 2021). As demonstrated in Table 15.1, the items for each construct are adequately measured (Chin, 1998).

Table 15.1. Cross Loading Criterion for the Results of the Discriminant Validity.

Items	Purchase Intention	Social Trust	Self-Efficacy	Network Stability	System Quality	Social Referral	Shared Goals
IA1	**0.876**	0.449	0.493	0.441	0.409	0.450	0.390
IA2	**0.869**	0.441	0.504	0.446	0.441	0.473	0.356
IA3	**0.888**	0.416	0.496	0.455	0.436	0.476	0.366
IA4	**0.880**	0.377	0.498	0.481	0.425	0.452	0.370
ST1	0.430	**0.762**	0.406	0.455	0.477	0.466	0.514
ST2	0.357	**0.818**	0.317	0.389	0.424	0.317	0.551
ST3	0.406	**0.789**	0.330	0.478	0.548	0.444	0.462
ST4	0.322	**0.807**	0.228	0.350	0.393	0.299	0.580
SE1	0.515	0.342	**0.820**	0.371	0.400	0.366	0.310
SE2	0.423	0.340	**0.836**	0.406	0.457	0.445	0.235
SE3	0.416	0.338	**0.820**	0.394	0.452	0.397	0.338
SE4	0.487	0.305	**0.783**	0.373	0.463	0.364	0.302
NS1	0.507	0.502	0.415	**0.862**	0.685	0.524	0.451
NS2	0.419	0.479	0.364	**0.856**	0.613	0.448	0.411
NS3	0.413	0.390	0.438	**0.830**	0.702	0.493	0.386
NS4	0.393	0.394	0.384	**0.815**	0.556	0.469	0.359
SQ1	0.386	0.473	0.397	0.567	**0.793**	0.400	0.400
SQ2	0.300	0.497	0.408	0.728	**0.845**	0.518	0.437
SQ3	0.326	0.466	0.487	0.603	**0.828**	0.511	0.413
SQ4	0.369	0.493	0.507	0.612	**0.843**	0.469	0.390
SR1	0.463	0.440	0.400	0.516	0.479	**0.866**	0.391
SR2	0.489	0.347	0.459	0.530	0.518	**0.888**	0.293
SR3	0.446	0.387	0.409	0.483	0.496	**0.856**	0.306
SR4	0.415	0.485	0.388	0.446	0.481	**0.827**	0.424
SG1	0.386	0.544	0.397	0.469	0.470	0.426	**0.815**
SG2	0.300	0.595	0.408	0.344	0.367	0.300	**0.831**
SG3	0.326	0.499	0.487	0.380	0.396	0.346	**0.811**
SG4	0.369	0.528	0.507	0.381	0.391	0.284	**0.821**

For the second criterion, Fornell and Larcker (1981) suggested using the comparison between the AVE and the square root of correlation values among the latent variables. The AVEs should be greater than the squared correlation estimates. Table 15.2 shows that the square root of AVE of each construct is

Table 15.2. Fornell and Larcker (1981) Criterion for the Results of Discriminant Validity.

Constructs	Purchase Intention	Network Stability	Self-Efficacy	Shared Goals	Social Referral	Social Trust	System Quality
Purchase Intention	**0.878**						
Network Stability	0.519	**0.841**					
Self-efficacy	0.567	0.474	**0.815**				
Shared goals	0.422	0.481	0.364	**0.819**			
Social referral	0.527	0.574	0.482	0.414	**0.860**		
Social trust	0.480	0.530	0.407	0.662	0.485	**0.794**	
System quality	0.487	0.760	0.543	0.496	0.574	0.583	**0.827**

notably greater than the correlations of all the other constructs. An additional evaluation for convergent and discriminant validity tests is to examine the outer loadings of each indicator. Each indicator should load higher than 0.4, with values close to 0.7 indicating adequate discriminant and convert validity (Hulland, 1999). In all cases, the tests confirmed the satisfactory discriminant and convergent validity.

Structural Model

The theoretical model and the hypotheses were analysed using 5,000 iterations of the bootstrapping technique (Chin, 1998). First, we checked the potential problems of multicollinearity by assessing the value of the variance inflation factor (VIF). To ensure the complexity of the model, the VIF values should not exceed 5 (Hair et al., 2021). No VIFs were greater than 2.7 (Table 15.3), suggesting that the model did not establish any problems of multicollinearity. Second, we evaluated the R^2 value of the endogenous latent variables. Third, we examined these specific hypotheses using a two-tailed test and a significance level of 0.05 to assess the t-statistics and the *p*-values.

The R^2 for the purchase intention was 0.4. The effects of social trust ($\beta = 0.30$, $p < 0.01$) and self-efficacy ($\beta = 0.45$, $p < 0.01$) on individuals' purchase intention are significant and thus support *H1* and *H2*. The R^2 for social trust was 0.54.

Table 15.3. Descriptive Statistics and Correlation of Constructs.

	Mean	Std Dev	VIF	1	2	3	4	5	6	7
1 Purchase Intention	3.73	0.85	n/a	1.00						
2 Social trust	3.42	0.71	1.20	0.47	1.00					
3 Self-efficacy	3.86	0.68	1.20	0.56	0.40	1.00				
4 Network stability	3.82	0.69	2.59	0.52	0.52	0.48	1.00			
5 System quality	3.86	0.67	2.63	0.49	0.58	0.54	0.76	1.00		
6 Social referral	3.84	0.80	1.21	0.53	0.47	0.48	0.58	0.57	1.00	
7 Shared goals	3.52	0.72	1.40	0.42	0.67	0.36	0.47	0.49	0.40	1.00

Note(s): Correlations > 0.15 significant at the 0.05 level and > 0.20 significant at the 0.01 level (two-tailed). Descriptive statistics are based on the participants ($N = 373$).

There were four proposed direct links with social trust, namely, network stability (*H3*), system quality (*H4*), social referral (*H5*) and shared goals (*H7*). The results confirm the positive effects of system quality ($\beta = 0.24$, $p < 0.01$), social referral ($\beta = 0.12$, $p < 0.05$) and shared goals ($\beta = 0.47$, $p < 0.01$) on social trust. In contrast, the results show an insignificant link between network stability and social trust, rejecting *H3*.

Finally, the R^2 for self-efficacy was 0.27. We proposed two direct links, including individuals' perception of social referral (*H6*) and shared goals (*H8*). These two paths were positive and significant, indicating that the samples support the contention that an individual's social referral ($\beta = 0.40$, $p \leq 0.01$) and shared goals ($\beta = 0.20$, $p < 0.01$) will increase their self-efficacy. Table 15.4 illustrates the results of the hypothesis testing.

Next, we used Cohen's (2013) recommended approach to evaluate the effect size (f^2); the value of f^2 shows the strength of the relationship between the constructs. According to the guidance provided by Cohen (2013), our results indicated that both self-efficacy (0.27) and social trust (0.12) reached the medium level towards purchase intention, while among the constructs towards social trust, shared goals (0.34) showed the largest effect followed by system quality (0.05) and social referral (0.02). In this test, network stability did not reach the minimum level. Finally, the social referral towards self-efficacy reached the medium level at 0.18, followed by the small effect of shared goals (0.05).

Finally, we applied the blindfolding procedure to assess the Stone-Geisser Q^2 value (Hair et al., 2021). The Stone-Geisser Q^2 value indicates the extent to which a construct can predict the model's endogenous latent variable. The omission

Table 15.4. Results of the Model With Interaction Terms.

Hypothesis	Beta	*p* Values	Results
H1: Social trust → purchase intention	0.30	0.00***	Supported
H2: Self-efficacy → purchase intention	0.45	0.00***	Supported
H3: Network stability → social trust	030	0.41	Not supported
H4: System quality → social trust	0.24	0.00***	Supported
H5: Social referral → social trust	0.12	0.02**	Supported
H6: Social referral → self-efficacy	0.40	0.00***	Supported
H7: Shared goals → social trust	0.47	0.00***	Supported
H8: Shared goals → self-efficacy	0.20	0.00***	Supported

Note(s): *Significant at 0.05 level, **Significant at 0.01 level, ***Significant at 0.001 level.

distance was set to seven as recommended by Geisser (1974). According to the recommendation by Hair et al. (2021), our results show that all the constructs reached at least the medium value of Q^2 (Table 15.5). In particular, social trust was the highest (0.33) in predicting individuals' purchase intention in CC.

Robustness Checks

The final step of the data analysis was to carry out robustness tests to ensure that the results are adequate and avoid mistakes in drawing empirical conclusions. As suggested by the recent literature (Hair et al., 2021; Sarstedt et al., 2020;

Table 15.5. Results of Structural Model Assessment.

Constructs	*f2*	*R2*	*Q2*
Network stability	0.002		
System quality	0.049		
Social referral	0.180		
Shared goals	0.336		
Social trust	0.123	0.537	0.328
Self-efficacy	0.273	0.265	0.173
Purchase intention		0.396	0.297

Note(s): f^2: Small effect size ($f^2 < 0.02$), Medium effect size ($0.02 \leq f^2 < 0.15$), Large effect size ($f^2 \geq 0.15$); R^2: Weak explanatory power ($R^2 < 0.2$), Moderate explanatory power ($0.2 \leq R^2 < 0.5$), Strong explanatory power ($R^2 \geq 0.5$); Q^2: Model lacks predictive relevance ($Q^2 < 0$), Small predictive relevance ($0 \leq Q^2 < 0.25$), Moderate predictive relevance ($0.25 \leq Q^2 < 0.5$), Strong predictive relevance ($Q^2 \geq 0.5$).

Zaefarian et al., 2017), robustness checks should be a mandatory standard before reporting the results obtained from PLS-SEM. The tests should include endogeneity bias check, quadratic effect (nonlinear effect) and unobserved heterogeneity bias.

Endogeneity Bias

This research takes the possible endogeneity bias into account to ensure that the constructs are not correlated with the error term of the exogenous variable, sample selection bias and no reverse causality between the constructs (Sarstedt et al., 2020). The potential endogeneity bias was addressed by performing a Durbin-Wu-Hausman test (Nakamura & Nakamura, 1985) with the help of EViews 13 software. This test has also been used in recent studies to address endogeneity issues (e.g. Zaefarian et al., 2017). As shown in Table 15.6, it is confirmed that endogeneity bias is not a problem in our data.

Quadratic Effect

As suggested by Sarstedt et al. (2020), this thesis assessed nonlinear effects using Ramsey's regression specification error test (RESET), endogeneity bias check using Durbin-Wu-Hausman test and unobserved heterogeneity using FIMIX-PLS. First of all, a recent study claimed that the relationships between the constructs are usually assumed to be linear; however, this is not always the case (Ahrholdt et al., 2019). When a relationship is nonlinear, the size of effect between the two constructs not only does not increase or decrease according to the estimates in the exogenous construct but also depends on its value (Hair et al., 2021). To identify whether or not the relationships in our model are nonlinear, we used Ramsey's

Table 15.6. Assessment of Endogeneity Bias Using the Durbin-Wu-Hausman Test.

Test	Coef (β)	p Value	F-statistic	Bias present
NS → ST	0.534	0.000**	0.000**	No
SQ → ST	0.617	0.000**	0.000**	No
SR → ST	0.425	0.000**	0.000**	No
SR → SE	0.210	0.000**	0.000**	No
SG → ST	0.192	0.000**	0.000**	No
SG → SE	0.341	0.000**	0.000**	No
ST → PI	0.169	0.012**	0.012**	No
SE → PI	0.400	0.000**	0.000**	No

Note: **Significant at 0.01 level.

Table 15.7. Assessment of Quadratic Effects.

Structural Path	Coef(β)	p Value	t-Statistics
Social trust → purchase intention	0.376	0.060	1.856
Self-efficacy → purchase intention	0.585	0.090	1.693
Network stability → social trust	0.035	0.554	0.592
System quality → social trust	0.194	0.126	1.532
Social referral → social trust	0.077	0.184	1.330
Shared goals → social trust	0.356	0.072	1.800
Shared goals → self-efficacy	0.225	0.322	0.992
Social referral → self-efficacy	0.420	0.290	1.059

RESET. The results are presented in Table 15.7, with values of $p > 0.05$, indicating the linear effect's robustness in the model.

Unobserved Heterogeneity Bias

Unobserved heterogeneity can be a major threat to the empirical results; therefore, an examination of unobserved heterogeneity bias was included in robustness checks. Unobserved heterogeneity occurs when all participants are assumed homogeneous rather than heterogeneous (Hair et al., 2021). In addition, research failing to consider the examination of unobserved heterogeneity is bound to produce incorrect results (Hair et al., 2021; Sarstedt et al., 2020). In order to assess this potential issue, we conducted finite mixture PLS (FIMIX-PLS; Hahn et al., 2002). Following the guideline provided by Sarstedt et al. (2020), this thesis considered all demographic characters of the sample (gender, education, household income, user and non-user and age) along with the constructs within the model. When selecting the number of segments, researchers should jointly consider the modified Akaike's information criterion with factor 3 (AIC$_3$) (Bozdogan, 1994) and consistent AIC (CAIC; Bozdogan, 1987) (see, e.g. Hair et al., 2021; Sarstedt et al., 2020). Moreover, the entropy statistics (EN) should be larger than 0.5 and the segment sizes should meet the minimum sample sizes. The full results from FIMIX-PLS are demonstrated in Table 15.8. Although all segments met the criteria (EN > 0.5), five-segment and four-segment solutions did not meet the minimum sample size. The minimum sample size was determined with the help of G*power software. However, when examining the criteria (AIC + AIC$_3$), all segments fall into the $k = 1$ criteria, indicating that the unobserved heterogeneity does not exist in the dataset and does not affect the empirical results (Sarstedt et al., 2017).

Table 15.8. Assessment of Unobserved Heterogeneity Using FIMIX-PLS.

Criteria	Number of Segments				
	$k = 1$	$k = 2$	$k = 3$	$k = 4$	$k = 5$
AIC	2605.348	2530.682	2514.587	2357.426	2311.048
AIC_3	2622.348	2563.682	2564.587	2424.426	2395.048
AIC_4	2639.348	2596.682	2614.587	2491.426	2479.048
BIC	2672.015	2660.094	2710.666	2620.172	2640.46
CAIC	2689.015	2693.094	2760.666	2687.172	2724.46
HQ	2631.82	2582.069	2592.447	2461.759	2441.853
MDL_5	3074.682	3441.742	3894.982	4207.155	4630.111
LnL	-1285.674	-1232.341	-1207.293	-1111.713	-1071.524
EN	NA	0.688	0.522	0.690	0.77
NFI	NA	0.718	0.516	0.649	0.718
NEC	NA	116.216	178.229	146.618	85.666

Note(s): AIC: Akaike's information criterion; AIC_3: modified AIC with Factor 3; AIC_4: modified AIC with Factor 4; BIC: Bayesian information criterion; CAIC: consistent AIC; HQ: Hannan-Quinn criterion; MDL_5: minimum description length with factor 5; LnL: LogLikelihood; EN: entropy statistic; NFI: non-fuzzy index; NEC: normalised entropy criterion.

Solutions and Recommendations

This study is the first attempt to investigate the antecedents of social trust and self-efficacy in a labour-market-based CC platform where individuals share their personal skills rather than providing access to their properties, as is the case with platforms like Uber or Airbnb. While Uber and Airbnb require individuals to share their personal properties, the labour-market-based CC platform, such as TaskRabbit, operates on a different premise by enabling users to share their personal skills without the need for accessing the seller's property and explains how social trust and self-efficacy together drive purchase intention. Prior studies have assessed the antecedents of social trust in organisational management (Qu & Yang, 2015) and community development research (Delhey & Newton, 2003). While the concept of self-efficacy has been examined frequently in different domains, it has not been fully understood in the CC domain. It is also important to note that contextual factors, such as the unique characteristics of the platform and the specific user base, can influence the dynamics of social trust, self-efficacy and purchase intention. By theoretically explaining and empirically examining how trust in the collective entity and trust in one's own ability to navigate the collective entity together drive purchase intention, our research explains the critical role that trust plays in driving consumers' use of CC, extending existing understanding of CC.

Our results reveal that seven out of the eight proposed hypotheses were supported. The bootstrapping method confirms that both perceived social trust and self-efficacy have significant and positive effects on users' purchase intention in TaskRabbit. Shared goals prove to be the strongest antecedent to social trust, followed by perceived platform system quality and social referral, reinforcing the findings of the previous literature (Chow & Chan, 2008; Inkpen & Tsang, 2005). However, network stability has no relevance to social trust, which suggests that although network stability promotes long-lasting cooperative behaviour and affects how people evaluate the overall value of using a particular CC platform (Eckhardt et al., 2019), network stability does not have a direct relationship with users' evaluation of other CC members' trustworthiness.

Compared to social trust, self-efficacy has a stronger effect on the purchase intention in TaskRabbit. This finding shows that people's confidence in their own ability to navigate and utilise TaskRabbit has a more significant impact on their purchase intention. Furthermore, the findings also confirm social referral and shared goals as two significant antecedents to self-efficacy (Tamjidyamcholo et al., 2013). In particular, social referral has a higher influence than shared goals on self-efficacy, showing the importance of social recognition and inclusion in determining a person's evaluation of their own capability in utilising the TaskRabbit platform to achieve the required tasks.

This chapter contributes to the CC literature in three ways. First, this research discusses how social trust drives purchase intention. By going beyond discussing users' motivation to purchase intention, using self-determination theory, this research acknowledges the importance of social trust using social capital theory and explains how social trust drives purchase intention, as it is affected by shared goals, system quality and social referrals. In this regard, it enriches the extant CC research and offers a more in-depth understanding of individuals' purchase intention.

Second, by including self-efficacy and testing its effect in driving purchase intention based on data collected from TaskRabbit, this chapter reveals that self-efficacy is the key driver that affects a user's evaluation of whether to purchase via the CC platform, even more so than his/her social trust. The finding confirms the work of Zhu et al. (2017) regarding the importance of self-efficacy in CC. However, rather than focusing on the individual's self-efficacy on ridesharing (Zhu et al., 2017), this chapter discusses self-efficacy in using the platform, thus providing a different dimension to understand how self-efficacy drives purchase intention, in the CC literature.

Finally, this chapter also discusses four important antecedents to social trust and self-efficacy in driving purchase intention, illustrating that individuals' social trust could be increased by perceived shared goals, social referral and platform system quality. These results are consistent with prior research in the e-marketplace, providing additional evidence that promoting social referral is an approach to leverage the existing social networks between individuals (Lai et al., 2017). Individuals acknowledged that recommendations and information from these people are trustworthy (Lee & Turban, 2001). In essence, social referral serves as a channel for delivering trustworthy recommendations and advice, which reinforces the classic aspects of social capital that are critical to the characteristics of CC.

Managerial Implications

The research offers practical insights for CC platforms to enhance their promotion. For platform suppliers, it's recommended to highlight and communicate the positive outcomes of CC usage to increase awareness and attract potential users. In platforms focusing on skill-based exchanges where offerings are intangible, establishing familiarity is key; thus, implementing referral programs and forming partnerships with complementary services can aid in attracting and retaining users. Additionally, maintaining transparency about service accuracy and benefits of collaboration can bolster social trust among users. For service providers within skill-based exchange platforms, building social trust and self-efficacy is paramount. This involves showcasing skills, emphasising professionalism, offering responsive support and continuously improving skills and seeking feedback to enhance user confidence and outcomes in the collaborative consumption context.

Future Research Directions

- The research focuses on a specific labour-market-based CC platform, limiting the generalisability of the findings. Future studies should explore these relationships in other contexts.
- Longitudinal studies are recommended to track changes in social trust and self-efficacy over time within the CC platform, providing insights into user engagement and platform sustainability.
- The data collected did not show significant effects when examining the mediating role of the studied constructs and multiple mediation. Larger sample sizes and investigation in different labour markets are necessary.
- Future research should consider additional factors, such as cultural factors and social participation, to better understand their influence on social trust. Expanding the framework and exploring alternative theoretical perspectives would enhance understanding of the antecedents of social trust in CC platforms.

Conclusion

This chapter provides a comprehensive overview of the research conducted, highlighting its contributions and limitations. It discusses the specific labour-market-based CC platform under investigation and suggests future research directions, including longitudinal studies and exploring additional variables. The analysis revealed three key findings. First, the model confirmed that social trust and self-efficacy each plays a significant role in influencing purchase intention. Second, an individual's perceived shared goals have a strong impact on his/her social trust and self-efficacy. Third, an individual may feel that there is a shortage of service providers and a poor system quality, thus highlighting the importance of balancing the triadic model of CC. This chapter emphasises the need to consider contextual factors and expand the framework to better understand social trust in CC platforms. In conclusion, while the research makes valuable contributions, further investigation is necessary to enhance understanding and address the identified limitations.

Case Study

In today's dynamic consumer landscape, collaborative consumption stands as a revolutionary concept reshaping traditional notions of ownership and consumption patterns. Sarah, a young urban professional, intrigued by its promise of sustainability and community engagement, embarks on a journey to explore collaborative consumption platforms.

Sarah's exploration begins with a desire to uncover the essence of collaborative consumption. Immersing herself in platforms facilitating the sharing and exchange of resources, Sarah experiences firsthand the transformative power of collective action. From sharing economy giants to niche platforms catering to specific interests, Sarah witnesses the diverse array of opportunities that collaborative consumption offers.

She stumbled upon a platform where neighbours lent and borrowed tools, from power drills to gardening equipment. Intrigued by the idea of community sharing, Sarah dove into the platform, eager to see how trust played a role. As she interacted with fellow users and perused reviews, Sarah's exploration extended to a community garden initiative, where users shared gardening tools and expertise. Initially hesitant to participate due to her lack of gardening experience, Sarah found herself surrounded by a supportive community eager to share knowledge and resources. Through hands-on learning and positive feedback from fellow gardeners, Sarah's self-efficacy flourished. Empowered by her newfound skills, she not only contributed to the community garden but also inspired others to join, fuelling a cycle of empowerment and participation.

Case Study Questions

(1) How does social trust influence individuals' willingness to engage in collaborative consumption activities?
(2) How can collaborative consumption platforms foster self-efficacy among users, and what are the potential implications for user engagement and adoption?
(3) Discuss the significance of shared goals and system quality in shaping users' experiences within collaborative consumption platforms. How do these factors contribute to building trust and promoting sustainable consumption practices among users?

Key Terms and Definitions

Collaborative Consumption: a socio-economic system that facilitates the sharing, renting, borrowing, trading and lending of resources, both tangible and intangible, among individuals or communities through technology-enabled platforms to enhance resource utilisation, sustainability and mutually beneficial relationships.

Network Stability: the frequency of membership changes within a network, indicating the level of user dropouts and steady growth in registered members.

Purchase Intention: an individual's inclination or willingness to engage in a future buying behaviour, indicating their likelihood to make a purchase or consume a product or service.

Self-efficacy: an individual's belief in their own capabilities to perform a specific behaviour or task, influencing their trust in their ability to participate effectively on a collaborative consumption platform and their intention to make purchases.

Shared Goals: common objectives or aims that are mutually pursued by individuals within a collaborative consumption network, fostering cooperation and collective efforts towards achieving desired outcomes.

Social Referral: the sharing of valuable information or knowledge within or outside a network, often through social ties.

Social Trust: the confidence in the reliability and integrity of others within a network, influencing engagement and cooperation in collaborative consumption platforms.

References

Abdar, M., & Yen, N. Y. (2020). Analysis of user preference and expectation on shared economy platform: An examination of correlation between points of interest on Airbnb. *Computers in Human Behavior, 107*, 105730.

Ahrholdt, D. C., Gudergan, S. P., & Ringle, C. M. (2019). Enhancing loyalty: When improving consumer satisfaction and delight matters. *Journal of Business Research, 94*, 18–27.

Akbar, P., & Hoffmann, S. (2022). Collaborative space: Framework for collaborative consumption and the sharing economy. *Journal of Services Marketing, 37*(4), 496–509.

Arnould, E. J., & Rose, A. S. (2016). Mutuality: Critique and substitute for Belk's sharing. *Marketing Theory, 16*(1), 75–99.

Bandura, A. (1986). *Social foundations of thought and action: A social cognitive theory.* Prentice Hall.

Bandura, A. (1997). *Self-efficacy: The exercise of control.* Freeman.

Bandura, A. (2001). Social cognitive theory: An agentic perspective. *Annual Review of Psychology, 52*(1), 1–26.

Barber, B. (1983). *The logic and limits of trust.* Rutgers University Press.

Bardhi, F., & Eckhardt, G. M. (2012). Access-based consumption: The case of car sharing. *Journal of Consumer Research, 39*(4), 881–898.

Belk, R. (2007). Why not share rather than own? *Annals of the American Academy of Political and Social Science, 611*, 126–140.

Belk, R. (2014). You are what you can access: Sharing and collaborative consumption online. *Journal of Business Research, 67*(8), 1595–1600.

Benoit, S., Baker, T. L., Bolton, R. N., Gruber, T., & Kandampully, J. (2017). A triadic framework for collaborative consumption: Motives, activities and resources & capabilities of actors. *Journal of Business Research, 79*, 219–227.

Bozdogan, H. (1994). Mixture-model cluster analysis using model selection criteria and a new informational measure of complexity. In *Proceedings of the first US/ Japan conference on the frontiers of statistical modeling: An informational approach* (pp. 69–113). Springer.

Bozdogan, H. (1987). Model selection and Akaike's information criterion (AIC): The general theory and its analytical extensions. *Psychometrika, 52*(3), 345–370.

Butschek, S., Amor, R. G., Kampkötter, P., & Sliwka, D. (2022). Motivating gig workers – Evidence from a field experiment. *Labour Economics, 75*, 102105.

Celata, F., Hendrickson, C. Y., & Sanna, V. S. (2017). The sharing economy as community marketplace? Trust, reciprocity and belonging in peer-to-peer accommodation platforms. *Cambridge Journal of Regions, Economy and Society, 10*(2), 349–363.

Cha, M. K., & Lee, H. J. (2022). Does social trust always explain the active use of sharing-based programs?: A cross-national comparison of Indian and US rideshare consumers. *Journal of Retailing and Consumer Services, 65*, 102515.

Chin, W. W. (1998). Commentary issues and opinion on structural equation modeling. *MIS Quarterly, 22*(1), vii–xvi.

Chiu, C. M., Hsu, M. H., & Wang, E. T. (2006). Understanding knowledge sharing in virtual communities: An integration of social capital and social cognitive theories. *Decision Support Systems, 42*(3), 1872–1888.

Chow, W. S., & Chan, L. S. (2008). Social network, social trust and shared goals in organizational knowledge sharing. *Information and Management, 45*(7), 458–465.

Cohen, J. (2013). *Statistical power analysis for the behavioral sciences.* Routledge.

Coleman, J. S. (1988). Social capital in the creation of human capital. *American Journal of Sociology, 94*, S95–S120.

Compeau, D., Higgins, C. A., & Huff, S. (1999). Social cognitive theory and individual reactions to computing technology: A longitudinal study. *MIS Quarterly: Management Information Systems, 23*(2), 145–158.

Delhey, J., & Newton, K. (2003). Who trusts? The origins of social trust in seven societies. *European Societies, 5*(2), 93–137.

Eckhardt, G. M., Houston, M. B., Jiang, B., Lamberton, C., Rindfleisch, A., & Zervas, G. (2019). Marketing in the sharing economy. *Journal of Marketing, 83*(5), 5–27.

Ert, E., Fleischer, A., & Magen, N. (2016). Trust and reputation in the sharing economy: The role of personal photos in Airbnb. *Tourism Management, 55*, 62–73.

Felson, M., & Spaeth, J. L. (1978). Community structure and collaborative consumption: A routine activity approach. *American Behavioral Scientist, 21*(4), 614–624.

Fornell, C., & Larcker, D. F. (1981). Evaluating structural equation models with unobservable variables and measurement error. *Journal of Marketing Research, 18*(1), 39–50.

Fukuyama, F. (1996). *Trust: The social virtues and the creation of prosperity* (1st ed.). The Free Press.

Gawer, A., & Cusumano, M. A. (2014). Industry platforms and ecosystem innovation. *Journal of Product Innovation Management, 31*(3), 417–433.

Geisser, S. (1974). A predictive approach to the random effect model. *Biometrika, 61*(1), 101–107.

Hahn, C., Johnson, M. D., Herrmann, A., & Huber, F. (2002). Capturing customer heterogeneity using a finite mixture PLS approach. *Schmalenbach Business Review*, *54*(3), 243–269.

Hair, J. F., Hult, G. T. M., Ringle, C. M., & Sarstedt, M. (2021). *A Primer on Partial Least Squares Structural Equation Modeling (PLS-SEM)* (3rd ed.). Sage.

Hamari, J., & Koivisto, J. (2015). Why do people use gamification services? *International Journal of Information Management*, *35*(4), 419–431.

Hartl, B., & Hofmann, E. (2021). The social dilemma of car sharing – The impact of power and the role of trust in community car sharing. *International Journal of Sustainable Transportation*, 1–24.

Hartl, B., Hofmann, E., & Kirchler, E. (2016). Do we need rules for "what's mine is yours"? Governance in collaborative consumption communities. *Journal of Business Research*, *69*(8), 2756–2763. https://doi.org/10.1016/j.jbusres.2015.11.011

Hsu, M. H., & Chiu, C. M. (2004). Internet self-efficacy and electronic service acceptance. *Decision Support Systems*, *38*(3), 369–381.

Huang, S., Yu, Y., & Jiao, Y. (2022). *Customer-product matches in online social referrals: A graph embedding approach*. https://doi.org/10.2139/ssrn.4125028

Hulland, J. (1999). Use of partial least squares (PLS) in strategic management research: A review of four recent studies. *Strategic Management Journal*, *20*(2), 195–204.

Inkpen, A. C., & Tsang, E. W. K. (2005). Social capital, networks, and knowledge transfer. *Academy of Management Review*, *30*(1), 146–165.

Lai, C. Y., Li, Y. M., & Lin, L. F. (2017). A social referral appraising mechanism for the e-marketplace. *Information and Management*, *54*(3), 269–280.

Lamberton, C. P., & Rose, R. L. (2012). When is ours better than mine? A framework for understanding and altering participation in commercial sharing systems. *Journal of Marketing*, *76*(4), 109–125.

Lee, K., Hakstian, A. M., & Williams, J. D. (2021). Creating a world where anyone can belong anywhere: Consumer equality in the sharing economy. *Journal of Business Research*, *130*, 221–231.

Lee, M. K. O., & Turban, E. (2001). A trust model for consumer internet shopping. *International Journal of Electronic Commerce*, *6*(1), 75–91.

Lei, Y. W. (2021). Delivering solidarity: Platform architecture and collective contention in China's platform economy. *American Sociological Review*, *86*(2), 279–309.

Leismann, K., Schmitt, M., Rohn, H., & Baedeker, C. (2013). Collaborative consumption: Towards a resource-saving consumption culture. *Resources*, *2*(3), 184–203.

Milanova, V., & Maas, P. (2017). Sharing intangibles: Uncovering individual motives for engagement in a sharing service setting. *Journal of Business Research*, *75*, 159–171.

Möhlmann, M. (2015). Collaborative consumption: Determinants of satisfaction and the likelihood of using a sharing economy option again. *Journal of Consumer Behaviour*, *14*(3),193–207.

Nadeem, W., Juntunen, M., Shirazi, F., & Hajli, N. (2020). Consumers' value co-creation in sharing economy: The role of social support, consumers' ethical perceptions and relationship quality. *Technological Forecasting and Social Change*, *151*, 119786.

Nakamura, A., & Nakamura, M. (1985). On the performance of tests by Wu and by Hausman for detecting the ordinary least squares bias problem. *Journal of Econometrics, 29*(3), 213–227.

Nahapiet, J., & Ghoshal, S. (1998). Social capital, intellectual capital, and the organizational advantage. *The Academy of Management Review, 23*(2), 242–266.

Newton, K. (2001). Trust, social capital, civil society, and democracy. *International Political Science Review, 22*(2), 201–214.

Ozcan, P., Möhlmann, M., & Krishnamoorthy, C. (2017). *Who shares and who doesn't? Results of the UK Sharing Economy Consumer Survey.* Available at: https://wrap.warwick.ac.uk/103410/

PwC. (2015). *Sharing or paring? Growth of the sharing economy.* Available at: https://www.pwc.com/hu/en/kiadvanyok/assets/pdf/sharing-economy-en.pdf

Qu, W. G., & Yang, Z. (2015). The effect of uncertainty avoidance and social trust on supply chain collaboration. *Journal of Business Research, 68*(5), 911–918.

Ringle, C. M., Sarstedt, M., & Straub, D. W. (2012). A critical look at the use of PLS-SEM in MIS quarterly. *MIS Quarterly: Management Information Systems, 36*(1), iii–xiv.

Sarstedt, M., Ringle, C. M., Cheah, J. H., Ting, H., Moisescu, O. I., & Radomir, L. (2020). Structural model robustness checks in PLS-SEM. *Tourism Economics, 26*(4), 531–554.

Sarstedt, M., Ringle, C. M., & Hair, J. F. (2017). Treating unobserved heterogeneity in PLS-SEM: A multi-method approach. In *Partial least squares path modeling* (pp. 197–217). Springer.

Sundararajan, A. (2016). *The sharing economy: The end of employment and the rise of crowd-based capitalism.* MIT Press.

Tamjidyamcholo, A., Baba, M. S. B., Tamjid, H., & Gholipour, R. (2013). Information security–Professional perceptions of knowledge-sharing intention under self-efficacy, trust, reciprocity, and shared-language. *Computers & Education, 68*, 223–232.

Ter Huurne, M., Ronteltap, A., Corten, R., & Buskens, V. (2017). Antecedents of trust in the sharing economy: A systematic review. *Journal of Consumer Behaviour, 16*(6), 485–498.

Tsai, W., & Ghoshal, S. (1998). Social capital and value creation: The role of intrafirm networks. *The Academy of Management Review, 41*(4), 464–476.

Tschang, F. T. (2021). Platform-dependent entrepreneurs: Participants in an expanding universe of platforms? *Academy of Management Perspectives, 35*(4), 696–701.

Tóth, Z., Nemkova, E., Hizsák, G., & Naudé, P. (2022). Social capital creation on professional sharing economy platforms: The problems of rating dependency and the non-transferability of social capital. *Journal of Business Research, 144*, 450–460.

Tripp, J., McKnight, D. H., & Lankton, N. (2022). What most influences consumers' intention to use? Different motivation and trust stories for Uber, Airbnb, and TaskRabbit. *European Journal of Information Systems*, 1–23.

Tussyadiah, I. P. (2016). Factors of satisfaction and intention to use peer-to-peer accommodation. *International Journal of Hospitality Management, 55*, 70–80.

Van Den Bulte, C., Bayer, E., Skiera, B., & Schmitt, P. (2018). How customer referral programs turn social capital into economic capital. *Journal of Marketing Research, 55*(1), 132–146.

Venkateswaran, V., Kumar, D. S., & Gupta, D. (2021). To trust or not': Impact of camouflage strategies on trust in the sharing economy. *Journal of Business Research, 136*, 110–126.

Ventura, M., Salanova, M., & Llorens, S. (2015). Professional self-efficacy as a predictor of burnout and engagement: The role of challenge and hindrance demands. *The Journal of Psychology, 149*(3), 277–302.

Werts, C. E., Joreskog, K. G., & Linn, R. L. (1973). Identification and estimation in path analysis with unmeasured variables. *American Journal of Sociology, 78*(6), 1469–1484.

Williams, A. (2006). Tourism and hospitality marketing: Fantasy, feeling, and fun. *International Journal of Contemporary Hospitality Management. 18*(6), 482–495

Yao, Q. M., Baker, L. T., & Lohrke, F. T. (2022). Building and sustaining trust in remote work by platform-dependent entrepreneurs on digital labor platforms: Toward an integrative framework. *Journal of Business Research, 149*, 327–339.

Yi, M. Y., & Hwang, Y. (2003). Predicting the use of web-based information systems: Self-efficacy, enjoyment, learning goal orientation, and the technology acceptance model. *International Journal of Human-Computer Studies, 59*(4), 431–449.

Zaefarian, G., Kadile, V., Henneberg, S. C., & Leischnig, A. (2017). Endogeneity bias in marketing research: Problem, causes, and remedies. *Industrial Marketing Management, 65*, 39–46.

Zhu, G., So, K. K. F., & Hudson, S. (2017). Inside the sharing economy: Understanding consumer motivations behind the adoption of mobile applications. *International Journal of Contemporary Hospitality Management, 29*(9), 2218–2239.

Zhai, M., Chen, Y., & Wei, M. (2021). Influence of trust and risk on peer-to-peer investment willingness: A bidirectional perspective. *Internet Research, 2016*(18).

Zhang, T. C., Jahromi, M. F., & Kizildag, M. (2018). Value co-creation in a sharing economy: The end of price wars? *International Journal of Hospitality Management, 71*, 51–58.

Zhang, R. J. (2020). Social trust and satisfaction with life: A cross-lagged panel analysis based on representative samples from 18 societies. *Social Science & Medicine, 251*, 112901.

Zhou, T. (2012). Understanding users' initial trust in mobile banking: An elaboration likelihood perspective. *Computers in Human Behavior, 28*(4), 1518–1525.

Chapter 16

Digital Customer Knowledge Management and Ethical Innovation Strategy

S. Asieh H. Tabaghdehi[a] *and Hossein Kalatian*[b]

[a]Brunel University London, UK
[b]University of Northampton International College, UK

Abstract

In today's rapidly evolving digital era, the focus on Customer Knowledge Management (CKM) has emerged as a critical endeavor for businesses aiming to enhance the customer experience, strengthen customer relationships, and secure future engagement, particularly as they navigate the complex landscape of digital transformation. The integration of innovative and ethical digital transitions has the potential to significantly influence the CKM process, ultimately reshaping the very essence of the business model in terms of performance, productivity, and sustainability within the market. The core objective of this chapter is to explore further the complex domain of digitalization and its profound impact on businesses, with a specific emphasis on Small and Medium-sized Enterprises (SMEs). Through the lens of CKM, we will explore how leveraging digital tools and strategies can empower businesses, especially SMEs, to foster digital innovation within their CKM initiatives and subsequently attain and sustain a competitive advantage in an increasingly dynamic and competitive marketplace.

Keywords: Customer knowledge management (CKM); small and medium enterprise (SME); digital innovation; customer experience and engagement; privacy; transparency; inclusivity

Introduction

The rapid technological revolution has impacted significantly in most organizations and consumer experiences. Digital advancement has a fundamental effect on the way businesses engage with their customers. The spread of digital channels,

Business Strategies and Ethical Challenges in the Digital Ecosystem, 357–368
Copyright © 2025 S. Asieh H. Tabaghdehi and Hossein Kalatian
Published under exclusive licence by Emerald Publishing Limited
doi:10.1108/978-1-80455-069-420241016

data analytics, and artificial intelligence (AI) has unlocked the access to customer insights. CKM, which entails the systematic collection, management, and application of customer information, has become the essential of effective customer-centric strategies. It allows businesses to not only understand the unique needs, preferences, and behaviors of their customers but also to anticipate future trends and demands, all while tailoring their products and services accordingly. The existing literature emphasizes that digitalization made the knowledge management processes effect on innovation, the market and financial performance significantly (Raguseo & Vitari, 2018; Saldanha et al., 2013, 2017). It is inevitable that the digital transformation has challenged the innovation and organizational learning theories (Berger & Kuckertz, 2016).

The strategic integration of digital tools and platforms into CKM is indeed transformative. It enables businesses to capture, analyze, and derive actionable insights from vast volumes of data, whether through social media sentiment analysis, purchase history, or browsing patterns. This data-driven approach provides businesses with the ability to personalize interactions, recommend relevant products or services, and optimize pricing, ultimately enriching the overall customer experience. Moreover, digitalization facilitates real-time engagement, offering customers seamless and immediate access to information, services, and support. The upshot is that businesses can establish deeper and more meaningful relationships with their customers, which are key to fostering loyalty and future engagement.

The technological revolution necessitates firms to enhance their knowledge management processes, resulting in increased innovativeness (Escribano et al., 2009; Laursen & Salter, 2006; Mazzola et al., 2016; Natalicchio et al., 2017; Passaro et al., 2018). However, it is essential to underscore the ethical dimension of this digital transition and innovations, particularly in SMEs. Furthermore, after the recent global pandemic, the emergence of digital platforms for managing organizations, achieving objectives, and, most importantly, surviving in the market has become the primary concern for every business, especially Small and Medium Enterprises (SMEs). Both the OECD (2019) and the EU Commission (2019) have published reports on the economic and social consequences of technologies, raising questions about societal readiness for new technological advancements (Szczepański, 2019). Hence, it is crucial to understand how SMEs can effectively (Zairis, 2020) and, more importantly, responsibly manage and coordinate digital activities. Furthermore, online customer knowledge management (CKM) and ethical business innovation can enhance the competitive strategy for all stakeholders. A recent study by Ye et al. (2018) revealed that businesses with a higher inclination toward advanced technology and digital platforms could compete more efficiently and improve their market share. Therefore, it is vital to focus on CKM and business innovations through the advancement of their soft skills for better economic and social impact.

Digitalization has brought significant attention to ethical concerns, such as discrimination, inclusion, and privacy, in SMEs. For instance, existing literature emphasizes the importance of addressing discrimination and inequality issues in the workplace (Howcroft & Rubery, 2018). A further study by Janssen and van den Hoven (2015) indicates that adopting transparency and data privacy mindsets can restructure organizational and social issues. Therefore, it is of utmost importance to investigate how ethical issues can reshape CKM and digital innovation in today's digital society. It remains relatively unexplored how technology-enriched strategies could assist businesses, particularly SMEs, in enhancing their CKM strategies. For SMEs with limited digital literacy and resources, ethical digital innovations can help them improve their customer relations responsibly while creating economic and social impact. The responsible handling of customer data and the respect for privacy are not just regulatory requirements but pivotal elements in building and maintaining trust. Businesses that demonstrate ethical and transparent practices in their CKM processes tend to earn not only the loyalty of their customers but also their advocacy.

By implementing ethical CKM strategies, they can achieve sustainable progress in the rapidly growing digital market. Thus, it is crucial to understand the processes required to enhance businesses' understanding of responsible digital innovation to achieve sustainability initiatives in SMEs. Sustainability, often considered in terms of both environmental and business continuity, is a vital element of this digital transformation. Digitalization reduces the environmental footprint by decreasing the need for physical infrastructure and travel, and it can enhance the resilience of businesses by providing them with the capacity to serve customers remotely during unforeseen disruptions. Hence, the digital era has ushered in a new paradigm for CKM, providing businesses, including SMEs, with the tools and strategies necessary to unlock unprecedented value from their customer data. This chapter seeks to explore how these innovative and ethical digital transitions can be harnessed by businesses to fortify their CKM strategies, fostering innovation and, in turn, achieving a sustainable competitive advantage. By aligning digitalization with ethical principles, businesses are not only poised for growth and adaptability but also capable of cultivating enduring and meaningful relationships with their customers in an ever-evolving marketplace.

Digital Transformation in SMEs

It has been significantly observed that SMEs have been using digital technologies in various forms to improve their resilience, performance, competitiveness, adoption, and innovation. Digital technologies and AI are helping SMEs enhance their market share by providing them with boundless access to new markets, customers, and opportunities. This implies that SMEs can achieve economies of scale by reducing business costs, improving productivity, and increasing efficiency. All of these benefits have been realized through the adoption of digital technologies in their operations and management, especially after the COVID-19 outbreak, which acted as an accelerator for SMEs' digitalization. However, digital transformation poses some challenges and barriers, particularly for SMEs. These challenges include a shortage of skills, resources, infrastructure, and most importantly, awareness at different scales. Government support through supportive policies and strategies is crucial for SMEs' adoption, survival, and innovation in this fast-developing market. A report by BusinessTechWeekly explored that SMEs are uncertain about how to get started with digital transformation in their business. They emphasized that SMEs need to focus on three key strategies.

First, they need to prioritize their business goals and develop the required strategy based on the importance and urgency of each segment in their business structure. For instance, they may need to start with front-end transformation, where they deal directly with customers (e.g., customer relationship management or CRM), and then progress to back-end transformation, such as human resource (HR) or information technology (IT). Second, SMEs need to carefully plan how their business will transition to a digital platform, ensuring that employees and customers are not overwhelmed by the changes. This requires thorough planning and control over the change process, which can minimize the risk of disruption in business functionality and budget. Third, it is crucial that SMEs' staff are prepared for the digital transformation. Employees need to understand the value of digital transformation in their business and how their smooth adoption can enhance business productivity. Like any other transformation, effective communication plays a crucial role in the success of these changes.

Similarly, digital transformation can only succeed if employees embrace the transformation and the adoption of the new platform. When it comes to SMEs' digital transformation, several factors come into play, including the size of the SMEs and the industry in which they operate. According to an OECD report in 2021, most SMEs intend to start their digitalization with their marketing and administrative departments, but they face challenges when it comes to data security, analytics, and the use of cloud computing. These challenges are partly due to weak internal capabilities, skills gaps, and financing gaps. Experts have also highlighted that policymakers and government intervention play a vital role in assisting SMEs with their digital adoption and development.

Customer Knowledge Management (CKM) and Digital Innovation in SMEs

Digital adoption and technological solutions assist SMEs in a range of activities, including product design, processes, best practices, and innovation in the rapidly growing digital market (Gil-Gomez et al., 2020). Digital platforms improve customers' accessibility to a vast range of products in a very convenient manner, leading to a better purchasing experience for customers in the digital market. Furthermore, the digital market provides a highly competitive platform where customers can purchase products at the lowest prices. On the other hand, SMEs are under significant pressure to compete effectively and maintain long-term relationships with their customers. Therefore, knowledge is a vital resource for businesses (Friedrich et al., 2020; Uden & He, 2017), and CKM in the digital era plays a crucial role in the survival of SMEs in the market.

While the digital platform enables businesses to capture extensive data on customer tastes and behavior, it can be particularly challenging in the digital market, especially in industries like the creative industry (Eisenhardt & Martin, 2000; Lusch et al., 2007). Organizations require an effective set of skills to create, store, and transfer knowledge about customers (Alegre et al., 2013) to gain a competitive advantage, boost productivity, and drive business growth (Chua & Banerjee, 2013; Pil & Holweg, 2003). However, Castagna et al. (2020) show that SMEs tend to use traditional technologies more rigorously to support their CKM processes rather than innovative digital technologies, primarily because they perceive digital innovation as more expensive.

In contrast, the digital platform in giant businesses such as eBay and Amazon has dramatically enhanced customers' purchasing experience, improved their decision-making processes, and reformed their interactions with businesses since the start of the COVID-19 pandemic. The continuous excellence of these giant companies sets a high bar for SMEs in enhancing their customer relationships to improve their market share. Therefore, accessing customer information and implementing knowledge management can significantly help businesses in their innovation process (Adams & Lamont, 2003; Cardinal et al., 2001; Darroch & McNaughton, 2002; Dias & Bresciani, 2006; Mao et al., 2016; Pyka, 2002). However, SMEs find it challenging to keep up with rapidly evolving innovation. As indicated by Najafi-Tavani et al. (2018), this situation has led businesses to become more collaborative, encouraging knowledge-sharing for further innovation. Furthermore, knowledge can be combined in various ways that can result in innovation (Du Plessis, 2007). Therefore, recombining CKM, especially in the digital era, can assist businesses in achieving more innovation, maximizing their resources, enhancing their performance and process management, and increasing their competitive advantage (Costa & Monteiro, 2016; Martín-de-Castro et al., 2011; Zack et al., 2009). Thus, there is a lack of studies on the theoretical foundations of different types of digital businesses (such as e-commerce, the freemium model, peer-to-peer, on-demand, and ad-supported models) that could assist businesses, particularly SMEs, in CKM, customer experience management, customer relationship management for the exploitation of responsible digital innovation at various levels.

The Role of Ethics in Digital Customer Knowledge Management (DCKM)

Ethical concerns have taken center stage in the integration of digital technologies into everyday human lives, particularly in issues related to transparency, equality, inclusion, and privacy. As societies and individuals continue to grapple with the evolving relationship between humans and technology, understanding unethical behavior and how to mitigate it is paramount in today's world. The growing reliance on technology has significantly enhanced CKM processes and business innovation strategies. However, it has also drawn considerable attention to ethical concerns aimed at preventing inequality, exclusion, and unfair practices across various industries. CKM and business innovation in the digital era have the potential to empower customers. Still, they come with potential consequences, particularly in terms of ethical data management over the long term.

One crucial issue pertains to the ownership of data. It is vital to identify who has ownership rights over the data created through digital interactions. Furthermore, it is equally important to consider how to efficiently and ethically handle customers' information while striving to enhance the customer–business relationship. Transparency, equality, inclusion, and privacy are at the core of these ethical concerns, and they can significantly impact the relationship between digital businesses and consumers. Customers who create data through their interactions with digital platforms often express concerns about various aspects of their data. They question how their information is collected, used, and disseminated to third parties. Addressing these concerns is essential for maintaining trust and ethical practices in the digital business landscape. To foster strong and ethical relationships with consumers, businesses must navigate these complex issues surrounding data management and privacy.

Conclusion

Digital customer knowledge management (DCKM) plays a pivotal role in shaping the trajectory of SME digital transformation and, consequently, influencing overall performance. The impact is multifaceted, spanning various aspects of the business landscape. DCKM empowers SMEs with the tools and insights needed to understand their customers at a granular level. By leveraging digital platforms and analytics, businesses can gather comprehensive data on customer behavior, preferences, and expectations.

The real-time data provided by DCKM enables agile decision-making in the digital transformation process. SMEs can swiftly respond to market changes, customer feedback, and emerging trends, ensuring that their digital strategies remain adaptive and effective. Furthermore, with in-depth customer knowledge, SMEs can tailor their products, services, and interactions to meet individual customer needs. Personalization, facilitated by DCKM, enhances the overall customer experience and fosters loyalty. DCKM supports SMEs in creating targeted marketing campaigns and sales strategies. By understanding customer preferences, businesses can deploy more effective digital marketing efforts, reaching the right audience with the right message.

Access to comprehensive customer knowledge fuels innovation and product development. SMEs can use customer insights to identify gaps in the market, discover unmet needs, and develop new digital products or services that align with customer expectations. Therefore, DCKM aids SMEs in optimizing their digital channels, ensuring that online platforms align with customer preferences. Whether through websites, social media, or mobile apps, businesses can tailor their digital presence for maximum impact. DCKM provides valuable data for evaluating the performance of digital initiatives. Key performance indicators (KPIs) related to customer engagement, conversion rates, and satisfaction can be tracked to measure the success of digital transformation efforts.

This leads to managing customer knowledge effectively and contributes to higher customer retention rates. By anticipating customer needs, resolving issues promptly, and maintaining personalized engagement, SMEs can build lasting customer loyalty. Therefore, SMEs leveraging DCKM gain a competitive edge in the digital landscape. The ability to harness customer insights for strategic decision-making positions businesses as industry leaders, driving sustainable growth and success. DCKM acts as a catalyst for SME digital transformation by aligning digital strategies with customer expectations and market dynamics. The symbiotic relationship between DCKM and overall performance underscores the pivotal role it plays in the success of SMEs in the digital age.

The ethical considerations and responsible practices associated with the collection, use, and management of customer data in digital environments plays a crucial role in DCKM. Upholding ethical standards in DCKM builds trust and confidence among customers. When individuals believe that their data is handled responsibly, with respect for privacy and security, they are more likely to engage with businesses and share valuable information. For instance, digital ethics ensure that customer privacy is prioritized in the collection and utilization of data. Adhering to ethical guidelines helps prevent intrusive practices and assures customers that their personal information is handled with care.

The ethical DCKM involves transparent communication about data practices. Businesses should provide customers with clear information about how their data will be used and seek explicit consent. This transparency fosters a positive relationship and empowers customers to make informed decisions. Moreover, digital ethics advocate for fairness in data usage. It is essential to avoid discriminatory practices, ensuring that customer data is not used to perpetuate bias or discrimination. Also, it promotes inclusivity and equal treatment of all customers. Particularly, SME's ethical considerations emphasize the importance of maintaining accurate and reliable customer data. Businesses should take measures to ensure data integrity, preventing inaccuracies that could impact customers adversely.

For instance, ethical DCKM includes robust security measures to protect customer data from unauthorized access, breaches, or cyber threats. Prioritizing cybersecurity safeguards customer information and mitigates the risks associated with digital interactions. Therefore, there is an urgent need for the ethical DCKM principle and guidelines that should be aligned with legal and regulatory frameworks governing data protection and privacy. Businesses must comply with laws such as the General Data Protection Regulation (GDPR) to avoid legal consequences and demonstrate a commitment to ethical practices. Ethical guidelines provide a framework for addressing potential dilemmas related to DCKM. Businesses can proactively anticipate ethical challenges and establish practices to mitigate risks, ensuring responsible and ethical decision-making.

Ethical behavior in DCKM contributes to the long-term reputation and brand image of businesses. Customers are increasingly conscious of ethical considerations, and businesses that prioritize digital ethics are likely to be viewed positively by consumers. Embracing digital ethics as part of DCKM reflects an organization's commitment to sustainable and responsible business practices. This commitment is increasingly valued by customers and stakeholders in the digital era. Digital ethics in DCKM are paramount for building trust, protecting privacy, ensuring fairness, and upholding responsible business practices. Businesses that integrate ethical considerations into their DCKM strategies are better positioned to navigate the evolving digital landscape while fostering positive relationships with their customers.

Case Study

Ethical Concerns in the Digital Business–Consumer Relationship

In the fast-growing landscape of digital businesses, the relationship between these enterprises and consumers is heavily influenced by a myriad of ethical concerns. Transparency, equality, inclusion, and privacy play pivotal roles in shaping this relationship. This case study explores the ethical challenges faced by digital businesses and how addressing these concerns can enhance the connection between digital businesses and their consumers. Technology Man ltd. (assumed company name) is an international tech company that specializes in developing and selling innovative software applications and serves a diverse customer base. Their leading product is a productivity app that has gathered millions of users worldwide. Technology Man ltd. prides itself on its innovative approach to software development. Over the years, the company has striven to stay ahead of the competition by introducing cutting-edge features and functionalities. However, this continued innovation has raised concerns among both employees and consumers regarding ethical issues including Transparency; Data Privacy; Equality and Inclusivity. Transparency and data privacy are one of the primary ethical concerns within Technology Man ltd., where several cases came to light that the company was accused of collecting more user data than what was explicitly mentioned in their privacy policy. Consumers expressed unease about their personal information being harvested without their knowledge.

Furthermore, Technology Man ltd. faced criticisms for a lack of equality and inclusivity in their development teams. Some employees and consumers pointed out that the company's development teams were predominantly male, which might have led to unconscious biases in the development process, potentially affecting the inclusivity of their products. After a short-term exercise of market research, the company recognized the importance of these ethical concerns and took immediate steps to handle them. To address the concerns around transparency and data privacy, they initiated a comprehensive review of its data collection practices. They revamped their privacy policy to make it more accessible, clearer, and, most importantly, aligned with the actual data collection practices. This step increased transparency significantly, making consumers feel more inclusive and in control of their personal information. Additionally, they enhance equality and inclusivity in its development teams by launching the diversity and inclusion programs aimed at fostering a more diverse workforce. They also established an ethics committee to take closer look into the day-to-day practice and be responsible for scrutinizing product development processes to identify and rectify potential biases. This initiative not only ensured a broader perspective in product development but also sent a strong message to consumers that their concerns about inclusivity were being taken seriously and relevant action being taken. Notably, by proactively addressing these ethical concerns enhanced their relationship with their consumer.

The revised privacy policy and transparent data collection practices enhanced consumer trust and users appreciated knowing that their personal information was being handled responsibly. Moreover, the commitment to inclusivity led to a more diverse and innovative workforce, which had a direct impact on product development. The company's products began to reflect the values of inclusivity, and consumers noticed the positive change. This led to higher consumer satisfaction and loyalty in the long term. This indicates that the critical role of addressing ethical concerns such as transparency, data privacy, equality, and inclusivity should not be viewed as mere ethical obligations but rather as opportunities to build a deeper, more sustainable connection with consumers. By proactively embracing these values, digital businesses can ensure the trust and loyalty of their customers while continuing to drive innovation in their respective industries.

Case Study Questions

(1) How did Technology Man ltd. address concerns around transparency and data privacy, especially in response to accusations of collecting more user data than explicitly mentioned in their privacy policy?
(2) What specific measures were implemented to enhance transparency, and how did these measures contribute to building consumer trust?
(3) In response to criticisms regarding a lack of equality and inclusivity in development teams, Technology Man ltd. launched diversity and inclusion programs. How did these initiatives contribute to fostering a more diverse workforce?
(4) In what ways did the establishment of an ethics committee further address potential biases in product development?
(5) Explore the long-term impact of addressing ethical concerns on consumer satisfaction and loyalty. How did the revised privacy policy, transparent data collection practices, and commitment to inclusivity contribute to higher consumer satisfaction and loyalty?
(6) In what ways did consumers perceive and appreciate the positive changes in the company's products and values?

Key Terms and Definitions

Data Privacy: Data privacy refers to the protection of individuals' personal information and the control they have over how it is collected, used, and shared by organizations and other entities.
Transparency: Transparency refers to the practice of openly sharing information, processes, decisions, and actions in a clear, honest, and accessible manner.

Equality and Inclusivity: Equality and inclusivity refer to principles and practices aimed at ensuring fair treatment, opportunities, and representation for all individuals, regardless of their differences or backgrounds.

Digital Customer Satisfaction: Digital customer satisfaction refers to the level of satisfaction or contentment experienced by customers in their interactions with digital channels, platforms, and services provided by businesses or organizations.

References

Adams, G. L., & Lamont, B. T. (2003). Knowledge management systems and developing sustainable competitive advantage. *Journal of Knowledge Management, 7*(2), 142–154.

Alegre, J., Sengupta, K., & Lapiedra, R. (2013). Knowledge management and innovation performance in a high-tech SMEs industry. *International Small Business Journal, 31*(4), 454–470.

Berger, E. S., & Kuckertz, A. (2016). Female entrepreneurship in startup ecosystems worldwide. *Journal of Business Research, 69*, 5163–5168.

Cardinal, L. B., Alessandri, T. M., & Turner, S. F. (2001). Knowledge codifiability, resources, and science-based innovation. *Journal of Knowledge Management, 5*(2), 195–204.

Castagna, F., Centobelli, P., Cerchione, R., Esposito, E., Oropallo, E., & Passaro, R. (2020). Customer knowledge management in SMEs facing digital transformation. *Sustainability, 12*(9), 3899.

Chua, A. Y. K., & Banerjee, S. (2013). Customer knowledge management via social media: The case of Starbucks. *Journal of Knowledge Management, 17*, 237–249.

Costa, V., & Monteiro, S. (2016). Key knowledge management processes for innovation: A systematic literature review. *VINE Journal of Information and Knowledge Management Systems, 46*(3), 386–410.

Darroch, J., & McNaughton, R. (2002). Examining the link between knowledge management practices and types of innovation. *Journal of Intellectual Capital, 3*(3), 210–222.

Dias, R. T., & Bresciani, S. (2006). R&D and knowledge: A theoretical assessment of the internationalisation strategies. *International Journal of Technology, Policy and Management, 6*(1), 1–32.

Digital Transformation for SMEs- The Ultimate Guide, BusinessTechWeekly. (2023). https://www.businesstechweekly.com/operational-efficiency/digital-transformation/guide-to-digital-transformation-for-smes/#How-can-SMEs-start-the-digital-transformation-of-their-organisations

Du Plessis, M. (2007). The role of knowledge management in innovation. *Journal of Knowledge Management, 11*(4), 20–29.

Eisenhardt, K. M., & Martin, J. A. (2000). Dynamic capabilities: What are they? *Strategic Management Journal, 21*, 1105–1121.

Escribano, A., Fosfuri, A., & Tribo, J. A. (2009). Managing external knowledge flows: The moderating role of absorptive capacity. *Research Policy, 38*, 96–105.

Friedrich, J., Becker, M., Kramer, F., Wirth, M., & Schneider, M. (2020). Incentive design and gamification for knowledge management. *Journal of Business Research, 106*, 341–352.

Gil-Gomez, H., Guerola-Navarro, V., Oltra-Badenes, R., & Lozano-Quilis, J. A. (2020). Customer relationship management: Digital transformation and sustainable business model innovation. *Economic research-Ekonomska istraživanja, 33*(1), 2733–2750.

Howcroft, D., & Rubery, J. (2018). Automation has the potential to improve gender equality at work. *The Conversation*, 11.

Janssen, M., & van den Hoven, J. (2015). Big and Open Linked Data (BOLD) in government: A challenge to transparency and privacy? *Government Information Quarterly, 32*, 363–368.

Laursen, K., & Salter, A. (2006). Open for innovation: The role of openness in explaining in-novation performance among U.K. manufacturing firms. *Strategic Management Journal, 27*, 131–150.

Lusch, R. F., Vargo, S., & O'Brien, M. (2007). Competing through service: Insights from service-dominant logic. *Journal of Retailing, 83*, 5–18.

Mao, H., Liu, S., Zhang, J., & Deng, Z. (2016). Information technology resource, knowledge management capability, and competitive advantage: The moderating role of resource commitment. *International Journal of Information Management, 36*(6), 1062–1074.

Martín-de-Castro, G., Delgado-Verde, M., López-Sáez, P., & Navas-López, J. E. (2011). Towards 'an intellectual capital-based view of the firm': Origins and nature. *Journal of Business Ethics, 98*, 649–662.

Mazzola, E., Bruccoleri, M., & Perrone, G. (2016). The effect of Inbound, Outbound, and Coupled Open Innovation practices on firm performance: Empirical evidences from bio-pharmaceutical industry. *International Journal of Technology Management, 70*, 2–3.

Najafi-Tavani, S., Najafi-Tavani, Z., Naudé, P., Oghazi, P., & Zeynaloo, E. (2018). How collaborative innovation networks affect new product performance: Product innovation capability, process innovation capability, and absorptive capacity. *Industrial Marketing Management, 73*, 193–205.

Natalicchio, A., Ardito, L., Savino, T., & Albino, V. (2017). Managing knowledge assets for open innovation: A systematic literature review. *Journal of Knowledge Management, 21*, 1362–1383.

OECD. (2019). *Artificial intelligence in society*. OECD Publishing. https://doi.org/10.1787/eedfee77-en

OECD. (2021). *The digital transformation of SMEs*. OECD Publishing. https://www.oecd-ilibrary.org/sites/bdb9256a-en/index.html?itemId=/content/publication/bdb9256a-en

Passaro, R., Quinto, I., Thomas, A., Chase, R., & Secundo, G. (2018). The impact of higher education on entrepreneurial intention and human capital. *Journal of Intellectual Capital, 19*, 135–156.

Pil, F., & Holweg, M. (2003). Exploring scale-the advantages of thinking small. *MIT Sloan Management Review, 43*, 33–39.

Pyka, A. (2002). Innovation networks in economics: From the incentive-based to the knowledge-based approaches. *European Journal of Innovation Management, 5*(3), 152–163.

Raguseo, E., & Vitari, C. (2018). Investments in big data analytics and firm performance: An empirical investigation of direct and mediating effects. *International Journal of Production Research, 56*, 5206–5221.

Saldanha, T. J., Melville, N. P., Ramirez, R., & Richardson, V. J. (2013). Information systems for collaborating versus transacting: Impact on manufacturing plant performance in the presence of demand volatility. *Journal of Operations Management, 31*, 13–329.

Saldanha, T. J. V., Mithas, S., & Krishnan, M. S. (2017). Leveraging customer involvement for fueling innovation: The role of relational and analytical information processing capabilities. *MIS Quarterly, 41*, 367–396.

Szczepański, M. (2019). Economic impacts of artificial intelligence (AI). *Briefing.* European Parliamentary Research Service (EPRS).

Uden, L., & He, W. (2017). How the Internet of Things can help knowledge management: A case study from the automotive domain. *Journal of Knowledge Management, 21*(1), 57–70.

Ye, Y., Lau, K. H., & Teo, L. K. Y. (2018). Drivers and barriers of Omni-channel retailing in China: A case study of the fashion and apparel industry. *International Journal of Retail & Distribution Management, 46*(7), 657–689.

Zack, M., McKeen, J., & Singh, S. (2009). Knowledge management and organizational performance: An exploratory analysis. *Journal of Knowledge Management, 13*(6), 392–409.

Zairis, A. G. (2020). *The effective use of digital technology by SMEs. Entrepreneurial development and innovation in family businesses and SMEs* (pp. 244–255). IGI Global.

Chapter 17

Ethical Governance of Digital Footprint Data: A Journey Towards a Responsible Society

S. Asieh H. Tabaghdehi

Brunel University London, UK

Abstract

In the rapidly evolving digital landscape, the ethical governance of digital footprint data has emerged as a critical domain, influencing privacy, trust, transparency, accountability and overall digital well-being. Here we provide an overview of key considerations and challenges in this realm, emphasising the need for a robust ethical framework to guide the responsible use of digital footprint data. We explore the interconnected dimensions of trust, transparency, accountability and digital well-being in the context of digital footprint data. Trust is paramount in the digital age, and individuals entrust vast amounts of personal data to online platforms. Establishing and maintaining trust necessitates ethical practices in handling digital footprints, ensuring that individuals feel secure in their online interactions. On the other hand, transparency becomes a cornerstone in fostering trust, as individuals demand clarity regarding data collection, usage and sharing practices. An ethically governed approach involves providing users with accessible and comprehensible information about how their digital footprints are utilised, empowering them to make informed decisions about their online engagement.

It is inevitable that there is an urgent need for a comprehensive ethical framework such as Digital Footprint Ethical Regulation that addresses trust, transparency, accountability and digital well-being collectively. By emphasising the local and global dimensions of ethical governance, the abstract underscores the importance of education, training, support, resources and a regulatory framework to efficiently and ethically manage digital data, ensuring a harmonious coexistence with evolving technologies.

Business Strategies and Ethical Challenges in the Digital Ecosystem, 369–379

Copyright © 2025 S. Asieh H. Tabaghdehi

Published under exclusive licence by Emerald Publishing Limited

doi:10.1108/978-1-80455-069-420241017

Keywords: Digital footprint data; responsible business; SME; trust; accountability; privacy; digital well-being

Introduction

Since the last decade, the emergence of digitisation in the business environment has generated a vast amount of data traceable online, known as digital footprint data. The term 'digital footprint' refers to the electronic information that each employee or organisation creates, transfers or receives in the form of emails, document-sharing, calls or chats (Hitt, 2019). A digital footprint represents the actual data and information of individuals or organisations that are publicly available on various digital platforms. With a 40% increase in remote working due to the COVID-19 pandemic (ONS, 2020), digital interactions have become obligatory, transforming everything we say and do into digital data, creating evidence.

There are two types of digital footprints: passive and active. A passive footprint is created when information is collected from the user without their knowledge, raising concerns about ownership and the need for individuals to review, eliminate or prevent the commercialisation of their own digital data. On the other hand, an active digital footprint is where the user deliberately shares information about themselves, either through social media sites or websites. In an active digital footprint, there are an unlimited number of shareholders for your digital data, making digital data users accountable for their footprint.

Companies have been actively involved in monitoring, tracing and storing digital data generated by individuals both online and offline through integrated technologies. The primary objective behind these efforts is to comprehend customer needs, wants and desires, thereby enhancing customer engagement (Banerjee et al., 2011). However, this practice presents a considerable challenge, particularly for Small and Medium Enterprises (SMEs). Prior research has demonstrated that digital footprints are not only utilised for selecting internal employees based on performance (Gloor et al., 2020) but also serve as tools for surveilling fraudulent activities (Xiong et al., 2018). Moreover, Abril et al. (2012) highlighted that maintaining a digital presence on public platforms, such as social media, introduces potential risks to the privacy of both individuals and organisations. Noteworthy instances, like Facebook's use of personal information for 'political propaganda campaigns' in the United States and United Kingdom, underscore the ethical concerns associated with the misuse of user information, revealing a need for responsible actions (Bowcott & Hern, 2018).

Despite these challenges, the ethical dimensions surrounding the handling, monitoring and regulation of digital footprints remain ambiguous. Previous studies have suggested that the evolving relationship between humans and technology may result in a lack of awareness regarding ethical implications (Coeckelbergh, 2013). Likewise, numerous ethical and policy-related challenges, encompassing privacy, trust and ownership of data management (Pardo & Siemens, 2014), have surfaced. Fundamental questions emerge, such as the classification of information about a person's way of life without divulging personal details as personal information. Additionally, the impact of monitoring employee profiles on aspects like privacy, equality, personal engagement and transparency warrants careful examination.

Breaches of data privacy can result in economic harm (Ives, 2019), and unregulated digital privacy may have significant costs for organisations, economies and societies, given the longstanding recognition of personal data as essential economic assets (Janeček, 2018). The issue of data privacy has prompted governments and policymakers to reassess laws, regulations and policies related to data privacy and security. In 2018, the European Union General Data Protection Regulation (GDPR) addressed personal data seriously, emphasising individual privacy rights and enhancing consumer control and access to data (Voight & Bussche, 2017). Regulators are concerned that if digital footprints compromise individuals' (consumers/employees) privacy and trust, it could lead to serious social consequences affecting employees' well-being and performance, customer behaviour and relationships among organisations and individuals. Additionally, there is an increased risk of privacy issues such as fraud and illegal hacking. Consequently, unregulated digital privacy poses potentially substantial costs for organisations, economies and societies.

However, the rapid digital transformation triggered by the COVID-19 outbreak has fundamentally altered how individuals and organisations operate. Our continuous online engagement has become a ubiquitous phenomenon, leaving behind a trail of digital data, whether actively or passively. Ethical risks and privacy concerns stemming from digital footprints are of utmost importance. The misuse of digital footprints can result in widespread problems such as discrimination, exclusivity, inequality and the misleading of customers (e.g. Cambridge Analytica). For the average customer, employee or employer, challenges related to data protection and security are complex. Key questions about the ownership of Digital Footprint Data, employees' skills in protecting customers' data online, and how SMEs are addressing ethical issues surrounding digital footprints are primary concerns in the ongoing digital transformation. These questions underscore profound ethical implications for SMEs' digital footprints during and beyond the COVID-19 outbreak. It is crucial to understand how SMEs manage the vast data collected from various digital platforms without infringing on the digital privacy and data security of other stakeholders. Yet, it is not clear how regulators, organisations and individuals can enhance their digital skills and ethical understanding to establish clear responsibilities in a responsible and sustainable society.

Ethical Governance of Digital Footprint Data

There has always been concern about digital information and its contribution to the digital footprint. Digital footprints encompass all online activities and hold commercial value (Dwork & Mulligan, 2013). Any personal information available online or on digital platforms, such as social media, becomes public information. Article 19 of the United Nations Human Rights Council states that the same rights people have offline must also be protected online. Therefore, insufficient regulation, policy and law enforcement related to the digital footprint can lead to the loss of societal self-esteem (Donaldson et al., 1994; Gostin, 1994), a loss of trust that could damage personal and professional relationships (Putnam, 2000) between organisations and individuals, an increase in privacy risks such as fraud and illegal hacking (Buil-Gil et al., 2021) and issues of well-being.

The pandemic has ushered in a swift digital transformation in our professional lives, making constant online engagement a natural aspect of our daily routine. In this digital landscape, whether we are customers, employees or employers, our online activities generate a valuable commodity – our digital footprint. This newfound ubiquity raises significant challenges, including data privacy, security, surveillance, GDPR compliance and web tracing. Questions abound: Who owns the data within digital footprints? Do employees possess the knowledge to safeguard customers' data? How do SMEs navigate the ethical complexities? Hence, organisations access digital footprint data generated by customers for various commercial objectives, raising ethical issues such as data privacy, security, surveillance and web tracing (Abril et al., 2012). Particularly SMEs, despite limited resources, bear responsibility for implementing effective policies for handling digital data, facing challenges such as financial constraints, a knowledge-technology gap, digitally skilled labour shortages and the absence of handling digital data policies.

Establishing clear boundaries between professional and personal online activities is essential. However, the prospect of organisations monitoring employees' personal activities raises doubts about the feasibility of such separation. Despite SMEs grappling with limited resources, they share an equal responsibility for data handling and processing with larger organisations. Key challenges include financial constraints, knowledge-technology gaps, shortages in digital skills, and a lack of established policies and procedures. Various incidents of online trolls, associated with psychopathy and sadism (Sest & March, 2017), can affect one's well-being, raising concerns about how individual trials online are used to predict one's way of living. This type of online behaviour can create new opportunities for new types of antisocial behaviours, which, if not governed by clear ethical considerations, may contribute to a dysfunctional way of living in the community. The key challenge in developing new regulatory approaches is to balance individual privacy and limit the harm of the digital footprint (Barth-Jones, 2012; Cohen & Mello, 2018; Rothstein, 2020). Hence, there is a need for policymakers to develop an ethical framework to efficiently manage the worrying consequences of misusing the digital footprint that creates discrimination (e.g. insurance pricing), exclusivity, inequality and consumer harm (e.g. Cambridge Analytica) (Cadwalladr & Graham-Harrison, 2018). What is required is a more nuanced understanding of the clear implications of online trials and impressions and how individuals can ensure their trials are managed ethically without jeopardising their way of living and social engagement. For instance, Bari and O'Neill (2019) and Clayton et al. (2019) identified that multi sectoral regulatory approaches are required for individual's privacy protection.

Another issue related to the digital footprint is accountability for individuals' digital information and how individuals can be given the opportunity to review, eliminate and prevent the commercialisation of their own digital data. With hyper-connectivity and digitisation, employees are expected to work anytime and from anywhere. Research has highlighted how employees may raise issues related to functional affordance (the relationship between users and technology and the possible uses or how it can or should be used) (Grgecic et al., 2015). This includes, for example when employees have four functional affordances online: visibility, editability, persistence and association when using social media (Treem & Leonardi, 2013). The risk increases when the boundary between work and personal space blurs, allowing employees to invite colleagues for social interaction online and extending an invitation for people to share, retweet, vote or like a post (Lankton et al., 2015; Majchrzak et al., 2013). This poses a further risk of unethical behaviour due to the unclear boundaries between the digital trails of an employee or an organisation.

Undoubtedly, the COVID-19 outbreak has led to a significant shift to the digital world, consequently causing massive challenges to the protection of human rights. For example, Fama Technologies provided its corporate clients with more than 11 million pieces of publicly available content from employees and job seekers (Financial Times, 2018). Approximately 14% of the content warned of sexism, and 10% for racism or hate speech. Yet, after almost four years, the transparency discussion of digital footprint is still lagging. Hence, this study plans to develop insights and a framework for organisations and policymakers to use digital footprints ethically and safely in creating business and social value.

Trust and Transparency in the Digital Landscape: Impacts on Customers, Employees and Employers

Transparency and trust are critical issues associated with remote work and online engagement, impacting customers, employees and employers alike (Schnackenberg & Tomlinson, 2016). Research indicates that risk concerns and issues related to trust significantly hinder the widespread adoption of business-to-customer (B2C) e-commerce in the banking sector (Yousafzai et al., 2003). Ambiguity surrounding rules, roles and regulations can result in negative consequences, whereas a transparency-based sharing framework produces positive results (Köbis et al., 2021). Perceived security and privacy significantly influence customer trust, and future research holds managerial implications for increasing transparency without jeopardising trust-based commercial sharing (Köbis et al., 2021).

Furthermore, accountability becomes a contentious issue in the context of employee anonymous online dissent (EAOD) in modern digital environments, raising ethical and accountability concerns (Ravazzani & Mazzei, 2018). In the digital era, advanced artificial intelligence (AI) systems render informed consent less effective, as businesses increasingly rely on data-trained algorithms for decision-making (Kim & Routledge, 2020). Thus, individuals are concerned about protecting their privacy and personal data online, but practical actions often fall short. Recent research suggests that consumers are less likely to protect their data or leave social media even when they distrust its safety (Chamorro-Premuzic & Nahai, 2017). Chamorro-Premuzic and Nahai (2017) argue that the concept of 'personal' once meaning 'private' no longer exists, given that online data is widely available in public domains. Making personal data more secure might restrict our ability to enjoy free and personalised services online, emphasising the role of informed consent in determining what to share and what not to share online.

The high level of involvement in the current social media environment raises questions about separating personal and professional life. Ethical consequences of digital footprint data extend beyond business, impacting social behaviour, users' image, identity, and community roles. Responsible digital footprint management requires defining new roles/responsibilities within SMEs to promote transparency and accountability in data processing. As technology rapidly advances, educational institutions must address knowledge-technology gaps to provide adequate training and education. Policies on data privacy, surveillance, GDPR and cybersecurity are crucial for SMEs to create value, requiring a collaborative approach between employees, employers and customers to establish boundaries between professional and personal activities on digital platforms. Therefore, lack of control over data shared with key partners has ethical consequences regarding transparency and accountability, necessitating a collaborative ethical approach to address digital data ownership issues without compromising privacy and security. As the ethical concerns around digital footprint is global – but the solution starts at the local level Particularly SMEs require education, training, support, resources and a regulatory framework to manage digital data efficiently.

Digital Well-being: The Impact of Artificial Intelligence (AI) on Workforce Welfare

The concept of 'digital well-being' encompasses the profound influence of technological advancements on citizens' lives and overall well-being (Burr et al., 2020). In recent years, the workforce's inclusivity and future security have encountered challenges due to the widespread adoption of digital platforms and AI. The consequences and implications of technological progress on the well-being of the workforce have emerged as a central concern for policymakers in our rapidly growing digital society. AI's role in shaping the future of the United Kingdom as well as the global digital economy introduces various risks, particularly concerning workforce well-being and rights in establishing an inclusive workforce with equitable tasks and responsibilities. Consequently, there is a pressing need to develop an analytical framework that aids the government, decision-makers and organisations in comprehending the intersection of AI, productivity and workforce well-being in an increasingly digital economy. It is pivotal for generating insights at both organisational and individual levels, fostering the ethical and responsible use of AI to create an inclusive labour market.

For instance, addressing the ethical, societal and economic dimensions of technology in societal lives is imperative to raise awareness of the swift diffusion of technology. Noteworthy reports from both the OECD (2019) and the EU Commission (2019) delve into the economic and social consequences of AI and machine technologies, emphasising pertinent questions about societal readiness for this technological advancement. Therefore, developing a set of effective policies, strategies and regulations becomes crucial to promoting the ethical use of AI, particularly in SMEs globally. These measures aim to enhance the workforce's proficiencies for the benefit of humankind and society at large. Policymakers face the challenge of comprehending the applied perspective of AI on the future workforce in a digital economy, considering fairness and safeguarding measurements for workforces. Striking a balance between encouraging the design, development and use of AI to foster growth and competitive advantage while simultaneously prioritising workforce well-being remains a formidable challenge for governments.

Conclusion

The accelerated digital transformation triggered by the COVID-19 pandemic underscores the imperative for societies to adopt a more focused and comprehensive policy and regulatory approach. The ethical risks and privacy concerns emanating from the widespread use of digital platforms emphasise the need for rigorous exploration, discussion and dialogue. To address these challenges, there is a call for the development of new ethical frameworks that empower regulatory authorities to safeguard individual privacy and mitigate the potential harm associated with digital footprints on a national scale. Proposing the establishment of what can be termed as 'Digital Footprint Ethical Regulation (DFER)', the advocacy is for widespread adoption and stringent enforcement in every ethical and efficient society.

In our quest for a digitally informed society, both individuals and organisations aspire to benefit fairly from sharing digital information on various platforms while ensuring the protection of digital data privacy linked to digital footprints. Achieving this vision necessitates a comprehensive understanding of digital ethical regulations, underscoring the importance of robust digital footprint strategies. Creating a safer digital environment for businesses and individuals to operate ethically and fairly demands a well-informed populace adhering to digital ethical regulations.

To ensure transparency and accountability in the handling and processing of digital data, organisations are encouraged to designate a dedicated individual responsible for managing the digital footprint data. While larger organisations possess the necessary resources and capabilities, a critical question arises regarding whether smaller organisations can uphold the same standards of trust, privacy, transparency and ethics in managing digital footprints internally.

The evolving landscape of technology has outpaced public knowledge, highlighting the urgency of bridging the knowledge–technology gap through continuous education and training initiatives led by policymakers. SMEs, in particular, face a pressing need to institute new roles and responsibilities internally to manage data effectively, fostering transparency and accountability. As we address global ethical concerns surrounding digital footprints, the journey towards a solution must begin at the local level. SMEs stand in need of comprehensive support, encompassing education, training, resources and a regulatory framework to empower them to efficiently and ethically manage digital data in the ever-evolving digital landscape. In doing so, societies can collectively embrace the ethical challenges posed by digital footprints, paving the way for a more responsible and equitable digital future.

Case Study: Digital Footprint Data and Well-being

In the rapidly evolving landscape of the digital era, the concept of the digital footprint has emerged as a crucial element shaping individuals' lives and overall well-being. Assume a diverse group of digital citizens, including professionals, students and senior citizens, each navigating the digital landscape in their unique ways. Their daily interactions with various online platforms contribute to the creation of extensive digital footprint data, capturing a wide array of personal, professional and social activities.

The participants engage in diverse online activities, such as social media interactions, online shopping, educational pursuits and professional networking. These activities generate a wealth of digital data, forming intricate digital footprints that reflect their preferences, behaviours and interactions. Participants express concerns about the extent to which their digital footprints are tracked and utilised by online platforms. The fear of potential misuse and unauthorised access to personal information raises questions about the impact on mental and emotional well-being. Participants share experiences of the positive and negative effects of social media on their mental and emotional well-being.

Whereas, students discuss the impact of their online activities on educational opportunities and the challenges of maintaining a balance between digital engagement and academic success. Also, professionals discuss the implications of their digital presence on career opportunities and professional relationships. In some other cases, the ethical considerations surrounding the collection and use of digital data raise dilemmas about individual autonomy and consent. Participants highlight a general lack of awareness regarding the extent and implications of their digital footprints. There is limited understanding of privacy settings and data management that contributes to heightened concerns. Participants grapple with the trade-off between personalised online experiences and the potential risks to their well-being. This implies that the social media interactions play a significant role in shaping social connections and influencing self-esteem. There is a significant need for online platforms to prioritise ethical design principles. Designing systems that prioritise user well-being, consent and autonomy can contribute to a more positive digital experience.

As individuals continue to navigate the digital landscape, it underscores the importance of fostering awareness, advocating for ethical practices, and developing solutions that prioritise the holistic well-being of digital citizens. So, as individuals continue to navigate the digital landscape, it underscores the importance of fostering awareness, advocating for ethical practices and developing solutions that prioritise the holistic well-being of digital citizens. The experiences and insights shared by participants contribute to a broader conversation about the ethical considerations surrounding digital footprints in our rapidly evolving digital society.

Case Study Questions

(1) How an individual's professional digital footprint can influence job prospects, networking and career progression.
(2) How algorithms shape individuals' online experiences and influence the content they encounter.
(3) What is the impact of algorithmic curation on individual mental and emotional states.

Key Terms and Definitions

Digital Footprint Data: Digital footprint data refers to the traces or records left behind by individuals' online activities, interactions and behaviours across digital platforms and devices.

Digital Literacy: Digital literacy refers to the ability to navigate, understand, evaluate and effectively use digital technologies and tools for various purposes.

Digital Well-being: Digital well-being refers to the state of optimal health, happiness and balance in individuals' lives in relation to their use of digital technologies and online activities.

Ethical Governance: Ethical governance refers to the principles, practices and processes by which organisations, institutions and governments ensure that their decisions, actions and policies adhere to ethical standards and values.

References

Abril, P. S., Levin, A., & Del Riego, A. (2012). Blurred boundaries: Social media privacy and the twenty-first-century employee. *American Business Law Journal*, *49*(1), 63–124.

Banerjee, S., Bolze, J. D., McNamara, J. M., & O'Reilly, K. T. (2011). How Big Data can fuel bigger growth. *Accenture Outlook*, (3), 28–35.

Bari, L., & O'Neill, D. P. (2019). Rethinking patient data privacy in the era of digital health. *Health Affairs Blog.* https://www.healthaffairs.org/do/10.1377/hblog 20191210.216658/full/

Barth-Jones, D. (2012). The debate over re-identification of health information: What do we risk. *Health.* https://www.healthaffairs.org/do/10.1377/hblog20120810. 021952/full/

Bowcott, O., & Hern, A. (2018, April 10). Facebook and Cambridge Analytica face class action lawsuit. *The Guardian.* https://www.theguardian.com/news/2018/apr/ 10/cambridge-analy tica-and-facebook-face-class-action-lawsuit

Buil-Gil, D., Miró-Llinares, F., Moneva, A., Kemp, S., & Díaz-Castaño, N. (2021). Cybercrime and shifts in opportunities during COVID-19: A preliminary analysis in the UK. *European Societies, 23*(Suppl. 1), S47–S59.

Burr, C., Taddeo, M., & Floridi, L. (2020). The ethics of digital well-being: A thematic review. *Science and Engineering Ethics, 26*(4), 2313–2343.

Cadwalladr, C., & Graham-Harrison, E. (2018). Revealed: 50 million Facebook profiles harvested for Cambridge Analytica in major data breach. *The Guardian, 17*, 22.

Chamorro-Premuzic, T., & Nahai, N. (2017). Why we're so hypocritical about online privacy. *Harvard Business Review*. https://ipc.kingscollege.edu.np/wp-content/uploads/2022/03/H03N00-PDF-ENG.pdf

Clayton, E. W., Evans, B. J., Hazel, J. W., & Rothstein, M. A. (2019). The law of genetic privacy: Applications, implications, and limitations. *Journal of Law and the Biosciences, 6*(1), 1–36.

Coeckelbergh, M. (2013). Drones, information technology, and distance: Mapping the moral epistemology of remote fighting. *Ethics and Information Technology, 15*(2), 87–98.

Cohen, I. G., & Mello, M. M. (2018). HIPAA and protecting health information in the 21st century. *JAMA, 320*(3), 231–232.

Donaldson, M. S., Lohr, K. N., & Bulger, R. J. (1994). Health data in the information age: Use, disclosure, and privacy—Part II. *JAMA, 271*(18), 1392.

Dwork, C., & Mulligan, D. K. (2013). It's not privacy, and it's not fair. *Stanford Law Review, 66*, 35. Online. https://heinonline.org/HOL/P?h=hein.journals/slro66&i=35

European Commission. (2019). *Economic impacts of artificial intelligence (AI)*. https://www.europarl.europa.eu/RegData/etudes/BRIE/2019/637967/EPRS_BRI(2019)637967_EN.pdf

Financial Times. (2018, October 12). Shannon Bond, A messy digital footprint can cost you a job. https://www.ft.com/content/87cfe2ee-bfeb-11e8-84cd-9e601db069b8

Gloor, P. A., Colladon, A. F., & Grippa, F. (2020). The digital footprint of innovators: Using email to detect the most creative people in your organization. *Journal of Business Research, 114*, 254–264.

Gostin, L. O. (1994). Health information privacy. *Cornell Law Review, 80*, 451.

Grgecic, D., Holten, R., & Rosenkranz, C. (2015). The impact of functional affordances and symbolic expressions on the formation of beliefs. *Journal of the Association for Information Systems, 16*(7), 580–607. https://doi.org/10.17705/1jais.00402

Hitt, E. L. (2019). You're on [post] did camera: Third parties' expansion of employees' digital footprint. *University of Pittsburgh Law Review, 81*, 405–436.

Ives, M. (2019). Data breaches dent Singapore's image as a tech innovator. *New York Times*. https://www.nytimes.com/2019/01/29/world/asia/singapore-data-breach-hiv.html

Janeček, V. (2018). Ownership of personal data in the Internet of Things. *Computer Law & Security Report, 34*(5), 1039–1052.

Köbis, N., Soraperra, I., & Shalvi, S. (2021). The consequences of participating in the sharing economy: A transparency-based sharing framework. *Journal of Management, 47*(1), 317–343.

Lankton, N. K., McKnight, D. H., & Tripp, J. (2015). Technology, humanness, and trust: Rethinking trust in technology. *Journal of the Association for Information Systems, 16*(10), 880–918. https://doi.org/10.17705/1jais.00411

Majchrzak, A., Faraj, S., Kane, G. C., & Azad, B. (2013). The contradictory influence of social media affordances on online communal knowledge sharing. *Journal of Computer-Mediated Communication, 19*(1), 38–55. https://doi.org/10.1111/jcc4.12030

OECD. (2019). *Artificial Intelligence in Society*. OECD Publishing. https://doi.org/10.1787/eedfee77-en

Office of National Statistics (ONS). (2020, April). *Coronavirus and homeworking in the UK: April 2020*. https://www.ons.gov.uk/employmentandlabourmarket/peoplein work/employmentandemployeetypes/bulletins/coronavirusandhomeworkingintheuk/april2020

Pardo, A., & Siemens, G. (2014). Ethical and privacy principles for learning analytics. *British Journal of Educational Technology, 45*(3), 438–450.

Putnam, R. D. (2000). Bowling alone: America's declining social capital. In *Culture and politics* (pp. 223–234). Palgrave Macmillan.

Ravazzani, S., & Mazzei, A. (2018). Employee anonymous online dissent: Dynamics and ethical challenges for employees, targeted organisations, online outlets, and audiences. *Business Ethics Quarterly, 28*(2), 175–201.

Rothstein, M. A. (2020). Predictive health information and employment discrimination under the ADA and GINA. *Journal of Law Medicine & Ethics, 48*(3), 595–602.

Schnackenberg, A. K., & Tomlinson, E. C. (2016). Organizational transparency: A new perspective on managing trust in organization-stakeholder relationships. *Journal of Management, 42*(7), 1784–1810.

Sest, N., & March, E. (2017). Constructing the cyber-troll: Psychopathy, sadism, and empathy. *Personality and Individual Differences, 119*, 69–72.

Treem, J. W., & Leonardi, P. (2013). Social media use in organizations: Exploring the affordances of visibility, editability, persistence, and association. *Annals of the International Communication Association, 36*(1), 143–189. https://doi.org/10.1080/23808985.2013.11679130

Voight, P., & Bussche, A. v. d. (2017). *The EU General Data Protection Regulation (GDPR): A practical guide* (1st ed.). Springer Publishing Company, Incorporated.

Xiong, F., Chapple, L., & Yin, H. (2018). The use of social media to detect corporate fraud: A case study approach. *Business Horizons, 61*(4), 623–633.

Yousafzai, S. Y., Pallister, J. G., & Foxall, G. R. (2003). A proposed model of e-trust for electronic banking. *Technovation, 23*(11), 847–860.

Printed and bound by CPI Group (UK) Ltd, Croydon, CR0 4YY

19/11/2024

14595529-0003